Understanding China:
New Viewpoints on History and Culture

book in **Understanding China** series provides a short and
ible guide to the research highlights of an active field of
se studies. Focusing on interdisciplinary work that bridges the
nities and social sciences, the books introduce readers to the
ct, discuss the major problems and, by critically analyzing
eting solutions and taking up new viewpoints, draw readers into
ebates. The books are written in language accessible to readers
e Chinese studies, but are sufficiently informative, current and
cative also to engage the specialist reader.

rs: David Faure, The Chinese University of Hong Kong and
    University of Oxford

Helen F. Siu, Yale University and the Hong Kong Institute
of Humanities and Social Sciences

in the series:

na and Capitalism: A History of Business Enterprise in Modern China
d Faure

"A brilliant piece of synthetic research as well as a delightful read, it offers
a history of the Chinese book to the eighteenth century that is without
equal."

— Timothy Brook, University of British Columbia

"Writers, scribes, engravers, printers, binders, publishers, distributors,
dealers, literati, scholars, librarians, collectors, voracious readers — the
full gamut of a vibrant book culture in China over one thousand years
— are examined with eloquence and perception by Joseph McDermott
in *The Social History of the Book*. His lively exploration will be of consuming
interest to bibliophiles of every persuasion."

— Nicholas A. Basbanes, author of *A Gentle Madness, Patience and Fortitude,*
A Splendor of Letters, and *Every Book Its Reader*

A SOCIAL HISTORY OF THE CHINESE BOOK

Books and Literati Culture in Late Imperial China

In this learned, yet readable, book, Joseph McDermott introduces the history of the book in China in the late imperial period from 1000 to 1800. He assumes little knowledge of Chinese history or culture and compares the Chinese experience with books with that of other civilizations, particularly the European.

Yet he deals with a wide range of issues in the history of the book in China and presents novel analyses of the changes in Chinese woodblock bookmaking over these centuries. He presents a new view of when the printed book replaced the manuscript and what drove that substitution. He explores the distribution and marketing structure of books, and writes fascinatingly on the history of book collecting and about access to private and government book collections.

In drawing on a great deal of Chinese, Japanese, and Western research this book provides a broad account of the way Chinese books were printed, distributed, and consumed by literati and scholars, mainly in the lower Yangzi delta, the cultural center of China during these centuries. It introduces interesting personalities, ranging from wily book collectors to an indigent shoe-repairman collector. And, it discusses the obstacles to the formation of a truly national printed culture for both the well-educated and the struggling reader in recent times.

This broad and comprehensive account of the development of printed Chinese culture from 1000 to 1800 is written for anyone interested in the history of the book. It also offers important new insights into book culture and its place in society for the student of Chinese history and culture.

*   *   *   *   *

Joseph P. McDermott is presently Fellow of St John's College, Cambridge, and University Lecturer in Chinese at Cambridge University. He has published widely on Chinese social and economic history, most recently on the economy of the Song dynasty for the *Cambridge History of China*. He has edited *State and Court Ritual in China* and *Art and Power in East Asia*.

A SOCIAL HISTORY OF THE CHINESE BOOK

Each
access
Chine
huma
subje
comp
the d
outsi
prov

Edit

Also

Chi

Da

A SOCIAL HISTORY OF THE CHINESE BOOK

Books and Literati Culture in Late Imperial China

Joseph P. McDermott

香港大學出版社
HONG KONG UNIVERSITY PRESS

Hong Kong University Press
14/F Hing Wai Centre
7 Tin Wan Praya Road
Aberdeen
Hong Kong

© Hong Kong University Press 2006

Hardback	ISBN-13:	978-962-209-781-0
	ISBN-10:	962-209-781-2
Paperback	ISBN-13:	978-962-209-782-7
	ISBN-10:	962-209-782-0

Secure On-line Ordering
http://www.hkupress.org

British Library Cataloguing-in-Publication Data
A catalogue record for this book is available from the British Library.

Printed and bound by Kings Time Printing Press Ltd., in Hong Kong, China

To

H. T. M, *s. q. n.*

Contents

List of Illustrations

List of Abbreviations

CSJC	*Congshu jicheng*
SBBY	*Sibu beiyao*
SBCK	*Sibu congkan*
SKQSZB	*Siku quanshu zhenben*
SKQSCMCS	*Siku quanshu cunmu congshu*
SKWSSJK	*Siku weishou shu jikan*
XXSKQS	*Xuxiu siku quanshu*

Acknowledgements

This book has had a long gestation. For many years, I had indulged an interest in the history of Chinese books and printing by buying most of the few books that appeared on the topic in any language. The prospect of actually doing research on the subject, nonetheless, remained daunting, not least because I kept on recalling the wise counsel of that great sinological bibliophile, Piet van der Loon. Over thirty years ago, as he shared with me his afternoon tea and cigarette smoke, he spared no words in warning me off the subject for doctoral research. The Chinese documentation explicitly on the topic was scant, the information dispersed and sometimes contradictory, and many of the books not readily available for inspection even in East Asia. Far better, he advised, to file away the scraps of information one came across in the next few decades of reading, so that in due course one might write a book on this difficult, if important, topic.

In the last few years, what changed my mind about the prospects for such research was not just the requisite passage of time. I also had the good fortune of receiving a series of generous invitations from friends wishing me to talk and write about the topic. I wish to express my deepest gratitude to them for dragging me away from my normal rounds in Chinese villages for a rewarding excursion into the world of paper, ink, and woodblocks. First credit goes to Cynthia Brokaw, who, in the mid-1990s, asked me to comment on papers at a conference she was involved in organizing on late imperial Chinese book culture. As I prepared for this task, I soon became aware that major advances had recently occurred in this field. Reading the work of Zhang Xiumin, Ōki Yasushi, Lucille Chia, and especially Inoue Susumu prompted me to submit an essay for the conference's volume. This she read with customary insight, and since then she has generously encouraged me and commented intelligently on my forays into related topics.

Next, in response to a request from another old friend, Choi Chi-cheung, I took the opportunity to pursue my revived scholarly interest by giving lectures on the topic in early October 2002, in Hong Kong and Guangzhou. Three of these talks were presented at the South China Research Center he runs at the Hong Kong University of Science and Technology, and one at Zhongshan University in Guangzhou, where I was the privileged guest of Liu Zhiwei, Chen Chunsheng, and Maybo Qing. The lively discussions that followed each of the talks, the liberal hospitality lavished on me by Professor Choi and his assistants, and the evident breadth of interest in the subject strengthened my belief that the subject of Chinese book history encompassed a wide variety of fascinating specialties that gained greater significance when studied together rather than when approached from their separate disciplinary bailiwicks.

Thirdly, at international conferences held in Tokyo (2000) and Sendai (2003), I had the good fortune to give invited talks at the request of Professor Isobe Akira and his Center for Northeast Asian Studies at Tohoku University. These meetings on the theme of publishing culture in East Asia introduced to me much fine work being done in Japan and Korea, some of which has found its way into this volume. These conferences drew together scholars from no fewer than twelve countries, confirming claims of the breadth of scholarly interest in the subject. If my findings here help to promote this cause that Professor Isobe has so selflessly promoted, then I will be grateful.

Thus, portions of the first four chapters have appeared in print in separate essays I wrote for Cynthia J. Brokaw and Kai-wing Chow, eds., *Printing and Book Culture in Late Imperial China* (Berkeley: University of California Press, 2005); *Orientations* (Fall 2002); and Isobe Akira, ed., *Higashi Ajia shuppan bunka kenkyū, niwatazumi* (Tokyo: Nigensha, 2004). I wish to express my gratitude to these publishers for allowing me to make use of some of this material here.

Not long after I left the warmth and learning of these audiences in East Asia, I received the last of my invitations, when David Faure generously asked me to contribute the text of my Hong Kong talks to a new series of volumes he was editing on Chinese history. Three of the original lectures (Chapters 2, 4, and 5) have thus been expanded for inclusion here, and three further chapters and an introduction have been added to complete the story with research and writing done largely since the original lectures.

In revising these lectures, I have been fortunate to air my ideas at seminars and panels in Oxford, the Academia Sinica, the History Department of Beijing University, the British Library, the annual meeting of the Association of Asian Studies in 2003, SOAS in London, and the Department of East Asian Studies at Princeton University. Colleagues in all these places helped me further my understanding of the issues by questioning my views and poking holes in my argument. While I cannot claim to have persuaded all those in attendance, they all have been instrumental in revising and, I hope, improving my analysis.

Some others also have helped me along the way. In Hong Kong, Dr Cheung Sui-wai and Puk Wing-kin, as well as Professors Billy So and Chu Hung-lam of the Chinese University of Hong Kong hosted me with great cordiality. Elsewhere, on two continents, Sören Edgren provided good company and instruction, as did Lucille Chia and Martin Heijdra. These three excellent scholars provided exemplary models for listening patiently and arguing generously with some views they did not always share. Professors Wang Xiaofu, Deng Xiaonan, Wang Tianyou, and Zhang Xiqing at Beijing University welcomed me with a warmth hard to match, and Professors Liu Ts'ui-jung, Ch'en Jo-shui, Hsiung Ping-chen, Ch'iu Peng-sheng, Wang Fan-shen, Huang Kuan-chung, and Lau Nap-yin helped me settle into library work during two highly enjoyable stays at Academia Sinica.

Back in Cambridge, Peter Burke, Jack Goody, Stefan Reif, and many other fellows of St John's College made me alert to new work on similar problems in the West and elsewhere; the excellent staff at the library of St John's College (especially Jon Harrison) shared with me their rich collection of writings on Western books; Corey Byrnes compiled the Glossary–Index for the book; and, within the group of Chinese history scholars in Cambridge, David McMullen, Roel Sterckx, and Denis Twitchett read through part or all of the manuscript, pointed out some questionable statements, and made wise recommendations. Others who pointed out errors and gave helpful advice for which I am grateful include Evelyn Rawski, Danny Gardner, Beverley Bosseler, Mark Halperin, Bruce Rusk, Frank Dikötter, Jonathan Israel, Heinrich von Staden, and Zhang Ling.

Last but not least, I have benefited greatly from the staff of the major libraries I have repeatedly turned to during this research: the Cambridge University Library, the Bodleian, the Tōyō bunko, the

Tōyō bunka kenkyūjo, the Naikaku bunko, the Fu-ssu Nien Library at Academia Sinica, the Needham Institute of East Asian Science and Technology, and the Gest Library at Princeton. Names are invidious when thanking such selfless work, but several in particular deserve to be mentioned: my old friend, Shiba Yoshinobu at the Tōyō bunko, unfailingly eased my way to the books in his care; and Charles Aylmer, Koyama Nobuo, and John Moffett at Cambridge and David Helliwell at the Bodleian. They all have been consistently understanding of my frequent and troublesome queries and requests.

If, then, this book shows greater wisdom than if I had tried to write it as a fledgling graduate student, it is in great part due to the help I have received from all these friends. I hope that Piet van der Loon would not have been too disappointed with this consequence of following his advice.

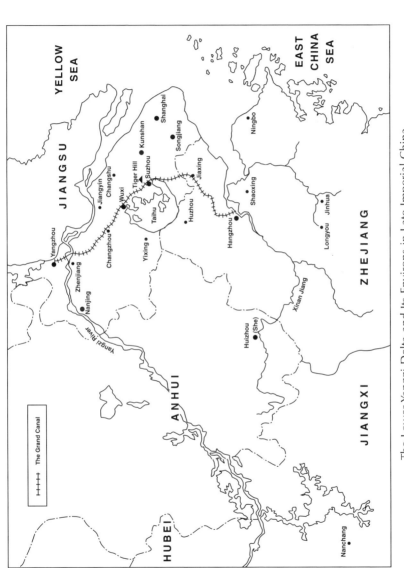

The Lower Yangzi Delta and Its Environs in Late Imperial China

Introduction

In the northwestern suburbs of the city of Suzhou, situated near the center of the lower Yangzi delta, there is a small hill that overlooks narrow streets crowded with shops, shrines, and homes. Known as Tiger Hill (*Huqiu*), it has for well over a millennium been the subject of innumerable poems, paintings, and stories, all recognizing it and its buildings as a symbol of the wealthy and civilized city it graces. Its leisurely slopes have drawn countless visitors from near and afar and become the final resting home of famous monks, celebrated women, and successful scholar-officials. One of these honored dead, laid to rest over two centuries ago among the shrubs and grasses at its western foot, was a shoe repairman named Qian Jinren (see Figure 1).

Figure 1   The grave of Qian Jinren, at Tiger Hill, Suzhou, Jiangsu Province

What won this busy cobbler a seemingly incongruous place on this celebrated hill of literati leisure was his ardent love of books and learning. Orphaned when young, Qian was taken in by a cobbler household too poor to pay his school fees but practical enough to teach him the trade of repairing shoes. Eventually, when a young adult with a paltry income, he learned how to read, according to one account, from neighborhood children who were attending school. His practice was to pay his informants one copper cash for each Chinese character they taught him to identify. He then did work for Suzhou bookstores and temples, which allowed him at his request to borrow and read their books in lieu of the normal cash payment. This arrangement, even as he continued to do his work as a shoe repairman, lasted for some forty or fifty years, and, as his own book collection grew, he slowly acquired in this center of classical scholarship something of a reputation for his knowledge of Confucius' *The Analects* and a popular intermediate text, *The Classic of Filial Piety* (*Xiaojing*). Some well-known Suzhou scholars visited him and talked of their shared concern with books. When in his old age his feet grew ulcerous and left him bedridden, one of these scholars, Wang Bing, came to the rescue. Wang had abandoned his early dreams of repeating his father's success in the civil service examinations and had become a doctor respected for both his Confucian learning and medical practice. With the approval of his family, Wang took Qian into his home to grow old and die. And so, this surprisingly literate artisan ended up being called a teacher (albeit, "the Shoe-Repairman Teacher") and honored with a gravesite at a place associated with the rich and famous of this cultured city. Moreover, the carving onto his gravestone of the calligraphy of the province's high-ranking surveillance commissioner publicly confirmed his admission into the city's cultural élite. Qian's life, then, would seem to have epitomized that traditional Chinese dream, whereby any man could rise in station from poverty to fame due solely to his command of the written culture of his country.[1]

Yet, there is another account of his life, specifically, his manner of death, that does not sit well with this tale of social success. In 1792, a year of poor grain harvests, Qian died, directly or indirectly, not from ulcerous feet but from a food shortage that struck the city of Suzhou. It was only after Qian could not leave his house due to the food shortage that this Confucian doctor, Wang Bing, moved Qian out of the cramped half-room he had rented for much of his life into the more comfortable quarters of Wang's own home. Some 100 days later, Qian died there at the age of 76 *sui* without a son, without a bed, without a chair and table, and even without a pot and pan to his name. As he left nothing but his shelves of tattered books, several scholars from Suzhou chipped in to rescue him from the disgrace of burial among the forgotten and displaced, in the six public graveyards in the vicinity of Tiger Hill.[2] Tens and hundreds of literati came from all directions to attend his burial at the foot of their Tiger Hill, thereby honoring a man who had venerated them and their learning for his entire adult life.[3]

Which image or impression is true? At this distance it is hard to say. But, regardless of which is true — and possibly both are — this pair of tales merits our attention for underlining the lure and power of the book in late imperial Chinese culture and its complex relation to China's social and economic hierarchies. In examining these two themes, this book tries to discern what the history of the Chinese book can tell us of important changes in technology, learning, and social relations between 1000 and 1800.

To many observers inside and outside of China, such an effort will seem odd. What else is an old Chinese book but a treasured artwork? Placed apart on a shelf and wrapped in elegant clothboard, it exudes a sense of the quiet diversions of the study rather than of the contentions of history. Yet, scholars of Chinese bibliography (*banxue, muluxue*) have for generations helped to undermine this idealized fantasy by researching essential facts about these books, such as the publication date, location, publisher, and collectors, for their original and subsequent printings. Here, by making use of the writings of these bibliographers, as well as more recent research on book production, distribution, and consumption, I would like to replace this precious image of the book with one that does justice to the book's centrality in the evolution of Chinese culture from the eleventh through the eighteenth centuries. In each of the following chapters, then, I want to consider a variety of social and economic issues too seldom associated with the history of the Chinese book. Firstly, how was a book most commonly printed and why did this method of woodblock printing remain the predominant technology for book printing for so long in China? Secondly, when and how did the imprint — that is, the printed book — replace the manuscript as the principal form of book in China? Thirdly, what changes did this adoption of the imprint bring about for the distribution, consumption, and use of books in late imperial times? Fourthly, when and how were Chinese scholars able to overcome problems of access to books and thereby constitute what we today might call a sizeable "community of learning"? And, finally, what were the understandings of the uses of literacy and books that the literate and illiterate held in late imperial China and how did they cut across social divisions?

If these questions about book history appear to be bookish, then my aim in writing this book will have been misunderstood. It is my belief that the history of the book should lie at the heart of our understanding of China's élite culture. For at least the last thousand years, book learning has been central to the identity and legitimacy of this country's cultural and political élite, as determined by the state's written examinations as well as by that élite's definition of itself and its culture. Books, then, have had a profound impact on the social, political, and intellectual history of China as well as on the aspirations, obsessions, and living conditions of a sizeable number of its men and women, of its Qian Jinrens as well as his scholarly patrons. What we can learn about the production, spread, and use of books will go a long way to explaining not just the gradual ascendance of the imprint or the intellectual and literary impact of a book, an author, or a school. Our conclusions will also suggest how the literate élite's world of learning evolved and what role it may have played in the making of an empire-wide culture shared by literati and non-literati alike.

Consider for a moment the impact of writing and its various media on Chinese history. More than 3,500 years ago, the invention of writing in China helped to establish and strengthen political and social institutions that made knowledge more explicit and fixed, that transmitted it more successfully, and that nurtured experts in its contents. The bronze inscriptions of ancient China record the early efforts to create these institutions, just as the stone steles with inscribed texts of the Confucian classics demonstrate the antiquity of the commitment to make this approved knowledge available to literate men. The manuscript copy, greatly facilitated by the invention of paper, represented the fragile and repeated struggle to transmit written knowledge more privately in the making of a written culture. And, the printed book, a remarkable offspring of the basic Chinese inventions of paper and printing, expanded both the audience and contents of written works, making them more mobile, transferable, and useful to the educated élite and society at large. Thus, the study of when and how this particular form of communication known as the imprint gained priority in Chinese culture over manuscript copies can reveal how people dealt with bookish knowledge and how an already ancient written culture gained a wider and deeper role in the public and private life of its people, particularly the literate. In other words, the history of Chinese printing, as explained in the following pages, will cast light on the spread of Chinese learning, the evolution of its institutions, the activities of its experts, and the growth of groups with shared bodies of knowledge on both the local and imperial levels. Surely, such concerns cannot be dismissed as bookish.

This book's analysis, despite its breadth of concern, accepts two significant limitations, one spatial and the other social. Instead of trying to explain an eight-century history of the book for all of China, this book focuses on one region, the lower Yangzi delta, and on the one type of reader we know the most about, the literati. A regional focus is crucial for dating the transition from manuscript to imprint, if only because it brings into play local factors essential for this analysis, such as prices and distribution. For instance, in mid-twelfth-century China, the price for an imprint title could vary by as much as 600 percent, depending on where the text was published;[4] such variation effectively nullifies the utility of any empire-wide comparison of imprint prices for an analysis of how they may have influenced the production and trading of books. The focus on the lower Yangzi delta is also intended to tighten our analysis, since this region maintained an unquestioned centrality in the production, distribution, and transmission of books from the Song dynasty (960–1279) to the Qing dynasty (1644–1911). In the Song, the printing center of Hangzhou had only two serious national rivals in the book trade: Jianyang in northern Fujian and Chengdu in Sichuan. After the 1230s, however, Chengdu ceased to offer much competition; it was not until the eighteenth century that its printing industry recovered from the Mongol conquest in the mid-thirteenth century.[5] Jianyang remained a formidable rival, at least in the amount of book production, through the Yuan (1232–1367) and Ming dynasties (1368–1644).[6] But, for the Ming, less information on book culture, especially book consumption, survives from the area of Jianyang than collectively from Suzhou,

Nanjing, Hangzhou, and other book center cities of the lower Yangzi delta.[7] Thus, an account of book production and consumption in the lower Yangzi delta, particularly one concerned with this region's transition from a manuscript to an imprint culture and its residents' use of books, promises to provide the most complete, long-term picture of the Chinese book world from the eleventh to the eighteenth centuries. It may also serve to suggest for much of the rest of China a *terminus ante quem* for the retreat of the manuscript copy in the face of an ascending imprint culture.

A second restriction for our analysis concerns the primary type of writer and reader it discusses: the literati. This focus on the Chinese men who made the writing, reading, and collection of books central to their self- or family identity is determined by practical considerations. Extant books from these centuries and our knowledge of them derive overwhelmingly from literati or government collections and writings. The mass of popular imprints of almanacs, calendars, broadsheet ballads, prayers and other religious texts, as well as newspaper sheets (*xiaobao*) and tax forms put out for the "utilitarian reader" have by and large not survived. While our concentration on longer lasting materials will not bar us from eventually considering these usually ephemeral publications, the evidence and conclusions presented here in most of the chapters refer predominantly to just the most literate portion of the largely illiterate population in arguably the wealthiest, most heavily commercialized, and most culturally advanced area of China during these eight centuries. When, in the last chapter, we return to the case of Qian Jinren, our understanding of his situation will be transformed by what we have learned of the life and learning of the literati and scholars whose writings he fervently admired. We can then proceed to see what these two worlds of the artisan and the literati shared in their perceptions of literacy and the book.

These restrictions, even when put this strictly, will, I believe, have their own rewards. At this stage of our understanding of the Song, Yuan, and Ming book world, the process of moving from relatively certain information to less certifiable speculation is more promising than repeating the broad, unfounded generalizations that glut most books on the printing history of China. A regional and literati perspective will in the end provide us with a reasonable chance of clarifying the proportion of imprints to manuscripts in the most important governmental and private libraries, the difficulties that even major book collectors encountered in acquiring copies of famous works, and changes in the social status of these collectors, in their collecting focus, in their social composition, and even in some reading practices in the seventeenth century. This approach will also allow us to analyze the reasons for the imprint's eventually permanent ascendance from the mid-Ming, as well as to determine how the world of Song and late Ming publishing may have differed. The last chapter, after offering a brief account of Qian Jinren's learning and literacy, explores the various understandings of the benefits of literacy and the book in late imperial times and then compares Qian's appreciation of them with that of his literati admirers in Suzhou. We may not end up certain which account of Qian Jinren's final days is more likely to have been true. But, we will, I hope, better understand the critical role of the book, especially the imprint, in the making of Chinese culture and society from the eleventh to the eighteenth centuries.

1 The Making of an Imprint in China, 1000–1800

Throughout the past century, the invention of printing has ranked, in the eyes of Chinese scholars, as one of their country's greatest contributions to the history of humankind. The view of the present doyen of Chinese book history, Zhang Xiumin, could have been expressed by any scholar and bibliophile in China over the past four generations: "As everyone knows, our country not only invented the art of paper making but also invented the art of printing, woodblock as well as moveable-type, and thereby has made a very important contribution to the development of world culture."[1]

Minus its remarkable assertion that a country can invent something, this piece of cultural self-congratulation does contain a fair amount of truth on the centrality of China in the discovery of paper and printing and in the development of book culture. And yet, as one reviews the Chinese writing on woodblock printing, the oldest and most common type of traditional Chinese printing, an odd fact slowly emerges. The Chinese historical record contains strikingly little direct commentary about this invention, especially in its first few centuries. It fails to identify the date of the invention of this type of printing and the name of the putative Chinese man or woman who invented it.[2] It reveals very little concrete information about the early spread of this invention throughout the empire during its first 250 years; it is likewise surprisingly quiet about its use during the next six centuries, from being adopted to print the Confucian classics between 932 and 953 in the southwestern region of Sichuan, to the sudden appearance of some very detailed accounts of the late sixteenth-century book world. And, it tells us precious little about the organization of book production operations and the relation among the different parties involved in such work. In fact, we have strikingly few accounts of how Chinese woodblock books were made, even though printing, along with the two other inventions of gunpowder and the compass, would become, in Francis Bacon's famous words, one of the three inventions (all Chinese) that "have changed the whole face and condition of things throughout the world in literature, in warfare, and in navigation." [3]

The difficulty of studying this invention, then, begins with the obscurity of its own beginning. Ever since the Song dynasty, the origin of printing has been traced by commentators to the Tang dynasty (618–907) or to the mid-tenth-century printing of the Confucian canon in Sichuan.[4] These views, seldom based on extensive research, have, over the last hundred years, given way to fresh interpretations. Drawing on more concrete evidence, these modern discoveries have turned simple questions about the early history of printing into a hornets' nest of complexity about books, charms, and non-Chinese printed items.

Consider, for instance, the issue of the first printed book. Tang records indicate the printing and availability of imprints and other printed materials in the major urban centers of northern and central China during the ninth century. They refer to almanacs privately printed in 835 in Sichuan and the Huainan area in the lower Yangzi valley, to an imprint on the medical techniques of moxibustion by no later than 861 in the capital of Chang'an (present Xi'an), and to the printing of writing on monastic rules by 873–79 in probably the other capital of Luoyang. They also tell of a poetry collection printed in 847–49 in Jiangxi Province and of printed reading-primers, character lists, and dream interpretation and divination books for sale in Sichuan in 883.[5] But, about fifteen years ago, Zhang Xiumin, drawing on the reading notes of a nineteenth-century scholar, announced that a sixteenth-century source related how the Tang court had carved and printed (*zixing*) a book in 636 or slightly later. A collection of essays about model Chinese women compiled by a deceased empress, this book was judged by Zhang to be the earliest known imperial imprint and possibly the oldest printed book in world history.[6] Yet, as Zhang himself admitted, no Tang source, including those that mentioned this essay collection, confirmed his claim of its being printed. Furthermore, although these Ming and Qing sources take us closer to the supposed event, they remain no closer than nine centuries away from it[7] (as if the only English reference to the Norman invasion of England had been written in the twentieth century). Support for Zhang's claim of the discovery of the practice of printing by the early seventh century comes instead from another Tang report, stating that the Buddhist Monk Xuanzong (d. 664) had a Buddhist image printed up for distribution in large numbers after his return to China from India in 645.[8] Interestingly, none of these sources claims that this empress's compilation is China's oldest printed book, a silence that perhaps makes the information more credible. Even more recent research by Timothy Barrett has traced the first practical and public use of woodblock printing to a slightly later date, to an early eighth-century effort by the Tang dynasty Empress Wu (r. 670–710) to print Buddhist prayers and images. Barrett even raises the possibility that printing may have been in use in China at least a century earlier, but his scholarly restraint keeps him from stretching the evidence.[9]

Thus, while it is clear that activities at least similar to printing were occurring in Tang China, not least at its court, this evidence still leaves us in the fuzzy world of speculative scholarship.[10] In search, then, of something more concrete, we fortunately can turn to an actual surviving Tang imprint, a copy of the *Jingang jing* (Diamond Sutra; Vajracchedikā), published with a date of 868, that seems to merit the accolade of being the world's oldest extant printed book. Discovered about a century ago among 40,000-odd documents in a cave at the Dunhuang Buddhist monastic complex in far northwest China, this sixteen-feet long scroll has a quality of carving that bespeaks at least a few generations of experience and tradition. Not surprisingly, it turns out to be not the oldest extant example of Chinese printing. That honor — since early printing was not used solely, and not necessarily primarily, for books — arguably goes to a Buddhist charm discovered in 1944 in a tomb in Sichuan's provincial capital of Chengdu and dated by modern scholarship to sometime after 757. But even this Chinese charm is not for sure the world's oldest extant example of printing, since ancient charms discovered in Japan and Korea may well deserve that title. Certain Buddhist charms printed in about 770 in Japan survive today, and a Korean Buddhist one dates from between 704 and 751. Unearthed in 1966 in a temple stupa in Kyongju in southeast Korea, this Korean Buddhist scroll of about fourteen feet (originally, it stretched probably to more than twenty feet) may actually be the world's oldest surviving example of printing.[11] Its retention of this title for the past four decades has prompted some Koreans to claim that printing itself was an original

Korean invention, but few researchers outside of Korea have taken this suggestion seriously. Some Chinese and Western scholars even claim, without any convincing evidence, that this scroll was of Chinese origin. In sum, evidence of printing in China and in Chinese dates from no later than the mid-eighth century and possibly from half a century earlier.

If dates and names in printing history are problematic, so then is information on how a woodblock book was actually made. In the words of the well-known Chicago historian of the Chinese book, Professor Tsien Tsuen-hsuin, "unlike papermaking, the technical procedures of printing have scarcely been documented in Chinese literature. No information on how printing blocks were made ... is available, except for occasional remarks made by a few foreign observers and writers." The first reasonably detailed Chinese description of the work involved in any of the four stages of woodblock printing of books — transcribing the text to be printed, carving it into prepared woodblocks, printing sheets off the carved blocks, and binding the printed sheets into a book — was recorded from an oral interview held in China only in 1947, at least some 1,200 years after the discovery of printing.[12] Even as recently as 1987, Tsien felt this lacuna in the Chinese documentary record so sharply that he visited woodblock printing shops in Beijing and Shanghai in order to write a firsthand account of this production work that he had spent a half century studying from afar.[13]

Reasons for this gap can be readily imagined. Chinese artisans, it may be thought, kept their artisan skills to themselves and their offspring. Yet, they were not the only persons involved in book production, as many scholars from the eleventh century onwards privately sponsored book publication and distribution but never described such work in their writings.[14]

Such an omission may then be attributed to these scholars' reputed aversion to recording technical information on manual labor and manufactures. Even the eleventh-century polymath, Shen Kuo, was faulted with his arithmetic by a mid-thirteenth-century author, who concluded, "Few are the scholar-officials who know the art of calculating."[15] Yet, on four closely related techniques, that antipathy is hard to discern. For instance, the earliest surviving complete description of how a Chinese artisan mounted a scroll of calligraphy and painting was written in 847 by a scholar-artist from a collecting family; this comparison is not arbitrary, since the spatial arrangement of the different parts of a hanging scroll served as a model for the distribution and location of blank space and characters on a printed sheet (hence the frequent use of the same terms for sections of a scroll and a printed sheet).[16] Furthermore, detailed manuals for first builders and then other types of carpenters were written and distributed as early as the tenth and thirteenth centuries,[17] and the techniques of papermaking were described generally in the late tenth century and then in great detail in the 1637 work, *Tiangong kaiwu* (*The Creations of Nature and Man*).[18] Although this late Ming book on technology in general paid no attention to printing of any sort, the Chinese invention of moveable-type printing was described by Chinese scholar-officials, first in the mid-eleventh century by Shen Kuo and then, in far greater detail, in the early fourteenth and mid-eighteenth centuries by highly informed scholar-officials.[19]

In all likelihood, then, the most persuasive explanations for the prolonged absence of such a record in Chinese about the production of woodblock printing are the most obvious. Initially, some detailed descriptions of printing may have appeared in writing and perhaps print, but they do not survive. Meanwhile, workers with special skills for producing good quality imprints had little reason or interest in sharing such valuable knowledge with non-family members. The general skills and technology, however, were so simple and, by the Song, so widespread that literate people regarded them as too commonplace to write about. In the words of one mid-nineteenth-century Chinese scholar, "It is far from certain that the invention of woodblock printing was hard. Since antiquity there have been charms and seals that could have taught this idea. Really, for this invention there was no waiting for a strange and clever idea."[20] In other words, the vast majority of Chinese readers would have agreed with Francis Bacon that the craft of printing is mainly obvious and straightforward but would have, at least up until the early twentieth century, regarded his assessment of their vital significance in human history as uninformed and eccentric.[21]

When, then, was such a detailed description of woodblock printing first recorded? The answers to this question are perhaps the oddest, and least expected, of all in this extraordinary tale. Firstly, the earliest extant record, in detail, of how a Chinese woodblock book was made appeared in print in 1820. Secondly, this account of printing technology and work was written and published outside of China, in Malacca. And, thirdly, it was authored by a Scottish Protestant missionary, William Milne (1785–1822), then based in Malacca, in his English language book, *A Retrospect of the First Ten Years of the Protestant Mission to China.*[22]

All these landmark events in the historiography of Chinese printing result from early nineteenth-century missionary activities supported in East and Southeast Asia by the London Missionary Society. In the first half of this chapter, I wish to introduce and discuss Milne's exceptionally informative early nineteenth-century account of woodblock book production. In making use of a book that has so far escaped the attention of virtually all earlier studies of the Chinese book (the main exception is the noted French expert on the Chinese book, Jean-Pierre Drège),[23] my aim is more than bibliographical. My interest in Milne's work is not due to its rarity and originality but to the quality of its analysis of issues that have long bedeviled the study of Chinese book history. Thus, I first present Milne's account of the different stages in the production of woodblock imprints and explain their implications for workers' wages and book prices. The next section then seeks to explain the relative cheapness of woodblock imprints, by examining certain late fifteenth- and sixteenth-century technical changes in Chinese imprint production that simplified and hastened the production process. Then, in the final section, the focus falls on the life of the workers themselves, especially the carvers, and how they responded to the changing technical and economic circumstances of their craft in the sixteenth century.

Milne's Account

In 1812 the London Missionary Society, a voluntary association established in London in 1795 to promote the spread of evangelical Protestantism to all corners of the globe, sent William Milne as its second missionary to China. Even before he arrived in East Asia, Milne was acutely aware of the challenge he and other missionaries faced in trying to convert people to the word of God, without the aid of a fully translated Bible. The London Missionary Society's first China missionary, Robert Morrison, had succeeded in translating the New Testament into Chinese by 1807, but Milne, even after translating into Chinese many books in the Old Testament, recognized the inadequacy of his and Morrison's accomplishment. A student of the Chinese language needed to have "bones of brass, lungs of steel, heads of oak, hands of spring-steel, eyes of eagles, hearts of apostles, memories of angels, and lives of Methusaleh!"[24] Even then, a good Chinese translation of the Bible was not enough. It still needed to be printed and widely distributed to a people who preferred the use of the mission's printing budget for their more practical needs and in a country that closed its doors to Protestant missionaries and forced them to rely on Chinese servants to distribute their books at night and in secrecy.[25]

What, then, was the best — the most efficient, effective, and inexpensive — way to print this translation? To help its governing committee to make this decision, the London Missionary Society asked its representatives in the field to report on the relative feasibility and costs of the alternative technologies of woodblock printing and moveable type. Milne, conscious that the committee of his financial supporters back in London was largely ignorant of Chinese woodblock printing practices, took upon himself the task of explaining and assessing for them the workings of this craft. Fortunately, he had been apprenticed, and successful, as a house carpenter for several years back in Scotland,[26] and had, in 1817, brought from Canton to Malacca Chinese men, including printers.[27] He then became closely acquainted with Chinese printing practices, by either running or supervising the Mission's publishing operation there until his death in 1822.[28] Moreover, he did so usually along Chinese lines, relying on Chinese woodblock printing methods to publish anything written in Chinese, and, in the eyes of one disgruntled British junior, managing the workforce of eighteen men (including one Chinese for Chinese publications) as if they were all Chinese: "As to the principles on which the mission was conducted, I believe it to be purely Chinese gathered from the rules and maxims of the Four Books of Confucius, which is the principle of a father and his family, where the father alone has power to act and direct. And the seniority and juniority which has created so much bitter dissention [among some missionaries] has been the strict adherence to the Chinese doctrine of elder and younger brothers."[29]

In drafting his report, Milne was aided by all his experience in the carpenters' and printers' shops as well as by consultations with

Chinese and non-Chinese experienced with woodblock printing.[30] Consequently, his extended account of Chinese printing practices in *A Retrospect of the First Ten Years of the Protestant Mission to China* provides the first detailed account in any language of Chinese printing methods (the first detailed East Asian discussion of woodblock printing technology would appear in the 1929 Japanese publication, *Nishikie no hori to suri* (*The Carving and Printing of Colored Woodblock Prints*).[31] What follows, then, is a review of Milne's 1820 text, interwoven with passages from an 1838 account of Chinese printing by a missionary-printer successor to Milne, Walter Henry Medhurst.

The simplest, and rarest, kind of woodblock printing practiced by Chinese in Malacca (and presumably in parts of southeast China) required the very quick preparation and carving of assorted wooden strips: "... when an urgent affair occurs, a number of workmen are called in, and a small slip of wood, with space for one, two, or more lines, is given to each, which they cut with great expedition, and when all is finished, join together by small wooden pins." Used to print recent news and other ephemera for handbills, court gazettes, and local announcements, this form of printing clearly did not require the participation of highly skilled carvers.[32] Another kind of quick carving-to-order relied on softer surfaces such as beeswax and resin, or clay, or pulverized gypsum; the first of these entailed "spreading a coat of wax on a wooden frame, after which, with a graving tool, they cut the characters thereon ..." Though seldom practiced in Malacca (Milne and his Chinese workers there claimed never to have observed it), this method was used to issue gazettes and other ephemera in Canton, Ningbo, and Beijing.[33]

The kind of woodblock printing, which in Milne's view "almost universally prevails,"[34] was far more complex, at least in its initial stages. It made use of wooden blocks that were far sturdier and longer lasting than the wooden slips. It also demanded considerable care from the artisans using these thin rectangular slabs of wood:

> The process of preparing for and printing with the blocks, or in the stereotype way, is as follows. The block, or wooden plate, ought to be of the Lee 梨 [i.e., the Chinese character meaning pear] or Tsaou 棗 [i.e., the Chinese character meaning jujube] tree which they describe thus:—"The Lee and the Tsaou are of a fine grain, hard, oily, and shining; of a sourish taste; and what vermin do not soon touch, hence used in printing." The plate is first squared to the size of pages, with

the margin at top and bottom; and is in thickness generally about half an inch. They then smooth it on both sides with a joiner's plane; each side contains two pages, or rather indeed but one page according to the Chinese method of reckoning; for they number the *leaves*, not the pages of a book. The surface is then rubbed over with rice, boiled to a paste, or some glutinous substance, which fills up any little indentments [*sic*], not taken out by the plane; and softens and moistens the face of the board, so that it more easily receives the impression of the character.[35]

Some knowledge of the different types of wood and their particular features was clearly required, if only to facilitate their preservation and the work of the artisans involved in making imprints from them:

> The transcriber's work is, first to ascertain the exact size of the page, the number of lines, and of characters in each line; and then to make what they call a 格 Kih, or form of lines, horizontal and perpendicular, crossing each other at right angles, and thus leaving a small square for each character — the squares for the same sort of character, are all of equal size, whether the letter be complicated as to strokes, or simple: a letter or character with fifty strokes of the pencil, has no larger space assigned to it than one with barely a single stroke. This makes the page regular and uniform in its appearance, though rather crowded, where many complicated characters follow each other in the same part of the line. The margin is commonly at the top of the page, though not always so. Marginal notes are written, as with us, in a smaller letter. This form of lines, being regularly drawn out, is sent to the printer, who cuts all the squares leaving the lines prominent; and then prints off as many sheets, commonly in *red ink*, as are wanted. The transcriber then with black ink, writes in the squares from his copy; fills up the sheet; points it; and sends it to the block-cutter, who, before the glutinous matter is dried up from the board, puts the sheet on *inverted*, rubs it with a brush and with his hand, till it sticks very close to the board. He next sets the board in the sun, or before the fire, for a little, after which he rubs off the sheet entirely with his fingers; but not before a clear impression of each character has been communicated. The graving tools are then employed, and all the white part of the board is cut out, while the black, which shews the character, is carefully left. The block being cut, with edged tools of various kinds, the process of printing follows.[36]

The modern reader, aware of the multitude of beautiful East Asian books made in this manner, can only marvel at the simplicity of this process of preparing and carving woodblocks. For this work, the carver employed only a handful of simple tools that, as Milne aptly observed, "may be carried in the workman's hand, in a tolerably large pocket handkerchief ..."[37] Among these "graving tools" Milne includes "a joiner's plane" and "edged tools" which he does not identify,[38] probably because they were the ordinary iron knives, chisels, groovers, sharpening stones, scrapers, and planes commonly found in the traditional carpenter's kit.[39] Since the materials likewise were chosen not for expense but for durability and practical utility, the quality of woodblock carving essentially depended on the manual dexterity of the practitioners — in other words, their artisanal training, experience, and interest in the job.

Milne, unfortunately, provides no detail on the methods of these carvers. For such instruction, we must turn to Medhurst's 1838 book on the contemporary situation in China and its reception of Christian books. Originally trained as a moveable-type printer in England, Medhurst keenly favored the adoption of this kind of print for the mission's Chinese printing. Nonetheless, he paid close attention to the actual work practices of Chinese woodblock carvers and came away impressed:

> The block, after having been smoothly planed, is spread over with a glutinous paste; when the paper is applied and frequently rubbed, till it becomes dry. The paper is then removed, as much of it as can be got away, and the writing is found adhering to the board, in an inverted form. The whole is now covered with oil, to make the letters appear more vivid and striking; and the engraver proceeds to his business. The first operation is, to cut straight down by the sides of the letters, from top to bottom, removing the vacant spaces between the lines, with the exception of the stops. The workman then engraves all the strokes which run horizontally; then, the oblique; and, afterwards, the perpendicular ones, throughout the whole line; which saves the trouble of turning the block round, for every letter [i.e., character]. Having cut round the letters, he proceeds to the central parts; and, after a while, the page is completed.[40]

The skill of Medhurst's carver would seem to lie in his ability to cut into the woodblock rapidly and cheaply. His goal was not to reproduce the expressive shape of the character or the flow of ink presumably evident in the original brushstrokes; it was simply to carve a recognizably similar form of the character as quickly as possible.

The two remaining stages in book production, printing and binding, appear, if anything, simpler in Milne's account:

> The block is laid on a table; and a brush made of hair, being dipped in ink, is lightly drawn over the face.[41] The sheets being already prepared, each one is laid on the block and gently pressed down by the rubbing of a kind of brush, made of the hair of the Tsung [i.e., 棕 palm] tree. The sheet is then thrown off; one man will throw off 2,000 copies in a day. Chinese paper is very thin, and not generally printed on both sides, though in some particular cases that is also done. In binding, the Chinese fold up the sheet, turning inward that side on which there is no impression. On the middle of the sheet, just where it is folded, the title of the book, the number of the leaves, and of the sections and also sometimes the subject treated of, are printed, the same as in European books, except that in the latter, they are at the top of the page, whereas here, they are on the front-edge of the leaf; and generally cut so exactly on the place where it is folded that one in turning the leaves, sees one half of each character, on one side, and the other half, on the other. The number of sheets destined to constitute the volume, being laid down and pressed between two boards, on the upper one of which a heavy stone is laid, they are then covered with a sort of coarse paper — not with boards as in Europe; the back is then cut, after which the volume is stitched, not in our way, but through the whole volume at once, from side to side, a hole having been previously made through it with a small pointed iron instrument. The top and bottom are then cut, and thus the whole process of Chinese type-cutting, printing, and binding is finished.[42]

All this work was sometimes executed by just one person[43] but far more commonly by separate specialists in each of the four stages.[44] Although by probably the mid-thirteenth century and no later than the early fourteenth century, some workers, including carvers, were women or children, they usually were adult males.[45]

The overall cost of this work has long confounded Western commentators (traditional Chinese records very rarely mention the issue), and on this matter Milne expressed to London his own perplexity. Firstly, "there are always a great many incidental expenses, which cannot at first be brought into any calculation."[46] More troublesome was the great number of variables for every aspect of the printing stages, creating a confusing tangle of figures and prices that undermine the validity of any clear-cut conclusion on prices and thus on the key issue of the relative costs of printing with woodblocks or with moveable type:

> Not having a sufficient series of facts on both sides of the subject, to form proper data, I choose rather to propose this in the form of question, than to affirm any thing relative to it. Without seeing both methods fairly developing their advantages, no man can be a proper judge of their merits; and without a full, clear, explicit, and merchant-like statement of all and every item of expense attending both methods, for *a given quantity of work,* (say an edition of thirty thousand copies of some standard book,) there is no means of coming to a correct decision.[47]

A major complication to any calculation of production costs was the lifespan of woodblocks. Over time, their surface wore out, thereby limiting the number of clear copies they could make.[48] To postpone that inevitability, the printers would, "after making 2000 to 3000 copies, … gently wash the plate, repeatedly dry the blocks and not allow their face to soften by being kept wet with ink for a long time, then let the blocks dry, so as to re-harden their surface and thereby extend their printing life."[49] Yet, the point at which blocks started to print blurred, unsellable copies was hard to determine in general, and Milne's conclusions are characteristically cautious and precise:

> The permanent clearness of a Chinese impression depends greatly on the quality of the wood of which the plate is made; on the goodness of the type cutter's work; on the proper tempering of the ink, and on the care of the printer. If, for example, the printer be a clumsy or careless workman, the very first thousand copies will appear blotted, and the blocks will not last any length of time — perhaps they will not bear casting off 6 or 7,000 copies without being renewed, or at least repaired. I am not able to say with certainty, *what number* of copies, good blocks will bear to be cast off: our printers there affirm, that *thirty thousand* can be printed from the same plate, if it possess the quality and advantages above mentioned. From some that we have used, in the service of the Mission, upwards of *ten thousand* copies have been printed, and they seem perfectly able to bear another edition of the same number, if carefully treated.[50]

Two decades later, another missionary raised Milne's top figure of 30,000 by roughly a third: "It used to be supposed by foreigners that not more than 15000 or 20000 copies could be taken from a set of [wood]blocks. But from recent experiments it appears that more than 40000 copies may be struck, giving very fair impressions."[51]

In the end, this basic issue of the maximum size of a print run remains for both Milne and us too complex to permit just one figure. The variables of quality he indicated for wood, ink, and print work are too great to allow any single conclusion, but rather a set of maximum estimates of, say, 6,000 for poorly carved and tended blocks, a maximum of roughly 40,000 copies of well-cut blocks of very hard wood, and, far more commonly, runs of 15,000 to 30,000. And, to muddy the water even more, these woodblocks, even while still capable of printing readable copies, could themselves be sold off to be replaned for the carving of another book.[52]

After presenting his readers with all these complexities, Milne is aware of woodblock printing's disadvantages. He mentions the length of its production time, its seeming inappropriateness for miscellaneous ephemera, the storage problem created by the accumulation of woodblocks, the declining clarity of a used woodblock's impressions, the expense from the repetitive labor required to carve the same character many times, the uselessness of worn-out wooden blocks, and the difficulty of including other languages' writing in columns of Chinese characters. Yet, in the end Milne does not disguise his conviction that woodblock printing in some if not many instances is both cheaper and more suitable than moveable type for printing in Chinese. Admittedly, he is largely ignorant of the variety of earlier Chinese successes in using moveable type (he seems unaware that moveable type was invented four centuries earlier than Gutenberg by Bi Sheng [c. 990–1051] in the 1040s)[53] and of the considerable drop in book prices from the mid-eighteenth century to the early nineteenth.[54] Moreover, wooden moveable type, according to a sophisticated analysis recently presented by Martin J. Heijdra, was arguably the cheapest means of printing books with very small runs, of roughly a hundred or fewer. Milne, most likely due to his interest in achieving large runs for the Bible and his religious tracts, ignores this possibility and so focuses, like virtually all the missionaries, on metal moveable-type versus woodblock printing, to reach a conclusion he considers valid for all runs regardless of their size.[55] And, he completely neglects the advances of stereotyping[56] and especially the attractions of lithography, a very late eighteenth-century invention that represented the first major innovation in Western printing technology since Gutenberg's time.[57]

Despite these weaknesses in his analysis, Milne distinguishes himself from most of his British contemporaries by calling attention to the important cost advantages of woodblock printing for Chinese-language texts. Firstly, Chinese woodblock publishers, unlike their Western counterparts, had no need of a foundry for casting type, or expensive and complex machines for printing and binding, or premises (with costly rent) for housing equipment and products (they had only to house the woodblocks).[58] In addition to a handful of simple carving tools, carvers merely required a small table and odd stool. Moreover, this pair of wooden furniture pieces could be located virtually anywhere, be it temporarily designated space in a domestic or temple courtyard, the corner of a cellar or attic, alongside the bed in a small room, publicly accessible land alongside a field or road, or even the deck of a traveling ship.[59] Consequently, a publisher's overhead and rent were minimal, as would also be the initial layout of capital and interest payments.[60]

Secondly, the casting and cutting of Chinese characters into metallic type was, at least initially, more expensive than the purchase and carving of woodblocks, not least because the Chinese language consisted of tens of thousands of distinct characters, some of which would have to be made in many copies for moveable-type printing. Long-term use of these fonts would cut their cost, but many beginning enterprises could not bear the heavy initial outlays or interest rates on loans to meet the starting costs of a printing press and type font. At this time, Milne was seeking funds to print in Chinese his *On the Exposition of the Epistle of Paul to the Ephesians*, and in a separate composition explains why printing this book with woodblocks would be far cheaper than with Western-style moveable type:

> The expense of preparing a set of good blocks for it will amount, I suppose, to £50 sterling at least. It contains about 86,000 characters. If to these the points and head-lines be added, they will amount to 90, 000. The expense of printing it with the defective font of moveable characters which we possess, would amount, I think, to much more than four times that sum; for there are, as you will see, three different sizes of letter, which could require as many different sizes of character. This would necessarily be very expensive. On the Chinese mode, the different sizes of character are all cut on the same block, by the same hand, with the same ease, and at nearly the same price. But indeed, in our circumstances, and with our views of the subject, we are fully satisfied that the Chinese method of printing is the most suitable to their language, and best adapted to our purposes.[61]

And, thirdly, labor costs for woodblock production were noticeably cheaper than for moveable-type printing. The block cutters' "only business is to follow their copy. Of this latter sort, there are many in China, females particularly (for they also cut as well as men), who cannot read a single word; and yet they earn their daily bread at this work. But such could not be employed as [moveable-type] compositors," since a compositor needs to have some knowledge of reading: "A tolerably educated Chinese cannot be employed for much less than double the wages of a mere mechanic; and I am persuaded that men of tolerable education are necessary to carry on this work with expedition."[62]

The low wages of these woodblock workers, as well as their efficiency, astonished Milne, as they had all Western commentators on Chinese printing ever since the Jesuit missionary Matteo Ricci noted "the ridiculously low" price of Chinese books in the late sixteenth century.[63] Milne estimated that, over the course of a year, a good carver could cut on average 150 characters a day, and two Chinese workers, each printing from a separate block, will between them run off 2,000 paper copies a day. This Chinese pair, if compared with the production level of an English press using a form of only four pages for each impression, could produce "about as many sheets in a day as the two men at the English press can, supposing both parties equally qualified in regard to skill and strength."[64] Medhurst, in coming to the conclusion that "the rapidity with which [the Chinese] carve their intricate and complicated characters is really surprising, and not to be imitated by European artists, in the same style of execution," lowered the first of these figures to 100 characters a day for the carver but raised the second to 3,000 copies a day for one printer.[65] Equally striking to Medhurst was the cheap cost of Chinese labor: "A London engraver was surprised when he learned, that what could cost sixty or eighty shillings in England might be accomplished by a Chinese workman for half-a-crown [i.e., 2.5 shillings, or less than 5 per cent of the London cost]."[66]

Yet, once again Milne shows a sharp awareness of the complexity of labor costs by noting the great range in Chinese carvers' pay. Whereas the famous Haechang Temple in Canton hired carvers by the day for one cash per carved character for its handbills, public notices of festivals, and religious tracts,[67] he notes that his colleague Morrison at the start of the nineteenth century had received from several workers in Canton greatly varying estimates for the price ("in

Spanish [i.e., Mexican] dollars") of three grades of work involved in carving 10,000 woodblock characters: top-best quality: 30, 21, and 11; second-best quality: 20 and 15; and, third-best quality: 12 and 7.5. Westerners often had to pay more than Chinese, not least because the Chinese government banned the printing of their religious tracts in China and thus obliged Milne to set up his press in Malacca rather than Canton. Nonetheless, the second of Morrison's estimates approximates the carving expenses Milne paid in Malacca in c.1820.[68] When compared with the cost of printing by moveable type, it does seem to have been cheaper, particularly when the publisher was not willing to make a long-term investment in his printing enterprise.

After his death in 1822, Milne's recommendation would eventually lose out to arguments in favor of using moveable type for printing Chinese texts. The advocates of this technology held that moveable type was actually cheaper once its machinery was in place and once an adequate type font had been made for Chinese characters. Furthermore, they believed that the operation of this Western technology, since it needed little if any aid from Chinese workers, would free the mission from Qing dynasty controls over Chinese carvers and thus enable it to schedule more regular publication of its books.[69] But, I suspect that what won the London committee over to this "Westernization" printing plan was the committee's evangelical drive to save the souls of 450,000,000 Chinese with its translated version of the Bible. Type fonts had their inadequacies,[70] but their runs far outstripped those of any Chinese woodblocks with maximum runs of, say, 40,000 cheap impressions. Salvation, then, lay with the technology of the printing press, and, by the mid-nineteenth century, its font was ready and its machinery had been moved to Hong Kong and then Shanghai. Virtually, without notice, the woodblocks made for the missionaries' translation of the Bible fell into disuse, and two Western methods of printing, first lithography and then moveable type, came to replace woodblock printing for the great majority of urban publications by the second and third decades of the twentieth century.

If Milne's recommendation of woodblock printing won few Western supporters during the nineteenth century, his analysis nonetheless remains highly valuable for its account of the process and economics of woodblock production on the eve of the introduction into China of modern Western printing methods, lithography as well as moveable type. It enables us to understand why knowledgeable Chinese, aware of the potential of moveable type, still preferred woodblock printing and why its advocates in China were often hardheaded men of business as well as literati and scholars.

Changes in the Production of Woodblock Imprints

Milne's claims of low production costs for woodblock printing are, it must be said, supported by a variety of Chinese descriptive accounts and some price data from the mid-Ming onwards. These sources indicate the introduction of significant drops in production costs for each of the four stages of production during the sixteenth century. Consider first the matter of binding. The stitched binding of books mentioned in Milne's description was a method that originated between the late ninth and late tenth centuries but was widely adopted only from the sixteenth century, in part, to make books more durable.[71] In contrast to the two kinds of book binding more commonly used from the tenth to the sixteenth centuries — that is, wrapped-back binding and butterfly binding with a stiff cover and pasted spine — stitched binding avoided the troublesome pastes that all too often in these other binding methods failed to hold the folded paper sheets together. Instead, it relied on puncturing the folded sheets with a sharp awl and threading them, with the aid of a press, into an evenly tied collection of pages. The production of such flexible but tightly bound volumes, moreover, required fewer workers and permitted a lower level of skill than did other binding methods. These books also proved more convenient for shipping and storing, with or without the protection of a clothboard box cover.[72] Consequently, the widespread adoption of this kind of stitched binding, even for Buddhist texts, can only have cut book production expenses.[73]

Printing costs, as far as I can discern, fell not due to any simplification of the printing process itself but due to a significant reduction in the price of printers' paper.[74] In the Song dynasty, paper had been expensive enough to warrant its regular recycling, as the late Ming scholar Zhang Xuan confirmed when, to his surprise, he discovered writing on the backside of pages in Song imprints stored in the Ming imperial library.[75] Song court offices even relied on the sale of used paper to finance a banquet or increase their revenue.[76] Then, in the fifteenth and sixteenth centuries, the greater production of cheap (and sometimes improved) bamboo paper from Fujian and Zhejiang Provinces and the exploitation of once distant forests in Jiangxi Province greatly increased the supply of cheap paper in south China.[77] So inexpensive did paper become that the walls of villages in the southeast were soon festooned with government paper posters and shrines and temples lit up by the constant burning of paper money.[78]

But, the major factor in reduced book production costs during the middle and late Ming came from falling labor costs in reproducing the script carved into woodblocks. As such, these savings were most evident in the transcription and carving stages of the production process, two stages that, together, account for most production costs in the known woodblock printing budget estimates from the late Ming and the nineteenth century.[79] Whereas up to the early Ming the transcriber of a literati text onto the paper sheets destined for a woodblock might be the author of the text, his disciples, his friend, his son, or even a respected calligrapher,[80] from the latter half of the Ming the transcriber even for literati works was normally a "mere transcriber." He was, as Milne noted, not a scholar or literatus but a lowly scribe with a few circumscribed skills: "To write this form of the character, is of itself an employment in China. There are men who learn it of purpose, and devote themselves entirely to the labor of transcribing for the press. Few of the learned can write it: indeed they rather think it below them to do the work of a mere transcriber."[81] The transcribers were expected to write characters in a calligraphic style that blended and simplified the brushstroke styles of Tang dynasty calligraphers famous in the Song dynasty, such as Ouyang Xun (557–641), Yan Zhenqing (709–85), and Liu Gongchuan (778–865). Commonly known, therefore, as "Song dynasty characters" (*Songti zi*) — this is the very term Milne uses to name the kind of characters written by transcribers in his analysis[82] — this homogenized style is more accurately described by its alternative name of "artisanal characters" (*jiangti zi*). Nondescript and impersonal, it relied on the manipulation of a brush to form square-like characters out of five kinds of straight, flat, and upright strokes (一, 丨, 丿, 丶, and 一). The resulting box-like uniformity of characters facilitated carving and legibility as well as imparted a balance to the look of the page.[83] But, it paid little attention to the dynamic interplay in the original brushstroke order and style of the calligraphy, and the imprint looked significantly less like a manuscript (see Figures 2, 3 and 4).[84] Predictably, the eyes of literati readers were not pleased.

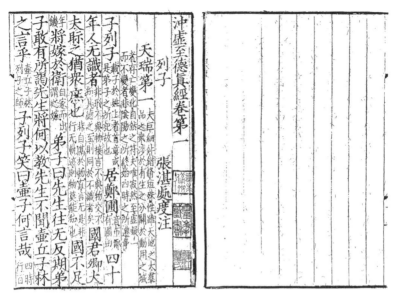

Figure 2   Zhang Zhan, annot., *Chongxu zhide zhenjing zhu* (Northern Song imprint), in Yan Lingfeng, comp. *Wuqiu bei zhai Liezi jicheng* (Taipei: Yiwen yinshua shuguan, 1971), v. 2

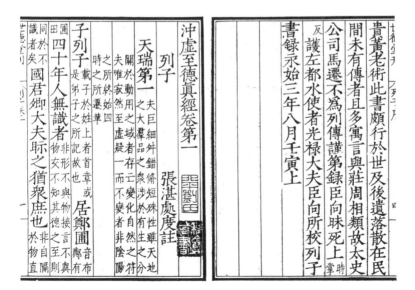

Figure 3   Zhang Zhan, annot., *Liezi zhu* (1530 imprint), in Yan Lingfeng, comp. *Wuqiu bei zhai Liezi jicheng* (Taipei: Yiwen yinshua shuguan, 1971), v. 2

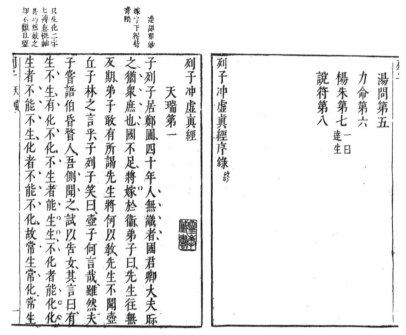

Figure 4   Sun Kuang, annot., *Liezi chongxu zhide zhenjing ping* (1621–27 imprint), in Yan Lingfeng, comp. *Wuqiu bei zhai Liezi jicheng* (Taipei: Yiwen yinshua shuguan, 1971), v. 8.

This change of calligraphy style had clear implications for woodblock scribal and carving work beyond the concerns of aesthetics.[85] In Lucille Chia's view, it cut costs, since it allowed the publisher to squeeze more characters onto the surface of a woodblock.[86] The severe restriction it placed on the range of a scribe's strokes and carver's cuts further lowered costs, since it reduced the range of calligraphic and carving skill demanded of their work. Able thereby to farm out some of this work to family members less gifted with cutting tools, the carvers seem to have gone about their work more quickly and cheaply but also in a strikingly different way. The clearest guide to the scale of savings is found in the wages prescribed for the scribes and carvers engaged to write or carve three different calligraphy styles for the Imperial Household Department (*neifu*) in the eighteenth century:

Calligraphy Style	Scribe, per 1000 Characters	Carver, per 100 Characters
Song [or, Artisanal]	2 *qian* of silver	8 *fen*
Ou[yang Xun]	4 *qian* of silver	1 qian 6 *fen*
Standard (*kaishu*)	3 *qian* of silver	1 qian 3 *fen*[87]

The drop in the labor costs of these two relatively expensive stages of book production of 50 percent (shifting from the standard to artisanal style) and 100 percent (shifting from the Ouyang Xun to artisanal style) points to significant savings that, in a competitive market, must have eventually led to considerable cuts in the cost of books for customers.

This change in the calligraphy style of an imprint also led, it seems, to a different method of carving, if not in this project then in other carving assignments. Just as a scribe reproduced a limited array of brushstrokes easy to carve, so did a carver cut on a single woodblock all examples of one type of brushstroke before cutting the rest. Each stroke in a character functioned as a reproducible part within what Lothar Ledderose has aptly termed "the module system" of Chinese script and art.[88] Once carved and printed, this script invariably resembled metal or wooden type more than the calligraphy of the famous masters it was said to imitate. In hindsight, then, the widespread adoption of these artisanal characters for literati imprints from the mid-Ming onwards represents a significant step in the long-term evolution of Chinese printing styles from manuscript-style to type-style script.[89] This shift would culminate in China with the widespread switch to lithography in the late nineteenth century and then to moveable-type printing in the twentieth century. Eventually, it would lead to the virtual demise of woodblock printing by the middle of the twentieth century.[90]

While we have no Ming description of the carvers' actual division of their labor (and Milne's own Chinese printer did all four stages of the work in Malacca), Medhurst's 1838 account presented above clearly has a carver cut a woodblock's characters in a stroke order — first the horizontal strokes, then the oblique, and finally the perpendicular (i.e., the vertical) — very different from the order in which they would have been transcribed. Three twentieth-century accounts generally confirm and clarify the workings of this carving process. A field survey report on traditional practices observed in

Yangzhou in 1999 indicates that each of the five artisanal strokes used for writing characters would be completely carved in turn for an entire sheet and woodblock, not for just each character in turn.[91] Such a reconstitution of the work process had potential implications for the carvers themselves; that is, once this work was divided in this way, more than one carver could in theory share in the work of carving the text of a single woodblock. In fact, this type of division of labor into distinct work modules was observed by Tanaka Shishō on a visit to China before World War II. The hard work (e.g., the horizontal strokes) was done by accomplished carvers and the relatively easy work (e.g., the vertical strokes) by their apprentices and other less experienced carvers, thereby relying on as many as four workers to carve the text of a single woodblock.[92] A recent report from Huizhou prefecture in southern Anhui confirms the general point of Tanaka's account, as woodblock carvers there are said to have divided up the carving work for a single woodblock among themselves according to the five separate strokes of the artisanal characters (no mention was made of a reliance on apprentices, but their use cannot be automatically ruled out).[93]

Since the first detailed Chinese account of the process of book production dates from 1947, the lack of any Ming or Qing source confirming such a division of carving labor need not rule out its practice then. Indeed, late Ming China boasted of far more detailed divisions of labor (up to 400 workers were used in as many as twenty-three stages in the production of porcelain at the Ming imperial kiln in Jingdezhen),[94] as well as of a trend for the adoption of simplified carving techniques for the related art of lacquerware (this change has been attributed to a shift of the work to large studios where carving assignments were parceled out to different carvers).[95] In sum, we should allow for a variety of carving practices associated with the increasing use of the artisanal characters from the mid-Ming, as determined by availability of carvers, their varying levels of expertise, their work schedules, the production budget, and other local factors. While the more advanced practices of labor division may have originated after the Ming, even the use of a single carver for artisanal characters in the latter half of the Ming would have generally simplified the previous work process, making it quicker and cheaper. Thus, the late fifteenth and early sixteenth century changes in book publishing skill, especially carving, confirm the first half, though not the second half, of Francesca Bray's general assessment of Ming technology: "the overall technological trend was towards smaller, not larger, scale, and toward more skilled methods."[96] Even though the writing and carving of artisanal characters required their own special skills, the latter claim of Bray's statement held only for up-market editions of literati imprints and their prefaces, a share of the total imprint market that declined greatly over the course of the Ming.

The claim of lower production costs and cheaper books is confirmed by the very limited price data we have on carvers' wages and book prices from the Song through the Yuan and Ming dynasties. These figures are notoriously hard to interpret accurately, since prices for the same title and amount of work could vary greatly according to the quality and availability of labor and materials, the place of production, and the infernally complex irregularities of metallic currency changes and depreciations over the seven centuries of these three distinct dynasties. Nonetheless, the price data for carving 100 characters in the Yangzi delta show a remarkable drop from, on average, about 35 *wen* in ca.1250 to 3.5 *wen* in ca.1600.[97] This fall in so crucial a component in book production costs, when combined with the other production savings we have considered, can only have meant a considerable drop in the overall cost of producing and buying books. High-cost versions of new and old titles continued to be published, but far cheaper versions of these were now available and in far greater numbers. These production and price changes would have, as we shall see, a considerable impact on the great expansion of commercial publication that took place in the last century and a half of the Ming.

The Worlds of Woodblock Carvers

What, then, was the impact of this fall in the cost of carving and other imprint production factors on the condition and organization of labor during the sixteenth century? By itself, perhaps little. But, thanks to some official records, to information in the imprints themselves, and to apparent changes in the way work was recorded on the woodblocks and their printed sheets, we can attempt an answer to this difficult question for the carvers. Unfortunately, our sources are seldom informative about the other kinds of artisans involved in imprint production.

Tucked away in printed books on the fold of sheets, at the end of prefaces, chapters, and introductory remarks or in the corners of illustrated prints, are the names of some 3,000 woodblock carvers from the Song and Yuan and another 6,000-odd from the Ming.[98] Their names appear in only a small portion of the surviving imprints of these dynasties — for example, less than four per cent in the Ming.[99] They also tended to appear more in some areas' imprints than in others'; for example, far more often in publications of Hangzhou and Hubei in the Song and Suzhou in the Ming than in those of Nanjing, Guangdong, Fujian, and the regional princely establishments in the Ming.[100] They are far more numerous than the names found so far for individuals involved in the production of other types of Song, Yuan, and Ming dynasty handicraft goods, such as porcelain, jade, ivory, and lacquerware. Also, they far outnumber the names of other book workers. For instance, for the Song we know the names of no more than twenty-two printer artisans and fewer binders, and just five printer artisans and seven binders in the Ming.[101]

This information, when used to reconstruct the working career of these carvers from their listed involvement in various book publications, shows that a carver's life in certain dimensions did not change significantly from the Song through the Ming. Carvers tended to congregate in centers of book production. By the mid-thirteenth century, thus, they worked in at least ninety-one prefectures in south China, but mainly in Hangzhou, Jianyang in northern Fujian, and Chengdu in Sichuan.[102] In the Jin and Yuan dynasties, the centers of production were Pingyang prefecture in southern Shanxi Province and, once again for southeast China, Hangzhou and Jianyang.[103] By the late Ming, the lower Yangzi delta, mainly Suzhou and Nanjing, would dominate along with Jianyang. By the early seventeenth century, carvers would also have found their way to provinces that, in the Song and Yuan, had produced only a few books (e.g., Hunan, Shaanxi, and Guangdong) but had recently started to print a fair number of imprints for the book market.

Conversely, many woodblock carvers from Song times onward were journeymen.[104] Their tools, as already seen, were few and portable. The demand for their labor in a single location or establishment could be unreliable and intermittent,[105] lasting perhaps a few days but also stretching out at intervals for as long as a century.[106] And, many prefectures had a shortage of artisans with the necessary skills for quality work,[107] so that much low-grade carving was done as secondary work by locals normally engaged in agriculture and other occupations. In the Song and Yuan dynasties, many traveling carvers appear to have been born in Hangzhou and Fujian.[108] In the Ming, many still came from Fujian but also from Zhejiang and, perhaps primarily, Jiangxi[109] (the Ming transcribers often came from Suzhou, or at least claimed to).[110] The range of their movements was extensive, a single Ming carver working in places as distant and varied as a Suzhou commercial printing house and a Mt. Wutai monastery off in northern Shanxi Province[111] (one suspects the involvement of labor or monastic brokers). The labor market for woodblock carvers in southeast China by the late twelfth century had started to become integrated, with, for instance, Hangzhou-based carvers finding work in 1177 alongside local carvers in Fuzhou, Jiangxi Province.[112] By the early fourteenth century, and even more during the sixteenth and seventeenth centuries,[113] that process had further developed, so that by the late sixteenth century as many as 387 carvers (as well as 84 scribes and 3 illustration carvers) from over 50 counties in 5 southeastern provinces might work in Hangzhou prefecture for the publication of an extensive collection of Buddhist texts.[114]

We can also note three changes that mark off the organization, division of labor, and social status of carvers in the sixteenth century from what they had been in the early Ming. Firstly, Ming artisan households acquired, by the late fifteenth century, greater independence from state control than they had known up to the late fifteenth century. As one type of artisan household, carvers' households, particularly those resident in or near large cities with publishing houses, like Nanjing, Beijing, and Hangzhou, would have been obliged to carve woodblocks for state printing publications for as much as two months every two years. For instance, 150 carvers were assigned to the Directorate of Ceremonial in the initial Ming capital of Nanjing on regular two-year assignments, as were 312 binders and 58 printers on regular one-year assignments.[115] By the end of the first century of Ming rule, such government work duties had begun to be replaced by cash payments, and by 1531, the number of artisans in this Directorate who were listed as engaged solely in publishing had more than doubled, to almost 1,300. Of these, 48 were brushmakers, 62 papermakers, 77 illustrators (or painters), 77 ink-makers, 80 cutters, 134 printers, 189 paper-sheet folders, 293 binders, and, as the largest group, 315 carvers. Quite likely, many of these workers did not work full-time and paid someone else to do this work for them. Nonetheless, it is clear that, by 1582, the woodblock carvers in Beijing had their own guild, as the emperor then granted a tax exemption to a woodblock carvers guild (*kanzi hang*) and thirty-one other guilds, including those for book workers (*tushu*), gazette copiers, intermediaries, and brush sellers, in the two metropolitan counties of Beijing.[116] For south China, a woodblock carvers guild is first recorded in 1739 in Suzhou.[117] The precise governance of these guilds, organized at least in part to ease the payment of taxes levied collectively on members, remains unclear. Yet, the state's role would certainly have receded, to allow for the increasing demands of the commercial publishing houses from the sixteenth century.

Secondly, as government controls weakened, the carvers seem to have formed more of their own work groups. Carvers had routinely worked in groups as just one of the various types of artisans engaged in imprint production, and each had regularly done just a small number of the pages in an imprint since at least the Song. As many as 134 carvers were hired for a Southern Song (1127–79) printing of the 102-chapter (*juan*) collected writings of the neo-Confucian master Zhu Xi, and, arguably, 80 carvers worked regularly in the relatively large publishing establishment of Mao Jin, The Hall of Drinking from the Well of Antiquity (*Jigu ge*), in the mid-seventeenth century.[118] Yet, beginning in the Yuan dynasty and increasingly evident from the late fifteenth century was, in the view of Nagasawa Kikuya and Tanaka Shishō, another form of carvers' work group: the carver whose name was cut into the woodblock had actually become the head of a group of carvers. As head, he arranged not just his own employment but also that of the other carvers in his group, both the experienced and the apprentices. The evidence for this claim about changes in work arrangements is largely circumstantial; that is, the declining frequency of the inclusion of a single carver's name on woodblocks and the sheets from the Song, when it was often on every printed sheet, to the Ming, when it was on but a few printed sheets and sometimes just on the final printed sheet of a chapter.[119] Since many artisans working for commercial publishers in the Song would also have had their own young apprentices, it is hard to think of such a group arrangement as new. But, it may be that the increased use of commercial printing in the Ming made it more common and allowed the head to arrange work for other experienced carvers as well as his apprentices, including younger family members and relations.[120]

Far less speculative is the evidence of greater stratification within the ranks of woodblock carvers by skills, location, and connections. Within the overall process of imprint production from Song times onward, the carvers as a group accounted for most of the wages paid to the four types of artisans involved in imprint production. Yet, even if their share might total nine or ten times more than, say, the payment for scribes, the average scribe nonetheless could do the work far more quickly than a carver (transcribing, by one estimate, 2,500 characters a day)[121] and on an annual basis would probably have earned considerably more than the ordinary carver. Furthermore, the scribe was literate and the carver often was not, thereby letting the scribe, even when younger, receive more face than the carver.[122] During the Ming, such distinctions among these different kinds of book production artisans persisted. Significantly, however, they were supplemented by increased distinctions in pay and status among the carvers themselves. While such economic and social differences had undoubtedly existed earlier in the Song (when these workers might have held the same tools and jobs and came from the same native place), in the late Ming we see a far wider social span, some carvers at the top, and less typical, end of the social hierarchy of their craft, distinguishing themselves as literati artisans.

The clearest examples of literati carvers were the Huangs of She county, Huizhou prefecture, in southern Anhui Province. Between the mid-sixteenth and the mid-seventeenth centuries, hundreds of them gained fame and fortune for themselves and their lineage by means of their delicate thin carving.[123] First recognized as the regional Huizhou style, their skilled use of the carving tools eventually influenced carving styles elsewhere in the empire. This popularity not only enabled the Huangs to replace a rival lineage as the dominant group in their native village and in the Qing dynasty to secure a special niche in the printing of lineage genealogies.[124] But also, it won much demand for their work as woodblock carvers and even small publishers in Nanjing, Hangzhou, and other cities of the Yangzi delta.[125]

These Huangs generally made no effort to disguise their lowly origins as farmers, carvers, or even book merchants.[126] Yet, many of these males preferred, like some highly respected late-Ming potters, gardeners, and bamboo-carvers, to present themselves as literati rather than as artisans[127] (at least in the nineteenth century, ordinary woodblock carvers in north and south China worshipped the god Wenchang, better known as the god for literati and civil service examination candidates).[128] Admittedly, no Huang seems to have imitated the artisan Zhu Gui by carving a book he had written.[129] Yet, their work, often included as illustrations in the flourishing literati genres of drama, fiction, drama, and print albums, won favor in literati circles. Understandably, then, many Huangs adopted a literati persona, taking on at least one style name (*zi*) and one soubriquet (*hao*) in the manner of any aspiring literatus. Some achieved local fame for their calligraphy and transcribed the texts they proceeded to carve.[130] Others became known for their compositions, their prose style, and their medical knowledge.[131] Others were skilled in the literati arts of painting, portraiture, calligraphy, and music.[132] And yet others became heads of small publishing concerns.[133] Many regularly traveled back and forth between their Huizhou village and the cities of the Yangzi delta, taking up work assignments and long-term residence in urban literati centers like Suzhou, Nanjing, and, especially, Hangzhou.[134] If no Huang carver actually passed the civil service examinations beyond the local student school level, some of their kin did gain official appointments, a certain Huang Quan even becoming a painting aide in the Ministry of War and a scholar in the Ministry of Rites.[135] To cite just one example, Huang Yingcheng (1565–1640) revised the family genealogy, wrote fine prose, composed a preface to a lineage genealogy, and carved illustrations for at least one known imprint.[136]

How different was the compensation for the successful literati carvers like the Huangs from that for the ordinary carver? At present, it is impossible to say. But, clearly their reputation and higher salary derived from the eminence that more than thirty of them achieved as carvers of illustrations (*huike*).[137] Despite the excellence of some Song illustrated prints (often to accompany Buddhist texts), this specialized term and category was first applied to carvers of woodblock illustrations, I believe, in the late Ming, as recognition of their distinctive craft.[138]

At the bottom, more typical, end of the scale, one finds artisans with poor working conditions and low pay. Working on short-term jobs, perhaps as brief as a day, they would be hired to carve between 100 and 150 characters a day. They were paid per diem or for each 100 characters they carved; calculated either way, their wages were low, varying in several sixteenth-century cases from 2.5 to 3.5 *fen* of copper cash per 100 characters.[139] A full day's work of, say, 150 characters, would earn a carver between 3.8 and 5.2 *fen*, along with a hard bed and a meager board of two meals. If his work was judged insufficiently skilled or not in line with the requested specifications, then, according to two late Ming contract forms for hired labor (both of which were published in the lower Yangzi delta), he was to lose a portion of his already paltry pay.[140] Although the wages for carvers, according to early nineteenth-century reports, accounted for between a third to a quarter of all the production costs for buying, cutting, and printing books off woodblocks,[141] the carvers then and earlier could barely scrape together a living for themselves (in the late Ming, 1 *fen* was needed to pay for one day's humble fare for a Buddhist monk).[142] Consequently, these itinerant workers rarely had any savings and at least a sizeable minority had no family of their own (a single imprint title often has carvers of the same surname, and it is likely that they were kin, but few of the 6,000 Ming woodcarvers we know of are identified as father and son). When marrying, many carvers, particularly the journeymen, may well have been unable to pay for the service of that respect-conferring busybody so well known to readers of Chinese fiction as the go-between.

The most insightful guide we have to the life and circumstances of such carvers is a short, but remarkably personal, biography written by the Suzhou literatus, Tang Shunzhi (1507–60), about a hired book worker (*shuyong*) named Hu Mao.[143] Fortunately, his name is not a literary dead-end, as Tang's appreciation of Hu's work opens a window onto the otherwise unrecorded experience of workers involved in the production of books, in this case principally the stage of binding, probably in Suzhou, the city reputed to do the best binding work.[144] Born in the southern Zhejiang county of Longyou, Hu Mao lacked the funds required to continue in the occupation of his father and elder brother(s), of trading in used books. But his skill at collating and binding books, particularly at ordering the mass of texts for printing sheets and piercing the sheets with a sharp awl, astonished many contemporaries in the book trade, not least because the pace and quality of his work were not deterred by his inability to fathom the meaning of the text. Initially, his talent won him much work in bookstores and in scholars' homes, both of which often printed books. Otherwise, his sole interest throughout his life was liquor: "The cash pay acquired by hired book workers is not much, and he used it all up in liquor. Hired book workers do not ask about being paid in cash; they invariably ask about whether the liquor can be enough or not. Mao had no wife and son. He was a hired book worker for several decades, and he had no pile of tiles where he might perch his body. Other than being permanently drunk, he was aware of nothing."[145] Later on, he made a living in the homes of various scholars, but his skill with books went unused. Fearing, then, that Hu had made no preparations for his burial, Tang ended up buying him a coffin made of fine cypress (*shan*) wood and composing a brief memorial to honor his skilled work. The response of Hu Mao and other Ming workers with woodblocks to these working conditions, when they were sober, can easily be imagined. Yet, no Ming account records any collective activity by them other than for, perhaps, religious worship and mutual support. They certainly did not engage in collective efforts to raise their salary, such as were attempted, in vain, by Suzhou's papermakers in 1755 and printing employees in 1845.[146]

This vignette of "a proto-industrial proletarian" suggests a sharp social divide between woodblock carvers and the literati authors of the texts they cut. Often that must have been the case, Tang Shunzhi's sympathy being more the exception than the rule. But, in the late Ming also the boundaries between artisan and literatus were blurred not only by artisans like the Huangs but also by Yangzi delta literati like Wen Peng (1498–1573). This painter, the son of sixteenth-century Suzhou's most famous literatus, Wen Zhengming (1470–1559), took up a chisel and knife to carve seal stones and secured a very successful career as a seal carver, with no loss to his reputation as a literatus.[147] Even with woodblock carving, one can note a few signs of this trespassing, as when some students at the National University in Nanjing during the last half of the sixteenth century carved woodblocks that were eventually used to print the university's edition of three dynastic histories (neither their Song nor Qing counterparts appear to have engaged in such labor).[148] In the commercial printing world of Mao Jin's publishing establishment, Jigu ge, the 200 men who were hired to produce books printed in the "artisanal character" style worked alongside literati who also became friends of their employer.[149]

Yet, such crossovers into artisanship, even for literati painters who carved seal stones and sold them to others, were relatively few.[150] We know of a certain Mu Jinwen, a Nanjing man registered in Suzhou, who, upon giving up his *shengyuan*, or district, degree and his hopes for an official career, set up his own shop to support himself in the latter half of the eighteenth century. His business work had him personally carving woodblocks, at least sometimes for books dealing with ancient calligraphy and inscriptions, that his shop would then print from and sell. Similar cases of literati turning to the work of artisan are seldom recorded (his son, for example, succeeded to his job, but no claim is made for him of any examination success)[151] and probably occurred more often than our sources suggest. Yet, carving the woodblocks of ordinary imprints was, unlike the carving of seals on order from individuals, impersonal work and of no status. Also, the work was quite often collective, obliging literati to associate with artisans engaged in the other stages of print and imprint production. By its nature, it would have been particularly otiose to many status-conscious literati, including those without the lowly district degree.

The future of woodblock production, however, lay with the artisans. In the eighteenth century, the simplicity, portability, low production costs, and low demand on skills enabled many poorer families to enjoy the benefits of its technical promise and its potential social reach. For the first time, many parts of China printed cheap individual illustrated sheets that met the demand of a far larger market for a more plebian treatment of popular subjects.[152] The world of literati-ish carvers like the Huangs lost out to the world of Hu Mao and ordinary carvers.[153] Not only would there emerge in the large cities of the lower Yangzi delta a greater divide between some readers of literati books and their artisan producers, a gap that an artisan like Qian Jinren would try to bridge. But this world of cheap and numerous imprints would also impress Qian's near contemporary, William Milne, and prompt him to write his graphic account of how these books were made.

Appendix 1.1

A late sixteenth-century imprint of the Buddhist canon in the lower Yangtze delta details the budget for different stages of publication. Note that the cost of paper, printing, and binding is not included, presumably because anyone receiving an offprint from these woodblocks was expected to pay these charges and services by himself or herself. Nonetheless, the prominence of carvers' wages in this budget (about three-quarters), combined with what we know of lower costs at this time for paper and binding, suggests that carvers' wages were the principal cost in this woodblock publishing venture. A photograph and transcription of this text, reproduced in the Japanese reprint of this canon, can be found in Inoue, *Chūgoku*, pp. 223–4:

- For each 100 characters the scribe receives 4 *li* of silver and the carver 3 *fen* and 5 *li* of silver.
- For each single woodblock, the transport from the place of purchase up to the temple is altogether 3 *fen* and 4 *li*, its planing work is 2 *li* of silver, and its margin-making work is 2 *li* of silver.
- For each woodblock, both faces have 20 columns. One column has 20 characters, so that each woodblock, upon the completion of the work on two sheets of the sutra, will altogether have a total of 800 characters [when a block has its full 800 characters, the carver would be paid 2 *qian* and 8 *fen* of silver].
- When both faces of each woodblock are carved and full of columns, the total expense [per woodblock] is 3 *qian* and 4 *li* of silver.

Appendix 1.2

Walter Henry Medhurst, *China: its State and Prospects*, pp. 569–71:

1. By Block Printing, at Malacca:	£	s.	d.
The passage of nine workmen, to and from China	72	0	0
Two thousand blocks, at £1 per hundred	20	0	0
Tools, gravers, &c	10	0	0
Transcribing 2,689 pages, at 9d. per page	100	16	9
Engraving 1,160,548 characters, at 1s. 3d. per hundred	725	6	10
Printing and binding 5,378,000 pages, at 1s. 8d. per thousand	448	3	4
Two hundred and ten peculs of paper, at £2. 10s. per pecul	525	0	0
[Total]	1901	6	11

The foregoing is the charge generally made for work done at Malacca, Batavia, and Singapore; in China the prices to Europeans are about two thirds of the above; but as we cannot now print with safety at Canton, we are obliged to take the estimate of work done in the colonies. The time occupied in the above undertaking, by nine type-cutters, and five printers and binders, would be somewhere about three years.

2. By Lithography, at Batavia:

	£	s.	d.
For two lithographic presses, with stones	100		
Materials, repairs, &c.	100		
Transcribing 2,689 pages, twice over, at 9d. per page	201	13	6
Printing 5,378,000 pages, at 1s. per thousand pages	268	18	0
Binding the above, at 3d. per thousand pages	67	4	6
Paper, the same as in the first statement	525	0	0
[Total]	1262	16	0

The above is the charge for printing by lithography at Batavia, where labour is cheap. The folding and collating would cost less for sheets worked off at a press, than for separate pages printed by the hand, according to the Chinese mode. The time occupied in the work, by one transcriber, four pressmen, and one binder, would be two years.

3. By Typography

	£	s.	d.
Cost of 3000 punches, or matrices, furnished by Mr Dyer	425	0	0
Ditto of one thousand pounds weight of metal, at 2s. per pound	100	0	0
One iron press, cases, furniture, &c	100	0	0
Composition of 2,689 pages, at 2s. per page	268	18	0
Printing 5,378,000 pages, at 6d. per thousand pages	134	9	0
Binding the above at 3d. per thousand pages	67	4	6
For 168 peculs of paper, at £2.10s per pecul	420		
[Total]	1511	11	

My Dyer's types being somewhat smaller than those used in the octavo edition of the Bible, less paper will be required. If, however, the French types be used, not only will the original cost be less, but a saving of one half the price of paper will be effected. The time required for the punch cutting cannot be precisely stated; but supposing the types ready, the printing of two thousand copies of the Chinese Bible would occupy four compositors, two pressmen, and one binder, one year.

Thus the entire cost being reckoned, the balance will appear at first in favour of lithography, but permanently in that of typography; in addition to greater speed and superiority of execution. When the first two thousand copies are struck off, if executed by means of xylography, we possess a set of blocks adapted for printing the scriptures alone, already much worn, and capable of working only five more editions, at one half of the original cost. If the work be performed at a lithographic press, we possess after its completion, only the presses and the stones, very much the worse for wear. But if metal types be employed, we have, when the work is done, a set of punches and matrices, from which millions of types may be cast, sufficient to supply the whole world; besides an iron press, and a complete fount of types, from which fifty more editions can be taken, at a lower rate, than that at which each edition could be printed from the wooden blocks.

2 The Ascendance of the Imprint in China

After the invention of woodblock printing by the early eighth century, the printed book, or imprint, gradually became a fixture of Chinese social and cultural life. The widespread popularity of the Song dynasty's civil service examination system, we regularly read, so stoked the demand for books that the imprint drove the handcopy off the shelves of most readers and bookstores by the eleventh or twelfth century. While this explanation may hold true for the texts tested in these examinations, what was the fate of the far more numerous titles that were not included in the narrow curriculum for these examinations? When and how did the imprint come to replace the manuscript as the principal form of book for these other titles and indeed for Chinese books in general? And, what changes in the production, distribution, and consumption of books then came about with this ascendance and eventual conquest of the imprint?

To help us answer these questions and to explore the implications of our findings, we might try to rephrase these questions in quantitative terms: when and how did imprint copies become more numerous than manuscript copies? Or, more concretely, when and how did a specific title more commonly exist as an imprint rather than as a manuscript? Alas, these questions are far easier to ask than to answer. For most Chinese book titles, we lack clear means to distinguish between those printed and those merely written or transcribed; only rarely do our most informative sources on books, the prefaces (which often survive apart from the book), specify whether the book in question is being printed. But even if we had what is now impossible to compile — a comprehensive list of all book printings from the late Tang to the nineteenth century — we would still have no way of knowing how many copies of these printed books were ever made. Over the thirteen-century span of pre-modern Chinese printing history, we know for less than 0.1 percent of all printed titles how many copies were made from any set of woodblocks. And, when forced to speculate, our conclusions on this matter in the previous chapter can only advise caution. Educated estimates of the maximum number of sheets printable from any woodblock vary very widely, from 6,000 to 40,000 copies, and yet the number of copies actually printed might range between none at all and the 30,000 or so copies I suspect was often the maximum run for a woodblock's clear impressions. Obviously, such diverging figures do not allow a quick and easy answer to our questions.

A second quantitative approach, focusing on the surviving manuscripts and imprints themselves, is slightly more helpful. The existence of these books constitutes undeniable evidence that these particular titles had become books and some copies of them even printed. In theory, then, we can compare the number of these surviving imprint copies with the number of surviving manuscript copies and so acquire a rough idea of their relative quantity and importance. Two Chinese scholars have recently used this simple approach to determine that, of some 12,000 surviving copies (*bu*) of pre-1912 books on Chinese medicine, the majority were manuscripts.[1] In other words, in the field of Chinese medicine, the traditional imprint may well have never replaced the more traditional manuscript, or rather it may have done so only in certain ways yet to be clarified. Another scholar, focusing on plays written a millennium after the discovery of woodblock printing, discovered that manuscript copies accounted for most of the eighty-odd surviving scripts of sixteen playwrights active in Suzhou prefecture in the seventeenth century.[2]

Fortunately, we have a more comprehensive and historically nuanced survey of Chinese imprints, that charts the varying production levels for all four traditional categories of books over time. By charting the publication date of surviving imprint titles from the Southern Song to the mid-Ming, that is, from 1131 to 1521, Inoue Susumu has given us a rough idea of imprint production levels at different times during these four centuries.[3] Overall, his two sets of figures — the first based on imprint holdings in the (Beijing) National Library and the National Library in Taipei, and the second on a recent Chinese catalogue of rare book holdings in numerous mainland China libraries — show a clear increase in the number of extant imprint titles from the early Southern Song into the Yuan, an

initial drop and then a further decline in the first half-century of the
Ming, and thereafter an increase that slowly mounts and then surges
upward from the last third of the fifteenth century into the first
quarter of the sixteenth. The longterm publishing record for each
of the four categories of imprints — classics (*jing*), histories (*shi*),
philosophy (*zi*), and belles-lettres (*ji*) — varied considerably (see
Appendices 2.1, 2.2, and 2.3). The number of classics titles peaked
in the Yuan dynasty (primarily due to an interest in popular
examination manuals) and regained such heights only in the early
sixteenth century. History titles rose in number gradually, through
to the very early Ming, fell back in the early fifteenth century, but
then surpassed their earlier peak in the last third of that century.
Philosophy titles increased from the Song to the Yuan, suffered a
severe setback in the first half-century of Ming rule, surged around
1430, but could permanently surpass this level only about a century
later. Even the belles-lettres titles, at this time essentially the literary
collections (*wenji*) of scholars and officials, suffered an early fifteenth-
century drop from an otherwise steady rise throughout these four
centuries. In short, the printing of titles in the Confucian classics,
history, and philosophy noticeably increased only in the latter half
of the fifteenth century, while those in belles-lettres did so only after
1500. Thus, in contrast to the conventional scholarly wisdom, Inoue
concludes that the imprint replaced the manuscript permanently as
the primary means for transmitting written culture in the lower Yangzi
delta only during the middle of the sixteenth century, not in the late
eleventh or twelfth century.

To Inoue's work we can now add Katsuyama Minoru's recent
statistical review of the extensive data on Ming publishing contained
in Du Xinfu's *The Comprehensive Record of Ming Dynasty Printed Volumes*
(*Mingdai keben zonglu*). Published in 1983, Du's catalogue lists some
5,200 Ming imprint titles culled along with their date and house of
publication from forty-four Chinese book collection catalogues for
all of the Ming (Inoue's statistical survey stops at 1521). Du's data,
despite the many omissions, still rank as the most comprehensive
single compilation of Ming publishing information and so allow
Katsuyama to propose a three-stage development of Ming publishing
activities. In the first century of Ming rule, all ten-year stretches
produced an average of fewer than ten titles a year but for the last
decade, between 1458 and 1468. Over the next century, this average

figure more than tripled, the rise occurring mainly between 1508 and 1528. The third period begins in 1561, when the number of published titles per decade shoots up to as much as fifty-three by the close of the sixteenth century, only to collapse by the dynasty's end in 1644 to early sixteenth-century levels of production.[4]

Over the rest of this chapter, I hope to demonstrate the general validity and significance of Inoue's and Katsuyama's statistical claims, but only after stressing the considerable coincidence of the overlap of these figures with the actual general trends. Inoue's figures omit a considerable number of surviving imprints published between 1131 and 1521 (they unexpectedly omit the major Japanese collections of rare Chinese imprints in the collections of the Seikadō bunko, Sonkeikaku bunko, and Naikaku bunko), and Katsuyama's even wider survey for the entire Ming draws on a work that is based on very incomplete, now out-of-date catalogues of book collections stored in just a few Chinese cities, mainly in Beijing and the Yangzi delta. The figures of both authors also tell us nothing of the far more numerous imprints whose copies have not survived, and of course they reveal nothing of the size and distribution of any imprint run between the early Song and late Ming.

This last lacuna is particularly important for assessing the success of woodblock printing, since the economics of the technology arguably promoted the reprinting of old titles rather than the publication of new ones. Woodblocks not only could regularly be expected to produce many times more impressions than moveable-type runs but also were, unlike the frames of moveable type used in Western printing, kept long after the first run, for further impressions on demand. In other words, a woodblock carved in one century could produce copies of a text in the following century. Also, any woodblock impression could at anytime readily serve as the transcription copy needed by carvers for the recarving of the same text into another set of woodblocks, a practice that would have reduced the cost of reprinting an old text as opposed to printing up a new one. Thus, overall, the use of the number of woodblock imprint titles to indicate book output tends to underestimate the scale of production levels and the extent of readership for Chinese books in these centuries.

Moreover, by themselves these woodblock title figures do not prove the relative success of the imprint, since no corresponding chart exists to indicate a concurrent decline in the production and use of manuscripts. The Song was the first period with a widespread use of printing when many scholars certainly did not consider the imprint a blessing.[5] Many of their own works, if we can judge by the number of surviving Song texts that were carved at most once in the Song, seem never to have been carved and printed. Indeed, unprinted Song writings may well have outnumbered Song imprints of both pre-Song and Song titles. Thus, although the compilation of a comprehensive list of manuscripts produced in the Song of both pre-Song and Song texts is impossible today, the great number produced then of both of these types of manuscript titles makes it wise to refrain from generalizing about and dating the relative importance of imprint and manuscript copies on the basis of Song imprint statistics alone. The same reservation is valid, if less so, for evaluations of imprint and manuscript production in the Yuan and Ming dynasties as well.

Finally, this focus on imprints alone, however tempting, only fosters the erroneous assumption that the popularity of the imprint necessarily entailed a corresponding decline in manuscript production and eventually its disappearance. As any library's rare book catalogue shows, that was decidedly not the case. Manuscript copies of Chinese books were still being made in the late twentieth century, not just in the twelfth or the fifteenth. Manuscripts, regardless of when we date their decline and demise, remained active begetters of other manuscript copies as well as of imprint copies right up to our time, and as I stress in this chapter's concluding remarks, they continue to shape the contents of Chinese imprints even today. Any attempt to date and explain the ascendance and eventual conquest of the imprint must see the manuscript and imprint as continuing partners in the creation of Chinese books well after any ascending set of imprint statistics might suggest the decline of the manuscript as a book form.

If these two comprehensive quantitative approaches then promise few or no certain rewards on their own, the historian must do his or her work with less comprehensive figures and, most importantly, non-quantitative sources. Here, as usual, the evidence is seldom satisfactory, although the research of Inoue, Zhang Xiumin, and some other Chinese scholars will prove valuable for our study.

The few Song generalizations on the increase of book printing and consumption, when not politically motivated praise for an emperor's rule, show a slow start, the printing focused on a limited range of writings in a few areas of the country. Even Buddhist establishments, despite their early use of printing in the Tang, made strikingly limited use of this technology at least up to the early eleventh century. Of the 8,000-odd items in the Stein collection of Dunhuang material (all reportedly pre-1020), only twenty are printed; the 1,000 items of similar material catalogued for the Pelliot collection contain just two. Not surprisingly, the distinguished Dutch historian of Chinese Buddhism, Erik Zürcher, has concluded that "even after at least a quarter of a millennium the role of the art of printing in the production and spread of Buddhist texts still was absolutely marginal."[6]

These same turbulent centuries from the mid-Tang to the early Song dynasty had reportedly seen a great loss of old books in general,[7] and so the early Song government felt a compelling need to print copies of books that had become alarmingly rare.[8] Thus, over the course of the eleventh century, it printed, or had printed, a large number of medical texts, the Confucian classics, the Buddhist canon, imperial edicts, almanacs, contract forms, tax forms, and ephemeral sheets on the examination results, all of which became widely available.[9] By the end of the twelfth century, printing was flourishing in northern Fujian, the center of cheap popular printing; the city of Hangzhou, a center for high-quality printing; and, perhaps most of all, in the city of Chengdu, in Sichuan.[10] Arguably, then, for these types of writing (minus the medical texts), the imprint largely replaced handcopy alternatives in people's reading and collections by c.1200 in these three places.[11]

Yet, elsewhere in the Song empire, even elsewhere in the cultural and economic center of the Yangzi delta, that shift was far from evident. Highly knowledgeable bibliophiles of the sixteenth and seventeenth centuries, such as Hu Yinglin and Xu Bo, argued that imprints first became numerous not in the Song and Yuan dynasties but only in the latter half of the Ming dynasty.[12] Some modern scholars, like Poon Ming-sun, Susan Cherniack, and Jean-Pierre Drège, have suggested similar views but so far have not presented detailed evidence to support their hypothesis.[13]

To test the validity of their claim as well as Inoue's research, it is useful to turn this single question of when the imprint replaced the manuscript in China into four more answerable, if circumstantial, questions: what was the size of government and private libraries, the portion of imprints in these libraries, the availability of specific titles, and the relative cost of manuscript and imprint production? When these four topics are addressed for the social stratum and region we are best informed of, the literati of the lower Yangzi delta, our analysis will be limited, unfortunately, to just the best educated men in the area of China with arguably the greatest cultural and economic resources during these eight centuries. These limitations nonetheless will help us avoid the unfounded generalizations found in all too many books on Chinese printing. They will also lead us to conclude that, for literati readers, the imprint became ascendant over the manuscript form of book in no more than a few parts of China by the early thirteenth century and that this ascendance (but for certain books like the Confucian classics) was secured in the entirety of the lower Yangzi delta, the Jiangnan region, only in the sixteenth century, that is, some eight centuries after the invention of woodblock printing. Even then, the manuscript will be seen to have persisted in shaping the form and contents of the Chinese imprint well into subsequent centuries.

Size of Libraries

The best surviving clues to the relative scale of Song book production are probably the number of chapters (*juan*) — the measuring unit of preference for Chinese book collectors — in separate Song book collections, especially the larger ones. The biggest library in the Song and Ming dynasties up to the sixteenth century was, with perhaps a few exceptions,[14] usually their Imperial Libraries.[15] But, if we assume that the character *juan*, usually translated as "scroll" for pre-Song texts, constituted the equivalent of "a chapter" in a Song or later book, then at no time did any Song collection's holdings outnumber those of the Imperial Libraries of the Sui and Tang dynasties or even the earlier Liang dynasty (502–57) at their respective peaks.[16] Wars, human errors, and natural disasters explain this fate. The sacking of Chang'an in the mid-eighth century and again in the late ninth century, along with the subsequent turmoil of the Five Dynasties in north China, led to the disappearance of much of the Tang Imperial Library's holdings.[17] At the start of the Song dynasty, the new Imperial Library held just 13,000 *juan*.[18] Subsequent Song seizure of rival states' collections and other acquisitions increased it considerably, but a highly destructive fire in 1015 and poor management kept the holdings at just 30,669 *juan* in 1041 and roughly 45,000 *juan* later on in the eleventh century.[19] This library was lost to the Jurchen invaders during their conquest of north China in 1127, and the relocated Song court built anew, having 44,486 *juan* by 1178 and 59,429 *juan* by 1220. The highest estimated figure we have for the holdings of all Song imperial court collections is 72,567 *juan* in probably 1177.[20] In sum, five and a half centuries after the An Lushan Rebellion had destroyed the great Tang Imperial Library, the Song Imperial Library's holdings numbered fewer *juan* than the Tang court's Library of the Academy of Assembled Worthies had contained — i.e., some 89,000 *juan* — in 731. The greater use of printing in the Song — assuming once again that the shift in the meaning of *juan* from "scroll" to "chapter" does not undermine the validity of comparing these figures — would appear not to have assured a larger size for the Song Imperial Library than for its immediate predecessors that had existed solely or overwhelmingly in a world of manuscripts.

The early Ming Imperial Library inherited sizeable portions of imperial palace and court book collections of the Song, Jin, and Yuan dynasties, transported at court orders from Beijing to Nanjing.[21] The first and third emperors several times ordered imperial book hunts and made numerous book purchases, so that, in c.1420, the Imperial Library contained about 20,000 titles and about 100,000 volumes (*ce*). In the next two centuries, as we shall see in Chapter 4, this remarkable collection would deteriorate greatly in quality and quantity, ending up by the dynasty's close as a mere shadow of its former self.[22]

For private collectors, the story is more complicated. In general, the Song saw an increase in the number of private collectors and in the size of the average collector's collection, but only from the sixteenth century do we find a large number of collectors with sizeable collections of over 20,000 *juan*. Whereas in the fifth and sixth centuries a family might retain a reputation for scholarship by reading or preserving just several hundred *juan* of books,[23] in the mid-twelfth century, "the family of a serving official of slight distinction invariably has several thousand *juan* of books."[24] Yet, the size of large private collections rose and changed less dramatically between the eighth and early sixteenth centuries. In the Tang, a collector gained celebrity for having 20,000 or 30,000 *juan*.[25] As was recently demonstrated in Fan Fengshu's extensive survey of the 214 largest private libraries in the Song, the number of Song collectors of 10,000 or more *juan* was considerably more than in previous dynasties (interestingly, slightly more of their collections were located in present Jiangxi Province than in the Yangzi delta).[26] Yet, of the 192 of these collections which are even roughly quantifiable, over two-thirds (130) had 20,000 or fewer *juan*. Less than a tenth (17) definitely had more than 20,000 *juan*; the rest were described as having "several 10,000 *juan*", i.e. anywhere between actually less than 10,000 up to 40,000 *juan*. Even the holdings of the great historian Sima Guang (1019–86), by his own counting, amounted in 1073 to "merely over 5,000 *juan*."[27] With the possible exception of two very well-placed Kaifeng holdings,[28] the five famous private Northern Song collections whose catalogues had been inspected by Ye Mengde (1077–1148) contained no more than some 40,000 *juan*.[29] None of these large collections was located inside the Yangzi delta, where holdings of just "several thousand *juan*" or "up to 10,000 *juan*" won some Suzhou men a reputation for being book collectors.[30] The largest delta collection in the eleventh century, that of Zhu Changwen (1041–ca.1100), came to just 20,000 *juan*, that of Ye Mengde himself in the early twelfth century to some 30,000 *juan* (a fire consumed close to half of his holdings in 1147), and the largest in the latter half of the twelfth century, that of the Wuxi collector You Mao (1127–94), also to 30,000 *juan*.[31] By the thirteenth century, the size of book collections in the delta had recovered from the destruction inflicted by Jurchen invaders in 1129 and 1130. But, according to the sixteenth-century book expert Hu Yinglin, all Song collections went no higher than some 40,000 *juan*.[32] The principal thirteenth-century exception was the collection of Chen Zhensun (1183–1261) of Huzhou: his catalogue's 49,700 (or, 51,180-odd) *juan* apparently made his holdings the largest private collection in the Southern Song.[33] But, coming at the end of the dynasty, when a vice-prime minister might build a special hall to house just "several thousand *juan* of books,"[34] it points to future rather than past trends.

This future, however, would not be evident for a few more centuries. In Hu Yinglin's view, "woodblock imprints (*banben*) were still few in Yuan times," and the largest known Yuan collection, of some 300,000 *juan*, was grossly bloated by the inclusion of multiple copies that disguised its real size of merely 30,000 distinct *juan*.[35] The delta's biggest collector in the thirteenth and fourteenth centuries, Zhuang Su (1245–1315) of the Shanghai area, had enough books, 80,000 *juan*, to cast doubt on Hu's hasty dismissal of all sizeable Yuan collections; the same holds true for the largely inherited 50,000-odd *juan* library of Chen Jimo in early fourteenth-century Yangzhou and the "several tens of thousands of *juan*" in the collections each of Yang Weizhen (1296–1370) and a man known as "the scholar outside the Blue Gate" in Hangzhou.[36] Suffice it to say that the scale of these collections was quite unusual for both of these centuries. More typical in the delta were notable collections of about 10,000 to 20,000 *juan* — even the wealthy literatus-painter Ni Zan (1301–74) of Changzhou had just several thousand *juan*, consisting largely of transcribed texts.[37] Seen in a long-term perspective, the distinctive feature of Yuan book collecting is less the contents or size of the collections than indications that the practice of serious book collecting had spread to lower social statuses: the owners of at least two Yuan collections came from quite inferior social backgrounds, one born into the family of a butcher, and the other into a cloth-trading family.[38]

An early Ming decline in the overall size of private book holdings is suggested by the reduced scale of the two largest family libraries then. The libraries of the Ge family in Yangzhou and the Li family in Ji'nan prefecture in Shandong Province *together* contained fewer than 42,750 *juan*.[39] In the latter half of the fifteenth century, the largest private collection in the lower Yangzi delta, that of Ye Sheng (1435–94), numbered just 22,300 *juan*, less than half of the peak figure for Chen Zhensun's collection in around 1250.[40] Since the early Ming government abolished the Song and Yuan procedures and institutions for pre-publication review and cancelled all imprint taxes,[41] this drop in the size of large private libraries may come as a surprise. Yet, the ravages of the mid-fourteenth century wars in the middle and lower Yangzi Valley had destroyed many libraries. Also, the first Ming emperor profoundly distrusted the delta's scholar-official élite and adopted fiscal policies highly destructive of their social and economic position. Timber (and thus paper) prices were high. And, Hangzhou, having been reduced at the fall of the Song dynasty to the level of a mere provincial seat, never recovered its premier position as the center of élite book production and consumption. All these factors persisted through the first century of Ming rule and help to explain the protracted decline in the delta's printing production.[42]

Evidence of a significant transformation of book collecting came only in the sixteenth century, when minor bibliophiles were commonly said to have 10,000 to 20,000 *juan*, and collectors like He Liangjun, Jin Pei, Fan Qin, Wang Shizhen, and Hu Yinglin gained fame only after acquiring at least two to three times more.[43] The peak Ming figure for a private collection was reached in the early seventeenth century by the Shaoxing collector Qi Chengye (1565–1628). A fire in 1597 destroyed all his inherited collection of some 10,000 *juan*, but by 1613, he had personally collected two to three times that figure. And, by 1620, his collection consisted of 9,000-odd titles and more than 100,000 *juan*.[44] Two similar cases of rapid book collecting took place when a recent metropolitan degree winner acquired over 3,000 titles between 1567 and 1574 and when a mere scholar at the National University in Nanjing succeeded in building up a huge book collection in just the three years between 1631 and 1634.[45] The rise of these private collections was recognized already at the close of the sixteenth century when the Ming Imperial Library, known as the Hall of Literary Profundity (*Wenyuan ge*), was judged to be "less than half the size of a scholar's collection of books."[46]

What, then, would a reasonably large private library, of some 10,000 *juan*, have consisted of before the publishing boom of the sixteenth and seventeenth centuries? Largely, the 9,000 *juan* in the standard writings of official learning: the thirteen Confucian classics and their commentaries, the *Shiji* (Records of the grand historian), and the eighteen dynastic histories written before 1100 would have totalled 2,750 *juan*; then the 3,000 or so *juan* in the early Northern Song collecteanea (*congshu*), and another 3,000 or so *juan* in the ten-odd collecteanea printed during the Southern Song. These texts, in the view of one Ming bibliophile, probably constituted the core contents of most major private collections from the last century of the Song through the Ming.[47] Only in the sixteenth century does the range noticeably widen.

Imprint Share

Information about the imprint share in these collections is hard to determine, but little suggests that, before 1500, the proportion of imprints was as high as many modern scholars have assumed. In the mid-eleventh century, the Kaifeng court officials Wang Qinchen and Song Minqiu regularly handcopied books, manuscripts, and imprints that they acquired, thereby assuring a high percentage of manuscripts in their collections.[48] One generation later, Su Song formed his collection largely on the basis of handcopies,[49] and in 1135, Ye Mengde described his own collection of c.20,000 *juan* as consisting "often largely of what I have copied myself."[50] In the latter half of the twelfth century, the collector You Mao, of Wuxi county in Changzhou prefecture, formed the most highly regarded collection of his generation: by modern calculation over nine-tenths of the items were manuscripts.[51] In 1177, the Song Imperial Library, including the main collection and the Imperial Archives collection, consisted of 59.5 percent of handcopies, 32 percent of unprocessed works, and just 8.5 percent of imprints (a less detailed breakdown puts the handcopy share at 91 percent of the *juan* and 92 percent of the volumes [*ce*]).[52] In the Ming, the Hall of Literary Profundity's holdings in Beijing consisted of 70 percent manuscripts and 30 percent imprints.[53] In the Yangzi delta, the Suzhou collector Shen Fang (1394–?) had holdings of several thousand *juan*, "all [of which] he personally had copied and collated to instruct his descendants."[54] The situation slightly later in the delta, in 1483, is suggested by the fact that books demanded by the eunuch Wang Jing on the subjects of astrology and divination were to be handcopied — i.e., neither bought nor printed — in Suzhou and Hangzhou.[55] In the mid-sixteenth century, the overall number of imprints had increased, but not necessarily enough to change their proportion in major private collections. For instance, for two private Ningbo collections of the eleventh and twelfth centuries, the breakdown had been fifty-fifty,[56] and it would remain so for the famed Tianyi ge collection in Ningbo in ca.1561 (even though its founder Fan Qin claimed that eighty percent of the holdings were imprints and just twenty percent were manuscripts).[57] Slightly later, however, a change is evident: in the late sixteenth century, Hu Yinglin's collection contained seventy percent imprints and thirty percent manuscripts,[58] and a handwritten catalogue of Niu Shixi's collection (of possibly just his rarest books) in Shaoxing prefecture lists fewer than fifteen percent of its titles and just eight percent of its *juan* as manuscripts.[59]

Availability of Books

Key changes in the availability of books also date from the sixteenth century. Until that time, both rich and poor constantly bemoaned their inability to find books. The Jurchen invasion of the lower Yangzi delta destroyed many Northern Song collections, making it hard to find copies of "the various histories of the Han and the Tang."[60] Faced with such shortages, mid- and late twelfth-century readers, such as the poet Lu You (1125–1210), traveled over 1,000 miles to as far west as Sichuan in order to hunt down books not available in the Yangzi delta; Lu returned with his boat carrying nothing but books.[61] Although one northern Sichuan collector in c.1165 spent his salary to acquire in Hangzhou books not available in his native province,[62] the Emperor Xiaozong (r. 1163–89) in 1179 ordered his officials to search for books in Sichuan's government offices and schools. He believed that these institutions and their copies of Northern Song government publications had escaped the disruptive rebellions and invasions that had destroyed so many important book collections in most of the rest of China during the 1120s and 1130s.[63] Not surprisingly, Lou Fang, the scion of a celebrated Ningbo family, admitted that, before acquiring a *jinshi*, or metropolitan, degree in 1193, "I had no books I could look at and even had to borrow the *Hanshu* and *Hou Hanshu* from others."[64]

Admittedly, by the close of the twelfth century, the imprint had become more available in the Song empire. Printed in just thirty-odd places during the Northern Song, books were published in over two hundred places (in at least ninety-one prefectures scattered in sixteen of the seventeen circuits, or proto-provinces) in the far smaller territory of the Southern Song.[65] This sixfold increase led to not only more books but also more areas with their own woodblock carvers, more regional exchange of these carvers, and more bibliographic details added to entries in book catalogues.[66] Whereas mid-twelfth-century catalogues at best distinguished imprints from manuscripts in their listings of the Confucian classics and the dynastic histories, one mid-thirteenth-century catalogue made this distinction for collected writings and philosophical works as well, and even took care to identify the place of publication for some of its imprints.[67] In 1202, the Hangzhou-based bibliophile Zhou Bida (1126–1204) noted the recent printing of the previously unavailable individual collections of many Tang authors like Han Yu (768–824) and Li Ao (774–836).[68] Private printing by bookstores, particularly of student primers, recognized classics and other sure sellers, quite possibly made such imprints more numerous than manuscripts in Jianyang in Fujian, Chengdu in Sichuan, as well as in Hangzhou.

But, certain genres, like gazetteers and pharmacopeia texts, were published in smaller runs than before, at least by government-funded printers.[69] And, in places as central and wealthy as Hangzhou and Ningbo, book and imprint shortages troubled even as elevated a figure as a future governor of Hangzhou and a vice-grand chancellor. When Yuan Shao acquired his metropolitan degree in 1187, he, being poor, still could not acquire books. "He often personally made handcopies (*shouchao*) of books and put them firmly to memory ... Afterwards, he was an official in the capital. In all, for twenty-five years he strove to collect books (*shu*) in order to achieve a long-cherished ambition. When the world did not yet have [a book], then he made transcriptions [of copies] in the Imperial Library and collections of old families and returned home. Therefore, his books for the first time were complete."[70] Yet, the persistence of shortages, even in areas very close to the capital, like Ningbo, is indicated by the report from a mid-thirteenth century devotee of Zhu Xi's philosophy, Huang Zhen (1213–80), that he drew no benefit from the supposedly universal availability of imprints of the Confucian classics. His copy of Zhu Xi's *Sishu jizhu* (Collected commentaries on the Four Books) was still a manuscript written in rough grass script, as he could not acquire an imprint copy from the official woodblocks kept in his native prefecture.[71] As we might expect, book shortages were also reported from more isolated inland areas like Qianshan county in Jiangxi Province.[72]

Most of the Yuan saw little break from Southern Song conditions and practices, though Inoue's figures on the holdings of the Yuan Imperial Library, as well as scattered evidence from other sources, suggest that the production of books in the delta increased somewhat at this time. Beijing officials, understandably, still looked on the southeast as the empire's best storehold of unusual books, even sending officials there to hunt down books in the early 1340s.[73] Hangzhou remained a vital production and distribution center for publishing, but it probably suffered a setback from its heights in the

Southern Song, when, as the capital, it had attracted a large number of students, scholars, and officials from throughout south China and had seen the imprint begin to dominate certain sectors of its book culture by the early thirteenth century. It is important to note, however, that this "progress" of the imprint over the manuscript was not extensive in Song and Yuan book culture of the delta at large, where its ascendance seems to have been restricted to this exceptional capital.

Even so, there was no severe setback for book printing and for the economy at large in the delta during most of the Yuan. An economic slowdown had occurred in the delta from the very late twelfth century, and the recovery was both intermittent and uneven in the thirteenth century, especially from c.1230 in Hangzhou.[74] But, Mongol conquest and rule from 1276 did not terminate "the Song economic miracle" — or, by extension, the expansion of printing — in the delta (though they certainly gave a severe blow to Sichuan's economy and printing industry).[75] According to recent studies separately undertaken by Shiba Yoshinobu and Richard von Glahn, significant retreat from late Song levels of economic development in the delta did not begin in earnest until the last chaotic decade or two of Yuan rule, in the mid-fourteenth century, and then that retreat was intensified by subsequent economic policies of the early Ming.[76] A recent study by Lucille Chia provides evidence to confirm this conclusion, by demonstrating that book production declined, particularly in the lower Yangzi delta, during the early Ming, not the Yuan.[77] In other words, the "retreat of book culture" in the lower Yangzi delta and Fujian can now be understood as a decline — not a collapse — of roughly one century — not two — and that primarily for the lower Yangzi delta under early Ming rule.

This first century of Ming rule was a time when carved woodblocks for books (all books?) are said to have existed only in the National University in Nanjing and the Jianyang region in Fujian and when the National University's blocks remained largely unused.[78] If so, it is not surprising that imprints from places in the delta were uncommon. Even half a century later, at the end of the Zhengde era (1506–21), only the princely establishments, government offices, and the printing houses of Jianyang reportedly possessed carved woodblocks. According to Gu Yanwu (1613–82), "As for what circulated among the people, it was no more than the Four

Books (*sishu*), the Five Classics (*wujing*), the [*Zizhi*] *Tongjian* (Comprehensive mirror [for government]), and books on moral nature (*xingli*). If any other books were printed, then they were stored up only by families who were fond of the past."[79] Popular materials suffered similar shortages. By law, government offices were expected to issue annual calendars to all households. But even at the end of the fifteenth century, many families in the capital still did not receive these printed copies, leading one literatus to complain: "Surely it is not only in the capital that families do not have calendars."[80]

A comprehensive explanation of this early Ming decline in publishing will require more detailed research. But, even if historians of the Chinese book need not explain a reversal from a predominantly imprint to a predominantly manuscript culture (such as no other culture is known to have experienced), the fact of the decline, whatever its causes, is indisputable. Acute shortages of books were widely reported both inside and outside of the delta in the fifteenth century. In 1429, a descendant of Confucius, Duke Kong Yanjin, had to go to Fujian to buy a book — and this turned out to be a manuscript copy.[81] In southeastern Jiangxi Province, the famous scholar-official Yang Shiqi (1365–1444) had acquired after twenty years of working as a teacher "only the Five Classics, the Four Books, and the poetry and prose of several Tang authors."[82] As we shall see in the next chapter, even after his rise to government office, his holdings remained small. Most scholars never attained his high office, his earnings, and his reputation as a book collector. As Lu Rong (1436–97) observed later in the fifteenth century, "Many poor scholars in out-of-the-way prefectures and minor counties have a desire to read books but cannot get even one sighting of them."[83]

In the lower Yangzi delta, similar difficulties confronted early and even mid-Ming readers seeking to acquire copies of famous books of literature and history. None of the writings of the four major Northern Song writers — Su Shi, Ouyang Xiu, Wang Anshi, and Zeng Gong — were available from commercial printing establishments in the early fifteenth century.[84] The works of Su Shi were hard to acquire right up to the Chenghua reign era (1465–87), while those of Wen Tianxiang (1236–83) reportedly survived, outside of the imperial palace, only in manuscript form even in his native Jiangxi.[85] The non-historical writings of Sima Guang proved equally hard to find, even for the largest book collector in the lower Yangtze delta during the fifteenth century. Ye Sheng had to spend more than twenty years to patch together a full collection of these non-historical writings of Sima Guang; he made copies from separate incomplete copies owned by three friends (none of whom in return seems to have relied on Ye's work to complete his own copy).[86]

The fate of the celebrated sixth-century collection of earlier Chinese poetry, *Wenxuan* (Anthology of Literature), is perhaps the most revealing example of this shortage of copies of well-known books in the early Ming. Its first publication during the Ming came as late as 1487 (Henan); other carvings then followed in 1522 (Beijing), 1525 (Shanxi), and 1549 (Suzhou), along with a few commentaries on its text in the Jiajing era.[87] Yet, up to the mid-sixteenth century, literati readers in the Yangzi delta repeatedly had trouble locating and owning a copy. Early on in the fifteenth century, Yang Shiqi reported that he had spent several decades trying to patch together a copy of this text from incomplete copies in the collections of over ten families. Nonetheless, his final, cumulative copy remained incomplete, prompting him to write a lamenting colophon addressed to his descendants: "In general, the woodblocks for books today often have omissions. If one wishes to get an entire book — and it is not only this book — there is labour in the printing and binding, supplementing and transcribing. It is not something that can be completed in a morning or evening."[88] Even a rich Suzhou collector like Yang Xunji (1458–1546) had to persevere for years before acquiring a full copy of this anthology.[89] He first transcribed an edition of it at the National University in Beijing, only to discover that this copy was incomplete. He bought a version in the marketplace, but it consisted only of the latter half of the full text. Eventually, only after handcopying the first half from a copy held by his good friend Wang Ao (1450–1524) did he put together a complete copy.

The works of the celebrated ninth-century Tang poets Bai Juyi and Yuan Zhen proved no different for fifteenth- and early sixteenth-century collectors. Yang Xunji had to borrow his friends' copies for his personal copy to be made.[90] Geng Yu (1430–96), a minister of the Board of Rites, was surprised to learn that copies of such famous books as *Jigu lu* (Collected ancient inscriptions), *Tangjian* (Tang mirror), and *Houshan ji* (Collected writings of Houshan) were still extant in his lifetime, as he had never seen these works.[91]

For famous history texts, the story was the same. Already, by the late twelfth century, complete imprint copies of Sima Guang's *Zizhi tongjian* were rare; readers reportedly preferred it rearranged by topic or abridged with a moralistic message.[92] Circulation in the early Ming appears not to have been extensive, and so the Songjiang native, Cao An, even after taking his *juren*, or provincial, degree in 1445, could acquire merely an abridged version.[93] The *Shiji* also was not widely available. After two printings in the Yuan (1288 and 1306), this most famous historical work of ancient China was carved only once in the first century and a half of Ming rule, i.e., 1463, in a government printing in Fujian.[94] Its circulation also remained highly restricted; the pre-Ming woodblocks in the National University in Nanjing were in poor condition and not widely accessible for use, and copies from the subsequent carvings and printings of 1515 and 1517 were available only to important officials located at major distribution points. It was only in 1525, when it was said that "a good edition of the *Shiji* was still lacking,"[95] that this text became available to poor scholars able to leave their village to buy this expensive book in a city.[96] And, the late Tang text, *Tongdian* (History of Institutions), was, according to Yang Shiqi, rarely seen in its complete version in the early Ming. Scholar officials instead had abridged versions.[97]

Likewise, the dynastic histories suffered long neglect until the late sixteenth and early seventeenth centuries. In the early Ming, complete copies of the *Song shi* (Dynastic history of the Song) were few, and even as late as 1534, the avid Suzhou collector and painter Qian Gu (1508–78) found that a copy of it made by the celebrated Suzhou literatus Shen Zhou (1427–1509) was missing thirty-four *juan*; Qian had to copy these out from another copy on his own.[98] Thus, Gu Yanwu's observation that the *Twenty-One Dynastic Histories* began to enter the libraries of scholar officials only after they were printed in Nanjing during the Jiajing reign and in Beijing during the Wanli reign (1573–1619) largely rings true.[99] Gu's comments on the limited circulation of scholarly books in general during the first half of the Ming, as given above, thus confirms the overall impression we have of a dearth of literati books in the Yangzi delta up to the middle third of the sixteenth century.

The evidence presented so far thus indicates that, up to the early sixteenth century, large private libraries were few; that they usually held between 10,000 and 20,000 *juan* and seldom more than 30,000 *juan* until the latter half of the sixteenth century; that normal scholar-official collections were considerably smaller; that even high officials in the capital of Hangzhou had trouble acquiring copies, including imprints, of well-known literati texts up to the thirteenth century; that the situation improved then in Hangzhou but not noticeably in large, nearby cities like Ningbo; and, that a shortage of books was reported in all these places from the fourteenth up to the early sixteenth centuries. These incidental details, however inconclusive when looked at separately, eventually add up to a general confirmation of a revisionist, skeptical assessment of Song book printing for most, but not all, of the lower Yangzi delta.

This set of conclusions, I believe, merits our belief, but only after we have answered two serious objections. Firstly, one can argue that complaints about the unavailability of texts from scholars like Yuan Shao and Huang Zhen are inconclusive. That is, when a Song reader complains about the impossibility of acquiring certain texts, we today are often not certain of precisely what he means: is it a lack of opportunities to acquire books, or merely a lack of access to copies in the collections of others loathe to share them? Since we have seen that, in the Song, large collections were few and few of them contained many books, complaints from individual readers about the difficulty of getting books were more likely to stem from a genuine sense of an overall shortage of books rather than from restricted access to them. Recall the woeful lament of the Jiaxing prefecture collector Cao Rong (1613–85) that no more than forty or fifty percent of the titles he had seen in ten-odd book catalogues from the Song and later were still extant in the mid-seventeenth century, and we can understand the despair brought on by the ongoing frustrations of Chinese readers unable to find titles they had long heard about.[100]

A second objection is harder to counter. This chapter's survey of Chinese titles that were hard to locate up to the sixteenth century has necessarily focused on what books were lacking. The choice of titles, moreover, reflects the concerns of literati scholars often interested more in past writings than in contemporary creations, in works of supposedly lasting merit than the ephemera that must have constituted the bulk of Chinese printing at all times. Thus, it has overlooked what books were actually printed and cannot by itself be said to constitute a full and accurate overview of Chinese printing culture and especially intellectual life during these five and a half centuries from the early Song to the mid-Ming. This criticism strikes me as valid. But, we can overcome much of its force and gain a reasonably persuasive overview of at least literati imprint culture by turning to a rich survey, once again by Inoue Susumu, that is based on the surviving imprints from these centuries in the published catalogues of the National Library in Beijing and the National Library in Taipei. Mindful that Inoue's description of these imprints necessarily ignores the numerous handcopies circulating in what we have seen was still an age of manuscripts, we can still use his review to gain a general idea of the books that people, especially literati in the Yangzi delta, were reading, or at least the authors and the topics they or publishers were interested in promoting through publication during the course of these centuries. Future research will almost certainly revise these findings, but in the absence of any other broad survey, this account remains a useful and important introduction to the world of the imprint for literati in the delta and elsewhere from the eleventh to the early sixteenth centuries. It also will not only confirm much of what we have discovered about the shortage of famous titles but also help to clarify the significance of the changes that would dramatically alter this situation from the early sixteenth century onward.[101]

Publications

By the tenth century, the types of books being printed seem to have expanded from a few Buddhist texts, medical writings, almanacs, government announcements, poetry, and divination books to include the collected prose and poetry writings of an individual; the first recorded publication in this genre was the collected writings of the Buddhist monk Guanxiu (832–912) printed in Sichuan in 923.[102] The range of topics that appeared in imprints further expanded in the early Song, with the publication of private political writings, ranging from poems making abstruse references to court politics, to actual discussions of contemporary political issues. Court officials, understandably, did not enjoy the public exposure of their views and activities, and so by 1009, they were imposing legal obstacles to the free and easy printing of books.[103] Yet, the resulting requirement that all books undergo pre-publication review, a form of censorship, did not prevent some clever persons from faking and then printing "imperial edicts" in Kaifeng in 1068, arousing thereby imperial ire as well.[104] Examination results and even successful examination compositions also readily won a market in eleventh-century Kaifeng, as did writings by a wide number of serving and posthumous scholar-officials like Su Shi and Ouyang Xiu.[105]

From the Southern Song onward, books in genres new to printing, such as dramas, arias, and fiction, were printed alongside a growing number of titles in the more traditional genres of classical studies, history, poetry, official memorials, divination, and medicine. Among Song imprints, what survives most among the philosophical books are works of Daoxue, "the Learning of the Way," the new Confucian teaching expounded by Zhu Xi and his followers; next come medical works. But once we enter the Yuan, medical texts predominate, followed by encyclopedias; these two genres account for almost sixty percent of all Yuan titles in the category of philosophy. Only then, reflecting the collapse of official and scholarly research on Confucian texts under Mongol rule, come writings based on the Zhu Xi school of neo-Confucianism. Among Song imprints of the belles-lettres category, most common were the collected writings of the Six Dynasties and Tang authors. But in Yuan times, almost no such works for Tang and earlier authors were printed, except for Du Fu (712–70) and Li Bai (705?–62). This unadventuresome concentration on the famous and the approved, stressing safe sellers, becomes even more evident in the early Ming.

Indeed, the early Ming seems to have seen a further narrowing of the range of texts printed. During the Yuan, government offices had sometimes printed literary works and the Confucian classics. But in the first century of the Ming, the classics imprints dealt with the Confucian classics and their commentaries, plus some popular simplifications of these classics, dictionaries, and rhyme books — and that is all. As for history studies, the *Tongjian gangmu* (Outline and details of the *Comprehensive Mirror*) and the *Xu tongjian gangmu* (Continuation of *Outline of the Comprehensive Mirror*) were printed, but not the *Zizhi tongjian* itself or even its abridged reworking as the *Tongjian jishi benmo* (Record of affairs, from beginning to end, in the *Comprehensive Mirror*). In fact, over this opening century of the Ming, the important history imprints were few and almost all printed by the government; for example, the *Yuan shi* (Dynastic history of the Yuan dynasty) (in the Hongwu era of 1368–98), the *Shiji* (in the Tianshun era of 1457–64), and the *Song shi* (in the Chenghua era of 1465–87). Early Ming imprints on history by private publishers are hard to find.

The belles-lettres imprints in the early Ming were similarly few. Of note were the *Zhuzi yulei* (Topically arranged conversations of Master Zhu), a Jiangxi official imprint of the Chenghua era, and the *Shanhai jing* (Classic of the mountains and seas), a National University imprint from Beijing. The list of preferred authors shows no change from that of the Yuan, since, for the first century of the Ming, no volume of the collected writings of a pre-Tang author was published; and the only Tang writers printed were Li Bai, Du Fu, Han Yu, Liu Zongyuan (773–819), Lu Zhi (754–805), and Lu Guimeng (ninth century). However, there was a gradual rise in the number of editions. More collected writings appear to have been printed in the early Ming than in the Song and Yuan: in the Song, 4.7 every ten years; in the Yuan, 4.8; in the Hongwu era, 6; in the Xuande era (1426–35), 12; and then 35.7 in the Chenghua era.

In the Hongzhi and Zhengde eras, there are a few sporadic signs of the publishing boom that was soon to follow in the sixteenth century. Old philosophical titles, such as *Huainanzi* (Master of Huainan), *Yantie lun* (Discourses on salt and iron), and *Duduan* (Independent judgments), begin to be published. Also, for the first time in the Ming, key neo-Confucian texts like the *Xiangshan wenji* (Collected writings of Lu Jiuyuan), the *Er Cheng quanshu* (Complete writings of the two Chengs), and the *Beixi ziyi* (Meaning of terms, as defined by Chen Chun) were printed. But the range of philosophical titles still remained fairly narrow, even within the confines of orthodox neo-Confucianism. Before 1565, an era which most intellectual historians consider the heyday of the orthodox Zhu Xi school of neo-Confucianism, virtually the only imprints related to "the Learning of the Way" school were Zhu Xi's commentaries to the Confucian classics and discussions of the principles of "nature and fate" (*xingming*). Far too little effort was made to encourage discussion of, not to mention debate about, this orthodoxy. Consequently, the tepid quality of intellectual life in the fifteenth century probably makes its thought less interesting and influential than that of any other century in the past thousand years of Chinese history.

Come the sixteenth century, a stronger desire for a more varied intellectual diet prompted an expansion of the philosophical concerns that were eventually reflected in imprints. Not surprisingly, the proliferation of imprints on a wider variety of philosophical topics coincided with the end of "the Learning of the Way" hegemony over Ming intellectual life and a surge of interest in the thought of Wang Yangming (1472–1529). The growing presence of the imprint in the book world of the Yangzi delta doubtless helped to spread awareness of new trends within neo-Confucian thought; these books often advocated practice over theory and spared no words in their denunciation of the bookishness of the "Learning of the Way" school, just at the time that the end of such bookishness ironically saw a vast increase in the number of books and readers even of other kinds of Chinese philosophical fare.

Similar changes occurred in the mid-Ming for non-philosophical publications as well. Publishers began to bring out new editions of a wide range of early history texts, which previously had not been extensively available in print: *Hanji* (Record of the Han), *Da Tang liudian* (Compendium of Tang administration), *Wenxian tongkao* (Comprehensive examination of written sources), and *Wu Yue chunqiu* (Spring and autumn annals of Wu and Yue). And they now also produced relatively recent histories, works like *Jin Wenjing gong beizheng lu* (Record of the northern campaign by Jin Youzi) and *Huang Ming kaiguo gongchen lu* (Accomplishments at the beginning of the august Ming dynasty), that could serve as roughly contemporary sources for Ming history. In the category of collected writings, a wide chronological range of texts was also published, including, as we have seen, texts like the *Wenxuan* dating from the Six Dynasties as well as more recent works. In the category of the Confucian classics, changes were less marked; but the publication of the *Yili* (Ceremonials and rituals) and the *Chunqiu fanlu* (Crown embellishments of the *Spring and Autumn Annals*) in the Zhengde period suggests a growing interest in less commonly reproduced classical texts.

These improvements, coming slowly but accumulatively, both in the fastidious world of scholarly texts and in the wider intellectual life of the delta, did not pass unnoticed by contemporaries. During the second quarter of the fifteenth century, according to the Taicang native Lu Rong, books (*shuji*) and printing blocks (*yinban*) were still not extensively available; only towards the end of the century, he says, did the situation improve.[106] Even up to 1521, as Gu Yanwu noted, the books which circulated among the people were "no more than the Four Books, the Five Classics, the [*Zizhi*] *Tongjian*, and books on moral nature."[107] In 1530 and as late as c.1550, certain Suzhou families and authors were still relying, perhaps because of relative prices, on the cheap publishing houses of Fujian to print their writings.[108] By the end of the Jiajing era, however, the situation had changed. Lucille Chia has found that more than nine-tenths of all surviving non-governmental Ming imprints, as listed in twenty library catalogues and thirteen other bibliographies, were published after 1505.[109] By the mid-sixteenth century, the literatus Wen Jia (1501– 83) would write that the appearance of unusual books no longer created the stir among Suzhou readers that it had at the start of the century.[110] What in the pre-1500 book world had been rare books, that most likely would not be seen again and might well disappear, began from around 1520 onward to be reprinted in increasing numbers, thus raising the likelihood of their eventual survival as an imprint. The modern editors of the *Sibu congkan* (Collection of the four branches of literature), known for their insistence on using only good imprint editions, would therefore draw very heavily on imprints produced in the second half of the Ming. Forty-four percent of the collection's titles were drawn from late Ming editions — this despite the common early Qing dismissal of Ming imprints as poorly edited.[111] Another set of figures shows the scale of the increase; whereas ten-odd book catalogues of private collections were compiled before the Song, sixty-odd were compiled in the Song and nine in the Yuan. But, come the Ming, the figure rises to 167, nearly three times the Song total.[112] With this surge in book publication came a greater number of private collections and privately held books than ever before in Chinese history. Predictably, some sixteenth-century scholars shifted the object of their complaints from the dearth of books to the excess. The Changzhou literatus Tang Shunzhi, at mid-century, complained, "If a butcher died, then his family, so long as it had the money, would have an obituary of him printed."[113] Others, such as the Suzhou writer Zhu Yunming (1461–1537), were not content with a derision of recent customs; they simply wanted the government to burn the mountain of objectionable books.[114]

Commercial Considerations

This shift to a world of far more imprints can be largely attributed to a great increase in the demand for two kinds of texts — examination cribs and certain genres of honorific and entertainment writing, especially "stories" (*xiaoshuo*) — the expansion of a commercial printing sector to meet this demand, and changes in the relative expense of woodblock printing vs. other book production methods. From the late fifteenth century, the number of candidates sitting for the examinations greatly increased, with a consequent boom in the demand for examination cribs and manuals. For instance, after a sub-prefect of Hangzhou profitably printed up successful examination essays in c.1480, printers in Fujian and elsewhere rushed to do likewise, and the publication of examination aids flourished even more than in the Southern Song.[115] Some authors — many of them failed examination candidates — made a living by writing and compiling works for this expanded audience. "In recent years," complained Li Lian, "unless a book is for the examinations, the commercial publishers (*shufang*) will not print it ... the market stores will not sell it and ... the scholars will not look at it."[116]

From the early sixteenth century, the popular demand grew as well for certain kinds of composition concerned with contemporary matters. These genres of writing included not just incidental writings honoring an individual's birthday, appointment, and departure for office, such as crowd many sixteenth- and seventeenth-century volumes of collected writings; such genres had existed before, if not in such profusion. Far more importantly, they include works of entertainment and the imagination, the novels and dramas that fired the literary passions of the late Ming. One recent Chinese study of the 1,056 commercial publishers of extant editions of Chinese "stories" from the Southern Song to the early twentieth century has found that all but four of these commercial publishers were active only after 1520 (140 were active sometime during the rest of the Ming),[117] while another has concluded that, of 1,507 such establishments, just three date from the Southern Song and Yuan and 185 from the Ming (the earliest Ming title appeared in c.1515 and the second in 1552).[118] The printing of over ninety-eight percent of these titles thus dated from and after the mid-sixteenth century explosion in the printing of books. Moreover, the harsh criticism they aroused in some literati circles was countered and eventually overcome by the generally warm welcome they met, if not always openly, from a wide spectrum of the scholar-official readership. In the words of the well-known Shandong collector Li Kaixian (1501– 68), "Scholar-officials generally take pleasure in stories, while the ancients' books explaining the classics often are shelved and do not circulate (*ge er buxing*)."[119] In the mid-seventeenth century, the unconventional author Li Yu poked fun at the hypocrisy of some of the objections of the Confucians about the popularity of his scandalous stories:

> Once my books are finished, everyone in the empire buys them and reads them. The only ones who are do not read them are simply the Teachers of "the Learning of the Way." But all of the real Teachers of "the Learning of the Way" buy and read them. Only there is a kind of fake "Learning of the Way" teacher who wishes to deceive people with his squareness and who merely does not dare to buy and go and read them. Or, some say, "It is merely that even if they do not dare to buy the stories themselves, they invariably hire others to buy them in their place and then read them and that even if they do not dare to read them in the open, they invariably read them privately behind the backs of others."[120]

This growth in demand for imprints during the Ming led to a significant change in the character of Chinese printing establishments, one that saw the government's traditional dominance give way to the irrepressible emergence of many private, often commercial publishers. From the tenth to the last third of the fifteenth century, government or official printing of élite books had accounted for virtually half of all imprint titles that survive in the National Library in Taipei.[121] More broadly, they account for 48 percent of the 210 surviving Song imprint titles presently catalogued in the collections of the National Library in Beijing, the National Library in Taipei, and Seikadō collection (54 percent in classics, 59 percent in history, 48 percent in literature, and 36 percent in collections).[122] Since government imprints were more likely to survive than non-governmental imprints, their share in overall imprint production between the tenth century and the last third of the fifteenth century, as well as in just the Song dynasty, is probably exaggerated by these figures. Nonetheless, their share of the imprint production in the century from 1465 to 1566 fell dramatically to just 26 percent. Moreover, this mid-Ming decline is evident in all four traditional categories of books. Only the share of history books, a scholarly subject of relatively little interest to early Ming authors and readers, remained fairly high, at 39 percent. But the government-sponsored imprints in the categories of classics and philosophy fell precipitously over the first two centuries of Ming rule, thanks no doubt to the popularity of guides to the classics and medical texts printed by commercial establishments.

The emergence of private, usually commercial, publishers on a large scale throughout southeast China represented a sea change in the character of Chinese printing. Admittedly, the designation "commercial printing establishments" (*shufang, fangke*) covers a variety of establishments, including longstanding household-based printers (like the Jianyang publishers), bookshop managers or book merchants who expanded into publishing, book collectors who began publishing some of their own works for profit, and possibly those literati families who turned to publishing as a respectable means of increasing their prestige and perhaps their income (these publications usually are more properly categorized as *jiake*). Indeed, these family publishers, according to Katsuyama Minoru, accounted for most of the mid-Ming publishers and publications and just under half of all Ming publishers and publications.[123] Katsuyama's distinction between commercial and non-commercial private publishers, taken over from traditional Chinese scholarship, is too rigid, particularly when even government offices printed books with an expectation of selling copies for profit for their officials, government schools, and students, and even for yamen construction expenses.[124] Nonetheless, his statistical survey of Ming printing shows that non-governmental publishing, in whatever guise, had clearly come to dominate the imprint culture of the Ming. The ascendance of these private, in particular the commercial, publishers in the world of Chinese publishing would survive increasing government censorship in the Qing and in the past century up to the 1950s.

A final factor in the ascendance of the imprint is the very complicated matter of cost. Imprints in the Song, Yuan, and the early Ming, in the view of Denis Twitchett and Inoue, were expensive. Since, as a consequence, the actual demand was not great, printers could not plan to make large print runs. The resulting rarety of Song and Yuan editions assured that, when the demand for books grew rapidly from the late fifteenth century onward, the price of these old imprints rose considerably.[125] Meanwhile, as seen in the first chapter, the price of new titles as well as of new issues of old titles dropped considerably in the sixteenth century, thanks to labor-saving and time-saving innovations in imprint production. These changes affected all the stages of book production that, in Hu Yinglin's view, determined the price: the quality of the paper, the accuracy of the transcription, the care shown with the binding and wrapping, the attention paid to the actual work of printing, the type of woodblocks used, and the fineness of the woodblock carving.[126] Yet, some of these price reductions mattered more for imprints than did others. For instance, reductions in the first four items in Hu's list would have reduced manuscript prices as much as imprint prices, and thus they could not have been crucial to bringing about a relative reduction in the production cost of an imprint. By contrast, the last two factors mentioned by Hu Yinglin concerned woodblock printing only, and so their price reduction mattered for the relative price of imprints. The larger and the more important price cut of the two would have been for carving, since carving accounted for much of the printing budget, as woodblocks themselves were not very costly, and since carving obviously was a cost not found in the budgets for the scribal production of books.

As the adoption of all the technical innovations mentioned in the previous chapter, especially that of the artisanal characters and their carving style, required no additional financial investment, no special skills other than a particular calligraphic style (indeed, it arguably allowed for inferior carving skills), and no new tools or technology, we may easily wonder why publishers took so long — roughly eight centuries — to adopt them. Here, the fate of the manuscript in Western Europe helps us to accept its persistent survival as well in lower Yangzi delta publication houses and collections up to and beyond the early sixteenth century. According to a recent estimate, Western European publishers had, by the end of their first century and a half of book printing (i.e., 1455 to 1600), issued a total of over 100 million volumes (the parallel figure for China's book production during its initial century and a half of printing is presently unknowable but was certainly far, far lower).[127] Nonetheless, manuscript copies remained in common use throughout Europe for at least two to three more centuries and in some countries for longer. In England, where in Europe the victory of the imprint was quickest and where most imprints were sold commercially without subsidy from as early as the start of the seventeenth century,[128] the number of imprint titles rose from 6,000 in the 1630s to more than 56,000 in the 1790s, and eventually to around 325,000 separate items in the 1870s. Meanwhile, the English manuscript was dying a very slow death:

> Throughout the sixteenth and seventeenth centuries, commercial manuscript circulation continued side by side with the book industry. The proportion of available manuscript texts compared to printed matter varied, as did the types of text produced by hand or print, but even in the eighteenth and nineteenth centuries the sovereignty of print was on occasion challenged by written communications.[129]

If, then, the more pertinent question becomes what price factors persuaded mid-Ming publishers to expand their book production in the delta, our focus should fall not just on the increased demand for books already mentioned but also on the competition that woodblock publishers faced from two methods of book production: moveable type and scribal copying. In other words, the key change that expanded the woodblock imprint share of the book market, and thus persuaded mid-Ming publishers to print more woodblock titles, would seem to have been the drop in the *relative* price of woodblock printing vis-à-vis these alternative methods of book production, thereby making these woodblock imprints more affordable and attractive items for purchase.

To understand the reasons for the widespread adoption of a new type of woodblock production, evidence about the competitive costs of moveable type in Ming China is highly suggestive, if not entirely convincing.[130] In the last third of the fifteenth century and first third of the sixteenth century, moveable-type printing won popularity among some delta publishers and literati (one of whom even rented type to print a book he otherwise lacked the money to publish with woodblocks). Two families in Wuxi county, the Huas and the Ans, put out, respectively, over twenty titles and several thousand *juan* of moveable-type imprints. Even though their books won considerable praise and attention, the overwhelming majority of other Chinese publishers did not switch to this method. Various explanations have been given for this reluctance. Some have stressed the conservatism of the Chinese scholar; yet, Zhu Yunming, an archetypical Ming literatus, wrote of the great interest of literati cognoscenti in this new method of book production. More persuasive are probably the technical obstacles to the easy and efficient adoption of this type of printing, such as the unsuitability of traditional Chinese inks for metal type, the uneven alignment of moveable-type characters on the printed page, their books' numerous textual errors, and the need for both small and big type fonts for each Chinese character and consequently the heavy increase in the initial outlay of capital. Yet, all these difficulties were resolveable (wooden type, for instance, remained the most popular variety of moveable type) through greater quality control and shared investment.

In the end, then, price factors seem to have mattered greatly in the eventually cool reception given moveable type, particularly in the last century of the Ming. As Milne's much later 1820 report to London would have us believe, moveable type was very expensive to establish — the Huas and the Ans were both very rich and made considerable investments in their printing enterprises — and very risky — the Huas ended up selling off a considerable amount of land due to their business losses. In addition, I would suggest that this method of printing possibly prompted price competition from woodblock publishers. The evidence for this claim is circumstantial: the cost-cutting innovations mentioned in the previous chapter were introduced in the same decades when the Huas and the Ans were promoting their new printing methods in Suzhou's neighboring prefecture of Changzhou. Thus, even if these woodblock changes were not intended to rival the Hua and An moveable-type publications, in the marketplace they certainly would have been in contention for the same circle of customers.

As discussed in Chapter 1, significant changes in transcription and carving methods in the mid-Ming led to a drop in the cost of preparing woodblocks for use in printing. While no Ming figures indicate the relative cost of artisanal characters and other types of carved characters, the already mentioned wage list for both scribes and carvers from the Four Treasuries project of the 1770s suggests that the adoption of artisanal characters for transcription and carving achieved savings of at least fifty percent in these two basic stages of woodblock production.

Such a drop would have also affected woodblock printing's longstanding rivalry also with another, hitherto the principal, method of book production, scribal work.[131] What, since the eighth century, had regularly kept handcopies cheaper than imprints was the low cost of scribal labor relative to the cost of woodblock carving. Hired to make copies sometimes in groups as large as thirty,[132] these scribes also worked as minor clerks, or were students in a local school and, most commonly, examination candidates.[133] These groups constituted a huge, permanent pool of cheap surplus labor that was largely responsible for keeping the handcopy cheaper than the imprint up until the sixteenth century. Here, I suggest, is a classic case of the prolonged delay that a technological advance in China might suffer before gaining widespread adoption: woodblock printing, an innovation of no later than the eighth century, failed to have an immediate and striking impact on book culture partly because of the continued low labor costs of traditional scribal work. It was eventually able to replace much of the manuscript book production, principally due to a greater demand for certain kinds of titles and due to price reductions brought on by technical changes encouraged, aside from a greater demand for certain kinds of books, by increased competition from moveable-type printing.

For more concrete information on comparative labor and production costs for manuscripts and woodblock imprints in the early sixteenth century, we very fortunately have comments made by the literatus Li Xu (1505–93) about scribal book production on the eve of the sixteenth-century publishing boom. During his childhood in Jiangyin commandery, at the northern edge of the lower Yangzi delta, Li tells us, he could not afford to purchase any of the imprints needed to study for the official examinations. He used only manuscript copies, made by scribes (from books in a friend's collection or at a book merchant's) for two or three *wen* of copper cash per twenty to thirty sheets of paper — i.e., 0.1 *wen* per handcopied sheet (of usually about 400 to 500 characters).[134] Clearly, no printed version, so long as it cost about 30 *wen* just to carve 100 characters on a woodblock, could compete with such a low cost of scribal reproduction for single copies.

To explore the implications of such a low scribal charge for the financial feasibility of printing multiple copies in the sixteenth century, it is useful to make two reasonable assumptions: firstly, that all their other costs for printing or handcopying were identical (but for woodblocks themselves) and did not change over the sixteenth century, and secondly, that one of Li's handcopied sheets costing 0.1 *wen* held roughly the same number of characters, 400 to 500, as did most woodblocks that would thus have very roughly cost 140 *wen* to carve. Under these conditions, a sixteenth-century commercial book producer would have been encouraged to shift his interest from copying to printing a book, only if he expected to sell a few thousand, rather than a few hundred, copies of its possibly 30,000 copy potential (although a well-carved woodblock was itself marketable after printing just these few thousand, or hundred, copies). In other words, the finances of commercial book publication, even with the lower costs of the late Ming, tended to discourage the adventuresome choice of new titles and to reward the printing of attested sellers for a reasonably predictable market. Aimed to please more than to instruct, these safe publications would have largely consisted of the works of a few famous poets and prose authors, examination manuals, medical advice books, "stories," miscellaneous anthologies of famous compositions, and the changing fashions and concerns of the day.

The late Ming publisher's interest would also have been stimulated by a change in his customers' taste. Readers increasingly tended to choose imprints over manuscript copies of the same works and appreciated handcopies less for the rarity of their contents than for their aesthetic qualities, especially their calligraphy.[135] This greater emphasis on the manuscript's hand rather than the title, contents, and price underlines the extent of the imprint's general ascendancy in the book trade of the lower Yangzi delta by the end of the sixteenth century.

In conclusion, let me stress that the ascendance of the imprint in the sixteenth century did not end the influence or the use of manuscripts in late imperial China. Firstly, even during and after this printing boom, the relatively well-to-do continued to report trouble finding some books they wanted to acquire and read. In the late sixteenth century, according to Hu Yinglin, literati still suffered from a shortage of books of Zhou dynasty (c.1000 BCE–221 BCE) texts, Tang poetry, and Song writings.[136] And, the travails of some important late Ming and early Qing collectors in the delta give ample evidence of this perhaps surprising claim. It took the wealthy Suzhou collector Shen Yuwen forty years before he could, in 1534, complete his handcopy of the Song work, *Henan Shaoshi wenjian lu* (A record of what was seen and heard by Mr Shao of Henan).[137] Thirty years passed between the first and second sightings of a well-known twelfth-century miscellany, *Qingbo biezhi* (Another record from Qingbo [Gate]), by the highly experienced editor Yao Zi (b. 1595); the first time Yao could not afford the asking price, since its owner regarded the title as a rarity and the second time he borrowed it and made his own copy.[138] It took a wealthy Suzhou collector over thirty years to put together, in 1584, a complete copy of the tenth-century work *Caidiao ji* (Collection of fine taste); and in 1579 he reported having similar trouble acquiring the Song dynasty work *Shuyuan jinghua* (The glories of a literary collection).[139] The major Suzhou collector Zhao Qimei (1563–1624) took eight years to acquire a full and accurate version of the *Luoyang qielan ji* (Record of the monasteries of Luoyang).[140] He also spent some twenty years trying to put together a full copy of the Song architectural treatise *Yingzao fashi* (Manual on architecture) in the Wanli reign era; he succeeded by buying an incomplete imprint and copying the remainder from an edition borrowed from the Imperial Library.[141] The late Ming Fuzhou collector Xu Bo, however well-traveled he was in the Yangzi delta, spent ten years searching for a copy of Tao Zongyi's mid-fourteenth century work, *Nancun chuogeng lu* (Record of when Tao Zongyi stopped farming), before he discovered that a friend had an incomplete copy which complemented his own family's incomplete copy.[142] Xu also spent another thirty years searching everywhere for a copy of the collected writings of Cai Xiang and eventually found a manuscript copy in an old book-collecting family in Jiangxi Province.[143] Even in the mid-seventeenth century, a devout Jiaxing follower of Zhu Xi, Zhang Lixiang, experienced similar frustrations in his attempts to obtain the *Jinsi lu* (Reflections on things at hand), an oft-quoted anthology of Song neo-Confucian writings compiled by Zhu and Lü Zuqian. After some trouble finding a copy, he had by chance acquired a not particularly good version of it from a book merchant. He soon loaned it to a friend who never returned it, and then had to wait over twenty more years before he could acquire another copy for his sons to read.[144] And, the early Qing literatus Zhu

Yizun (1629–1709), despite his success in accumulating a personal library of 80,000 *juan*, spent forty years looking for a copy of a Tang literary text (he eventually could copy just six of its twenty *juan*); he also spent many years handcopying from friends' copies in a vain effort to complete his version of the famous early Song geographical text, the *Taiping huanyu ji* (Gazetteer of the world during the time of supreme peace).[145]

These problems persisted well into the eighteenth century, though one senses that the problem then pertained primarily to specialized or originally rather unusual texts. Sun Yunqie, for thirty years, searched in vain for a copy of the *Xiyang chaogong dianlu* (A record of Western tribute); Wu Qian (1733–1813) spent several decades looking for and never finding Zha Shenxing's *Renhai ji* (An account of the human sea); Gong Cheng took thirty to forty years to look for but never find *Yixing zhu ji* (Collected writings on Buddhism by Peng Shaosheng [1740–98]); and Qian Daxin (1728–1804) searched another forty years and never found a copy of the Song geographical treatise *Yudi jisheng* (Famous recorded sites on the great earth). Further research, I suspect, will extend this list on and on, as we learn of the trials and tribulations involved in acquiring copies of rare books in the Qing dynasty.[146]

Thus, the unprecedented publishing boom of the sixteenth century may have significantly increased the number of texts in print and allowed the creation, for the first time, of many large private collections. But it still did not entirely alleviate book shortages for private collectors relying on the market. And, when necessary and possible, they turned to the manuscript as the next best solution to their shortage problem.

Not surprising, then, was the continued production and use of manuscripts in the Yangzi delta long after the imprint had come to dominate its literati book world. The appearance of a text as an imprint did not prevent readers from making a handcopy, or having a scribe make it, and then transmitting it as a manuscript to its next owner. Many Chinese scholars and book collectors like You Mao insisted that the best way of mastering or even reading a text was to make a brush copy of it.[147] Even if one did not fully understand what one was copying, one could reread it, memorize it, and eventually master it. Others, like the twelfth-century author Hong Mai (1123–1202), did so for reasons of scholarship; Hong reportedly made three manuscript copies of the *Zizhi tongjian*, one to research its errors and accomplishments, one to study its style, and yet another to master its Confucian learning.[148] And at a time when some thought that too many books were being published, an early seventeenth-century Suzhou advocate of handcopying claimed, "Writing a book is not as good as copying a book (*zhuoshu buru chaoshu*)."[149]

Scribal work done for others, of course, continued and even flourished in the late Ming, despite the abundant evidence of the ascendance of the imprint. One famous scholar-official, Huang Daozhou (1585–1646), for a brief period copied texts for a living. When imprisoned in Beijing for his political criticism, he supported himself by writing out, perhaps with his wife's assistance, copies of the *Xiaojing* that he sold for two *jin* apiece.[150] In Suzhou, a mid-seventeenth century examination failure, Jin Junming, though born into an official family, struggled to make a living by, among other things, writing text-copy manuscripts for publishers' woodblocks as well as calligraphy for the carved signboards of Suzhou temples and wine shops.[151] Even as late as 1769, the famous Beijing book quarter of Liuli chang was selling many manuscripts alongside its imprints; the man who reports this situation admits to passing most of his stay in the capital, borrowing and copying books.[152]

We thus need to recognize that the more book titles that were printed and the more extensive their distribution, the more likely it was that they gave birth to manuscript copies of a text in at least one stage of the transmission. So persistent and pervasive was this interplay that no sharp or absolute distinction can be drawn between manuscript and imprint in late imperial Chinese culture. The claim that the imprint first gained predominance over the manuscript in the Yangzi delta of the sixteenth century must then leave room for the continued vitality of a manuscript tradition that was not an evolutionary deadend but an important ongoing contributor to the formation of texts as we have come to read and know them today. As Dr James Hayes, the distinguished honorary member of the South China Research Center at the Hong Kong University of Science and Technology, reminded us two decades ago, village households in the New Territories tended to have, as late as the 1960s, manuscripts rather than imprints for their genealogies, their couplet collections, and their instruction manuals on family practices and social customs. For their books in other genres, such as geomancy and ritual texts, the manuscript copy was not predominant but still common.[153] May I suggest, then, that the findings here on literati culture in the Yangzi delta from the Song through the Ming may eventually prove valid for much of the book culture of ordinary readers as well, right up until recent times.

Finally, the manuscript tradition continued to shape not merely the appearance of woodblock imprints with the highly calligraphic styles that grace the frontispieces and prefaces of those books but also the contents of these imprints. Look at almost any traditional Chinese imprint, and it will usually read as a miscellany. More often than not, it turns out to be a collection of writings or comments by one or more authors, on one or more topics, to tell more than one story, just as if it had been assembled as a manuscript with items added or subtracted as the author(s) wished. If one or even many of the individual entries or sections in these books were dropped (and this holds true also for parts of many longer novels), then only a very knowledgeable reader would have been likely to notice the difference, even if he or she were reading an imprint edition rather than a manuscript copy. Such textual fluidity, so readily understandable in a manuscript-based literary culture, has long persisted as a Chinese imprint practice, from the pirate printers of the thirteenth century to the state printing houses of our day. In sum, the imprints that fill the shelves of our libraries bear, so to speak, the imprint of a rich manuscript culture that has persisted far longer and more pervasively in the world of Chinese books than many of us have suspected.

Appendix 2.1

Number of Extant Imprints by Period, from 1131 to 1521, National Library (Beijing) and National Central Library (Taipei) (Inoue, "Zōsho," p. 428).

Southern Song	(1131–1279)	Yuan (1271–1367)
Classics	50	75
History	48	59
Philosophy	39	51
Belles-Lettres	67	60
Total	204	245

	Ming (up to 1521)				
	1368–1402	1403–25	1426–35	1436–49	1450–56
Classics	2	5	4	7	2
History	18	6	5	3	5
Philosophy	10	8	6	5	4
Belles-Lettres	21	8	12	25	12
Total	51	27	27	40	23

	1457–64	1465–87	1488–1505	1506–21
Classics	0	7	9	18
History	3	20	25	34
Philosophy	6	27	38	36
Belles-Lettres	21	82	87	125
Total	30	136	159	213

Appendix 2.2

Number of Extant Imprints Printed in Every Ten-Year Period, from 1131 to 1521, That Are Presently in National Library (Beijing) and National Central Library (Taipei) (ibid.)

	1131– 1279	1271– 1367	1368– 1402	1403–25	1426–35	1436–49
Classics	3.5	6	0.6	2.2	4	5
History	3.3	4.8	5.1	2.6	5	2.1
Philosophy	2.7	4.1	2.9	3.5	6	3.6
Belles-Lettres	4.7	4.8	6.0	3.5	12	17.9
Total	14.2	19.8	14.6	11.7	27	28.6

	1450–56	1457–64	1465–87	1488–1505	1506–21
Classics	2.9	0	3	5	11.3
History	7.1	3.8	8.7	13.9	21.3
Philosophy	5.7	7.5	11.7	21.1	22.5
Belles-Lettres	17.1	26.3	35.7	48.3	78.1
Total	32.9	37.5	59.1	88.3	133.0

Appendix 2.3

Pre-1522 Imprints in Mainland Chinese Libraries, as Listed in *Zhongguo guji shanben mulu* (Inoue, *Chūgoku*, p. 181).

	1127–1274	1264–1367	1368–1402	1403–1435	Early Ming	1368–1435	1436–64	1465–87	1488–1505	1506–21
Classics	117 (8.1)	149 (12)	2 (0.6)	6 (1.8)	16	24 (3.5)	14 (4.8)	13 (5.7)	22 (12.2)	28 (17.5)
History	117 (8.1)	99 (8)	14 (4)	15 (4.5)	25	54 (7.9)	46 (15.9)	90 (39.1)	126 (70)	164 (102.5)
Philosophy	181 (12.6)	187 (15.1)	22 (6.3)	61 (18.5)	55	138 (20.3)	48 (16.6)	60 (26.1)	89 (49.4)	79 (49.4)
Collections	297 (14.4)	126 (10.2)	19 (5.4)	26 (7.9)	39	84 (12.4)	72 (24.8)	98 (42.6)	117 (65)	159 (99.4)
TOTAL	622 (43.2)	561 (45.2)	57 (16.3)	108 (32.4)	135	300 (44.1)	180 (62.1)	261 (113.5)	354 (196.7)	440 (275)

Notes:
1. The numbers in parentheses refer to the number of titles per decade within the designated period.
2. The Early Ming column contains titles whose precise date cannot be determined but whose general date of publication in the first seven decades of Ming rule is reasonably certain.
3. The figures for the 1368–1435 column are total figures for the three Ming dynasty columns immediately to the left of it.

3 Distribution of Books and Literati Culture

In the rich and lengthy historical record of China, where but perhaps among the biographies of Daoist hermits and Chan monks do we find as many endearingly or infuriatingly unconventional figures as in the ranks of its book collectors? From the Song, Yuan, and Ming dynasties alone, we find the single-minded bibliophile Xing Liang, who lived alone in three cramped and run-down Suzhou rooms, reading the books that covered the floor and ignoring the moss that dripped on his walls; the highly-regarded Ningbo scholar Feng Fang, who turned his bibliomania to the lucrative but disreputable business of making fake books; the Shaoxing student Yang Weizhen, who, in the early fourteenth century, removed the ladder to his second-floor room in order to devote five years solely to the study of books stored there in his family's collection; and, the tireless collector Yu Canzheng, who put his entire library on an island reachable only by boat, in part to drive away unwanted readers.[1] No wonder that the poet Lu You, an avid collector whose book-crammed study merited its name "Book Nest," held that "All the illnesses that a man has in his life come to a halt; only bibliomania can't be cured."[2] Equally perceptive was the remark of the late Ming bibliophile Xu Bo that, to find an unusual book, you needed only to find an unusual man.[3]

In this and the next three chapters, I want to examine important changes in book distribution and consumption through the eyes of both these unusual men and their more ordinary contemporaries from the Song through the early Qing. My aim is not to analyze these bibliophiles' bibliomania but to find answers to two questions they themselves obsessively asked: where and how might they acquire the books they wanted to collect? And, how might they gain access to read or copy books they otherwise could not acquire for themselves? If the second of these questions is concerned primarily with the immaterial act of reading, the first is concerned explicitly with the acquisition of a material object. And so, this chapter's focus on the first question examines the changing fortunes of two possible solutions to these collectors' problem of acquiring books — gifts and purchase — as well as late Ming changes in the social composition of their ranks. If the late Ming saw the ascendance of the imprint and commercial printing, it also saw the establishment in the delta of an extensive network of full-time bookstores, old bookstores, book catalogues, bookstalls, and private publishers, that provided many readers and collectors with a greatly expanded means of acquiring books. An analysis of the development of this market-based solution to the question of how to acquire books accounts for most of this chapter. We pay particular attention to seven distinctive book collectors of the last century of Ming rule — the bibliophile Hu Yinglin, the publisher Mao Jin, the boss-editor Chen Jiru, the editor-publishers Gu Yuanqing and Yin Zhongchun, the bookseller-publisher-collector Tong Pei, and the private collector Xu Bo — in order to examine how the distribution of books changed in commercial channels from the Song to the late Ming. The topics covered range from peddlers, lending libraries, bookstores and the types of books acquired, to changes in the social position of these collectors and the ways some of them found to use their collections. The focus, however, remains for us what it was for these men: how did one find and acquire the books one wanted to read and own?

Gifts

The history of gift giving remains an oddly neglected subject among sinologists. Chinese may have commonly resorted to gifts to consolidate ties and prepare persons for eventual requests, yet social and economic historians have chosen to pay far greater attention to the more "modern" means of distribution, such as market networks. Here, in a discussion of books, I would like to redress the balance slightly and explore both kinds of acquisition, gifts as well as purchases. In recent years, some anthropologists and historians have come to recognize the possibility of some mutual dependence of these apparent opposites, since the practice of gift giving has been seen to flourish in some commercial economies. Accordingly, in the increasingly commercialized economy of the Yangzi delta from the

Song through the Ming, gifts were not marginal activities. Books in particular played a vital form of gift — imperial, parental, or official — that involved, respectively, the court, the family, and officialdom in meaningful exchanges. While gift giving will be overall seen to have played only a secondary role in Song and Ming book distribution, it did so in particular niches important for certain kinds of books and for certain readers in certain situations.[4] It is these specifics that we try to determine in our account of how books were distributed and consumed from the Song through the Ming.

Perhaps the type of book gift most mentioned in our sources is the imperial presentation of imprints published by the court or another official agency. Initially, this contribution to book collectors was far from insignificant. In the Song, especially the Northern Song, book gifts from emperors built up at least sixteen sizeable private collections, thirty-odd princely collections (each of which contained between 10,000 and 50,000 *juan*),[5] and collections of some well-known private academies and needy prefectural schools.[6] In the Ming, the early emperors continued this practice on a reduced scale by donating imprint copies of both the Confucian classics to county and prefectural schools and their own writings to numerous princely establishments set up around the country.[7] From the mid-fifteenth century, this Ming imperial patronage dried up; perhaps the last notable contribution to an individual was the donation of 10,000 *juan* to the heirs of the influential Grand Secretary Qiu Jun (1418–95).[8] When imperial patronage somewhat revived in the late sixteenth century, it usually consisted of support from an empress dowager sponsoring the reprinting of the Buddhist canon and its distribution to major temples throughout the country.[9] Private collectors were not among her beneficiaries.

Also unreliable, perhaps surprisingly, was the fortune of those parental gifts known as bequests or inheritance. For males fortunate to be born in families with a tradition of book collecting, the prospect of inheriting and keeping a book collection would have looked attractive. We know of at least thirty-one such families from the Song, seventeen of whom held onto their collection for three or more generations. The most successful families were the Sun in Sichuan, which held on to their library for ten-odd generations from the late Tang to the early Southern Song, and the Han in Shandong, whose library survived fire, theft, warfare, and flood for ten generations from the eleventh century up to the mid-thirteenth century.[10] The lower Yangzi delta had a few sizeable hereditary family libraries in the Song, some more in the Ming, but mainly, it seems, in the Qing. For instance, Ye Sheng's library lasted in his descendants' hands for nearly 200 years, until the mid-seventeenth century.[11] Wu Kuan's (1436–1504) collection began to be broken up in the mid-sixteenth century and was finally dispersed only in the mid-seventeenth century.[12] Wen Zhengming's books began to be sold off by his descendants from the Wanli era, but many survived in their hands until the late nineteenth century.[13] Qi Chengye's collection was largely dispersed in the mid-seventeenth century, but some of his books remained in the hands of his descendants up until the 1950s.[14] The library of the Sun family of Changshu county of Suzhou prefecture, begun in the sixteenth century, remained largely intact up until the nineteenth century.[15] And, some famous libraries established in the late Ming or early Qing — twelve by one recent calculation — did survive to at least the early twentieth century. The most prominent example of these was the Tianyi ge Library. From its founding in c. 1560 up to the 1950s, this building and its book collection remained in the hands of the Fan family of Ningbo. Foreign invasion, lineage neglect, theft, and government confiscation all diminished the size of its holdings, mainly in the last century and a half. Yet, for at least the last three hundred years, it has ranked as the most famous private family library in China.[16]

But, these examples were exceptions. If a would-be collector was heir to such a collection of books, it was rare that he inherited it alone and that it survived repeated transmissions intact. Even if the books in a collection did not fall victim to the same natural disasters, political disorders, hungry worms, and the blind neglect that afflicted government collections, the Chinese practice of partible inheritance virtually assured that the heirs to a collection would soon divide the collection up and sell off whatever they individually wished. Collectors from the Song through the Ming and into early Qing regularly lamented the dispersal of a family's books, some even speaking of it as "a constant principle of things."[17] Often, this dispersal indicated the difficulty of the heirs in retaining the same level of income and wealth over several generations; for example, in the mid-sixteenth century it was said that, in Suzhou, few rich houses held onto their wealth for over a century and that its official families declined in a generation or two after their founding.[18] And, as the late Ming book collector Xu Bo knew all too well, the father's or grandfather's books were the first things his heirs would discard to maintain their standard of living: "I have seen that families who preserve their property (*chanye*) will often do so for up to six or seven generations, but those who preserve books will do so for no more than merely a generation or two." The major nineteenth-century collector Yang Jizhen echoed this view, by concluding that few family book collections remained intact after two generations.[19]

These judgments were not misguided. The sons of some book owners could not read them (*buwen*), had no interest in their father's books, and preferred to sell them off, even at ridiculously low prices.[20] In the Yuan dynasty, the major Yangzi delta collector Zhuang Su left his heirs 80,000 *juan*; they showed little interest in his learning, as they let worms, rats, and thieves make off with some of the collection. They burned some of the remaining books, when they feared that the books' content would anger local officials and endanger their own safety. And the rest of their father's collection they either sold off to pay their drinking and gambling debts or used to paste over gaps in the walls of their houses.[21] A Nanjing scholar's library in the fourteenth century suffered a similar fate, when his family's servants turned the pages of his books into shoe soles and bottle plugs. And, during the first half of the fourteenth century, the largest collection in the Zhedong area (i.e., most of Zhejiang Province) was inherited by heirs so negligent that they allowed over half of it to be stolen and sold by the family's servant manager or destroyed by the family's maidservants and concubines.[22]

In Ming dynasty Nanjing, wrote a saddened Gu Qiyuan, the major collections tended to be broken up and dispersed by their founder's children.[23] In Suzhou, the other major lower Yangzi delta center of the book world during the Ming dynasty, dispersals were as common as Shen Zhou's son suspected. The heirs of Shen Zhou's most distinguished disciple, Wen Zhengming, eventually sold off some sixty volumes of their father's poems and prose writings.[24] For the important collection of Yang Xunji, the dispersal came more quickly than even he would have predicted. This wealthy bibliophile had written, "If one has friends who read, / One ought to donate all one's books to them. / It is better than giving them to unworthy sons / Who would take them and sell them off for cash." Little did he realize that his own collection would suffer the truth of this advice to others:

within days of his death, his books were plundered and dispersed by relations, servants, and friends.[25] A son of the celebrated bibliophile Wang Shizhen, when pressed to pay his taxes, pawned his father's books to a Huizhou merchant.[26] The dispersal of the entire library of the heirless Qian Yunzhi at his death in the 1620s (it included the famous collection his father, Qian Gu, had built up from earlier Suzhou collections) ended, it was subsequently said, a Suzhou tradition of great book collecting.[27] And, though Zhao Qimei would double the size of the library he had inherited from his father, most of the 5,000-odd titles he listed in his collection's catalogue would pass upon his death into the possession of the famous collector Qian Qianyi.[28]

Some important collectors were resigned to such dispersal of their collection, and accordingly drew up a catalogue of their holdings explicitly to designate each son's share of this inheritable property.[29] Another collector, Xiang Yuanbian (1525–90), upon recognizing the inevitable, reportedly took the unusual step of writing on each item in his collection (mainly painting and calligraphy but probably also books, since he eagerly collected them as well), the price he had paid for it, lest his heirs forget the true value when they came to sell it (some later commentators held that Xiang marked his recorded price above his purchase price, since his real aim was to secure his descendants considerable profit when they sold off his collection).[30]

Many other collectors were not so fatalistic. An imperial prince in the fifteenth century had a book seal made with the legend ordering his heirs to keep and use his rare books "forever."[31] The eldest son of the famous Suzhou literati painter Shen Zhou reminded his own heirs that the family's books were heirlooms not to be sold off.[32] In the nineteenth century, Yang Jizhen had a seal legend carved with a 252-character long sermon to his heirs on how to protect his, or their, books, including the warning, "Do not sell off for cash, do not loan to others, and do not bequeath it to unworthy descendants."[33] A slightly earlier collector was even harsher: his book seal had the legend warning his heirs that, if they sold off any book from his collection, they thereby proved that they were not human and instead were like dogs and pigs. He promised them eviction from the lineage and a whipping.[34]

And, others repeatedly struggled, against the odds, to rebuild their family's dispersed collections. Consider first the book collection of the family of the twelfth-century scholar-official Wang Mingqing

(1145–1207). In the eleventh century, his grandfather reportedly brought back home several ten thousand *juan* of books collected during his long career as an official throughout the empire. During the chaos of the 1120s and 1130s, this entire collection, stored in two locations for safety from fire, was seized by a county magistrate more interested in plunder than in defending the county from rebellion and invasion. Unable to recover these books, the Wangs built up another large collection by the mid-twelfth century. But, since it was achieved at a time when the notorious Prime Minister Qin Gui was persecuting collectors suspected of holding books critical of his rule, the size of this new collection only revived the threat of political danger. Anxious to dispel all such suspicion (and thus save the rest of the family's property), Wang Mingqing's mother burned most of the new collection. "Whenever I think of it," confessed Wang, "my heart is pained and my head is sick." The volumes that escaped the fire were then stolen by relations or borrowed by others who never returned them. Consequently, by the close of the twelfth century, "less than ten percent of the bequeathed books survived." Wang continued his lament, "Whenever I return and inspect the old book boxes, I cannot bear to re-open them. I only shed a flood of tears."[35]

The book collection of Gu Yanwu's family from the mid-Ming to the early Qing, even though it overlapped a two-century publishing boom that saw the imprint replace the manuscript as the principal format for literati books in the Yangzi delta, experienced similar ups and downs. In c.1520, the collection numbered 6,000 to 7,000 *juan*. During the Jiajing era (1522–66), these holdings survived the Gu family's serious financial problems but not the raids by coastal bandits (*wakō*). Gu's great-grandfather then spent savings from his official salary to collect more books than his forebears had ever owned. Yet, since this collection, at his death, was divided up among his four sons, three generations passed before any of his descendants had a collection of as much as 5,000 to 6,000 *juan*. Then, under the stewardship of Gu Yanwu, China's finest historian since Sima Guang, two-thirds of its holdings were lost during the Qing conquest of the Yangzi delta in the 1640s. More than two decades later, Gu confessed that, in making use of an annual income from the family's tenants of 160 ounces of silver and living expenses of 100 to 130 ounces of silver (abetted by gifts and pay for editorial jobs), he had, in all his travels around north China, rebuilt the collection to no more than 2,000 to 3,000 *juan*, smaller than its predecessors in 1640 or even 1520.[36]

In sum, if fire, foreign invasion, and political factionalism did not destroy a family's collection, then the common practice of partible inheritance would have done the work, assuring that most major collections were whittled down in size over the course of just a few generations. The founder of a collection would have seen his parental gifts lead to dispersal rather than to preservation. His heirs, if keen to collect books, would have obviously benefited from his gift, but they still would have needed to rebuild the collection with their own efforts and resources. Imperial and official gifts, as seen above, would help, and did help in the Northern Song. But, at least in the Ming, such presents would rarely have been large and important enough to establish a family's reputation for scholarship. Where, then, might an aspiring scholar and collector have turned?

The answer depended on his circle. Among officials, imprints often served as presents to smooth their way through social occasions and into beneficial social relationships. Consisting usually of an official's own writings, those of a family member, or just a favored title, these books were published largely or entirely with government funds under the auspices of a government office. The practice dates to at least the mid-tenth century, when the high official He Ning had a government office print several hundred copies of a 100-*juan* collection of his own poetry and prose as presents to others whom he wished to impress.[37] This means of self-promotion attracted criticism from some Song scholars but eventually took root in a political culture that already tolerated examination candidates' presentation of sample writing compositions to their official examiners before the examinations from no later than the close of the twelfth century.[38] Zhu Xi himself criticized such government publications as a misuse of public funding[39] but was wise enough when denouncing one of his rivals, Tang Zhongyou, in 1182 to give far more attention to other charges, such as Tang's wasting time, money, and affection on a concubine.[40]

In the Song and Ming, provincial officials, especially traveling Ming censors, commonly relied on government salary funds and local government funds to print books, often for presentation to court officials.[41] By the late fifteenth century, Lu Rong wrote, "All the high officials give imprints as presents and often have all kinds of books printed. Some government departments are quite extravagant in this regard."[42] A century later, the bibliophile Hu Yinglin confirmed the prevalence of book giving among officials, and made clear one reason for the practice: such gifts were commonly exchanged when officials received appointments and promotions. The practice was especially appreciated by top-ranked officials, whose collections, padded largely with printed copies of the donors' examination writings, easily numbered over 10,000 *juan*.[43] From c. 1600, according to Gu Yanwu, this custom among officials went into decline, the officials more baldly presenting silver instead of books.[44] Yet, enough of the practice persisted for the late Ming Fujian collector Xu Bo to bemoan the presentation of books to officials for favors, saying that the recipients never read them and actually endangered their survival, since they put them on a shelf where they merely "fattened the ants and fed the rats."[45] And, of an official in the final years in the Ming, it was said that, when he attained an important position, his family increasingly had books presented to it.[46] Even in the late Qing, we learn from an early twentieth-century Beijing art dealer, provincial officials regularly directed book and art dealers in the Liuli chang quarter of Beijing to send books and art objects to court officials, presumably to gain a desirable placement in their next appointment.[47]

Yet, how common were such practices in the overall pattern of book distribution among officials in the Ming? According to Inoue, they were very common in the early Ming, as can be seen in the book-collecting activities of Yang Shiqi. A Jiangxi scholar who rose from poverty to become a Hanlin Academy scholar, a tutor to the heir apparent, and eventually Grand Secretary, Yang was probably the greatest private book collector of his generation, and has left us 302 book colophons. Once dated, three-quarters of these notes reveal two sharply different periods in his collecting life.[48] In his pre-official years, i.e., before 1399, he acquired at least forty-eight titles, only two of which were definitely imprints, whereas twenty-two were definitely manuscript copies (for twenty-four other titles acquired before 1399, this distinction between types of book is unclear). When Yang entered official life in 1399, the pattern changed dramatically. His definitely dated acquisitions increased three- or fourfold to no fewer than 184 titles. Of these, 134 can be identified as an imprint or a hand copy, and at least seventy percent of them were imprints. Almost all of these imprints were government publications that friends and acquaintances either gave him or arranged to be printed for him from woodblocks kept in government institutions in Beijing, Sichuan,

Jiangsu, Jiangxi, Anhui, and Zhejiang Provinces. By contrast, after 1399, he bought from individuals just seven titles, most of them released by officials leaving the capital for appointments elsewhere.[49] His purchases from market stalls and bookstores, even though he lived for at least two decades in Nanjing, amounted to fewer than six titles.[50]

Yang's colophons thus appear to portray an early Ming book culture that largely confirms other Ming evidence testifying to the decline of imperial book gifts to officials and the prevalence of book gifts in official circles, particularly as imprints circulating among official collectors. The educated commoner would by and large read and collect handcopies, whereas the high official would receive imprints that were usually printed by a government office. Furthermore, the official would acquire imprints either by direct purchase from other collectors and government institutions, or, far more often, as gifts from other officials, teachers, locals, friends, the sons, grandsons, and great-grandson of the author of a book, and friends with contacts at the National University.[51] One good friend presented Yang with a book every time they met, regardless of when they had last met.[52] By contrast, the only imperial gifts of writing that Yang records are the notices of his imperial appointment or examples of imperial calligraphy presented to him as special favors.[53] In sum, then, any book collector in the first fifty years of the Ming (and, by extension, some years before it) would have wasted a great deal of time looking for literati books in bookstores or waiting for imperial gifts, since imprints seem to have circulated and been distributed principally as gifts among interested officials.

This statistical analysis is highly suggestive but is nonetheless questionable on three counts. Firstly, Yang's colophons account for about 3,000 *juan*, only a portion — and probably a minor portion — of his collection, which is estimated to have eventually totaled 23,000 *juan*.[54] Even if we assume that Yang acquired more books in his final two decades after 1424 than in the two and a half decades before it, the collection of this ardent bibliophile in 1424 surely would have amounted to more than just 3,000 *juan* or to have been more than twice this figure. He claimed, in 1408, to have preserved all his acquisitions regardless of their condition and incompleteness — "Throughout my life I have never once not protected and loved old books and writings handed down to me, even if they were tattered and incomplete"⁵⁵ — and he proudly wrote a colophon for a ragged copy of an examination manual and a book given him by his teacher forty years earlier.⁵⁶

Secondly, as Yang makes clear in another colophon, he invariably took care to write colophons in books received from friends and acquaintances, indicating the origin of the book, but not to write so in books acquired as commodities (*huo*).⁵⁷ Thus, the total number of titles purchased after 1399 — fewer than thirteen from bookstalls, bookstores, and individuals — confirms not the prevalence of book giving in the distribution of literati books but merely what Yang had already claimed: his practice of recording the origin of book gifts from friends. In short, if his collection by 1423 totaled, as I suspect, more than 6,000 *juan*, most of them would not have been acquired as gifts.

Thirdly, Yang's colophons and numerous other writings disclose a great variety of ways an early Ming collector might build up his collection other than by gifts. Yang's account of his acquisitions proves to be particularly informative, since the nearly total destruction of his family's library in the Yuan-Ming transition obliged him to build up his collection virtually from scratch.⁵⁸ Inheritance thus meant little to him: the books his family had in his youth were just the *Four Books with Collected Commentaries* (*Sishu jizhu*) and *Transmitted Interpretations of the Book of Changes* (*Yi zhuanyi*).⁵⁹ One solution he resorted to was borrowing books: to read the *Shijing, Shang shu, Li ji, Chunqiu*, and *Zuozhuan*, he borrowed and transcribed the copies of others. And when it contained actually just half the text (as when at twelve or thirteen years of age he acquired a copy of the *Edited Commentaries of the Analects* [*Lunyu jishi*] from another villager), he still treasured it as if it were a huge ancient jade.⁶⁰ Later on in life, he would still copy books, even while traveling in a boat.⁶¹

Once he gained paid employment as a teacher, his anxiety about his basic expenses subsided enough to allow him to start buying books, such as the *Yi huitong* and *Yixue qimeng*.⁶² When he came across copies of the *Shilüe* and the *Shilüe shiwen* at prices far beyond his income as a village teacher, his mother ordered him to resort to a far older solution: to barter for the books with the family's sole chicken.⁶³ And, when he taught in Wuchang, he benefited from yet another ancient practice: the presentation of a copy of Liu Zongyuan's writings from a friend and the bequest of a copy of a neo-Confucian text.⁶⁴

Yet, overall, inheritance, borrowing, barter, and transcribing ended up mattering less than purchase. Once he entered official life in 1399, he started to acquire many books — this is where the story Inoue tells with his statistics is correct — but did so principally through purchase:

> I took on students for twenty-odd years and with all my accumulated diligence and energy I acquired only the Five Classics, the Four Books, and the prose and poetry writings of several Tang writers. As for the books on literature and history, I borrowed them from others to read. When I first received an imperial appointment, I was promoted to the Hanlin Academy, and I did not dare to waste the surplus from my official salary. All went to acquiring books. Only from then did my books and volumes become abundant.[65]

Even if Yang's "abundant" books still suffered serious gaps — he had no copy of the writings of the famous poet Xie Xuanhui (aka Xie Tiao)[66] and only incomplete copies of such famous works as the *Sui shu* (Official history of the Sui dynasty),[67] the *Liang Han zhaoling erji* (The two collections of the edicts and commands of the Former and Latter Han dynasty),[68] the *Tongdian*, and the *Wenxuan*[69] — his colophons show the limited role of gift giving even among bibliophile-officials in the formation of relatively large collections and the overall circulation of books in the early Ming. And, if purchase was the prevalent — though not the sole — means for a high court official to acquire books in the early Ming, then this practice must have been far more widespread during the latter half of the Ming when commercial publishing flourished greatly.[70]

Purchase

Where and how was a collector to buy books? Many Song, Yuan, and Ming collectors found these questions hard to answer satisfactorily. From Zheng Qiao in the twelfth century to Sun Qingceng in the eighteenth century, they preferred to stress the variety of obstacles, particularly in the late Ming, linked with purchase.[71] The options, at least according to the scattered references in pre-Qing sources, seem to have been few. Consider the troubles that awaited ordinary, inexperienced readers seeking to determine on their own what books to look for. They would have had precious few guides that were useful. Book catalogues compiled by booksellers existed since at least the middle of the eleventh century,[72] but we have little idea of how often they were used, and in what way and by whom, until the late Ming. Other book lists, notably those in the dynastic histories, would have helped scholars learn titles. But, as we have seen, the dynastic histories themselves were hard to find until the late sixteenth century. In theory, the catalogues of private collectors would have helped, but they tended to be published, if at all, only long after they had been compiled. Of the thirty-three catalogues of private book collections that are known to have been compiled during the Song, only four survive and none of these was published in Song times.[73] Furthermore, no fewer than 167 book catalogues of private collections were compiled during the Ming, but of these only 48 survive today, and few if any were printed during the Ming.[74] The most comprehensive catalogue of a private Song collection was first printed only in 1610, three and a half centuries after it had been compiled.[75] Likewise, the most comprehensive catalogue of a private Ming collector's holdings, valued principally for its holdings of Ming imprints, circulated in a small number of incomplete handcopies until it received its first printing, in 1913, only after the era of imperial China had ended.[76] Yet, even if these catalogues had been more available, they and their shorter counterparts seldom listed more than the title, author, and number of *juan*. Consequently, they would have provided only marginal aid for anyone maneuvering in a market notorious for incomplete copies and frauds.[77]

The most likely book outlets for Chinese readers would thus have been commercial: the book peddler, the lending library, and the bookstall and bookstores, all of which had a long history. Of the peddlers' practices, we unfortunately know very little; we know even less about any ties they may have had to publishing outlets or bookstores. One thirteenth-century source tells of peddlers whose boat rounds in the delta included both villages and cities in Hangzhou, Huzhou, and Xiuzhou. After months of peddling books intended mainly for female readers, he returned with his satchels full and his profits few: "The boat lost none of its weight, and the satchel [for his money] did not grow heavier. The insects got fat, and this man grew hungry."[78] By Yuan times, such "book boats" often originated in the delta prefecture of Huzhou. In addition to its boat production, book collectors, and publishing, this prefecture was famed for its large number of book merchants, who boated their books to the houses of collectors around the delta, and for its artisans, who produced books not just in Huzhou but also in other areas.[79]

Some peddlers who made periodic rounds of the same places could conceivably have run short-term lending libraries for regular customers. When they settled down in the larger towns and cities, these libraries would have possibly become a section of the operations of bookstalls and bookshops. The first written reference to a lending library tells of a stall, in the Suzhou county seat of Changshu in c.1370, which lent old and new books to customers of all ages, for a small fee.[80] Such lending libraries had probably first opened many centuries earlier, perhaps as early as the Latter Han (22–220) when there is the first extant reference to a market bookstall in Luoyang. And arguably they were widespread by the early fifteenth century. If as isolated and backward a prefectural seat as Qiongzhou on the island of Hainan boasted of a market stall that lent its books out to readers in the early Ming, then surely the same service was already available in the more prosperous cities and towns of mainland southeast China with far better access to the book production centers.[81]

For the scholarly reader, however, the reading fare of these libraries seldom offered anything of interest. Consisting of simple popular books suitable for unscholarly readers, these libraries tended to lend out reading primers, moralistic stories, fictional tales, historical romances in simple verse and prose, and entertainment works that, by the fifteenth century, were labeled "vulgar and heterogeneous stories" (*lisu boza zhi shuo*) and by the seventeenth century were denounced as "lewd songs and illicit tales."[82] In other words, the books in these lending libraries linked up more with local oral and popular culture than with scholarly or metropolitan written culture.

The operation of these libraries is very hard to research. But, three relatively late accounts from the nineteenth century, two from south China and the other from north China, confirm the impression that they provided for an adult readership that was far from scholarly. In c.1800, in the Fujian city of Fuzhou, the "vulgar and heterogeneous talk" in the lending libraries consisted overwhelmingly of handwritten copies of romantic ballads (*pinghua*), which found particular favor with female borrowers. Readers, female and male, could keep borrowed books for up to twenty-five days, paying a daily rate. Late returns suffered a daily overdue fine as well as the loss of the deposit (the amounts go unmentioned). The borrowers were not supposed to let others read or loan the books, but one suspects that these rules were often breached, as such prohibitions on usage were listed baldly at the back of the books. Charges were probably not very low, if only because the loan periods, usually from fifteen to twenty-five days, allowed the readers to make, or have made, their own copies and presumably be able to sell them on to others. Thus, loaning books might serve as a profit-making enterprise for lender and borrower alike.[83]

Slightly later, in the mid-1830s, the circulating libraries in the city of Canton in Guangdong Province dealt with a quite different gender of clientele and genre of books (the character of the books, however, showed less change). According to a Western missionary, at least some (and seemingly the majority of) the customers were male, whose reading fare consisted mainly of novels, at times "of a bad character." The circulating libraries, some stationary and others itinerant, loaned out their books cheaply for very brief periods. Out of one peddler's stock of more than 2,000 volumes (presumably the Chinese term is *ce*), eighty-five percent were on loan to customers, some of whom were "the servants and coolies of the factories [i.e., the Western companies there]."[84] The city reportedly had many other circulating libraries, and presumably they served the same plebeian sector of the urban populace.

The other place for which we have a relatively detailed account of lending library practices is late nineteenth-century Beijing, where lending libraries were often located in ordinary neighborhoods and run as a side business by steamed bun (*mantou*) shops. The range of reading matter here was only slightly wider than in Fuzhou — drum songs and collections of fictional legal cases — and thus once again of little use to an aspiring scholar. Confronted with the same abuses of reader theft and negligence as in Fuzhou, these Beijing lending libraries printed into their volumes legends that had a gusty vulgarity not matched by Fuzhou's shops (because the latter's customers were mainly women?):

> This shop loans out handcopies of legal case stories. What follows is clearly stated: The loan of a book is on a daily basis. If the book is not returned within half a month, the shop will confiscate the down deposit. If it is not returned in a month, then additional cash is charged by the day. If there are those who loan it and abuse it, who rip off its cover,

who rip up its binding, who rip out and use its paper, who write or sketch wildly into it, and who wildly change its characters, then these men are robbers and these women are bitches (*chang*). Do not be surprised to learn, sir, that they are the offspring of prostitutes (*jinü*).

More useful to literati and scholars, from at least the Song dynasty, were bookstores. From no later than the Han dynasty, Chinese readers had access to bookstalls, if not shops, where they could browse and read.[85] At first glance, shops dedicated solely to the book trade appear not to have been numerous, as many bookstores engaged in other trades, like stationery and paper money for funerals and ancestor worship.[86] Bookstores regularly and primarily engaged in the sale and printing of books appeared quite possibly by the sixth century in both north and south China. During the latter half of the eleventh century, a fair number were operating in Chengdu and Jianyang, as well as in the Song capitals of Kaifeng and Hangzhou.[87] In these two capitals, some bookstalls were located in the grounds of Buddhist temples (one Hangzhou temple in 1009 even printed up the writings of the celebrated critic of Buddhism, Han Yu).[88] In Southern Song Hangzhou, over twenty bookstores inside and outside the city walls are known to have printed and sold books.[89] The existence of many bookstores elsewhere can be inferred from the frequent inclusion of their name as the publishing house on the title page of an imprint. These establishments are thought to have held or had access to the woodblocks of a book, from which a copy could be ordered and then sold as if at a bookstore.

Nonetheless, according to Inoue, a Song or Yuan book collector, if he relied solely on bookstores to accumulate books, would have been hard pressed to form a sizeable collection of, say, 10,000 *juan*.[90] Instead, like Yang Shiqi in the early fifteenth century and Hu Yinglin in the late sixteenth century, he often acquired books, through purchase or transcription, directly from other book collectors or their heirs; or, like Li Rihua, he would buy them from book merchants who called on him at home (more than fifty such merchants visited Li between 1609 and 1616).[91] It is useful to recall that the great twelfth-century bibliophile, Zheng Qiao, when listing eight ways to acquire books (in all likelihood, relatively rare books), made no mention of bookstores.[92]

Perhaps, though, it is still surprising to see that stores which dealt primarily in the sale of books seem to have first become common in most of the Yangzi delta's cities only in the early sixteenth century (see Figure 5). Songjiang in particular appears to have developed very slowly. In 1234, after its prefect, Wang Yong, discovered that virtually the entire book collection of the prefecture's school library had been lost, he had such books as the *Shisan jing zhushu* (Commentaries to the Thirteen Classics) bought from a major surname group in Suzhou, presumably because he could find none for sale in Songjiang.[93] At the start of the sixteenth century, the Songjiang collector Lu Shen (1477–1544) had to go to Nanjing and Beijing to see many books (and even then could afford only incomplete, cheap copies).[94] By the 1530s, a change is evident: a Songjiang doctor with little land acquired within this prefecture 17,000 *juan* of books from peddlers and bookstores (recall that just two generations earlier, the scholar-official Ye Sheng's 22,300 *juan* constituted the largest collection in the delta).[95]

By the last third of the sixteenth century, similar changes were evident in prefectural seats in the middle and lower Yangzi Valley and Beijing. Bookstore quarters had grown up in Suzhou, Hangzhou, Nanjing, Beijing, and smaller cities like Kaifeng, Nanchang (in Jiangxi Province), and Wuchang.[96] According to a recent estimate, by c. 1600, Nanjing would have had no fewer than ninety-three commercial publishing establishments, Suzhou thirty-seven, and Hangzhou twenty-four; in the next four decades, up to the end of the Ming, the

Figure 5   Bookstore on Banjie Street in Suzhou, in the mid-eighteenth century, in Xu Yang, "Flourishing in a Prosperous Age" (*Shengshi zisheng tu*) (Beijing: Wenwu chubanshe, 1986), plate 53

figures for at least Suzhou nearly tripled.[97] Each of these establishments would have served as an outlet for their imprints. Furthermore, "old book stores" (*gushu pu*) dealing in books purchased from big private collections existed in Suzhou, Hangzhou, some other cities of Zhejiang Province, and even Nanchang in Jiangxi Province, by no later than the 1630s.[98]

For a description of the organization of this flourishing book market in the late sixteenth century, no better guide exists than the observations of Hu Yinglin. Born into a scholar-official family of modest means in the interior of southern Zhejiang, Hu as a child prodigy caught the bibliomania bug at the age of ten, when his father introduced him to Beijing's bookstores.[99] At the age of sixteen, he made the first of many visits to the cities of the Yangzi delta and then lived for five years in Beijing with his father, between his eighteenth and twenty-third years. Thereafter, for the next twenty to thirty years, he forsook food and comfort, borrowed money, pawned his clothing, and used his wife's silver hairpins, all to buy books in towns and cities along the Grand Canal and in the Yangzi Valley. By the age of thirty, his own collection, acquired mainly in Beijing and less so in his home area, amounted to some 20,000 *juan*. When combined with his family's previous holdings and the major Zhejiang library he subsequently purchased, it eventually totaled over 42,000 *juan*. Although it then consisted mainly of relatively cheap Fujian imprints, its size propelled Hu at a remarkably young age to the front ranks of Ming collectors, ahead of many of Zhejiang's old scholarly families.[100] Its rich holdings of prose and poetry also enriched the images and learned allusions in his writings, which thus won many admirers and supporters among the Yangzi delta's literati tastemakers, particularly Wang Shizhen and his brother, Wang Shimao. This powerful pair happily served as Hu's supporters in the delta's literati circles.

Acquiring a provincial examination degree but never taking up an official post, Hu seems never to have held a job, living off his father's official earnings and his family's lands.[101] In contrast to official collectors, Hu acquired relatively few books by gift from officials and by copying books in old family collections. Purchase, even crafty purchase, appears to have been his preferred method of acquisition.[102] The early seventeenth-century Fujian collector Xie Zhaozhe would claim that "no one was more skilled in the ways of searching for books than Hu,"[103] a skill that today is nowhere more evident than in his description of the sixteenth-century book market. Admittedly, his knowledge may not have been as extensive and accurate as he claims, since his stays in the south's book production and distribution centers of Suzhou and Nanjing were short, his visits to Yangzhou, Wuchang, and Huzhou very few, and he made no trips at all to Fujian and Huizhou. In particular, he may well underestimate the production level of northern Fujian, since he never visited it and was interested primarily in the production and distribution of books for élite readers like himself. Nonetheless, his description of the flourishing book markets of major urban centers in the Yangzi delta ranks not only as our best single guide to the organization and workings of the book trade of late Ming China but also as arguably the single most informative account of the market for any commodity in north and central China under Ming rule.[104]

In the late sixteenth century, Hu tells us, four cities stood far above all others as centers for the distribution of books: Beijing, Nanjing, Suzhou, and Hangzhou. Beijing, as the main imperial capital, attracted book merchants from all over the country, particularly at examination time. Its newly opened bookstores in the 1530s had given it a head start over most of the cities of the lower Yangzi delta. Yet, by the last quarter of the sixteenth century, Beijing's lead had faded, since it offered the customer just half of the titles available in Suzhou. Furthermore, it remained a backwater as a publishing center. Palace and government printings continued, but high paper costs made printing there three times more expensive than in Zhejiang. Its private publishing would not really flourish until the eighteenth century.

In the lower Yangzi delta, by the second half of the sixteenth century, the situation had changed unalterably. Hangzhou was still "a hub of the southeast." Its bookstores, up to "about thirty" from the total Southern Song figure of twenty-odd,[105] were concentrated at four major intersections in the city and found at temporary locations chosen to meet the seasonal demands of tourists, examination students, and temple visitors (its Buddhist imprints still drew customers to Shaoqing Temple, where all the booksellers were monks). Yet, for a keen collector like Hu Yinglin, its rare book market provided only occasional finds, and its newer imprint sector, for which its publishers often used easily carved poplar (*yang*) blocks, had not fully recovered from a nadir in carving quality reported earlier on in the century.[106] Its markets, moreover, were overwhelmingly dominated by imports from Suzhou, Nanjing, and Fujian.

The center for the production and distribution of quality imprints, the titles of which appeared in increasing numbers, had shifted indisputably to Suzhou, Nanjing, and Changzhou. Hu estimates that Suzhou and Nanjing each printed between five to ten times more books than the total number of books printed in Xi'an in Shaanxi Province in north China plus the three delta cities of Jiaxing, Huzhou, and Yangzhou. Sixteenth-century Suzhou city, according to a preliminary estimate, had no fewer than 650 woodblock carvers and roughly thirty-seven commercial publishers, mainly situated around Chang Gate and the Wu county yamen.[107] The quality of its carving, printing, and binding was rivaled only by Nanjing's, and its increased number of imprints (as well as Nanjing's) attracted book merchants from throughout the empire, particularly for encyclopedias. In fact, the volume of the book trade in Suzhou and Nanjing combined was, by Hu's perhaps questionable calculation, double the volume being produced then in Fujian.

Yet, in Hu's words, these two cities "were not places where books are gathered from elsewhere." A Fujian publisher might acquire woodblocks and open a bookstore in Nanjing, and Fujian carvers might occasionally find work in Suzhou.[108] Yet, less than three percent of the books on the shelves of Nanjing's and Suzhou's bookstores — this figure is in all likelihood far too low — are said to have come from elsewhere.[109] The cost of carving woodblocks in these two centers, even if carving in Suzhou cost only sixty percent of that in Beijing and twenty percent of that in the Imperial Household, was quite high. It was forty percent more than Hangzhou's and twice that of Fujian's. Consequently, Suzhou and Nanjing imprints, despite their occasional reliance on carvers from Fujian, had less market share the farther south they went, but were particularly welcome in the rest of the Yangzi Valley and in Beijing.[110] Their flourishing lasted, in the view of the celebrated observer of Nanjing life, Zhou Lianggong (1612–72), right up to the early Qing,[111] by which time there had emerged two levels of bookstores: small shops often clustered at major intersections in urban market areas (e.g., the Tiger Hill and Chang Gate areas in Suzhou, Three Mountains Street in Nanjing, Tiger Grove in Hangzhou), and wholesale outlets, located sometimes in temple courtyards (e.g., Cheng'en si in Nanjing), where the larger booksellers sold books to travelers and merchants from other provinces.[112]

The financing, management, competition and cooperation practices of these publishing houses, and their ties to writers, remain virtually unknown to us today. Future research will doubtless reveal how publishers bought and sold woodblocks and shared carvers, printers, and other workers; how certain houses established and maintained ties with certain writers; how they specialized in particular kinds of imprints; how some houses in the lower Yangzi delta distributed their books elsewhere in the country and perhaps even made anti-poaching agreements to keep competing versions of the same title from markets they could enter and dominate.[113] It would not be surprising if many publishers were active for only a short time, as the technology enabled very short-term investment and as workers were not permanently attached to a single "house" or publisher. We can even sensibly hypothesize that the place mentioned on the title page of a book as its publisher may sometimes have been merely the place where copies of this book could be obtained.

Yet, putting such speculation aside, we can summarize our present understanding of the mid-seventeenth century organization of the lower Yangzi delta's wholesale and retail book market along the following lines:

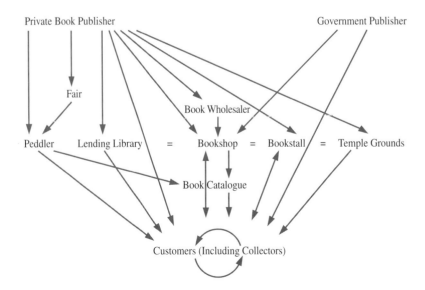

Literati

The broad description presented here of the late Ming book market masks profound changes in the role of literati-officials in the reproduction of élite Chinese culture. So far, I have used the term literati to talk about that group of educated men who spent much of their life reading, learning, memorizing, and transmitting texts, usually with the aim of acquiring the metropolitan degree and moving regularly in and out of government office. These men played a vital role in the production and transmission of Chinese culture from before the Song right up to the twentieth century. Yet, it is interesting to note that virtually all surviving collected writings (*wenji*) of Song dynasty individuals — and the overwhelming share of other extant materials — were written and collected by members of the literati-official stratum that held the metropolitan degree. In the Yuan, signs of a change were evident, when the prestige of Confucian learning plummeted thanks to the government's preference for other routes than just the official examinations to make its official appointments. The ranks of relatively important book collectors then included two men from very undistinguished social backgrounds: one was the son of a butcher, and the other the son of a cloth merchant.[114]

Social change in the ranks of the literati, however, became common in the latter half of the Ming, when the ranks of literati-official authors and collectors were joined by many men who never held an official post and yet now created, consumed, transmitted, and added to literati book culture.[115] Authors, editors, and collectors whose examination success never stretched beyond the lowest degrees, these district or imperial student (*gongsheng*) degree holders — men like He Liangjun, Feng Shu (1593–c. 1645), Lu Yidian (1617–83), and Qian Tong'ai (1475–1549) — come to mind, and one realizes that, for the first time in Chinese history, a significant portion of the major literati authors and private book collectors were neither themselves, nor from the families of, officials or high-degree holders. In other words, literati-official, or metropolitan degree holder, book culture was supplemented and complemented by what I wish to term, loosely, district degree and commoner book culture. Part of this sense of change is probably an illusion fed by the accidental disappearance of many publications by such people in earlier centuries. But it also reflects a greater number of readers for such books as well as changes in the character and contents of literati learning itself.

Of course, there were still many authors and large book collectors who passed provincial and metropolitan examinations. Without the writings of provincial degree-holders like Hu Yinglin, Huang Juzhong, Zhang Xuan, and Wen Zhengming, our knowledge of Ming book collecting would be seriously deficient; so, too, without the actual collections of metropolitan degree-holders like Ye Sheng, Lu Shen, Li Kaixian, Yang Xunji, Wang Shizhen, and Fan Qin, our own libraries would be much poorer. And, during the final decades of the Ming, the children and brothers of some provincial and metropolitan degree-holders would be responsible for the production of some of the marvels of woodblock printing throughout the world, over 100 titles of multicolored prints of the highest quality, apparently for educated and refined gentry.[116]

Also, some of these higher-degree holders engaged in book production for profit in a clear sign that the literary world of the delta had changed. In this more commercial, competitive, and varied world, where scholars might even express a wish for a type of proto-copyright,[117] the writings of some high-degree holders were up for sale. The provincial-degree-holder Zhang Fengyi (1527–1613) so despaired over his chances for a metropolitan degree and an attractive official career that he posted on the door of his Suzhou home a notice announcing the sale of his writing:

> "This household has no brush and paper for writing. If you are requesting standard script calligraphy all over a fan, it costs 1 *qian* of silver. If you want eight verses in running script, it costs 3 *fen* of silver. And, if you want poems and prose especially composed for a birthday, then it will cost several ounces per scroll." People vied in seeking them, and for thirty years it did not change.[118]

Such writings would eventually be compiled and published in their author's collected writings (the collection of the influential literatus Gui Youguang [1507–71], himself a metropolitan degree-holder and official, eventually included 170 prefaces, nearly a quarter of his total prose works).

Perhaps the literati writer for whom we have the most detailed financial information is Ai Nanying (1583–1646), a literatus who, upon gaining a provincial degree in the early 1620s, found his views and criticisms unappreciated in court circles then dominated by the notorious eunuch Wei Zhongxian (1568–1627). Whereas in the past such a degree-holder might have remained at home, in Jiangxi Province, and lived off his local landholdings, Ai enjoyed no such comfortable option. In 1621, he had broken up his father's estate with his elder brother(s) to inherit a total of 117 *mou* (some of which may have been land with tenancy rights rather than outright ownership). Since his annual income from this property came to 117 bushels of grain which, even after the division of his father's property, was intended to feed and clothe 50 people, Ai clearly needed to find other sources of grain and revenue. One solution was to buy cheap grain; hence, every year, in the eleventh lunar month, he purchased newly harvested grain for storage (and perhaps speculation?). But from 1628 to 1631, soaring rice prices underlined the fragility of such a strategy, as they not only prevented him from buying land but, in 1629, also led to the loss of some four *mou* of fields. Another, preferred, solution for Ai's financial troubles was an official appointment. Wei's death led to an edict summoning Ai to a metropolitan degree examination, but Ai ended up failing this test. A third, and more viable, solution proved to be writing. Ai advocated, and wrote in, an "ancient style" of composition that won him many imitators and, presumably, devoted readers, whose demand quite likely lay behind his frequent travels during these years to Suzhou, Beijing, and the Han River region in present Hubei Province. Having so little income from other sources, these travels seem to have brought him necessary income, letting him eventually entitle his collection of compositions *The Collected Writings of a Heavenly Hired Hand (Tianyong ji)* and buy back land that had belonged to two uncles.[119]

The ambitions of the far more numerous district degree-holders were particularly instrumental in expanding considerably the range of writings printed in the latter half of the Ming. As their low degree conferred only temporary relief from onerous service taxes, many strove for the stability and position offered by a higher degree. The odds, however, were against them. For instance, the eight counties of Suzhou prefecture had a total quota of 1,500 holders of the district degree, out of the tens of thousands of candidates taking this exam. Of these, just fifty could advance every three years to take the exam for the provincial degree.[120] The province-wide success rate for this exam was 11 percent in 1453 but fell to 3 percent in 1549 and 2 percent in 1630.[121] The low pass rate for the next rank, the metropolitan degree in an empire-wide competition, further reduced the chance of success, and then there might follow years of waiting, if lucky, for a lucrative appointment. Thus, even though Suzhou earned a reputation for producing top graduands in the metropolitan exam,[122] the vast majority of its candidates never qualified to sit for the provincial, let alone the metropolitan, exam and surely never received an imperial appointment.

This extremely high failure rate, combined with a paltry income as a lower degree-holder, forced many educated men to live off family wealth or their own labor. Few had the first option, and as many were more skilled at wielding the brush than turning the plough, these lower-degree holders often sought work in the booming world of commercial publishing for at least part of their income. Some did so for individual commissions, writing an endless stream of inscriptions, dedications, prefaces, and occasional verse for men with the money to pay (one literary collection was reputed to be two-thirds ghost-written).[123] Thus, along with some educated commoners who held no degrees at all, these lower-degree holders wrote, edited, compiled, revised, copied, published, and collected reading materials for a greatly expanded readership. Their books responded to and nurtured a widespread interest in "how-to books" for the examinations, medicine, prose and poetry composition, dictionaries, and numerous literati hobbies. They also put together collecteana and selections of the works of famous writers, wrote stories, or popular fiction, and composed whatever the person calling the tune wanted.[124] As men of letters (women authors and collectors were still far less numerous and not openly writing for the market),[125] they might be dismissed as profit-seeking vulgarians by some elevated literati.[126] Yet some commoner collectors, like Yao Shilin (1561–1651) — literate only from his early twenties and the eventual possessor of over 20,000 well-collated *juan*[127]— were feted by high-degree holders who previously would have circulated in separate social worlds.

The precise terms of remuneration that awaited these writers from their commercial publishers remain unknown, and it is likely that few could survive on book compilation or composition alone.[128] But the range and degree of literati and commoner involvement in the world of commercial printing can be understood by observing the activities of literati collectors in three different activities of book production: publishing, compilation, and sales. Literati had long been involved in the book business, often as family publishers but also as booksellers, by no later than the early eleventh century, when all the book merchants were said to be scholars (*shi*).[129] Even if an exaggeration, this view indicates how central this social group was to not just the consumption of books but also their distribution and production in the Song and Yuan dynasties.

To cite a few notable examples of literati book publishers and sellers from the Song and Yuan will, I hope, suffice. The famous literatus Mu Xiu (979–1032) not only had the collected writings of the celebrated scholar-officials Han Yu and Liu Zongyuan printed up but also sold them himself in the bookstalls of Xiangguo Temple in Kaifeng in the early eleventh century.[130] The celebrated neo-Confucian scholar Zhu Xi was so angered by the pirated printing of his own writings that, with the aid of his children and some disciples, he published about thirty-five of his own titles (mainly commentaries on the Confucian classics and other famous writings) for sale under his own name as publisher.[131] His rival, Tang Zhongyou, owned a Zhejiang bookshop that sold books that he published with government funds.[132] One twelfth-century publisher, Yu Renzhong, even advertised himself as a metropolitan degree-holder from the National University (*Guoxue*).[133] The poet Lu You and his son Lu Ziyu published fifty-one titles, and Yue Ke, a descendant of Yue Fei, published two books of family history, his own writings, and his own studies of Confucian classics and commentaries.[134] The Hangzhou book dealer Chen Qi (fl. early thirteenth century) had advanced to the metropolitan examination before opening a bookstore in the capital, where he sold, edited, and published books as well as befriended many scholars with good talk and fine wine. His political troubles, i.e., banishment for printing a poem some officials considered critical of the rule of Prime Minister Shi Miyuan, did not deprive him of the respect and affection of other officials, who addressed him as "a scholar" (*shi*).[135] The Shanghai collector Sun Daoming (1296–1376), the son of a butcher, handcopied several thousand chapters of books, which book and calligraphy collectors bought from him at hefty prices.[136]

What distinguished late Ming literati involvement in the publishing world was the number of such literati, the range of their commercial activities on behalf of others' books, and their detachment from the halls of exams and officialdom. The most famous publisher of the final years of the late Ming was undoubtedly Mao Jin. A student and disciple of the highly influential scholar-official Qian Qianyi and the son of a wealthy gentry scholar, Mao repeatedly failed to pass beyond the level of an imperial student in the examination system. Aided then by funds from his mother, in the 1620s he launched a publishing house, Jigu ge, that over the next forty years published close to 600 titles, many for the first time ever or for the first time in a large run. His editions relied initially on his own collection of the 84,000 volumes that he had inherited or purchased and subsequently on books borrowed from other natives of the Suzhou county of Changshu. His publishing lists largely focused on making available, if not always accurately,[137] modern versions of rare Song and Yuan editions of collected writings of Tang, Song, and Yuan dynasty authors, history titles, studies of the Confucian classics, and stories for a literati readership. For all this work he had twenty printers, a number which a recent study has estimated, on the basis of modern woodblock printing practice, to indicate a total workforce of about 200 regular workers.[138] All these workers were stationed at his home (the carvers were housed in two of the corridors, near the nine storerooms that contained the carved woodblocks). His son would carry on the work less successfully, and the business would come to a close after his grandson took charge. Despite the grandfather's warning that any male descendant who did not sell books would damage the family's reputation and be worth less than any beast or fowl, this grandson reportedly used woodblocks carved with Tang poems to heat up his tea water.[139]

Many late Ming publishers relied on outside editors to compile and edit books for publication. As they recycled and reprinted a striking number of older writings in new formats, they needed knowledgeable editors with access to collections whose books could be excerpted. In the Yangzi delta, the most celebrated of these "boss-editors" was Chen Jiru, a man whose successful literary career only underlined the fact that examination failure no longer prevented one from achieving high status in literati circles as well as wealth from commercial publications.[140] After repeatedly failing to advance beyond a district degree, Chen gave up his examination dreams at the age of twenty-nine and began a long and profitable career writing and especially editing books in large collecteana published with others' funds. The schoolmate of the influential painter-official Dong Qichang and the close acquaintance of other Songjiang literati, he used his extensive network of literati and official connections, his privileged access to the libraries and networks of his close friends, and his own large collection of unusual books to put together texts on literati subjects that interested the delta's publishers and readers. To do the editing, transcribing, and collating, he drafted teams of delta scholars attracted by his fame, connections, and promise of pay. In the end, the books appeared under his name as editor and compiler, even though the work was farmed out to others, including at times holders of the metropolitan degree (these men quite possibly passed on the assignment to their own underlings). Typically, he selected writings about literati life, its hobbies, pleasures, and history. His friends wrote prefaces that touted his rare abilities, and these publications rapidly became very popular among literati, merchants, and others anxious to learn about the culture that distinguished the scholar-official élite from just local literati.[141]

Some commoner collectors, like the Suzhou enthusiast for fiction Gu Yuanqing and the Jiaxing doctor Yin Zhongchun, actually did the editing and publishing work themselves, perhaps because they collected books in less prestigious fields of reading. Gu lived in the northwest suburbs of Suzhou city, where he published rare titles he had initially assembled for his pleasure. He showed particular interest in "stories," publishing two large compendia as well as a variety of shorter works.[142] Yin Zhongchun was a Jiaxing village doctor who turned his bibliomania about medical texts into a publication enterprise. He had from youth kept spare change in his pocket, on the odd chance of picking up incomplete, ravaged copies of medical books for a few pieces of copper cash. Eventually, he went off with his collection to Jiangxi Province, where several doctors joined him in compiling and publishing one of China's oldest extant specialist catalogues of medical works, the *Yicang mulu* (Catalogue of a medical collection), consisting of over 590 titles. In the end, his efforts won the admiration of many literati, Chen Jiru capping Yin's posthumous reputation by writing his biography.[143]

The combination of collector-editor-publisher was common in the late Ming delta. What made the career of Tong Pei special was that this commoner not only collected, edited, and published books but also actively sold them.[144] Without too much exaggeration, he could even be described as a book peddler. Although he seems to have spent considerable time in retirement in his home county of Longyou in the Zhejiang mountains, Tong was forced by the poverty of his family's fields to spend most of his life working away from home, mainly in the delta. There he acquired not only a Suzhou accent but also the personal and commercial connections in Suzhou that his father had developed as a bookseller. His father may have been able to afford a Suzhou woman as his concubine but he lacked funds to send his son to a local school. Consequently, Tong was taught by his father how to read and then taught himself, from books in his father's satchel, how to write classical verse. His eventual proficiency in poetry and even art connoisseurship is said to have aroused envy from some and offers of patronage from others, including gentry and officials eager to marry him to one of their kinswomen, introduce him to the court, and give him money. His rejection of all these offers in order to follow in his father's steps, selling and publishing books, signaled neither humility nor independence. Sometimes he lived at home; other times he traveled by boat to many places within the delta (a common mode of transport for many booksellers going from Zhejiang to Suzhou) and earned a living selling old books. His collection of 25,000 *juan*, said to have contained many rare individual titles, about a third of which were random, was listed in a catalogue that would have easily functioned as his commercial stock list as well (he is said to have loaned several old books to book dealers who paid him an annual interest, that he then passed on to his older brother).[145]

During trips to Shandong and Hunan, he wrote landscape and travel verse that he exchanged with literati friends back in the delta. Eventually, he edited several chapters of his county's local gazetteer and printed several prose and poetry compilations (some of which ended up in the Tianyi ge Library), while his own collected writings were arranged in six *juan* by a Suzhou literatus. His commercial endeavors proved successful enough to enable him to develop extensive friendships with literati (he extracted several from debt) and exchanged verse with some of them during his trips to Shandong and Hunan. Interestingly, his literati friends included major figures in the Yangzi delta's contending schools of literary style at the time. On the one hand, he became a disciple of the famous, Suzhou author, Gui Youguang[146] and a close friend of another leading figure in Suzhou's world of commercial publishing, Wang Zhideng (Tong conceivably sold their publications). Yet, he also associated closely with another Longyou bibliophile, Hu Yinglin, and was posthumously honored with an obituary by Hu's patron, Wang Shizhen, in the delta's high gentry circles. Thus, in a milieu where patronage was still necessary, Tong hedged his bets by becoming, in the words of one biographer, "a scholar secluded among merchants," capable of bridging very different literati circles.[147] How sharply this openness about a commercial career in publishing contrasts with the circumspection shown by a late fourteenth-century Wuchang scholar to even his close friends about his own activities as a bookseller.[148] Yet, unlike the late eighteenth and early nineteenth century literati book collectors Huang Peilie and Qian Tingmo, Tong never set up a stall or shop as a book dealer in Suzhou, from where he dispensed advice on the provenance of books that had emerged from private collections.[149]

Limitations

It is tempting to conclude this account of late Ming commercial book distribution with a remark made by an early nineteenth-century English observer that, in China, "the traffic in books is a lucrative and most honorable branch of trade."[150] Yet, for at least the late Ming, any claim that commercial printing and the book market had triumphed and replaced all of their rivals would be seriously inadequate. Recall two points already made — the flourishing practice of book gifts in official circles and the shortage of many book titles in major collections of the sixteenth and seventeenth centuries — and recognize the scarcity of late Ming bookstores. In Hu Yinglin's account, few, if any, are located outside the prefectural and provincial seats of government. Only in the eighteenth century do we see bookstores begin to appear in some numbers outside of these seats, as migrants from old and relatively new production centers established new commercial printing centers in inland market towns and even rural districts in Jiangxi, Hunan, Sichuan, and southern Fujian. The power of these migrants would be evident even in Beijing. In 1769, a recent visitor to the booksellers in Beijing's Liuli chang quarter wrote a detailed list of the shops and their owners, and found that these owners had largely come from Huzhou in Zhejiang, Suzhou in southern Jiangsu, and Jinxi county in Jiangxi.[151] But the limitations of book distribution by the market were more than structural. The imperial and government office patronage of publishing of the early Ming had dwindled by the mid-Ming, to be dominated not just by commercial printing but also by the high gentry patronage of literati and bibliophiles. One notable case is that of the late Ming collector and poet, Xu Bo (1570–1642).[152] Like Hu Yinglin, Xu suffered from a lifelong obsession with collecting and reading books, to the extent of using a great deal of his family's wealth to assemble a collection. Some rarely seen and hard-to-locate books he acquired by transcribing copies in other people's houses, by begging others for their copies, by being presented with them as gifts by friends, and often, as seen in surviving colophons to his books, by purchase. In addition, for several years he relied on a Fuzhou clerk, a fellow collector, to buy reportedly seven-tenths of all his book acquisitions.[153] In other years, he made at least seven extended visits to the lower Yangtzi delta cities of Nanjing, Suzhou, and Hangzhou, where he fraternized with many famous book collectors[154] and visited Nanchang in Jiangxi, She county in Huizhou in southern Anhui Province, and Yunnan Province in the far southwest.[155] He is known to have bought books at bookstores or bookstalls in Ningbo, Hangzhou, Nanjing, Nanchang and Jianyang in northern Fujian, and in a Quzhou temple in the Zhejiang interior.[156] Two particularly favorite haunts of his were Jianyang bookstores from 1599 to 1609 and a small bookstore in the Guanxian quarter of Fuzhou city.[157] He published his and others' collected writings as well as some fiction titles (and possibly sold them, even if the only commercial side of his book life that he writes about is the sale of old books).[158]

But what makes Xu interesting to a social historian of the book is actually his disinterest in the flourishing commercial world of book publishing. Like Tong Pei, he remained a commoner all his life, after repeated failures to acquire even a district degree. But, unlike Tong, he came from a family of officials (his father and brother were degree holders), and he used his family's collective holdings of 70,000 *juan* to forge contacts with well-known bibliophiles in the Yangzi delta and with a group of Fuzhou book collecting officials, especially Cao Xuequan (1574–1646). He formed his own poetry society with members from Fuzhou and the Yangzi delta.[159] Understandably, then, he persistently wished to be outside the commercial world.[160] Only a minority of his 145 book colophons indicate that these books had been purchased. Instead, more of the books with these colophons came as gifts from friends and as his own handcopies of rare books in the collections of others.

More importantly, he sought to be close to bibliophile officials who could serve as his patrons. In 1639, he agreed with the influential scholar-official bibliophile Qian Qianyi for the two of them to hunt down books and reconstruct two earlier collectors' book catalogues, only to see their plans dashed by the collapse of the Ming and the subsequent disorder.[161] His closest patron, however, was undoubtedly his book-collecting friend Cao Xuechuan. He traveled off to Hunan and Yunnan Provinces to visit Cao in his official headquarters. He and his brother wrote prefaces for books that Cao published, he co-headed poetry circles in Fujian with Cao, he brought Cao a Tang writer's work to be printed,[162] and he regularly exchanged poetry with him. Cao reciprocated in a variety of ways, including the construction of Xu's library to hold his books. In other words, this collector survived not simply from his family's inherited wealth but also from support from an even wealthier official patron who provided him with introductions to collectors elsewhere and the means to preserve his collection. The late Ming may well have seen a great expansion of commercial printing, but literati still sought and found patrons outside the market in political circles. Unlike the early years in the dynasty, however, the patron was not the imperial court but the highly placed official.

The importance of close personal ties in book collecting circles would exist also among book collectors anxious to locate and acquire books. Even when many copies of a book were held in different collections in a particular area, it is likely that at most only a few were accessible. The frequent dispersal of family book collections of one to ten generations' vintage allowed books to change hands, but there was no guarantee that either the old or new owner would make them available to others. Thus, this kind of circulation of books did not necessarily lead to the rapid dissemination of ideas and information or to any strong awareness among literati that their shared interests as scholars mattered more than their separate family ties. That struggle about access to books and its impact on the making of "a community of learning" are the topics of the next chapter.

4 The Problem of Access in the World of Chinese Learning

The creation of a book, a manuscript as well as an imprint, represents the detachment of a body of knowledge from the sole embrace of its author into eventually the hands of its readers. Compared with the age-old alternative of oral transmission from a teacher to his disciples, this sharing of learning tends, eventually if not initially, to foster a degree of impersonality in the transmission and preservation of knowledge. The printing of books further strengthens this tendency, since it multiplies the number of identical copies available for widespread distribution. Over time, the impersonality of this knowledge, that is, its divorce from its creator, becomes predominant, if only because imprints, virtually by definition, end up wandering into the hands of collectors and other readers unknown to the author or to one another. Willing to use the ideas and information of an imprint for their own purposes, these people may well make the book their own, in ways the original author would never have imagined.

In recent years, two models of book circulation have made use of such reflections to clarify key links in the spread of humanistic learning in the early modern West. One model, proposed by Robert Darnton, concentrates on the different human actors engaged in producing and distributing knowledge. Another, conceived by Thomas R. Adams and Nicolas Barker, prefers to deal with books themselves to analyze the circulation of these objects among institutional and individual collections for the use of readers. While these models recognize that the greater circulation of books tends to make knowledge more impersonal, abstract, and self-reflexive, they have also agreed that the market, through the activities of private publishers and bookshops, and institutions like libraries and universities, increasingly provided readers with access to desired knowledge. Even censorship could be conquered by an appropriate mixture of cash, guile, and pluck.[1]

Unfortunately, for an account of the circulation of Chinese books, these models are seriously flawed. They assume the smooth passage of books through a world free of serious bottlenecks other than a censorious state and costly prices, whereas in the world of learning from the Song into the Qing dynasty, scholars and students persistently complained about their lack of access to learned books in the collections of others. Books, once they were bought in any of the commercial outlets described in the previous chapter, were frequently put away, and shown to few if any non-family members until they re-emerged for resale or perhaps inheritance.

Yes, Chinese readers could usually acquire texts of the Confucian classics tested in the civil service examinations, some medical texts that the government and private parties in the eleventh century printed and distributed, and various texts (usually religious) that were made available, sometimes free of charge, by Buddhist and some other religious establishments.[2] Yes, if ranked as official teachers, students, officeholders, and degree holders, they had access to at least the libraries of some government schools.[3] And, yes, some readers would have known of books from booksellers' catalogues compiled for private readers by no later than the mid-eleventh century.[4]

But for other writings of literati culture — such as unofficial commentaries, histories, poetry and prose collections, and countless other literati titles — the liberating impact of print technology and market distribution was far more gradual than sinologists have usually believed.[5] Up until the sixteenth century, the problem can perhaps be primarily attributed to a shortage in the supply of imprints and handcopies as well as in the relatively small number of bookshops and stalls with the literati writings we have been considering. Yet, even after the ascendance and spread of the imprint had greatly increased the number of books and bookstores in the lower Yangzi delta, the problem of access there persisted. In fact, as we re-examine the pre-1600 record, the causes can be seen to be not simply the economic factors of cost and production levels. They also included the continued reluctance of collectors of learned books to allow their books to be read by others. The owners of these books tended to treat them as their own objects, almost as if they were their own creations, and as useful for controlling the transmission of the knowledge of these books along highly personal lines.

In other words, the study of book use can tell us much of the relative limitations of the state and the market in late imperial times in meeting the needs of readers and collectors desperate for institutions that might satisfy their demand better than the market. If, as we shall see in the next chapter, the Chinese state eventually had to play a crucial role in creating communities of knowledge far more encompassing than could be supported by any market-based distribution of learning, it does not mean that the state fulfilled this task successfully or that the private collectors lost their dominant position as brokers in the world of learning for most of the seven to eight centuries under study here.

Thus, in this chapter, I wish to describe this issue of literati and scholars' access to book collections, primarily in the Yangzi delta, from the eleventh to the seventeenth centuries. After a brief comparative survey of the problem in both pre-modern Western Europe and the Middle East, the focus falls on government libraries in China, especially their problems of management, rather than strictly access, at both the central and local levels. The discussion then concentrates on the larger private collections, describing their restrictive policies for reading and borrowing their books, especially, but not exclusively, their rare and old books. My aim is less to judge these practices than to explain and assess their extensive impact on the world of learning during these centuries, particularly for the formation and maintenance of any broad "community of learning" outside of state institutions. While my interest in this topic is shaped in part by my readings about the establishment of, in Erasmian terms, "a republic of letters" in early modern Europe,[6] the choice of the subject actually grows out of a wide reading of Chinese sources that repeatedly reveal a deep concern about access among Chinese readers and collectors alike. Although the object of our concern here — the world of learning as opposed to the more general world of literati books — is more narrow than that presented in the previous two chapters, it constitutes a problem that lay at the heart of not just the transmission of Confucian learning but also at any effort to realize the ideas and values of this learning outside of élite circles. It thus deserves to lie at the heart of any discussion of the world of learning during these seven centuries of great neo-Confucian influence.

A Community of Learning?

The introduction of the concept of "a community of letters" into the study of Chinese learning practices may well seem artificial and misdirected. Yet, its central notion — of a large group of educated persons collectively engaged in the study and development of a body of shared humanist learning outside the parameters of authorized knowledge of the state or a religious organization — is far from irrelevant to Chinese cultural and social history. Shorn of its implicit clerical-vs.-secular opposition and any Western political commitment, the concept of "a republic of letters" rephrased as "a community of learning" helps to establish a framework for analyzing the problems faced by scholars who, from no later than the third century, sought to assume the leading role in the transmission of Chinese written culture.[7] At times, this assertion by scholars inevitably placed them in competition, if not conflict, with those imperial courts intent on playing the same central role as creator and patron of learning and the arts. Though usually unable to match the courts in funds and other resources, these scholars, and especially book collectors, devised some solutions to their problems, solutions that by no later than the seventeenth and eighteenth centuries included the notion of a shared collection of Confucian learning, a Confucian canon (*Ruzang*).

The concept originated with none other than the well-known late Ming scholar-official Cao Xuequan, whom we met at the end of the last chapter as a patron of learning in Fuzhou prefecture in Fujian Province. As a book collector himself, Cao was sharply critical of the exclusive practices of other book collectors. By shutting off their holdings from others, they were, in his view, reducing the chances of the survival of these texts, since their rare copies remained vulnerable to threats from fire, flood, theft, and inheritance practices. To avoid these disasters, Cao called for the compilation and dissemination of a comprehensive body of Confucian learning that would be far more public (*gong*), in the manner of the Buddhist and Daoist canons. He wanted the family schools that had held private collections to cease being just for their members. Instead, these places of instruction were to attract from afar teachers and students who would study and propagate the learning of this comprehensive Confucian collection of books. For over ten years, Cao struggled to complete this compendium, but in vain. The fall of the Ming led to his death and the demise of his dream.[8] Some twelve decades later, the noted Shandong collector Zhou Yongnian (1730–91) revived Cao's ideal by announcing the opening of his own very large collection to other scholars and the need to establish a central library for them. Although he, too, would fail to attract sufficient support to make his collection truly complete and comprehensive, his ideal as well as Cao's would inspire Ruan Yuan's vast compilation of classical learning, the *August Qing Dynasty Exegesis of the Confucian Classics* (*Huang Qing jingjie*), published in 1829.[9]

The disparities between Cao's ideal and Zhou's proposal in many ways encapsulate key differences between the worlds of learning of the late Ming and the mid-Qing. Cao assumed a single center of storage and learning over which he, the gentry patron, would serve as a virtually imperial protector of learning in a world where knowledge did not quickly expand. Zhou, instead, sought to use state institutions to benefit local scholars throughout the empire at a time when knowledge about these texts was growing. Influenced by the success of the Qianlong emperor's Four Treasuries project to collect all Chinese books for his own collection, he wanted the magistrate and big lineages of each county to set up a charitable school endowed with its own fields and a library filled with book donations from local collectors. Each of these schools was to list its books and allow them to be copied by other schools, as well as to set up its own moveable type (*huoban*) to publish its rare books.[10] Despite their differences, then, both proposals have the great strength of being interested in establishing a non-court institution that would promote the preservation and dissemination of a certain kind of shared learning among those interested and literate. This ideal of "a community of learning" can help us understand the problems that learned Chinese had in creating a widely inclusive community of scholars up until the late eighteenth century. What then first appears as a mere problem of scholarly access will be seen as emblematic of the society's larger difficulties in institutionalizing the imprint's potential to depersonalize the ownership of knowledge for the benefit of a much wider readership and audience. Imprints may have escaped the personal ties and claims of their authors, but they definitely had trouble escaping the private claims of the persons who owned them.

Put in such terms, the issue of access to these private collections can easily be seen in stark black-and-white categories such as have been suggested by some recent Chinese discussions of this issue: was a particular collection open or closed?[11] Such a blunt approach tends to treat the problem as a morality tale of institutional weakness vs. private greed, or private hardship vs. government plunder, and, as such, represents a continuation of the basic assumptions and values that have for so long bedeviled efforts to resolve the problem that Chinese scholars and students have had in gaining access to books. While mindful of the difficulties sometimes caused by government censorship, persecution, and confiscation,[12] we still need to place the problem of access within a broader context concerned with a great number of variables: who is making what request to whom, for whom to do what? Is access requested merely to see? To read? To read and borrow? Or, to read and copy? For how many books? What is the edition of the requested book(s), its rarity, contents, condition, calligraphic style, quality of paper, and market value? And, how many people are making the request? This broader yet more precise approach has the great advantage of seeing the problem as institutional more than as moral and of focusing our attention on how private book collectors treated one another at a time when, in quality and quantity, their collective holdings often surpassed those in most, if not all, government libraries. We thus will be able to discern the practices of book collectors and scholars that obstructed and aided the exchange of learning that one might expect of any "community of learning."

Such a nuanced understanding can be usefully fostered by a brief consideration of the social history of the book in two other cultures, the Arabic and the Western European. In the Middle East, well before the first use of moveable-type print there by Jews for a Hebrew text in Constantinople in 1493, the problem of access to books was, at least in some places and periods until the nineteenth century, nowhere near as acute as in much of late imperial China. Despite the continued resort to the traditional practice of handcopying Arabic-language books until the early nineteenth century,[13] some very large repositories of Arabic books and other learning were established between the ninth and early twelfth centuries. In Cairo and Baghdad (as well as Córdoba in Islamic Spain), libraries said to hold between 200,000 and 500,000 volumes were managed by political or religious leaders, for readers of all social strata. After these libraries were closed down by the twelfth century, due to, among other factors, religious pressures, the major Arabic book collections were held in college libraries dedicated solely to the study of Islamic texts and open also to Islamic readers, or the faithful, of a very wide social spectrum. Totally private book collections seem to have been much less important. Holding far fewer books, they seldom attracted many students and readers, even though they seem not to have espoused the same exclusivity practiced by many Chinese private book collectors. In sum, the limited research so far conducted on the social history of the Arabic book suggests that some civil and religious authorities of the early Islamic world made their libraries accessible to urban Arab readers but eventually restricted that access to the Islamic faithful and to just Islamic, rather than also Hellenistic, learning.[14]

In Western Europe "public libraries," such as were founded in the Mediterranean world by Roman emperors and other men for all literate citizens,[15] did not exist in medieval times. A literate male's access to institutional book collections then was usually restricted by his religious, institutional, civic, and personal ties. Some Jewish communities in Italy, for instance, had their synagogues serve as their public libraries; members donated or deposited religious and secular books in these religious institutions for the use of other members wishing to fulfill the Jewish male's traditional duty of systematic study. In the words of a rabbi active at the turn of the eleventh century, "Books are not made to be stored away, but rather to be lent."[16] Yet, due to their religious and linguistic differences, the location of the books inside Jewish religious institutions, and a justifiable fear of the books' confiscation by Christian authorities, all parties seem to have assumed that non-Jews, or Christians, were not to use such libraries. The medieval Christian laity was also generally denied, it seems, easy access to Christian monastic or cathedral libraries. Even though large monasteries were "in the habit of lending books to persons who were not members of it and even to laymen,"[17] such a privilege for laymen would not have been conferred lightly or frequently. Books remained few and very costly; lay readers, if literate, were interested mainly in books of a more secular concern than those usually found in monastic and church collections; and, monasteries, if they loaned books, tended to loan them to other monasteries for copying. Indeed, despite a decree by the Council of Paris in 1212 to the contrary, many monasteries threatened excommunication for anyone who lent out their books.[18] From the thirteenth century, when reading was no longer a central practice of just the monasteries, some cathedral and especially university libraries thrived.[19] They opened their holdings more to their students and other persons attached to them.[20] But, these collections were still far from constituting anything like a public library, either for religious or secular texts.

From the fifteenth century libraries of generally secular Western institutions began to form a more varied and complex relation to their readers. In 1444, shortly before Gutenberg's invention of the printing press, what has been called the first Western public library since Roman times, that is, a library open to all "studious citizens," was established in Florence.[21] Some private collectors, including princes, gradually started to set up libraries for scholarly or city-based readers, some of whom might be allowed to borrow books freed of their chains.[22] Yet, paradoxically, as the number of readers, books, and especially rare books increased and as religious differences grew more contentious, scholarly libraries like the Vatican became less obliging to readers' requests.[23] In his celebrated 1627 work on libraries Gabriel Naudé reported that only three important European libraries — the Ambrosiana in Milan (from 1602), the Augustinian monks' Angelica Library in Rome (from 1620), and the Bodleian Library in Oxford (from 1612) — allowed scholars to have unimpeded entrance to their holdings. By contrast, the top five libraries in Naudé's survey of European libraries gave at best limited access to their holdings.[24] "From the sixteenth century nearly every university that was founded had a public library," but most university libraries were "only accessible to graduate students of the higher faculties and to teachers for a few hours per week," and their books seldom could be borrowed (the irregular exceptions were books used in lectures and by professors).[25] According to Reinhard Wittmann, most universities, as well as monasteries, towns, and courts, in Germany had a library policy that actively discouraged the reading of their books.[26] In Britain the Bodleian Library, despite its relative openness to non-Oxford scholars, banned all its readers, including Oxford professors and kings, from gaining access to its stacks and borrowing its books.[27] In the eighteenth century the Bodleian even barred all non-members of the university from examining a manuscript in its reading room unless they were accompanied by a holder of the university's Master of Arts or Bachelor of Civil Law degree. Visitors were permitted to consult the manuscript so long as this type of Oxford graduate sat or stood beside them.[28]

The practice of one Cambridge college, St John's College, reveals the extent of the obstacles that confronted both outsiders and insiders seeking to use libraries in European educational establishments between the sixteenth and the eighteenth centuries. Its 1530 and 1545 statutes allowed its fellows and scholarship students access to the library only by permission of the Master and President and allowed the fellows to take books out of its library only if they left "many, or better, books on the same subject in the library," had acquired written permission from the Master, President, or Dean, and had registered the loans before 9 October of that year. In 1617, the laws were tightened to bar all but fellows from entering the library and to bar the fellows from borrowing books without prior consent of the Master and College Council. In 1639 it was decided that "only one book was to be borrowed at a time, for 48 hours," and in 1650 it was ordered that no one without a Cambridge Master of Arts degree could study in the library and no fellow-commoner or holder of a Cambridge Master of Arts degree could borrow books. After 1654 no fellow or scholarship student was allowed to take any books out of the library without permission of the Master and the College Council. Come 1662, the protective chain around the books tightened, as henceforth fellows and scholarship students could borrow books only with permission of the Master and College Council.

These restrictions were composed in highly contentious times, when religious controversies erupted into civil wars, when books were burnt for their teachings, and when eventually very scarce surviving copies replaced only some of the lost volumes. Nonetheless, the upshot of all this contention and these rules was that ordinary students could neither gain direct access to the library nor borrow any of its books and that teachers could gain access and borrow books only with their seniors' permission. Doubtless, students could, and did, rely on the approved teachers to borrow books for them, with these teachers obliged to see that the books were returned on time. But it was only in the mid-nineteenth century, some four hundred years after the invention of printing had supposedly transformed European methods of study, that all students did not need permission to enter the library and borrow books on their own (fellows appear to have received these privileges towards the close of the eighteenth century). Needless to say, by this time the far more numerous and valuable old books were stored on a floor apart from the modern books that students commonly used. Although they were made available for research, they definitely were not for borrowing by anyone.[29] They were simply too old and too rare.

At the same time, away from the universities, some institutional libraries, particularly in national capitals like Paris, proved more accommodating to both known and unknown readers. Twice a week, for a weekly total of no more than ten hours, readers were welcome at the Bibliothèque Mazarine from 1644. Similar arrangements were made at the Bibliothèque de l'abbaye de Saint-Victor from 1652, the Bibliothèque des avocats from 1708, the Bibliothèque de la Doctrine chrètienne from 1718, and some other libraries of professions and religious orders from the mid-eighteenth century.[30] The Bibliothèque du Roi, on the way to becoming the national library of France, the Bibliothèque Nationale, followed a similar policy for scholars and even for the general public from 1692 to 1706 and then from 1720 to the present.[31] In German lands the Prussian State Library opened its holdings to the public in 1661, as did the Hofbibliothek in Vienna in 1726.[32] At a lower level, municipal and even parish libraries were formed by bequests from local dignitaries.[33]

In Britain the most publicly available collection was that of the British Museum, established according to its principal founder, Sir Hans Sloane, for "the improvement, knowledge and information of all persons." Yet, from 1759 to 1806 admission to its Reading Room required prior approval of initially the Trustees and later the Principal Librarian. During this half century its readers totaled a mere 160 or so.[34] As late as 1803 a visiting German could express amazement about the paucity of public facilities for scholarly books in Britain: "It will scarcely seem credible that there does not exist in the United Kingdom a single public library stored with the most important works in the various departments of literature."[35]

By contrast, private book collectors in Western Europe often proved remarkably willing to share their books and knowledge, clear evidence of the persisting impact of the Erasmian ideal of "a republic of letters."[36] They were exhorted and at times expected to share their learning and texts with others, as most memorably suggested in Jean Grolier's practice of embossing on the binding of his books, after his own name, the words "et amicorum" [i.e., and friends'].[37] In Tudor times as well as in the following two centuries, private English scholarly libraries were few, and serious scholars commonly made the rounds of some aristocratic collections in country houses which would show them, either freely or to those who agreed to sign a loan note.[38] From the seventeenth century, just as scientists often shared their discoveries through the public presentation of their verifiable research, so did humanists in the Erasmian mold engage in a regular exchange of imprints, manuscripts, and correspondence delivered throughout Western Europe, even during religious wars. At a time when the exclusive practices of a great many European universities and their libraries often made them less and less central to major European intellectual and cultural innovations,[39] scholars developed very extensive personal networks outside their universities and their countries. In the words of one recent study, "Lending books to friends seems to have been an integral part of the culture of the Republic of Letters since the beginning of the seventeenth century. A polite enquiry as to whether a friend had a certain book in his library was expected to be met with the equally polite offer to send it post-haste. The bigger and better the library the greater the obligation." The same service might even await strangers introduced by a close friend of the owner.[40] According to two expert French studies, by the late seventeenth century, private book collectors in Paris were increasingly opening their collections to visiting scholars with suitable introductions.[41] Yet, the most magnanimous example of scholarly exchange at this time was perhaps that provided by Leibnitz (1646–1716). Not only did he travel widely to meet other scholars throughout Western Europe, but also he wrote 15,000 letters in scholarly correspondence with over a thousand correspondents inside and outside of Europe (he even exchanged letters, though less regularly, with Jesuits in Beijing). In freely dispensing ideas and information usually not found in his publications, he sought to establish reciprocal and widespread networks of disinterested scholarly exchange.[42]

In all these cases "the public" remained no more than a small number of lettered males in the population of these communities. Arguably, for some of these libraries the number of their visitors and the variety of these visitors' nationality narrowed over time, due to the decline of Latin as a *lingua franca*, the concomitant rise of nation states and their separate national libraries and universities, and the declining appeal of Erasmian humanism and its tradition of a transnational "republic of letters." But, even if we forget the increasing international exchange among Europe's natural scientists engaged in the study of universal problems, we cannot fail to notice the emergence in Europe of a variety of libraries which opened their holdings to a larger number and wider range of men and even women in their political or social community. Royal collections evolved into national libraries, bishops' and aristocrats' collections were bequeathed to become municipal libraries, and even vicars' collections were turned into parish libraries, all of them somewhat accessible to both locals as well as outsiders.[43] Lending libraries and reading clubs also grew up in towns and cities, providing books to people regardless of their differences in religion and national origin. Social class, however, remained a hurdle for winning admission into some of these reading societies,[44] and copyright laws, at least in England, forced the ordinary reader to limit his or her reading habit to books out-of-copyright, if only because they were noticeably cheaper than either new publications or old titles still under copyright.[45]

This Western European experience from the sixteenth and seventeenth centuries onward was far more secular than that of the Middle East, and proves useful for examining what in part seems to be a mirror opposite world of book collectors' practices in China's world of learning between 1000 and 1700. In other words, the Western European pattern of higher educational institutions' exclusivity, the gradual appearance of more "public" libraries, and individuals' exchange of scholarly materials contrasts sharply with a Chinese pattern for forming book collections that seems to have encouraged far less institutional variety. In China the government in general provided government libraries for just its officials and would-be officials (i.e., its students), while private collectors commonly restricted other readers from having access to and sharing their book collections. And, when change came to these practices in the eighteenth century, it would benefit principally scholars and collectors rather than all the literate members of a community or profession. The following pages will describe these Chinese practices and analyze their problems, as well as assess the broader implications of the frequent inaccessibility of private book collections.

Government Book Collections

A Chinese reader's access to government book collections varied according to his status and the administrative regulations and practices of the institution whose books he wanted to see. As a rule, the most restrictive were the libraries assembled for and about the emperor and his family. In the Song dynasty, these private imperial book collections were stored in the imperial archives of each emperor's reign or in repositories of books, paintings, and writings acquired separately or cumulatively by Song emperors (the largest collection of the latter type, the Taiqing Pavilion, was expected to hold a copy of all books in the court library open to officials). In the Yuan and Ming dynasties, similar imperial libraries were set up at the court. Indeed, many of the books and woodblocks in the early Ming Imperial Library came from the Song, Jin, and Yuan imperial collections.[46]

In general, these private imperial collections were accessible to only the emperor and a few favorites specially granted access by him.[47] Even though their texts would sometimes escape the confines of the palace (as when many Yuan plays slipped out into private Ming collections and then into commercial publications),[48] far more representative of the government policy towards imperial repositories and their holdings was the treatment accorded the great encyclopedia, the *Yongle dadian*. Compiled by 1406, this vast compendium was intended to contain, in the words of the high minister Qiu Jun, "all the books of the empire." The Yongle emperor (r. 1402–25) ordered that two copies be made for storage at the Directorates of Education (*Guozi dian*) in Beijing and Nanjing. But his order was never implemented, ostensibly for reasons of expense. Shipped to the newly constructed palace buildings in Beijing in 1421, it was initially stored near the Zuoshun Gate, and from 1441, in the Hall of Literary Profundity (*Wenyuan ge*). Nearly a century later, it was placed in the newly constructed (1534) Imperial Archives (*Huangshi cheng*) along with the Veritable Records (*Shilu*) and Precious Instructions (*Baoxun)* of the reign of each Ming emperor. This sole copy was inaccessible to officials, a rule that was not dropped even after a serious palace fire in 1557 prompted the Jiajing emperor to order that two copies of it be made. The aim of the copying appears to have been simply to improve the likelihood of the encyclopedia's survival of any future fire; hence, the decision to locate each copy in a different place, the original returned to Nanjing, the main copy stored in Beijing's Hall of Literary Profundity, and a second copy stored in Beijing's Imperial Archives.[49] Thereafter, official appeals to gain access to any one of them, even when approved by the emperor in 1594, proved ineffective right to the end of the Ming dynasty, when the first copy in Beijing was lost to fire and the second suffered much damage during the dynastic transition.[50]

Far more accessible to scholar-officials between the tenth and seventeenth centuries were various government book collections set up in different central government institutions.[51] As we know far more about Song and Ming practice, my comments focus on these two Chinese dynasties. In the Song, for instance, the libraries of the Three Institutes (*Sanguan*), particularly that of the Historiography Institute (*Shiguan*), were accessible to the emperor, his retinue of top officials and their own followers, any high official or related personnel in a central government institution, and specially selected child prodigies. In addition, the ranks of favored readers at these most important official collections included in the early Northern Song the holders of both nominal and real low-ranking posts in the Palace Library (*Mishu sheng*) and in the Southern Song many men who did not hold even nominal posts in the government. In fact, in the Song, these libraries tended to become the rearing grounds of promising young scholars, who were allowed to spend a few years reading in these libraries before receiving an official posting.[52]

Other government institutions in the capital also had libraries for their own staff. To take the most obvious example, the Directorate of Education and the schools it administered in the capital provided books for their teachers and students and sometimes used them to make reprints for prefectural schools throughout the empire (these schools were expected to buy these imprints at production cost, out of cash grants from the government).[53] These local government schools, if they had a collection of books, sometimes banned any borrowing, as at the prefectural school in present Jiaxing prefecture in 1266, one even claimed, "Taking a book away is allowing it to be stolen."[54] More commonly, these schools permitted their students to borrow books, yet with clear reminders of the need to return them promptly. The following message was inserted in a copy of the *Zizhi tongjian* held by one prefectural school:

> It definitely is one of the hundred proper acts for a scholar-official, when borrowing a government-printed book, to show it constant love and protection. Have the authorities clearly record the loan in a register. Once every month the school is to record the loans in its register. The books are not to be loaned out for a long time. If in any case you damage or lose it, the school is to press you to pay for a replacement as far as is reasonable. The names of those who receive a book and hide it are to be publicized, and a fine is to be considered.[55]

Some local schools even printed books for sale to students and others.[56] These generally favorable terms of access let collectors long resident at the court (e.g., Su Song and You Mao) transcribe, or have transcribed, a wide range of titles for their private collections.[57] Such reading conditions, however, were easier to prescribe than to realize and especially to maintain. The problem was not that the Song government generally favored exclusivity (though by 1061, it had classified some of its holdings, such as military and astronomy texts, as secret and usually kept them away even from officials assigned to edit the texts of the collections).[58] The vast majority of books in the collections were free of such controls, and yet books in the Three Institutes often became lost. At times, the culprit was fire, as when, in 1015, the entire collection went up in flames and decades passed before the holdings were restored. At times, it was poor management: as of 1061, the collection still had no complete editions of texts as basic as the seven dynastic histories of the Southern Dynasties.[59] Even when the Historiography Institute's copies were first collated with copies in private hands and then woodblocks carved for a new edition, a court official as eminent as Sima Guang might complain that he was never able to have access to these books for careful reading, until he concentrated his work solely on his compilation of the *Zizhi tongjian* in 1073.[60] And, at times the problem was military misfortune. Virtually all the books in central government institutions were lost to the invading Jurchen upon their conquest of the Northern Song capital of Kaifeng. Forced to flee south to Hangzhou, the Song court had to expend enormous efforts to rebuild book collections of roughly equivalent size.[61]

Yet, even if fire, poor management, and political instability might unexpectedly reverse generations of efforts to preserve a government collection, a far more regular and persistent threat to the integrity and survival of the libraries of the Three Institutes was the rifling of their holdings by generations of emperors, imperial relations, special agents, high court officials, and other official personnel with authorized access.[62] In 999, the government issued its first ban against this abuse; at least seven others followed (in 1059, 1089, 1114, 1131, 1157, 1204, and 1228).[63] Sometimes, it exempted certain parties from the ban, such as the imperial palace itself in 1131[64] and officials engaged in collation work within the palace precincts in 1157 and 1204.[65] But, the bans generally applied to all of officialdom, and their frequent reissue suggests that they were often violated. In 1204, for instance, it was reported, "After scholar-officials had long become used to this ban, they came to view it as a dead letter, and those who sought to borrow books were very multitudinous. They borrowed them for a long time and did not return them."[66]

Consequently, when less than a third of their holdings were reported as surviving in 1060, many books in the holdings of the Three Institutes had ended up in the collections of scholar-official families. The two court libraries least scathed by these "borrowings," the Shaowen and the Academy of Assembled Worthies, escaped not because of extra vigilance but because "they have an imperial image in their building and one cannot enter them unless one is wearing court clothing."[67] In the first half of the Southern Song, the incidence of pilfering appears not to have been so severe; just thirty percent of all the titles listed in catalogue of these libraries, the *Chongwen congmu*, had disappeared by 1204.[68] Yet, slightly later, in 1228, book theft had become so common that some scholar officials were said to be flogging off for a profit the books they had removed from court libraries and then impressed with their private seals.[69]

During the Ming, the situation in the libraries for officials and students in central government institutions was, if anything, worse. Of at least six such institutional collections, the Halls of Literary Profundity in Nanjing and Beijing were the largest and most important for officials. Despite a ban on borrowing, their books were removed and frequently not returned by palace eunuchs, officials, and others.[70] After a fire in the Nanjing palace destroyed all the books in the Hall of Literary Profundity in 1449,[71] its counterpart in Beijing became the principal remaining Imperial Library for officials. Its fate, alas, was almost as dismal as if it, too, had been set aflame. In 1492, it was said that all its remaining books had been chewed up by worms and rats, and detailed suggestions were made to prevent further deterioration.[72] Slightly later, the culprits were identified as the archivists and officials. The first group had simply stolen them, and the second had failed to return those they had borrowed, usually without permission.[73]

However exaggerated these reports, several officials in the early and mid-sixteenth century were shocked enough by the continued deterioration of this library to put their sharply critical views in writing and in print:

> The books in the library of the Hall of Literary Profundity are looked after by eunuchs and illiterate idiots whose position is minor and whose rank is low. When officials borrowed books of the library for reading, they often did not return the original slipcase for books. Come the Jiajing reign era and afterwards, those in charge often did not follow the rules and no longer paid attention to inspecting and checking the books. Of the holdings in the Hall of Literary Profundity, over half then were lacking and lost.[74]

In 1609, when the Hall of Literary Profundity (here referred to as the Imperial Household library) retained reportedly fewer than ten percent of the titles listed in a library catalogue compiled for it in the Zhengtong reign era (1436-49),[75] a private collector relied on an acquaintance to remove from the Hall a book he would copy on his own for nearly twenty days.[76] This same collector would later, as an official, make his own handcopy of more than twenty books in this library.[77]

In the early seventeenth century, Wang Kentang, the holder of a 1589 metropolitan degree, made a particularly depressing assessment:

> The book collection of the Hall of Literary Profundity consisted entirely of books handed down from the imperial library of the Song and Yuan dynasties. Even if they were not refined [printings], they were all imprints from Song woodblocks. Accordingly, the books often helped the students. Since students did not know how to cherish and treat them as important and since the library's eunuch staff was negligent and did not inspect them, the books were often taken away by others. I once saw very many titles in the library of Mr Ma of Liyang, each volume of which had the seal imprint of the Hall of Literary Profundity.

In 1589 when I entered the library building, the library head Wang Jingshi told Jiao Hong and me, "You both are reputed to read books in the Imperial Library, so why don't you read [books here]? I will order the books to come by their title. When you want to look at them, it will be possible to have them arranged by title for you to ask for." A short while later, the books did come by using the book catalogue, but there were only four of them. All the others had become the books of Mr Ma that I had seen and that had already left the register. When I consulted the catalogue and requested [to see its books], less than a fifth or a tenth survived, many of them in tatters or incomplete. When I asked why, [Mr Wang] then said, "It is because in 1586 some persons received them, took them out, and have still not returned them."

Later on, the head of the library, Peng Yang, told me that they had been returned. Not having looked into and examined [what he had said], I asked a library clerk, who said, "They are now in the storehold." I was greatly delighted and swiftly gave an order for them to be taken out of the storehold. However, they had all been replaced by contemporary imprints and were not the old editions of the Imperial Library. I promptly ordered that they be returned and exchanged for [the original editions], but what now survives [of these original editions] is only one out of a thousand or ten thousand. And so, by the day and month the books have been disappearing. Within ten years it will inevitably reach the point that the library will have no sheets of paper but only characters.[78]

Other observant sixteenth- and seventeenth-century literati concluded that the library's fortune had fallen to the extent that the reduced number and quality of its holdings made it far inferior to any major collection then in private hands.[79] The Fujian collector Xie Zhaozhe was forced to wonder if, in a century, the Hall of Literary Profundity's Library would still survive.[80] And, by the very late Ming, the collection had lost two-thirds of even its woodblocks, thanks to their sale, their use for fires in cold weather, and their damage from rain, rats, and insects.[81] Such conditions hardly made for an environment conducive to serious scholarship or thought.

In the provinces, the best conditions were found at the libraries of some Ming princes, especially those in Zhou and Jin.[82] For instance, the seventeenth son of the first Ming emperor was a well-known bibliophile with a collection reportedly rivaling that of the Hall of Literary Profundity. Fond of copying others' rare books, he is said to have printed and distributed many literary and religious works on his own.[83] Elsewhere, the regulations on access to these princely collections varied. According to an eighteenth-century writer, "every day hundreds of people came to transcribe books" at the imperial prince's residence in Chengdu in Sichuan,[84] allowing it to play a critical role in the culture of the province's educated élite (like its counterparts in other regions, it was destroyed during the Manchu invasion of the 1640s and 1650s).[85] But, at least in the early seventeenth century, the imperial princes' book collections in the provincial seats of Kaifeng and Nanchang were not open to outside readers; in Kaifeng, they were also reported to be rotting away, and in Nanchang to be incomplete.[86]

The other major provincial government libraries were at government schools, but these often proved even less useful than the Hall of Literary Profundity. Before the Ming, government school libraries were uncommon and were almost always attached to schools in provincial or prefectural seats.[87] Those in the lower Yangzi delta were thought to have the most books, and when, in the first half of the fourteenth century, officials there had lists of the titles of these collections carved into stone, Yuan Dynasty officials fond of learning would often borrow the books in these libraries for their reading, partly because the collections in Beijing were so inferior.[88] The early Ming government irregularly distributed books in small numbers to prefectural and county schools.[89] Yet, only from the sixteenth century did such prefectural and county schools commonly have a library building. Even then, a decent prefectural school library would seldom have had over 2,000 *juan,* and a county school library far fewer (at a time when even minor Yangzi delta collectors would have had over 10,000 *juan*). Consisting originally of imprints issued by the state (usually, but not always, free of charge), these collections sometimes grew, thanks to later purchases and donations, and could usually be consulted by students.[90] But, over the long run, their books, even when stored in locked wooden cabinets, suffered neglect along lines already seen in the Hall of Literary Profundity in Beijing.[91] If the problem was not indifferent supervision by schoolteachers, it was the students' flagrant disregard of school rules that banned the removal of books from the library and of the school's subsequent demand for their return and threats of shame and punishment.[92]

In sum, at different times during the Song and Ming dynasties, the libraries of the Three Institutes and the Hall of Literary Profundity held an impressive quantity and quality of books, which court officials, members of the imperial family, and selected others seem to have been able to read and copy. Though officially barred from borrowing books from these libraries, these men seem to have done so with impunity. Libraries lower down the bureaucratic order also suffered severely from the disappearance and theft of books. Thus, overall, the greatest problem for their readers, especially in the Ming, was their caretakers' and other readers' rank disregard for the rules of these libraries on borrowing, and lack of concern for the survival of these books. In Ming times, these abuses were attributed to the low rank of the officials and eunuchs appointed to manage the library, and thus their inability to thwart the borrowing practices of higher-ranked officials. But, whatever the reasons, the libraries of the Chinese government were in no way essential centers of learning for much of the Song and for at least the last two centuries of Ming rule. That role and even the minor one of simply guaranteeing scholars and officials access to their culture's written heritage were assumed by private collections whose owners would assure that they generally remained private. For a part of the Song and most of the Ming, these owners had no serious institutional competitors as patrons of scholarship and holders of learning, an imbalance that would seriously impair the development of textual scholarship and, arguably, learning in general.

Private Book Collections

From the eleventh century to the last quarter of the eighteenth, imprints and manuscripts increasingly ended up in the hands of private parties. Relatively important private collections — numbering no fewer than 700 in the Song, 170-odd in the far shorter Yuan, 897 in the Ming, and most of the 2,082 in the Qing[93] — collectively constituted the most significant holdings and institutions of book learning throughout most of these eight centuries.[94] But, they proved far less welcoming to readers than did most government collections, even though it had been just such a practice of "manuscript culture" that had prompted the initial mid-tenth century printing of the Confucian classics:

> When Wu Qiujian was poor and menial, he once borrowed the *Wenxuan*
> anthology from an acquaintance. But this man was embarrassed [and

reluctant to lend it]. So Wu got angry [and thought], "If at another time I am titled, I ought to have it carved with woodblocks and transmitted on to other scholars." Afterwards, when he served the King of Shu as minister, he carried out these words and published [the *Wenxuan* and the Confucian Classics]. The creation of book printing was thereby made evident.[95]

But, for at least the next eight centuries, book collectors routinely remained deaf to the entreaties of many other readers wishing to read their books, especially the rare ones. The twelfth-century bibliophile Zheng Qiao observed, "Book-collecting families as a rule have two book catalogues. The one they show to others registers not a single unusual book. Unless the other party is completely sincere and completely courteous, are they going to be willing to show him anything rare?"[96] And, in the mid-seventeenth century, Huang Zongxi (1610–95) would complain, "Book-collecting families, unless they have reached the point of being troubled by poverty, all regard the showing of their books to others as a serious matter."[97]

Other book owners, sometimes lacking confidence in their descendants' dedication to learning, undertook a wide variety of measures to prevent undesired readers from gaining access. The simplest strategy was to reveal the existence of one's collection to no one but immediate family members; that was the practice of Qiu Ji (1523–1603) and Qian Yisu (1587–1646),[98] though Qiu Ji still took no chances. He had a twenty-seven-character seal legend carved, specifying the full address of his residence, just in case a volume ever escaped the citadel of his home.[99] Another practice was to hang in the library or at its entrance a plaque carved with a suitable warning to visitors and descendants, such as was favored by the famous fifteenth-century Suzhou collector Ye Sheng: "You must be diligent in your reading, tight in your locking, careful in your collecting, and must erect your building high."[100] Others, such as the Hangzhou collector Zhang Ao (b. 1394) and the noted Zhejiang collector Yu Canheng in the early sixteenth century, preferred the more desperate tactic of placing their locked-up libraries on islands. The former had guests use a boat to cross the pond to and from his library (nocturnal visits were banned); the latter was so opposed to the arrival of any guests that, every night, he removed the wooden plank that linked his library to land during the daytime. And, if anyone turned up on the island invited or uninvited, the visitor found a plaque hanging at the entrance to his studio: "The library does not invite guests, and books are not to be loaned to others."[101] The Song collector Chao Gongwu (1105–80) went one step further by turning away the rightful owner of his books. Having inherited in 1151 a valuable collection of 24,500 *juan* from his old friend Jing Du, Chao failed to obey Jing's injunction to return the books to his son when that son showed an interest in learning.[102]

The success that some collectors had in controlling access to their collection was demonstrated by the history of arguably the most famous private library of the Ming and Qing, the Tianyi ge (see Figure 6). Established in c.1560 by the rich Ningbo official Fan Qin,[103] it soon became celebrated for its impregnability against fire — thanks to its partially brick construction and its location within a special moat — and against book theft — thanks to its very restrictive rules on access. Thus, the library's founder rebuffed his own nephew's request to look at some of his books (this nephew, Fan Dache, went on to collect many rare books on his own, some of which reportedly ended up in the Tianyi ge),[104] as he permitted only his own direct male descendants to gain access to his books, and solely during the daytime. Even then, they had to satisfy strict conditions: each of the six branches of his offspring had to bring along the specially conferred key to open the library together, thereby preventing any single branch from controlling access to the library. These same six branches, even when a prefect supported a scholar's application to consult the books, all had to grant approval (and for one nineteenth-century applicant, that condition meant the assent of 102 equally empowered lineage members).[105] A surviving plaque, originating some time after the founder's death, details the penalties for violations of these restrictions on access:

> When descendants without good reason open the doors and enter the building, they are to be punished by not being able to join in the lineage sacrifices for three occasions. When they privately lead relations and friends into the building and willfully open the stacks to them, they are to be punished by not being able to join in the lineage sacrifices for one year. When they willfully take books of the collection and loan them off to in-laws and other surnames, they are to be punished by not being able to join in the sacrifices for three years. When they thereby pawn books off, they are to be pursued for disciplining and are to be permanently expelled and unable to join in the lineage sacrifices.[106]

Figure 6   Tianyi ge Library, in Ningbo, Zhejiang Province

This list of punishments suggests a history of infractions. But, for its first century the Tianyi ge and its collection survived largely if not entirely intact. Then, during the disorders of the Ming-Qing transition in the mid-seventeenth century it suffered losses. By c.1660, it had lost a fifth of its original holdings (most notably, half of its copy of the *Ming Veritable Records* [*Ming shilu*]).[107] It remained largely inviolate for another century, until it lost 638 titles to the Qianlong emperor's Four Treasuries project in the 1770s and suffered serious losses at the outbreak of military troubles in the mid-nineteenth century and then a break-in in 1913. The lineage's traditional exclusion of all non-lineage members from access to the library's books persisted up to the admission of the inveterate applicant Huang Zongxi in 1673.[108] Some later scholars also enjoyed this privilege. But, their number in the first two centuries of Qing rule was very limited, no more than ten by one account, and initially manifested the Fans' preference for local Ningbo scholars. Furthermore, their admission was granted only after they had been repeatedly rejected, after they had established a scholarly reputation, and often after they had expressed an interest in doing historical research (e.g., Wan Sitong for the *Draft History of the*

Ming [*Ming shi gao*]). Consequently, during the first two centuries after its founding, this important library, but for its printing of a twenty-*juan* work entitled *The Collected Books of the Tianyi ge of Fan Qin* (*Fan Qin Tianyi ge cangshu*), made very little contribution to the world of scholarship. And, in the second century, none of its books would be reprinted, although some privileged scholars would write of their visit.[109]

During these two centuries, the fame of the collection and its exclusivity spread, even though the first printed catalogue took much time to appear. Initially, a list had been drawn up by the founder, probably too short to cover all the collection. The two late Ming catalogues that mention the existence of a Tianyi ge book catalogue presumably were referring to one or more copies of this original list. In 1673, the situation began to improve, when Huang Zongxi drew up a list of the rare old books; yet, this catalogue was incomplete enough to need a supplement compiled six years later by Fan Qin's great-great grandson. The subsequent use of these catalogues is not clear, but the existence of two other manuscript catalogues for the collection, both written by the early eighteenth century, indicates growing, if limited, knowledge about the contents of the library, in some bibliophile and scholarly circles in the early Qing. Some mid- and late seventeenth-century scholar-collectors, such as Qi Chengye of neighboring Shaoxing and Xu Qianxue of Kunshan county in Suzhou, wanted their own collections to last as long as the Tianyi ge and so modeled their establishments along similarly exclusive rules and procedures.[110] The Qianlong emperor himself, when assembling his own imperial collection in the late eighteenth century, modeled its repository and grounds on the Tianyi ge's and declared it essentially off-limits to all but himself and his personal guests.[111] But, the first printing of a virtually complete catalogue for Tianyi ge was accomplished only after the provincial governor of Zhejiang had visited the library in 1803–04, ordered one of the Fans to compile a full catalogue, and then had a teacher at the Ningbo prefectural school collate and print it up in 1808.[112]

Meanwhile, local families also grew obsessed with this collection, particularly one early nineteenth-century family that married its daughter into the Fan family on the expectation that she would help them gain access to its books and acquire a special herb in its ownership. According to local hearsay, the library's founder had acquired in Huguang Province a herb that protected his books from the bookworms that plagued other collections in the Ningbo area, and he had predictably barred his descendants from ever sharing it with others. To her dismay, this young bride discovered that, as a woman, she was permanently barred from entering the library and thus obtaining this herb; she reportedly died of frustration, at her deathbed asking of her husband only that he bury her at the foot of the steps to the library.[113]

However extreme these access-denying measures were, they do not compare with the resolute refusals of very many collectors to loan their books. An old proverb, quoted by countless book collectors from Song times onward, succinctly summed up the Chinese common sense on the matter of loaning books: "To lend a book is stupid; so is it to return it."[114] Anxious that their heirs might forget this pearl of ancient wisdom, a large number of book owners embossed similarly blunt seal legends onto books in their collection. A famous seal legend introduced by the Tang collector Du Xian in his books —"To loan or sell off a book is an unfilial act"[115]— was also used repeatedly by later generations of collectors, such as the owner of the largest book collection in Songjiang prefecture during the Wanli era.[116] The seal legend of the sixteenth-century Suzhou collector Qian Yi went further: "If someone borrows and does not return this book, it will result in his execution by the gods. If my descendants do not treasure it, may they become real dunces!"[117] Even more extreme were the threats in the seals of two other collectors. Lü Kun (1536–1618) in 1579 had his book seal carved with a legend banning his sons from loaning or harming any of their father's books and promising their expulsion from the ancestral hall for any violation.[118] Two centuries later in Songjiang prefecture, the collector Wang Chang (1725–1806) has his seal legend read: "If some untalented [descendant] dares to sell and abandon my books, this means that he is not a human and is like a dog and pig. Evict him from the lineage and whip him."[119]

These admonitions, if not the threat of whipping, were not taken lightly, or so we are led to believe from the somewhat hyperbolic claim of one early seventeenth-century observer, Wang Kentang, that fewer than one out of 100 book owners heeded a famous pre-Tang scholar's advice that loaning books to others was to be the act of a scholar-official.[120] A few examples of the actual behavior of some scholars and scholar-officials add weight to Wang's claim. Thus, we learn that the very important twelfth-century Wuxi collector You Mao did not loan his books to others, and told his children not to do so either.[121] The Nanjing neo-Confucian Jiao Hong (1541–1620), according to his son-in-law, had the policy of loaning books to no one.[122] Zhao Qimei resolutely rejected requests to borrow his books from anyone but for three friends hailing from his local district in the Suzhou county of Changshu.[123] Qian Qianyi (1582–1664) built up a great collection, reputedly the size of the Imperial Household's, out of a lifelong pursuit of others' books, snapping up at least four large private collections.[124] Despite the warm words he showered on others who shared their books (e.g., Li Ruyi [1557–1630], whose books he would borrow), he failed to return books borrowed from others; he also prevented all guests to his library from borrowing his books and leaving it with even a sheet of notes.[125]

In fact, this very famous bibliophile, who was one of those literati with a seal legend reading, "To loan a book is unfilial," has left us perhaps the most depressing instance of bibliophilia turned to bibliomania. When living in north China, Qian had daily made use of the 6,000 to 7,000-volume collection of his fellow Yangzi delta book collector, Cao Rong. By letting Qian read and copy these books, Cao, naturally, thought that Qian would reciprocate. So, upon returning south to the lower Yangzi delta, he wrote to Qian, then back in Suzhou, to see if Qian might lend him his copies of two titles that he, Cao, had allowed Qian to copy. Qian agreed, but when Cao visited him in Suzhou, he denied that he had such books in his house. He dismissed his earlier assent as "empty talk" (*huhua*). Out of respect for someone older, Cao did not protest; he even refrained from ever again asking Qian to loan him a book. But, soon afterwards, in 1650, Qian's collection, thanks to a thoughtless servant, went up in flames, and when Cao paid him a visit to express his condolences, Qian lamented to him, "I have an obsession about loaning books. I fear that if they are loaned out, they will end up being lost. The two books you wanted to borrow, *The Treatise of the Nine Kingdoms* (*Jiuguo zhi*) and *A Chronology of the Ten Kingdoms* (*Shiguo jinian*), I actually had, but simply was not willing to lend them to you. Now after this conflagration, both these books are lost to mankind."[126]

Is it any wonder, then, that such exclusive practices, thriving nearly a millennium after the invention of woodblock printing and more than a millennium and a half after the opening of bookstores, would prompt Huang Zongxi's heartfelt lament about the difficulty of gaining access to libraries of major collectors, even though he was a celebrated acquaintance of theirs? His contemporary, the part-time writer Gui Zhuang (1613–73), viewed this exclusivity far more caustically:

> Books, publicly and privately owned, are carefully stored in boxes for a string of months and a series of years, and men do not see them. Forever separated from the wind and the sun, they permanently take leave of the table. This is called "secreting them away." Men all know the misfortune of the disappearance and loss of books, but nowadays they often take this so-called "secreting away" to mean that the owner loves books. They do not know that locking away and closing up things of use to the world is the height of misfortune.[127]

In justifying their reluctance to show and loan books, private owners in the Song, Yuan, and Ming resorted to explanations familiar to historians of the Song and Ming government libraries: soiling and damaging books, recurrent theft and loss, prolonged borrowing, and the failure to return books.[128] One Song observer complained, "Recently the scholar-officials, when borrowing others' books, do not transcribe, do not read, and do not return them. They make these books into their own. They also wish to assure that others do not have a copy (*ben*)."[129] More than twenty years before he died, Yang Shiqi reported that he had already lost five copies of the *Chuci* (*Songs of the South*), all loaned out and never returned.[130] The practice, according to a late sixteenth-century and early seventeenth-century Suzhou literatus, persisted: "Many are those who on borrowing another's book do not return it. Those who can follow the advice of the *Family Instructions of the Yan Family (Yanshi jiaxun)* [to loan their books as a proper scholar-official] are fewer than one out of a hundred."[131] And, at roughly the same time, the Hangzhou official Xu Xianqing (1479–1557) warned his offspring "not to treat lightly the showing of books and other family heirlooms to perversely covetous people."[132] Perhaps most notorious was the deception carried out by the early Qing dynasty collector Zhu Yizun. After his official demotion for bringing copyists into the Hanlin Academy Library to transcribe the records —"a beautiful demotion" it was called — Zhu was frustrated by the unwillingness of another collector, Qian Ceng, to show his copy of a rare book. Thereupon, Zhu bribed Qian's servant to open up his master's book chest and show this book to several yamen scribes Zhu had hired to copy it in a barely lit room. Meanwhile, Zhu spent the evening hosting a drinking party for the unwitting owner of the book and another famous scholar.[133]

These ruses and abuses, as surely all book owners would acknowledge, are known to all other book cultures, to government and private libraries alike. One can begin, in Western European history, with the medieval practice of chaining books to the book shelf, memorably explained by one modern English observer of the custom: "In the Middle Ages books were rare, and so was honesty. A book, it was said, was worth as much as a farm; unlike a farm it was portable property that could be easily purloined. Valuables in all ages require protection. Books, therefore, were kept under lock and key."[134] The Bodleian Library would maintain this practice for 1,448 old volumes until c.1761. Recall, also, the bull (and threat of excommunication) issued by Pope Sixtus VI against those who stole books from the Vatican Library and the moderate estimate by the 38-year-old Leigh Hunt in the nineteenth century that he had already lost six decent-sized libraries to borrowers. If that is not enough warning, then there is the bookplate legend that a nineteenth-century British collector had pasted into each of her books: "This book has been stolen from Lady Dorothy Nevill," or the fact that there survive today in the Bodleian just three of the original 279 manuscripts given by Duke Humphrey of Gloucester between 1439 and 1444 (one of these three bears the appropriate inscription: "If anyone steals this book may he come to the gallows or the rope of Judas").[135] For perhaps the most memorable example of such perfidy, we have to look no farther than a century and a half ago to the fate of French government-administered libraries supervised by Guillaume, comte de Libri Carucci (1803–69), the Inspector-General of Libraries under Louis Philippe. This greatest of French biblioklepts, while performing his duties, rifled the stacks of nationalized library collections of, in 1985 terms, 3,000,000 francs worth of books.[136] A Ming eunuch or official could have only gazed in envy at the scale of such bibliomaniac gluttony, even though French libraries did not suffer the same degree of loss as did the Song and Ming Imperial Libraries.

How, then, was the case of China, from 1000 to 1700, different? A useful initial analysis comes from the writings of Yao Shilin, a Jiaxing commoner who, in the late Ming, overcame a delayed start at education to become an exceptionally enthusiastic book collector.

His slow start may have only sharpened his observation of scholarly mispractice:

> Our prefecture has never been without book collectors, but it also has never had anyone famous for collecting books. In general, its book collectors merely knew that the storage of valuables might be considered [a means of] transmission. They did not know that distributing and sharing what one likes also is storage. Why is this? If one stores up valuables, then one's boxes and satchels will suffer a Qin-dynasty-style plunder which will mean that no one can learn from them. If they are distributed, then the spiritual principles [in them] will be transmitted by means of brush and paper. Thus, the difference between transmitting and not transmitting must be examined.
>
> There are four explanations for what is called "not knowing how to transmit." Generally, if among the teachings of past worthies there is something that will prompt a short-lived anger but will appear dignified after a hundred generations, the descendants, planning on behalf of the household, will not dare to transmit it. If in vanquishing [others] with their brilliance and in showing off their extensive learning, they take delight in privately knowing that others do not know [these things], then they will be conceited about their precious rarities and will not be willing to transmit them. If when a scroll is borrowed, there is no more patching up of its faults and correcting of its errors and if they alone practice the adage that to return [a book] is stupid, they will be worried about loaning it to be copied and so will not delight in transmitting it. If an old imprint is refined or a handwritten copy is elegant, then they fear that it will be copied and damaged and so they will not tolerate its transmission.[137]

Yao then takes this set of reasons for refusing to show, lend, and permit books to be copied — a family's reputation, the conceited desire to retain privileged access to rare knowledge, the protection of the text, and the protection of the book itself — and gives telling examples of such troubles from his own experience and that of his contemporaries.

Several points he omits, however, merit mention. Firstly, some collections would have almost certainly been located far into the private recesses of the house, where the women would have been situated; such collections would have been as off-limits as the women of their owners. Secondly, although concrete evidence is often lacking, it is my impression that only a few famous private book collectors, from the Song to the early Qing, were also major landlords or even major art collectors. In other words, very many if not most of them would appear to have put their funds into what they best understood, books, and predictably, in an increasingly commercialized society, sought to protect what was probably for them a major, if not the major, investment. The fact that books unlike land avoided all taxation made them an even more attractive investment, especially in a heavily taxed region like the lower Yangzi delta. Thirdly, these book collectors extended to their musty world of books the competitive spirit of the marketplace. These books represented their owners' social capital, wealth that had to be bolstered and increased through a persistent practice of exclusion. Readers had to learn, through gossip and reputation, of the existence of these collections and their rare titles, but, just as importantly, they had to be kept out, lest the books lose their social and economic value. And, finally, we see here the competitive spirit of that central arena of late imperial Chinese learning, the examination hall. Some, but far from all, of these collectors were degree holders; and, one cannot avoid suspecting that the acquisition of rare books and their rarer editions were meant to serve as a passport into the higher ranks of literati society for those collectors without a provincial or metropolitan degree. The accumulation of hidden rarities in private book collections was thus intended to compensate for some of their owners' repeated disappointments in the examination hall (e.g., Xiang Yuanbian, Zhang Yingwen, Qian Yunzhi, and Zhu Chaqing).

This lack of access to books in private collections had consequences that stretched far beyond the confining chambers of the examination hall and affected far more than the flow of gossip among private book collectors. In the education and intellectual life of the Song, Yuan, and Ming, it surely encouraged study through lectures (*jiangxue*), a fondness for dialogues over extended analysis, and a heavy reliance on memorization (what keen reader would not memorize a book that he might be prevented from copying, purchasing, or ever seeing again?).[138] It is striking that so few of the major Song, Yuan, and Ming thinkers up to the seventeenth century were actually major book collectors, a disjunction that probably lay behind the emphasis found in the writings of the celebrated mid-Ming thinker Wang Yangming and his numerous disciples on action over book learning.[139] It even can be held responsible for the already noted shallowness of Ming research into fields such as history and textual studies that benefit from reference to an abundance of texts. We should not be surprised by the charge of a mid-seventeenth century writer that the hoarding of books tended to discourage the active pursuit of learning:

> The old books that presently survive are complete. But what the court and the official offices pay attention to and what they are accustomed to looking at are merely the records of one dynasty [i.e., the present] and the books related to current affairs on military, penal, currency, and grain matters. Those who are said to be Confucian scholars seldom cast their eyes on books other than as writings for the civil service examinations. If one questions them of the events of previous dynasties and the names of the ancients, they do not understand even ten or twenty percent of the questions. There are definitely no gaps among the books in libraries. Those stored up in people's houses have not completely disappeared or gone out of circulation. But, I do not know how many of them have unfortunately been secreted away.[140]

Such "secreting away" thus helped to assure that this knowledge, whenever it escaped, tended to remain private. Though perhaps not as secret as other forms of Chinese knowledge (e.g., Daoist scriptures and rituals, carpentry and other trades),[141] it sometimes came to constitute bodies of learning that families kept to themselves. To other families, particularly those capable of retaining collections over generations of both success and failure in the civil service examinations, their books came to mean even more: they were manifestations of their otherwise contestable claims to social and cultural legitimacy.

Consequently, the major holders of this valuable knowledge became "culture brokers." Collectors could always use their books to make a living as teachers, if only because their collection would attract students able to afford a teacher but not a good book collection. In the last half of the Ming, however, collectors enjoyed an increasing variety of ways of using their books to support themselves and produce more books. We have already seen that some collectors, like Chen Jiru, edited and compiled books for publishers; some, like Jiao Hong, in addition advised other scholars on their texts and their research; others, like Wang Qi (a 1565 metropolitan degree holder), compiled, edited, and published his own works; and a smaller number, like Mao Jin, focused mainly on publishing their collection.[142] These men, if they wished, could occupy virtually all roles of the publishing process (other than that of the actual manual laborers involved in book production). Infinitely flexible, some of them became centers of learning far more important than any school or other local institution of their time. In fact, some late Ming collectors took over the cultural space once held by the government institutions and collections, and as private parties reigned over the development of literati culture. The book, despite the flourishing of commercial production, remained unexpectedly private, and access to its learning persistently dependent on personalities and personal ties.

It should be clear by now that the concept of a "community of learning" describes more an ideal than the reality of the world of learning in China between 1000 and 1700. Access to private collections in general was restricted, to the major private collections very exclusive, and borrowing from them even more difficult. One cannot but note that, before the latter half of the sixteenth century, only a few men took advantage of the convenience of boat transport and the absence of national boundaries to travel from throughout south China to the Yangzi delta to read books in private collections (how different is the history of rice circulation in these centuries!). Accounting for at least forty percent of all Ming collections with more than 10,000 *juan*,[143] these delta collections, as we have seen, often changed hands. But, when they did, only seldom are they reported to have left the delta before the second quarter of the nineteenth century.[144] To us, these Yangzi delta libraries are powerful symbols of China's rich tradition of learning. But, to Chinese coming from elsewhere, as outsiders from Hunan, Guangdong, and even Jiangxi Provinces, these book collections would have resembled nothing less than virtually locked vaults of knowledge which we too hastily rush to call "Chinese culture."

Such a judgment, however, may be too hasty and harsh. It may reflect the assumptions of our own time when private collectors can readily rely on the general willingness of large institutional libraries to open their collections to others and so provide an alternate route to research and learning. Book collectors in China could not enjoy such a comfortable assumption and so regularly admired collections like Tianyi ge for the high walls, moats, and rules their owners set up in defense of their books. Such steps to preserve books, however legitimate, were not easily balanced with the calls by other readers for greater access and dissemination, especially when so many literate men might request to see the books in a collection, and some of them not take care to protect them from harm or theft.

It is thus perhaps wise to conclude that, as literacy levels rose over the course of the Ming, these private collections fell under increasing pressure to function as public, or institutional, libraries in a society whose government was not willing to make such an institutional commitment. Indeed, the 1579 government ban on private academies actively discouraged collective gatherings of educated men outside of its own inadequate institutions. A generation later, the numerous informal literary clubs were more likely to publish the writings of their members than to form collectively held book collections.[145] It is not surprising, then, that the great majority of book collectors, even when we discard their self-interested justifications, balked at the suggestion that they open up their libraries to all interested readers. The "common sense" of their culture had taught them to do otherwise, and their government's inaction and actions largely confirmed the wisdom of such a decision.

5 Ameliorations and a Community of Learning

How, then, could a late imperial scholar, anxious to expand his knowledge without spending a fortune that he most likely did not have, escape this vise of often hapless government libraries and often unfriendly private libraries? The variety of solutions that Chinese scholars devised to cope with these persistent obstacles is the focus of this chapter, the emphasis placed on the formation of small coteries among book collectors to share their books and on the partial fruition of certain late Ming improvements in access only during the eighteenth century. Although attention is paid primarily to the efforts of these scholars from the Song through the Ming, a large part of the solution to their problems was achieved only outside their control, only in the Qing dynasty, and mainly in the realm of official and imperial policy towards élite culture and its artifacts.

Solutions

For some, the best hope lay in another's death and the inheritance. But, as we have already seen, the Chinese practice of partible inheritance, as well as the heirs' frequent disinterest in old books, regularly led to the dissolution of both major and minor private book collections within a generation or two of their formation. For striking testimony of how many heirs did not inherit their father's and grandfather's commitment to book collection, one need look no farther than the famous collectors' books themselves. Their pages are spotted with the seals of multiple owners, providing ample evidence that books in major collections frequently changed hands among collectors. Such transfers, it goes without saying, did not necessarily make these books more accessible to any reader other than the new owner.[1]

Many a scholar unwilling to wait for the news of the death or misfortune of others, actively sought to acquire copies of books in other collections. He might, of course, pay the owner for allowing him or his servant to make a handcopy, as was the case for Zhu Liangyu in 1515 and Li Wenzao over two centuries later.[2] In the Northern Song capital, Song Minqiu and Wang Qinchen earned a reputation for allowing other scholar-officials to consult and even borrow their books.[3] A few Southern Song collectors, such as Zhao Buyu and Lou Yue (1137–1213), are said to have opened their libraries to interested readers.[4] Whether their practice was really that simple or comprehensive is today unclear; Yang Shiqi took care to discriminate the potential borrowers of his books into those he did not approve of as men and those he regarded as "good men and committed scholars."[5] But in the late Ming, one collector became famous for his capacious generosity to inquiring readers: Li Ruyi. A frequent failure at the civil service examinations, he gained fame for carrying out his assertion that "one ought to share the fine books of the world with the readers of the world." Such a stance brought this wealthy commoner into contact with not just some of the most eminent scholar-officials of his day. He also allowed ordinary readers to borrow books from a collection that he had inherited and then expanded with his own acquisitions.[6]

At different times in the Sung and Ming, when private collectors observed that their number was increasing, the size of their collections expanding, and the price of the new imprints falling,[7] some of them attempted a much more direct solution to the problem of access. They donated their collection to others outside their family, who would otherwise have not inherited them. For example, as already mentioned, Jing Du, a north China refugee in Sichuan during the second quarter of the twelfth century, bequeathed all his books to his friend and fellow bibliophile Chao Gongwu.[8] Likewise, the doctor-monk Li Yanzhen gave Zhu Yizun over 2,500 *juan* in 1697.[9] Less common was the donation of books that accompanied the transformation of a family school into a private academy (*shuyuan*) that was open to aspiring students who were not direct family members.[10] Thus, for instance, Guo Qinzhi in Jinhua prefecture in Zhejiang Province in 1198 donated a sizeable collection of books to a private academy established at his wishes on his family's own land. More remarkable were efforts simply to create a library for students, as attempted in 1140 in Nanjing by the famous collector Ye Mengde[11] or in the late twelfth century by some men in southern Shanxi Province:

> Even though families do set up buildings for books and men look after libraries, I am nonetheless concerned that poor and rustic scholars with few resources will, despite their commitment, still lack books. Some will never avoid having to be diligent at borrowing books to read and at making handcopies. Yet, they will still not satisfy their collecting and reading, and they will lack the means to develop their allotted talents fully. My senior friend Chengqing wished to head a proposal to take on the responsibility to purchase books. The eminent in the county agreed to [the proposal] and matched him. Delighted to make a donation, they each provided money. Therefore, they acquired a certain number of volumes of the classics, history, and philosophy. And as for encyclopedias and dictionaries, they also provided amply for them if they were related to the examinations.
>
> Ah! This understanding is convenient not only for oneself but also for the masses. It is not only especially useful for the present but also transmits [books] to the future.[12]

Unfortunately, these privately sponsored libraries, usually intended to educate aspiring officials, were few and short-lived. Moreover, they seldom, if ever, had the quality and quantity of books required to foster important scholarly research. According to Qiao Pingnan, the book collections at large Song private academies numbered just several thousand *juan*.[13]

Sharing

The most commonly practiced solution to this dilemma was for scholars to share books, even if what was shared was only an inferior extra copy.[14] Private collectors were not always as resolutely deaf to requests as the warnings and rejections mentioned in the previous chapter might easily have been interpreted to indicate. As already noted, their response would have often been qualified. A reputation for refusing not only served to fend off unwanted requests but also functioned as a bargaining tactic to assure that the applicant was prepared to offer something in return. A policy of "no access" would have been understood by all parties as, to use a current phrase, "negotiable." Thus, the very proponents of "total closure" can sometimes be observed to allow others to use their collections, copy their books, and at times even borrow them. Witness the agreement reached by the founder of the Tianyi ge, Fan Qin, to share books with another important collector, Wang Shizhen,[15] as well as the thawing of a stern policy of refusal by the elderly Nanjing-based doyen of Ming scholarship, Jiao Hong. Having become a good friend of Chen Di, Jiao allowed this major Fukienese collector to spend a night in his library and even borrow some of his books. He let the large and important Suzhou collector Zhao Qimei borrow books from him. He also let a Huizhou man borrow for his Fuzhou bibliophile friend Xu Bo a copy of a very rare Song book that Jiao himself had acquired only by transcribing it in full in the Imperial Library. And, in 1609, he even agreed with Zhao Qimei and Mei Dingzuo (1549–1615) to form a book-copying club that would meet once every three years to copy out one another's rare books.[16] More surprisingly, perhaps, Qian Qianyi loaned some books to other Changshu natives Feng Shu and Qu Shisi.[17] He even agreed to allow Huang Zongxi to be a book-reading companion in his library (alas, Huang never put Qian to the test, since Qian's library went up in flames before Huang could arrange a visit).[18]

What grounds would persuade them to open and share their collections in this way? Firstly, collectors tended to show their libraries to people they already knew. Kinship ties were useful; for instance, the Huang family of Tandu in She county, Huizhou prefecture, decided to deposit their books inside the ancestral hall in order to stop them from being loaned out to non-lineage members.[19] In the late twelfth century, the famous collector Chao Gongwu was a cousin of the celebrated book collector Ye Mengde and the son of the sister of the great poet and book collector Lu You; all three of these men came from official families that had collected books for generations.[20] In Shaoxing prefecture, the young late Ming collector Shang Jun claimed that he often could look at books in the collection of his uncle, Niu Shixi.[21] And, in Ming Suzhou, where over half of the male descendants of Wen Zhengming married within the narrow confines of the Suzhou literati élite,[22] we see relations exchanging and loaning books to one another.

Friendship was another important tie that opened up otherwise inaccessible library collections, especially during the last century of the Ming, when literati commonly conferred greater significance to the concept of friendship in their social and political discourse.[23] Friends sometimes shared newly acquired books[24] and established numerous poetry and political discussion groups.[25] At times, a collector favored one or two particularly worthy or needy individuals, as when Su Song allowed Ye Mengde to copy his rare manuscripts, and Zheng Qiao loaned books to Fang Jian and Lin Ting.[26] In the Ming, Yan Qishan (1484–1507), too poor to buy books, sent his family's only servant to borrow books from friends for him to copy and read aloud day and night;[27] and in the mid-seventeenth century, Gu Yanwu, cut off in north China, regularly received books from friends back in Suzhou and Nanjing.[28]

But, far more commonly, friendship ties grew up among book collectors with something to share. The celebrated eighteenth-century poet Yuan Mei lamented that a poor reader encountered repeated difficulties when trying to borrow books from others.[29] What he needed could be a simple bottle of liquor or fish, gifts sent by the Song poets Huang Tingjian and Su Yangzhi when returning borrowed books to their owner;[30] or, it could be an expensive fur coat, as when the Shandong collector Li Wenzao sought permission from a secretive book dealer to copy one of his books.[31] Another lubricant was political influence; hence, the collectors tended to be receptive to inquiries from local officials,[32] even if fear kept them from showing their most treasured pieces.

But, probably the most effective, and certainly the most commonly adopted, currency a collector could use to gain admission to another's collection was his own book collection. Once inheritance, purchase, or scribal copying turned him, a mere reader, into a respectable collector, he would find curt replies of rejection from book collectors turning into letters of welcome. Their books serving as the key to entry into one another's libraries, these collectors would agree to a variety of book exchanges. Thus, to cite the more famous examples, in the twelfth century, You Mao shared books with Yang Wanli and Lu You,[33] as in the Ming did Ye Sheng and Liu Chang, Shao Bao, Yang Xunji, and Wu Kuan, Li Tingxiang and Li Kaixian, Liu Qian and Yu Bian, Zhao Yongjian and Huang Hongxian, Zhao Qimei and Feng Mengzhen, and He Dacheng (d. 1643) and Feng Shu.[34] At times, as in early sixteenth-century Suzhou, the motive might simply be to gloat in showing off one's latest unusual acquisition and so outdo friendly rivals.[35] Even then, some of these competitive collectors would exchange books, as surviving colophons reveal for Suzhou men like Tang Yin, Wen Jia, Yang Xunji, and Du Mu.[36] Often, such exchanges took place among equally placed bibliophiles: three early seventeenth-century Suzhou collectors — Feng Shu, Ye Shulian, and Lu Yidian — agreed to visit one another to consult each other's collection and borrow one another's books.[37] And, as time passed, the range of private libraries a well-placed individual might gain access to increased. Huang Zongxi, one of the foremost scholars of the seventeenth century, gained admission to at least fourteen major book collections in the Yangzi delta between 1613 and 1679. Twice he relied on a common surname, four times on common place-ties, and for the rest, on his and his family's network of friendship.[38] In his case, he seems to have shared not his books but his elevated status as an eminent scholar and his connoisseurship of any rare books shown him by hopeful collectors.

At no time do we read that one of these collectors allowed another to examine and copy all his books unconditionally. Indeed, at times, these exchanges were restricted to simply the viewing or copying of copies of books. Wang Qingchen showed only copies he, or others, had made of his acquisitions;[39] You Mao never allowed his books to leave his house;[40] and the late Ming collector Qi Chengye established a pact (*yue*) that allowed his literate descendants to enter the building of his huge collection and read the books there; they were explicitly barred from removing any book to a room of their own. Qi also allowed close friends to borrow his books to read, but only when there was a second copy; he made sure that his main copy never left his "secret garden."[41] His son, Qi Biaojia, adopted a more liberal policy for at least one favored guest. In 1639, Qian Qianyi asked him if he might borrow books from the collection. Initially, Qi Biaojia turned down the request, on the grounds that he had to follow his father's wishes in such matters and let no one borrow books at all. Four and a half months later — for unstated reasons — he reversed his decision and sent Qian Qianyi handcopies of the requested books.[42]

These scholarly practices doubtless enabled texts to be reproduced and thus reduce the chances of their elimination due to fire, flood, and other accidents. But, their long-term significance becomes clearer when they are considered as part of a larger, more formal network of book sharing. Sometimes, these networks would work along lines of teacher-disciple relations, as when the Suzhou writer Gui Youguang beseeched one of his disciples to negotiate for a viewing of two texts with the owner, who had several times rejected Gui's direct requests for access.[43] But the networking of collectors' ties would be most evident when the sharing collectors — men like Su Song, You Mao, Song Minqiu, Yang Shiqi, and Zhao Yongxian — had already enjoyed extended contact with the Palace Library in the Song and Ming.[44] Often holding court posts in the Palace Library, archives, or the Hanlin Academy, these collectors would, on their return home, often in the provinces, share their manuscript copies of Palace Library texts with one or more local collectors. In the last third of the eleventh century, Su Song served a total of nine years at posts at academies and institutes at the court, such as proofreader in the academies, sub-editor of the Academy of Assembled Worthies, and director of the Palace Library. According to his grandson, he daily transcribed 2,000 words from books in the libraries of these institutions, and, upon his retirement to the Yangzi delta, opened up his rare book collection of these manuscripts to Ye Mengde. Thus, even if a collection like Ye's suffered heavily from fire, and even if the heirs of these collectors did not open these books to interested scholars, their copies of these palace books had escaped the confines of the palace and would eventually circulate among private collectors, if only due to the heirs' wish to sell them off.

Sharing Pacts

The social, as well as the textual, implications of sharing would be made clearer when this practice was formalized into written rules. Qi Chengye, as we have just seen, made a pact with his male descendants about their use of his books. Yet, the sharing in this case was not mutual, as his pact resembles less a book pact than an extension of the venerable Chinese genre of family instructions (*jiaxun*) into the once arcane world of bibliophilia. Far more influential and revealing models were the formal, written pacts practiced by non-kin collectors, whereby book collectors specified the proper procedures for operating mutual lending associations so that they could read and copy one another's books. The first such formal pact I know of originated with two mid-eleventh century scholar-officials, Song Minqiu and Wang Qinchen.[45] Both had inherited famous libraries; Song's family library was particularly strong in holdings of collected works by individual Tang poets, books that he allowed Wang to look through and choose from for copying by office clerks. Both had already permitted some other officials access to their collections.[46] What distinguished this written pact, however, was its reciprocity. Each collector drew up a catalogue of all his holdings, showed it to the other, and allowed him to choose which books he wished to have copied for his own collection.

The immediate influence of this pact appears to have been minimal, since the next book pact, to the best of my knowledge, dates from nearly three centuries later, when the Henan collector Feng Mengzhou (c.1285–?) made his library available to "the literate of the village who were unable to have books." This pact, more a piece of philanthropy than a sharing agreement, had literate villagers return books when they finished reading them or when prompted to return them; they also were somehow to make up for any omissions.[47] Another two centuries would then pass before, in c.1570, we encounter the first mention ever of a mutual book-borrowing pact in the lower Yangzi delta. Coming at a time when men of all social strata were composing pacts for a very wide range of collective activities,[48] it lets us see how family libraries were opened up to select non-kin collectors on special terms. Wang Shizhen, probably the most famous literatus of his generation, proposed a book exchange to Fan Qin, the founder of the Tianyi gè, in clear-cut terms: "I wish that you and I each provide a list of our books and mutually make up for the omissions [in the other's list]."[49] As these men and their libraries were a couple of hundred miles apart, this agreement presumably required them to have their own scribes or servants copy out the desired books; if so, ready entrance to the library, borrowing, and personal reproduction of the text were still not negotiable. Like its Song precedent (whose terms may well have influenced it), this agreement was essentially a deal between two major collectors and no one else. The aim was mainly to improve the holdings of their collections, not to share widely or even assure the preservation of each other's books.

Shortly afterwards, book exchange agreements became more common. In c.1600, the dramatist and collector Mei Dingzuo made a pact with two other famous collectors — Jiao Hong and Zhao Qimei

— to meet up in Nanjing once every three years to show and share for reading and copying their rare and old books (presumably focusing on their finds in the previous three years).[50] Although this agreement was not carried out, a similar pact set up in the late Ming by three Suzhou collectors — Feng Shu, He Dacheng, and Wu Yifeng — actually was. This pact committed each member to allow the other members to borrow his newly purchased books for a set period before having to return them to their owner (previously held books were presumably not included).[51] Feng Shu also exchanged books with his friends Ye Shulian and Zhang Gongduan, though no role for a written pact is specified.[52]

Details of wide-ranging agreements on book exchanges survive in two pacts of the mid-seventeenth century. Their survival may have been arbitrary, but that cannot be said of their composition, which drew on the exchange pacts of other literati. The second pact also derives from a previous exchange agreement by one of the members of the pact and involved families already known to one another. Thus, the terms of these pacts give a nod to accumulated experience, as they were drafted for acquaintances that could even qualify as family friends.

The earlier of the two pacts was drafted by one of the major lower Yangzi delta book collectors of his generation, Cao Rong.[53] A native of Jiaxing prefecture like Yao Shilin, Cao was alarmed during the Ming-Qing transition by the disappearance of much of the country's written heritage.[54] In the mid-seventeenth century, he thus proposed a set of conditions for book exchanges that served as a model for later exchange agreements between book collectors:

> I shall now consider a simple and convenient method whereby each of two book collectors looks at the [other's] book catalogue and marks out what he lacks. First, there are the classics and their commentaries, then the histories official and unofficial, next the collected writings, and then the miscellaneous writings. The categories of the writings they are to look at are to be the same, the order for the dates [of the editions] they look at is to be the same, and the number of the chapters (*juan*) and slipcases they look at are to be the same. It is agreed the owner of a book will exchange books when one has a book and the other does not. The owners then are to give orders on their own to a servant in the house; a skilled worker, he is to copy [the books] and do the collation without error. And each is to hand over for mutual exchange what is copied during one or two months.

This method has several good points. Fine books will not leave
[their owners'] house. There will be merit for the ancients. What [the
owners] store up on their own will grow more abundant by the day.
And, [the pact] can be carried out in all parts of the country, in Chu
in the south and in Yan in the north.

I respectfully told [this proposal] to men who share my aims. They
assessed it and gave their approval. Some said, "This is a matter for the
poor and not for the wealthy." But, it reduces the expenses for
banquets, travel, and hobbies, can complete [the work of] the ancients,
give them an extension of life, and put out what has previously never
been printed and distributed. It will give long life to the jujube and
pear trees [used for the wood blocks]. At first, it will be a small volume,
then it will become a giant edition, and gradually it will expand. People
in all directions will definitely learn of the custom and be influenced
by it. They will regard as their own responsibility the commendation
of what merits honor and the distribution of its accomplishment.[55]

Four principles — safety, equity, self-interest, and preservation of
books — help to shape the terms of this pact. All books are to leave
each owner's house as copies and then be returned. Thus, the owner
would never show the original and so could have as much of it
included in the handcopy as he wished, no one else being the wiser
(later bibliophiles would criticize Cao for the numerous copying
mistakes in manuscripts once in his library).[56] Secondly, they are to
leave each owner's collection in equal numbers. Thirdly, the explicit
rationale is to improve one's own collection, prestige, and wealth —
note that the owner would actually have a second copy made for
himself as he loans it out (the other party would read and presumably
copy it as he wished, but only at his own expense). Fourthly, the
duration of the pact would seem to be short, as each side is to do
the copying for just one to two months. And, fifthly, the aim would
be the prolongation of the life of a book, as one more copy of it would
be made and so improve the book's chance of long-term survival. The
identity of the other party or parties in this pact is unclear, but two
later collectors with whom Cao agreed to copy one another's books
were the bibliophiles Zhu Yizun of Jiaxing and Lu Liao (1644–?) of
Suzhou.[57]

Also in the middle of the seventeenth century, another
celebrated book exchange pact was drafted by Ding Xiongfei
(1605–?) with another Nanjing collector, Huang Yuji (1629–91). This

pact, it is important to recognize, was not a spontaneous decision springing solely from a common addiction to bibliophilia. Both collectors came from families that had moved to Nanjing, Ding's from a county directly across the Yangzi from Nanjing, and Huang's from Fuzhou in distant Fujian Province.[58] Both men had fathers whose success in the examinations had raised their family's social status and introduced them and their sons to the influential circles and expensive interests of scholar-officials. Both families used their books for expanding their contacts and for raising their profile in a city rich with art, books, carefree officials, and colorful personalities. Both men knew Qian Qianyi and helped Gu Yanwu acquire books during his absence in north China. Huang had even collected three medical works by Ding Xiongfei's ancestor Ding Yi, as well as Ding's own catalogue to his family's book collection.[59] Thus, this pact is the slowly reached outgrowth of extensive contact between families who were long-term friends; such ties may well have been a necessary pre-condition for the inclusion in the pact of borrowing privileges that Cao Rong had explicitly ruled out for his unidentified co-participant.

The Dings had, from at least the fourteenth century, been renowned for their skill as doctors.[60] They lived in a county as close to Nanjing geographically as it was distant from it culturally:

> [In Jiangpu county] those who make a career out of poetry and books total less than a hundred-odd families in the county seat and environs. In the local market towns and poor villages, such households are fewer than one or two. How is it that they all lack the ability to teach their juniors? Poor scholars suffer financial hardships and cannot invite teachers for their sons and younger brothers. If they are rich, they are stingy with their wealth and cannot invite good teachers for their sons and younger brothers.[61]

By the late sixteenth century, Jiangpu's government facilities offered little support for learning: virtually all the books that the county school had received from the early Ming court had vanished, and the compiler of the local gazetteer wondered if the new arrivals of books would suffer the same fate in a few more decades.[62] By then, however, the Dings had left this backwater and moved across the Yangzi to Nanjing, which Ding Xiongfei, if not his biographers, regarded as his home.[63]

There, and later in Quanzhou in Fujian Province, when his father worked there as a local judge in the early 1620s, Ding Xiongfei acquired an interest in books. At the age of 19 *sui*, on his way back to Nanjing from Fujian, that interest developed into an obsession: "Once I arrived in Tiger Grove [Mt. in Hangzhou] and Tiger Hill [in Suzhou], I saw the bookstores crowded in rows and the books piled high like mountains. My insides shook, I gave a great shout, and I was about to go mad. I spent everything I had saved up to exchange for books." His wife shared his passion. Within ten days of their marriage ceremony, she handed over to him four packs of books from her dowry chest and later pawned and sold off pieces of her jewelry and clothing, presumably from the remainder of her dowry, all in order to support their "habit."[64] Their collection soon mounted to almost 20,000 *juan*. When combined with the great number of books he would soon inherit from his father, Ding's collection ranked as one of the largest in Nanjing.[65]

Even larger and grander was the Huang family's collection. Huang Juzhong was a widely admired collector who was repeatedly visited by Huang Zongxi and a host of others interested in reading and borrowing his books.[66] He himself collected some 60,000 *juan*, and his son Huang Yuji added another 20,000, together establishing the collection's distinctive strength in rare Ming imprints.[67] The son soon gained a reputation for loaning and showing his books to other officials and literati. He joined a classics and history reading society, loaned books to famous friends of his and his father's, and, in 1639, even agreed with the visiting Fujian collector Xu Bo to let each other look at books in their collections.[68] Thus, the pact that he signed with Ding Xiongfei in the early Qing actually formalized in writing long-term wishes and practices of his, and did so with a family of attested scholarly interests and official positions that the Huangs had already known and dealt with.[69] Furthermore, in 1654, the same year that Huang arranged his pact, a Suzhou native resident in Nanjing, Tang Huo, joined their pact and thereby accepted the following conditions:[70]

1. Each month, on the thirteenth day, Ding is to go to Huang and on the twenty-sixth day Huang is to go to Ding. Because the day is already set, one [need] make no other advance arrangements.
2. If an important task impedes one's visit, then one must give apologies in advance.

3. One does not bring in other friends; we fear that it would involve social intercourse with them (*yingchou*) and at the same time interfere with the inspection (*jianyue*) [of the books].
4. When [the guest] arrives, [the host is to provide] six dishes of fruit seeds; tea is not counted.
5. For the afternoon meal, provide one meat or fish dish and one vegetable dish; wine is not included. When there is a transgression of the quota, take away an unusual book and give a fine.
6. To each member of the sedan chair team, give 30 *wen* of copper cash; there are to be no more than three [such] persons.
7. Books cannot be borrowed for longer than half a month.
8. One cannot rely on others to return borrowed books.[71]

Unlike Cao Rong's pact, Ding and Huang's pact allowed each of them to borrow books and take them away but also specified that each must personally return the books he has borrowed (a rule doubtless facilitated by the proximity of their residences in Nanjing). Furthermore, it explicitly barred the participation of any other party; the fact that another Nanjing-based collector joined their pact within a year of its inception suggests that the main aim of this clause was to prevent any "free-rider" from enjoying these books, particularly if he had nothing to offer in return. In other words, any other participant had to commit himself to adhere to all the rules and responsibilities of the pact.

Yet, note what is missing from this pact. Written in 1654, it says nothing of politics, possibly because the early Qing government, in contrast to the late Ming government, had already outlawed political reading groups and thus reduced their number considerably.[72] The pact also mentions nothing of scholarship, although it (as well as many other types of late Ming pacts) ended up setting a model for the organization of the more collective scholarly efforts of the Qing world.[73]

Furthermore, so little of what we might expect to find in a book exchange pact passes without mention. How long is this pact expected to last (and how would one party be able to end it)? How do they choose their books (both collections had catalogues, but nothing is said of them)? How many books, and what kinds of books, can they borrow? Can the participants copy them? Each collector is to visit the other once a month and personally return the borrowed books within the next half-month. Yet, when does he return them — when the other party makes his next visit to his own house? If so, Ding would have had a borrowing period of just thirteen days and Huang of sixteen days, when the pact explicitly allows the borrowing to last for no more than half a month. How are we to make sense of this apparent inequality and violation of the pact? And, finally, what use will these collectors make, or be permitted to make, of the other's books? These details were perhaps considered small-minded concerns unworthy of generous men willing to initiate such a liberal exchange. Indeed, the visit is presented primarily as a social occasion, and the only fines mentioned are for failing to provide the set amount of food, not books.

In sum, these two collectors seem uninterested in practical or even scholarly uses of their books; they appear to be literati-bibliophiles, pure and simple, nurtured and appreciated by a late Ming literati culture that remained largely unaffected by a younger generation's calls for practical statecraft and textual and historical research. The late Ming ascendance of the imprint — its great multiplication of copies, its far lower prices, its extensive range of subjects, and the far larger size of its private book collections — encouraged some major book collectors, mainly in the lower Yangzi delta, to share their holdings with one another, despite their absence of kinship ties.

However novel and promising the use of written pacts may have been for book borrowing, none of them involved more than three persons. None seems to have led to any important collective writing or study, to an advance in learning, creativity, and possibly even the long-term transmission of these texts, or to the institutional innovation of a collectively owned library or library building (the modern notion of a public library, only hinted at in the discussions of the Confucian canon, was centuries away).[74] They thus are best seen as short-term ameliorations undertaken by coteries of literati bibliophiles faced with decidedly inadequate government libraries and often unwelcoming private libraries owned by people they did not know well enough to bother. Limited thus in scale and scope, these pacts have a historical significance that derives primarily from the simple fact that they existed in a world where a large and learned "community of learning," even in the late Ming, remained an ideal far divorced from reality. At best, we would have coteries of varying degrees of cohesion, their members enjoying different degrees of access for reading and borrowing books in any superior's or friend's collection. These coteries revolved around kin, friends, and other natives of the same locale, thereby helping to identify for us the limits to the notion of "the public" that was held and acted on by literate males in the late Ming for the sharing of their library and its learning.

Other Knowledge Bases

In addition to these "oligarchies of letters" so committed to the primacy of book learning, there co-existed a great variety of knowledge traditions that never reached the written or printed page and that did not derive their legitimacy mainly from an ancient text. The examples of such learning that come most readily to mind are perhaps the work practices transmitted by generations of artisans and peasants. In the late Ming, these bodies of practical knowledge interested some scholars and literati enough to prompt them to write books on long-novel topics ranging from gardening and cooking to weaponry and machinery. One particularly popular concern among educated men then was medicine, an interest that gave rise to the formation of the first medical association in Chinese history, The Benevolent Medical Association of Yiti Hall (*Yiti tangzhai renyihui*). Founded by the Huizhou doctor Xu Chunfu in c.1566 in Beijing, it obliged members to share and expand their medical knowledge together. Xu was dismayed that "the medical learning of the dynasty has been damaged by not meeting and lecturing, by not extending the search [for the causes of illness]." [75] Their principal topic of discussion, in addition to their study of the ancient medical classic, *The Yellow Emperor's Classic of Internal Medicine* (*Huangdi neijing*), was their study and experience as practitioners of medicine.

Although the sole surviving, incomplete record of this association includes neither its rules nor any account of its deliberations, a common interest in medicine seems to have mattered more to these men than the obligations of surname group, native place, and social station that, as already seen with scholarly book collectors, often divided Chinese from one another. For instance, the association's forty-six members as of 1568 came from eight provinces (only two were Beijing natives), bore thirty-two separate surnames, and included high court appointees as well as local county school students (many of them may well have been part-time amateurs rather than professionals).[76] And yet, they agreed as members to adopt mental attitudes, public practices, and private values that are commonly considered neo-Confucian: sincerity, study, benevolence, and unification with all of creation. Xu Chunfu warns them that the doctor who knows only medical texts is not as good as one who also knows the Confucian classics. In fact, he baldly states his distrust of doctors who do not read books and who base their knowledge solely on their experience. He has even fewer qualms about dismissing shamans as dangerous charlatans, not worthy of being spoken of on the same day as those like him, who are the heirs of medical knowledge from the ancient sages.[77]

Despite this streak of self-promotion, Xu places particular stress on the need for the members of the association to practice benevolence and reject self-interest:

> Medicine is a skill of benevolence. Sages write books, set up prescriptions, and save people from the pains of illness. When they wish to make benevolent men and gentle men know of [their discoveries], they carry out diligent study and clear examinations and then have [their learning] extended to those who do not understand. All this comes from the single-mindedness of a benevolent heart. If at first [this knowledge] is not set up for profit, then it will be passed on to later generations and men's minds will not become old. If they grow accustomed to pursuing profit, then in the end it will not be transmitted to later generations. It will perhaps for a time grow a bit, but it will be kept secret and will not be known by other men ... Some have weak points [in their practice of medicine], which they conceal to themselves and are embarrassed to be questioned about by others. They really fear to manifest the shallowness of their learning. To keep secret one's strong points is not benevolence, and even less is it benevolence to conceal one's weak points.[78]

Medical knowledge was to be spread through lectures and discussions in which sincere intentions, or honesty, were crucial.[79] Furthermore, the members of this association were expected to take on poor patients: "You especially must whole-heartedly give prescriptions to the poor and quickly relieve them of their pain. This is the basic work of one with a benevolent heart and benevolent skills." A member was to finance such charity work through extra high charges on his rich patients.[80]

This type of medical learning was clearly linked to the mastery of key medical texts, but it also derived its efficacy from experience. As such, its approach would, in the late Ming, be buttressed by a new type of learning, Western science. Introduced by Jesuit missionaries in the late sixteenth and seventeenth centuries, European knowledge of astronomy, mathematics, optics, physiognomy, artillery, and other natural science and technical fields helped to foster among some Chinese a greater interest in the material and natural sciences. The scholar Fang Yizhi (1611–71), for example, was, partly due to this Western learning, stimulated to extend the meaning of the *Great Learning*'s key phrase of *gewu* (i.e., investigate things) beyond the conventional neo-Confucian realm of human relations and moral principles to include material "things" not necessarily described in books.[81] For Xu Guangqi, a famous convert to Catholicism, an admirable feature of this Jesuit learning was its publicness (*gong*). Not only were the Jesuits generous in sharing their knowledge with others, but also their claims about the world were universally applicable and external.[82] Even if the Jesuits' presentation of Western science did not, in Jacques Gernet's view, "bear the mark of modern science or convey its spirit,"[83] it at least introduced an approach to the pursuit of scientific knowledge that was not primarily based on texts, even the Bible. In fact, this Western learning would be criticized by some Chinese for its divergence from the teachings written in their own Confucian classical texts.[84]

Longer-Term Solutions

In the Qing dynasty, these more hopeful trends of greater access to books and knowledge would initially represent just a sub-current. According to the great mid-Qing Suzhou bibliophile Huang Peilie (1763–1835), many of Suzhou's book collectors in the Kangxi (1662–1722) and Yongzheng (1723–35) reign eras, such as the Gus and Jiangs in Suzhou city, associated with literati and scholars, but "very deeply concealed their collections. Thus, few in the world knew that they were collectors."[85] Eventually, however, when efforts to open up the holdings of these and other important private libraries came to some fruition, it was due not only to their dispersal by heirs. The throne and its officials organized book-collecting projects that deprived the owners of their control over many rare editions that had entered their very exclusive private libraries formed during the late Ming and early Qing. More positively, the throne would be instrumental in the creation and institutionalization of government libraries open to all scholars. While some scholars would, in the late seventeenth century, still show interest in "reading the book without characters, the myriad things of heaven and earth,"[86] most scholars persisted in stressing the primacy of the text in Chinese learning. Their conviction would be nourished by the growing practice of some groups of Yangzi delta scholars to share their texts and debate their meaning in print. In fact, the emergence of the philological study of texts (known as the *kaozheng* school of learning) in the seventeenth century and its flourishing in the eighteenth century assumed a greatly improved access to texts and a wider dissemination of textual scholarship among scholars than in previous centuries. While the ordinary Qing reader was enjoying what Cynthia J. Brokaw has aptly described as not only a broader but also a deeper dissemination of texts in social as well as in geographic terms,[87] the Qing scholar was benefiting from greater dissemination of texts and their learning. Bibliography (*banben xue*) became, more than ever before, the core concern of not just the collector but also the committed scholar. And, if by the century's end ambitious students often could not acquire, even with money, current works explaining the classics, they still might purchase from book merchants several hundred *juan* of Song dynasty writings at prices that were "extremely cheap."[88]

This improvement in scholarly access was evident in four types of scholarly activity of the early and mid-Qing. Firstly, many Qing scholars liked to engage in extensive, far-flung correspondence with other scholars. In a society in which the circulation of scholarly letters functioned like the learned periodicals of contemporary Western Europe, the practice of letter writing enabled scholars to present their own ideas and information without great concern over government approval or its surveillance of the exchange. The most prolific scholarly practitioner of this art of letter writing was Qian Daxin (1728–1804), who, during his long life, exchanged letters with reportedly 2,000 friends and disciples, twice the number of Leibnitz's correspondents.[89] Some of the longer letters, as they probably did get shown around to other scholars, can be understood as scholarly articles in manuscript.

The second of these improvements involved the extension of the book-sharing practice that had been developed by late Ming scholars both as individuals and in groups. A bibliophile like Zhu Yizun succeeded, upon becoming an official, in gaining access to the Historiography Institute's collection. When dismissed from his Beijing position in 1684 for bringing a privately employed scribe into the Hanlin Academy Archives to transcribe official records for his private use, Zhu returned home to Jiaxing prefecture in the delta and soon won admission to at least seven of the delta's most important private libraries.[90] By gaining permission to transcribe rare works in all these collections, he built up a huge personal collection of over 80,000 *juan* and compiled a 300-*juan* survey of lost and extant copies of the texts of the Confucian classics (known as the *General Bibliography of the Classics* [*Jingyi kao*]).

By no later than the mid-eighteenth century, these individual practices blossomed into group exchanges. Whereas groups of scholars in the late Ming had most commonly favored the exchange of poems and formation of political associations, scholars of the mid-Qing liked to form and participate in scholarly reading and book-lending societies. In the city of Hangzhou, for instance, a group of not just two or three but seven bibliophiles shared their holdings with one another in a relatively informal manner. Meeting regularly and discussing their rare manuscripts and imprints, they let one another read, copy, and borrow their books. They wrote colophons for one another's books, collated variations in one another's different editions, and presented one another regularly with books to improve their libraries.[91] Such a practice was subsequently extended by at least one major private collector who, in late eighteenth- and early nineteenth-century Suzhou, began to open his library to visiting scholars and collectors he did not know and had not invited. While he continued to refuse to lend out his books, he made them available for inspection by these visitors in a reading room placed within his library.[92] We are thus not too far from the world of scholarship one encounters today in such private East Asian libraries as Seikadō bunko or even the reading rooms of ex-private libraries and smaller provincial libraries in China today.

The third and fourth types of scholarly activity were much more organized and, not surprisingly, involved official or even imperial support. The third type was evident in the over 150 editorial projects funded by the Qing Imperial Household during the first century and a half of the dynasty and especially by the Qianlong emperor (r. 1736–96).[93] The central goals of these activities may have been imperial acquisition, censorship, and preservation of written texts, but the process of text accumulation and editorial work unearthed and made known a great number of rare texts for the benefit of the scholars doing this editorial work. Although the scholars involved in the most famous of these compilation projects, the Four Treasuries, were eventually barred from copying and borrowing these texts, they were allowed, of course, to read the selected texts for their work; copies of some rare texts even leaked out into print.[94]

Then, from 1787, the government established rules far more supportive of text-based scholarship.[95] It allowed officials and literati with the appropriate credentials access to the entire body of texts in the copies of the Four Treasuries that were housed in specially built libraries in the three lower Yangzi Valley cities of Yangzhou, Zhenjiang, and Hangzhou. It also extended copying privileges to these same readers. This open-door policy, since it was supported by far more efficient library administration than in the Song and Ming, gives support to the claim of one knowledgeable twentieth-century Chinese scholar that, since the early nineteenth century, "there has been no scholar who did not partake of [the Four Treasuries'] riches or did not use it as a compass needle to find his way. Its accomplishments were great and its utility vast."[96]

Equally important for the growth of collaborative scholarship in the eighteenth century was official patronage. In the late Ming, as we have seen, wealthy officials and gentry had provided material support for one or two of their favorite scholars. In the mid-Qing, powerful official patrons, often provincial directors of education like Bi Yuan, Zhu Yun, and eventually Ruan Yuan, did so on a far grander scale. They used their official status, contacts, income, and other funds to support a series of editorial projects that employed hundreds of scholars and officials and that ended up publishing numerous influential editions of old books for scholars.[97] The ability of the state and private interests to form at least temporary institutional arrangements like these for collective scholarship suggests that the imbalance between private and public library interests so discernable in late Ming and early Qing China had been somewhat resolved by the late eighteenth century. This gain for scholars and scholarship in general, however, doubtless came at a cost to some private collectors and with the permanent loss of some books objectionable to the interests of the Qing ruling house.

Even then, the problems of book access and borrowing were not fully solved, particularly in scholars' interactions with one another. Many provincial students, as Alexander Woodside reminds us, lacked the wealth, connections, and leisure to acquire reliable copies of texts; the purchase of an adequate book collection was simply beyond their means.[98] Thus, in the early nineteenth century, a Hangzhou poet could still preface his poem, "A Poem on Borrowing Books," with comments that echoed the view expressed by Huang Zongxi a century and a half earlier: "Whenever book collectors acquire a rare book, they do not lightly show it to others. They transmit it to their descendants who never can completely protect it. Sometimes they keep it, but the rats harm it and the insects chew it. So, it will often end up incomplete."[99] By this date, the operative word in such a judgment may have become "rare" rather than "book." In fact, as the Suzhou bibliophile Huang Peilie suggests and as the Suzhou-born historian Gu Jiegang concludes, access to the holdings of the Four Treasuries appears to have rapidly transformed these once-rare volumes into "ordinary and commonly seen volumes." Private book collectors henceforth focused their energy and money on a fiercely competitive hunt for old editions, especially Song and Yuan imprints, and "those books not yet compiled into the Four Treasuries."[100] Thus, the overall improvement in access to scholarly books, especially to those in the care of the government, did not put an end to the intense sense of competition and the practice of exclusion among private book-collectors, even when they were old friends.

To sense the depth of such curatorial instincts, we have to do no more than consider the case of Huang Peilie himself. In four decades of actively collecting and selling books, Huang dealt with no fewer than thirty Suzhou collectors as well as some of his generation's most important textual scholars and book merchants. From them, as attested by a wealth of records, he regularly borrowed books, sometimes to copy and sometimes just to read.[101] Of this ensemble of eminent men, three were Huang's closest bibliophile friends, who, with him, formed, in the words of the title of their group portrait painted by the famous Hangzhou artist Chen Hongshou, "The Four Collecting Friends." With these men, Huang is said to have regularly shown, shared, and exchanged his books, as they did with him.[102]

Yet, when Huang purchased a Song imprint edition of the *Taiping yulan* (Imperial reader for the time of supreme peace) from one of these friends, the Suzhou collector Zhou Xizan, he locked away this huge encyclopedia and showed it to no one. Zhou himself had chosen to surrender ownership of this very rare edition of a well-known compendium, supposedly because he had become exhausted by the flood of requests to view it. Huang, pleading bibliomania, never unveiled it to Zhou or any other of his friends.[103] Likewise, Huang practiced prolonged restraint in making inquiries about the treasured books of others. Although he knew that the Suzhou collector Cheng Shiquan had acquired a Song imprint edition of the *Jianjie lu* (A record of injunctions), he was aware that this friend was unwilling to show it to others. Twenty years would have to pass before Huang asked to see it, and only after he had acquired enough cash to purchase it and not face the humiliation of a rejection (or the loss of Cheng's friendship).[104] The fact that these incidents — and they are not the only ones — occurred after the completion of the Four Treasuries project and the opening of its offshoot libraries in three Yangzi delta cities underlines the persistence of the problem of access to scholarly libraries. Is it any wonder that Mao Zedong is said to have acquired his deep hostility to Chinese scholars and their learning while he was working in the Beijing University Library?[105]

6 Literati Writings and the Case of Qian Jinren

The alert reader will have noticed that, over the course of this book, subtle changes have taken place in the type of reader under discussion. Whereas the first chapter considers woodblock imprints published for many types of readers, the second and third chapters deal largely with a variety of literati readers and writers, some far more concerned with entertainment than with scholarship. The fourth and fifth chapters narrow the range further, concentrating on scholarly book collectors and would-be scholars anxious to gain access to important collections of rare or valuable books. This contraction of the focus is accompanied by an emphasis on the difficulties that literati and scholars in the lower Yangzi delta had in acquiring books or even gaining access to them. Such obstacles persisted for these readers, until printed books became more numerous in the late Ming and until some important government and private collections became more accessible during the Qing.

And yet, the problems for the spread of literati learning and an expansion of its readership were far from solved. Some late Ming literati "descended to the market" to engage in commercial writing and publishing. The books they wrote and edited, regardless of whether they were put out by the government, a commercial house, or another type of private party, won a wider audience, drawing commoners, even artisans, "up" into the readership of what could loosely be called "literati writing." Even though these late Ming and Qing readers became familiar with a range of reading materials narrower than those discussed in the previous chapters, an expansion of literacy is, in the cautious judgment of the editors of a recent book on Qing education, "difficult to doubt."[1]

On the face of it, this increased literacy was expanding the readership for literati learning far beyond the ranks of the literati. Certainly, the literate would have encompassed some Buddhist monks, Daoist priests, military officers, boxing and fencing masters, medical men, geomancers, fortune-tellers, merchants, actors, private secretaries, clerks, schoolmasters, scribes, innkeepers, pettifoggers, shopkeepers, and artisan workshop heads.[2] Even moderately well-to-do tenants in the eastern stretches of the lower Yangzi delta had their sons learn how to read from as early as the middle of the twelfth century; the same skill was being acquired by the sons of "the small people in the countryside" there in the early seventeenth century.[3] In addition, some social and regional variations were recognized, such as that, in late imperial times, literacy was significantly more common among men than among women,[4] in south China than in north China,[5] and in cities than in villages.[6]

Yet, once an effort is made to quantify any of these categories with even a rough approximation, the concept of literacy becomes ever so nebulous and the analytical problems it poses to the social historian so troublesome. Chinese scholars have generally considered literacy to be the ability to recognize a certain number of characters.[7] But, they have sharply differed on the required number of these characters, some arguing for as few as 984 and others for over 3,000.[8] Furthermore, estimates of the literacy rate for adult males have varied so widely, from ten to forty-five percent and even higher,[9] that that one is forced to conclude that these figures are just "stabs in the dark" discussing and assessing quite different skills.

The concept of literacy, in other words, needs to be broken down into more useful categories. Helpfully, Evelyn Rawski and Wilt Idema have proposed different levels of literacy: the scarcely literate, the moderately literate, the fully literate, and the highly literate.[10] For the last two of these, Benjamin Elman has conceived the category of the classically literate, i.e., men with the ability to "read, explicate, and indeed memorize the canonical texts used in the civil-service examination system; and to write essays and poetry in classical style — whether or not they ever passed an examination."[11] In line with a figure suggested by F. W. Mote for Qing civil service examination candidates, Elman has proposed a roughly ten percent rate of classical literacy for adult males in Qing times.[12]

But estimates of literacy in Chinese need, as Rawski and others have recognized,[13] to go beyond designating these horizontally graded levels of competence and then adding up the share of the population with each of these skills. As the American missionary W.

A. P. Martin (1827–1916) observed, they also need to consider for written Chinese the co-existence of somewhat non-transferable functional literacies, each with its own distinctive characters and phrases and with its own distinctive meanings for shared characters and phrases:

> In the alphabetical vernaculars of the West the ability to read and write implies the ability to express one's thoughts by the pen, and to grasp the thoughts of others when so expressed. In Chinese, and especially in the classical or book language, it implies nothing of the sort. A shopkeeper may be able to write the numbers and keep accounts without being able to write anything else; and a lad who has attended school for several years will pronounce the characters of an ordinary book with faultless precision, yet not comprehend the meaning of a single sentence.[14]

Martin's observations were written in Beijing, but they were echoed for the southern province of Fujian by the English missionary Edward Joshua Dukes: "When I expressed to one of these [learned] men my surprise that he could not read a pamphlet which I had fairly well understood myself, he replied, 'How should I? I have never seen the book before!' "[15]

The ranks of the literate in China thus included not only a great number of busy, infirm, shortsighted, and unstudious men who had forgotten many of the characters they had learned in their youth. The ranks also included many adult readers who could not read the books written by other adult readers. Hence the great variation in Western estimates of "Chinese literacy" as well as the obstacles that David Johnson encountered in his far more sophisticated effort to quantify each of these functional types and levels of "literacy rate" and map with precision their social distribution among different communities of the empire.[16]

In place, then, of undertaking such a direct sociological analysis of the relation among different readerships, this chapter approaches the issue of literacy obliquely, by focusing on the question of what literacy, books, and book collecting meant to the literate and illiterate in the early and mid-Qing. It begins by reviewing common economic, moral, social, and religious perceptions of literacy, books, and book collecting, and then considers the extraordinary case of Qian Jinren. Introduced at the start of this book as the book-collector cobbler who was eventually buried at Tiger Hill, Qian had experiences as a reader and book collector that will easily seem marginal to the cultural concerns and activities of the literati and scholars of eighteenth-century Suzhou. Born into poverty and shortly afterwards orphaned, he learned to identify characters not from a teacher but from other readers paid for each character they taught him. He had access not to a school or private library but principally, through work, to books in Suzhou's bookstores, temples, and shrines. He thereby acquired a small collection of books and enough knowledge of the Confucian classics to impress a small group of Suzhou literati and scholars, such as Peng Shaosheng, Wang Jin, Wang Bing, and Xue Qifeng, with his love of learning. But, as we shall see in the last section of this chapter, Qian's use of his literacy ran counter not just to some widespread assumptions of his time but also to the far wider intellectual commitments of his literati admirers, particularly Peng Shaosheng. In the end, the case of this marginal figure will provide a useful, if indirect, way to examine the complex relations among the different levels and types of literacy in late imperial culture.

Perceptions of the Uses of Literacy and Books

The understandings of literacy and books that were current in late imperial China were largely positive. Admittedly, in the sixteenth century, some followers of Wang Yangming downplayed their significance for the necessary pursuit of sagehood, claiming that any man could become a sage and that to do so one need "just follow the way of 'ignorant men and women' who, without education, go about their daily tasks."[17] But by the seventeenth century, the influence of this Taizhou school of neo-Confucianism had largely receded, and throughout the eighteenth century, literacy and learning were once again appreciated and extolled widely, if not universally. Literacy and learning won favor not only for their cultivation of taste and discrimination but also, and probably more, for their improvement of a man's career chances, especially in the civil service examinations and official life. The successful candidates in these examinations could, in Samuel Johnson's memorable words, "smile with the wise and feed with the rich."

Over time, fewer and fewer of these educated men continued to think of success as limited to the examination hall. Despite the continuing allure of official life, the high failure rate in the examinations and the prospect of acquiring wealth through other careers persuaded many men to write of the usefulness of literacy outside of the study and the examination hall. Such expressions of literati appreciation of non-literati uses of literacy date to least the twelfth century, when Yuan Cai urged scholar-official families to educate their sons for non-official careers such as trade.[18] From the thirteenth century in north China and from no later than the seventeenth century in the lower Yangzi delta, some Confucian scholars developed a discourse that judged working for a living (*zhisheng*) to support one's family to have moral priority over reading books, particularly when an educated man could not gain an official appointment.[19] Although these scholars rarely specified the types of alternative employment they had in mind and their views represented a minor chord in the writing of the time, Ho Ping-ti has observed that many Qing scholars took on jobs "derogatory to [their] social status."[20] According to one Nanjing scholar at the close of the eighteenth century, financial hardship was driving nine-tenths of the scholars to live like commoners, working as merchants or clerks while concurrently retaining their degree.[21]

This linkage of literacy and commercial life eventually penetrated the rarefied world of rare book connoisseurship in the mid-Qing, when, for the first time, distinguished bibliophiles and collectors were operating as full-time dealers in the rare book trade. Huang Peilie, the influential collector, bibliographer, and book dealer discussed at the close of the previous chapter, is the most famous example; he opened his shop in 1825. Two other influential book men, Qian Tingmo (1750?–1802) and Qu Zhongrong (1769–1842), started dealerships in the vicinity of Tiger Hill in Suzhou. Towards the close of the eighteenth century, Qian Tingmo moved there from Huzhou to set up a rare-book store, elegantly called "The Study for Collecting Antiquities," which attracted many Suzhou literati and scholars.[22] In 1829, Qu Zhongrong, a well-known Changshu county book collector, also moved to Tiger Hill at the age of sixty to set up a dealership in books and antiquities in order to support his family.[23]

This increased penetration of the world of learning by commerce, of course, worked the other way as well. Just as literati engaged in commercial life, so did merchants and their family members engage in literati life and indulge in literati habits, such as

176 *A Social History of the Chinese Book*

collecting rare books. A few sons of merchants, including even a butcher's son, had become well-known collectors in the fourteenth century,[24] and merchants themselves (other than book dealers) became significant book collectors from the sixteenth century onwards, with the appearance of art and book lovers like Xiang Yuanbian. Yet, Xiang was the younger brother of a metropolitan degree-holder who shared his interest in collecting.[25] And so, the first significant book collectors in merchant families, outside of Huizhou and of the book trade itself, possibly date from as late as the Qing dynasty. Certainly, in Ye Ruibao's recent survey of Suzhou book collectors, the first collector labeled a merchant — that is, a merchant other than a book dealer, who, along with his family members lacked an examination degree — is Song Binwen (1690–1760).[26] This keen bibliophile, who, according to one account, engaged in the silver smelting business, substituted the traditional requirements for admission into élite bibliophile circles — a privileged education and/ or examination degrees — with his book collection and his book knowledge. Through purchase, he acquired a fine collection of handcopies of rare Song and Yuan editions of collected writings, and thereby developed a professional level of rare-book connoisseurship that won the admiration of literati and official collectors.[27]

This involvement of literacy and books with a wide range of knowledge outside of literati culture could in theory have forged more practical bodies of written and printed knowledge. Yet, such benefits and even the economic reasons for such literacy represent only a minor chord in the late imperial discussions we have of the benefits of literacy. Indeed, the most detailed such discussion, included in the seventeenth-century morality book, *Treasured Instructions on Examining the Mind (Xingxin baoxun*, pref. 1694), virtually neglects the economic benefits of literacy, to focus overwhelmingly on the moral and social benefits in ways typical of many other discussions of literacy.[28] Its simple style of composition indicates that it was written for intermediate readers like the inexperienced Qian Jinren, that is, moderately literate young males seeking far from complete classical literacy. The author takes care to address his remarks not to those too poor to study but instead to "those who could read but don't." To him, it is "as if they stand facing a blank wall, as if they recline with a covered head, and as if they go on a journey after extinguishing their candles. Their eyes are blind and their ears blocked. They are without knowledge and without learning." Such untalented men, "how can they be described together with Heaven, Earth and Man? I say, 'These men are hardly different from the birds and beasts'." Similarly harsh scorn falls on fathers and older brothers for not teaching their sons and younger brothers how to read.

To make clear the sharp moral and social distinctions between the literate and illiterate, this book details ten advantages of literacy and five disadvantages of illiteracy. Above all, it emphasizes the importance of acquiring a general literacy that enabled one to read books on morality. Such literacy is said to enable a person to understand morality and act morally ("those who do not know books often violate morality out of ignorance, while those who know books fear for their reputation and righteousness and so their violations of morality are few"). Literacy also improves a man's ability to reason clearly about moral principles and thus act morally ("those who read books do not turn their back on moral principle, while those who know books acknowledge obedience and seldom reject moral principle."). It teaches men how to control the movements of their body and thereby practice the proper etiquette and ritual that the illiterate cannot perform. It also teaches them shame, a sense of which marks "the difference between a gentleman and a petty man" ("the petty man does not know books and therefore he cherishes a mind without a sense of shame, while the gentleman knows books and has the capacity to perform acts that have a sense of shame"). And, it instills self-control, enabling a person to restrain his emotions and not show his joy or anger, regardless of whether he has been honored or disgraced.

This view of the moral benefits of literacy fits comfortably within the broad concerns and values of neo-Confucian thought, and derives primarily from the views espoused by the twelfth-century thinker Zhu Xi about learning. In arguing that book learning was crucial for "observing the intentions of the sages and worthies,"[29] Zhu had stressed the centrality of reading in attaining moral perfection: "In the Way of Studying nothing takes priority to the pursuit of moral principle, and the essence of moral principle invariably lies in reading books."[30]

The ability to read, according to the *Xingxin baoxun*, also conferred tangible social advantages that promised halcyon joys and blessings for the literate, the family, and the descendants, in five ways. Firstly, literacy leads to an increase of knowledge by letting one "check the past to judge the present"; the stories the book favors are the success-and-failure narratives that crowd Chinese books with strategies for gaining victory and avoiding defeat. Secondly, literacy is a means for securing posthumous fame. The written word preserves a person's reputation and record of accomplishments long after the bones have withered.

The three other practical benefits attributed to literacy are perhaps of greatest interest to us. For literacy, in this view, marks a person off from the vulgar, the stupid, and the unsuccessful. The distinctions it confers are more than moral and educational; they are social and visible:

> The appearance of those who do not know books is mean, their language base, their faces and eyes repulsive, so that they cannot be approached. As for those who read books, elegance will assemble on the peaks of their eyebrows, charm will come to life in the corner of their mouths, their spirits will be pure and standards elegant, so that one can really be intimate with them.

If that were not enough to win a young person over to literacy, then a fear of being stupid — or, worse, being considered stupid — should prove convincing:

> In dealing with friends, those who do not know books are afraid of everything and find it hard to practice tolerance. In verbal exchanges they are silent and make no reply. They have an earthen form and are a wooden doll; they are like a lump of a thing. Those who know books bow and give way and have a broad tolerance. In their social intercourse they show a sense of rank.

And, to crown it all, literacy will bring wealth and title (*fugui*). Ten years of hard work at reading will lead to success and fortune, give peace and pleasure, and bring honor to the kinsfolk and titles to the sons. Here the author appears to be referring to the consequences of examination success and an official career. But, overall, little is made of this practical goal and its rewards.

The advocacy of other practical and material dimensions of literacy is strengthened by the *Xingxin baoxun*'s listing of the dangers that literacy helps one avoid. Literacy helps assure that one's family will never lose the "family style" (*jiafeng*) of a wealthy and titled family. Learning will have a tradition, money will be transmitted, and copies of the classics will be read. Secondly, literate sons will escape quarreling about the care of their parents' food and clothing, thereby gaining rest for their own body and ease for their own mind. Literacy also will shield them from having to worry about food and clothing for themselves. It will give them numerous opportunities to learn from fine teachers and many schoolmates. And, it will let them have a quiet and secluded residence, set in a pure natural setting full of fresh and famous plants.

These practical moral and social reasons for becoming literate would lead to the moral order and social stability that Cynthia Brokaw has rightly judged to be a predominant theme in early Qing morality books.[31] *Xingxin baoxun* shares with these books, despite its appeal for the individual's moral transformation, a conservative rejection of social change and transformation. It insists that an individual's wealth, status, lifespan, and good fortune can all be ascribed to a fate that Heaven can change but — paradoxically and crucially — only after the individual has transformed his or her mind to know and accept the dictates of fate. Not surprisingly, in their appeal for greater literacy, these texts confirm the long-standing Chinese belief that the most literate men, the scholars, rightly held the highest social status, especially when they also attained government office.[32] Despite all the signs of the need for and reward of other types of literacy, many Chinese still linked literacy — i.e., classical literacy — to the study of the Confucian canon, the civil service examinations, and government office.[33] To adopt Donald Sutton's words about illiteracy, even moderate literacy in the classical language was "an index of social rank, a target of social snobbery ..."[34] A family might exempt half of its males from taking the exams for official appointment and have them work for a living.[35] But, in the words of an early Qing scholar from Suzhou, these males still had to be educated to read Confucian texts: "Even the stupid sons and grandsons must learn how to read the [Confucian] classics (*jingshu*)."[36]

This view was held with particular conviction by many commentators who survived the final decades of Ming misrule and the early decades of Qing order. To them, literacy — here we are talking about classical literacy — conferred moral benefits and a social distinction along some of the lines explicated by the *Xingxin baoxun*.

The late Ming Cantonese scholar-official Zhang Xuan wrote of literate men who wasted their literacy — "the number one means of a livelihood" — by "being content with being accustomed to the low-grade (*xialiu*)."[37] For the celebrated neo-Confucian thinker Liu Zongzhou (1578–1645) in Shaoxing prefecture, "the low grade of humans in the universe" was the carefree young men of his day who "are not fond of reading books."[38] A generation or two later, the Jiaxing scholar Lu Longqi (1630–93) wrote in strong terms to his sons: "I want you to read in order to understand the moral principles of the sages and to avoid being vulgar persons (*suren*). Reading books and being a man are not two [different] things."[39] His contemporary in Suzhou, Zhang Xikong warned, "Once the fragrance of books dies, the family's reputation will gradually fall into the base."[40]

Slightly later, a native of Hubei in the middle Yangzi Valley, Tu Tianxiang, added to the growing volume of scholarly concern by placing even stronger emphasis on literacy's role as a social marker:

> For a son or younger brother not to read books for one day is then to be close to petty men. How much more so if it goes on to the end of the year! Reading books cuts off the roots of being a petty man. Not reading books is on the way to being close to petty men. Moreover, if one reads books to the end of the year, then even if by chance one is close to petty men, still there will be days when one feels shame and regret [about what one is doing]. If to the end of the year one does not read, then one will daily be associating with petty men. One will fall into their ranks and not know it.[41]

For those who did not know which ranks of men were petty, a separate passage by this author made the identity clear: "In our family those who can read books are to be Confucian scholars and those who cannot are to work at agriculture. They are to be content with their station and practice self-discipline and thereby accept the aid of Heaven. They absolutely are not to hasten the censure of Heaven by having wild desires and violating their station."[42]

This exalted respect for literacy, the literate, and their elevated lifestyle was accompanied by a heightened respect for the printed book as a key signifier of this literacy and its social status. More often than in the Ming, families in the Qing were exhorted to retain their books in order to assure their survival as a scholarly family. It is as if the possession and accumulation of books were intended to relieve the anxiety that the heads of many official families rightly felt about their inability to prevent the decline and loss of their family's status. Even if the sons, as noted in Chapter 3, often ignored the father's appeals and sold off the books in order to preserve the family's living standard, the ideal of an old family library was certainly urged on readers by early Qing commentators like Zhao Minxian: "If for generation after generation the family does not make a break with the fragrance of books, then this will be a great good fortune for the family's status (*mendi*) and also be enough for it to become an old and hereditary family."[43] An arch neo-Confucian contemporary from Jiaxing prefecture, Zhang Lixiang, attributed to books even greater significance:

> The graves, the ancestral residence, the fields, and the books — these four the descendants are to guard. They are not to leave them even at the point of death. Such is what is meant by being a worthy. Invariably, when you have no choice, the fields can still be measured [for sale] and abandoned. But, the books definitely cannot be done without. Being without property merely means one is cold and hungry. Being without books means that one does not know righteousness and moral principles. How is one then different from the birds and the beasts?[44]

A century later, in a celebrated essay, the Suzhou bibliophile Sun Qingceng (1692–1767) called books "the greatest treasures of the empire." This district degree-holder, who eked out a living partly from the practice of medicine, reiterated Zhang's claim that their mere possession marked a man off from animals: "For one to have books is like a man's body having a soul (*xingling*). If a man does not have a soul, how then is he different from the birds and the beasts?"[45] What man, even a lowly artisan, could then ignore the moral and social significance of books?

This respect for books as a social and moral marker is complemented by a reverential, virtually religious, understanding of books as sacred objects that receives more attention in Qing sources than in those of earlier dynasties. Sun Qingceng, for example, develops his argument about the sacredness of books, to claim for them a role in the cosmological order: "If heaven and earth have no books, then how are they different from when at their beginning order had not yet been established?"[46] Among Qing scholarly circles, this religious impulse is most clearly evident in the high appreciation accorded ritual practices,[47] and particularly the ritual of a Suzhou book-collecting group centered on Huang Peilie. Aware that some literati had performed sacrifices to poems (*shi*) in the Tang dynasty and to ink in the 1650s, Huang decided to honor books in a similar manner.[48] On the last day of the year in 1801, 1803, 1805, 1811, 1816, and perhaps 1818, he carried out a sacrifice and rite of his own devising to honor rare books that he had specially arranged in one of his studies. The proceedings, called "[meetings to make] sacrifices to books" (*jishu, jishu zhi hui*), were attended by specially invited bibliophile friends, some of whom painted accounts of the ceremony.[49] Unfortunately, none of these descriptions is presently available, but it seems that Huang laid out his Song and Yuan woodblock editions as well as other important books in his collection. He then would offer some libation and food in their honor, the remnants being kept for a banquet held that night for his guests — all this done by a scholar-collector who would eventually open up his own bookstore in 1825 after dealing privately in books for many years.[50] The overall effect, it may be surmised, would have been a dignified ceremony not very different in spirit from the less formal versions of the better-known Japanese tea ceremony. In the Republican era, the ex-head of the Palace Museum, Fu Zengxiang (1873–1949), arguably China's greatest private book collector in modern times, is said to have carried on Huang's "sacrifice to books" with his own friends.[51]

As far as can be ascertained, these ritual activities garnered little attention in other Suzhou circles at the time. What instead caught the imagination and fired the passions of scholarly and commoner circles alike were two popular religious societies that promoted veneration of the written and printed word: the Cherishing Characters Associations (*xizi hui*) and the Wenchang cult. The practices of these associations can be traced to at least the sixth century, when educated Chinese were exhorted to show special care to books and any piece of paper bearing the name of a Confucian sage, a quotation from the Five Classics, or a Confucian commentary. By the mid-fifteenth century, scholars' respect for any paper with script had been designated a meritorious deed, and Ming scholars are sometimes described as collecting discarded scraps of used paper for cremation in special brick furnaces.[52] This essentially private custom of scholars, as Angela Ki Che Leung has perceptively argued, was transformed by no later than the last third of the seventeenth century into public acts that engaged scholars and others in the veneration of the written and printed word.[53] Cherishing Characters

Associations were formed initially in the Suzhou area and then grew popular throughout the Yangzi delta and the rest of the country. Their goal was to collect and then wash in water any scrap of paper their members found with Chinese characters, before burning it and placing the ashes into a ceramic container for release into a stream or the sea (see Figure 7).[54]

Figure 7   Paper Scrap Collector for Cherishing Characters Associations in Ningbo, in R. H. Cobbold, *Pictures of the Chinese, as Drawn by Themselves* (London: John Murray, 1860), p. 48

These associations in some cases had originally been formed by Buddhist monks in the early Qing and influenced by certain religious cults' handling of charms and religious texts.[55] Even these associations, however, soon came under the control and management of local Confucian scholars anxious to perform good deeds and thereby improve their chances and those of their descendants for success in the civil service examinations. Some associations took on a broader social agenda, such as helping to enforce government bans on lewd publications, destroy obscene woodblocks, and carry out acts of charity such as the provision of coffins and food to the needy.[56] Although these associations involved far more individuals of various social rankings than Huang Peilie's book-worship circle, they shared with the bibliophiles some cultural assumptions about writing and learning. In particular, they repeatedly elevated the scholars' use of paper — and by implication the scholars — over all other uses and statuses. Most vulnerable to these bouts of scholarly righteousness were artisans, as Cherishing Characters Associations wanted a general ban on artisan recycling of used paper for, among other things, candlewicks, umbrellas, fans, pottery, and shoes.[57] At least initially, when membership charges were not cheap, the poor and rich, whom some claimed could run these voluntary associations, clearly intended to include manual workers, like the cobbler Qian, mainly as their scrap collectors. Nonetheless, the practice of showing respect to writing spread widely both inside and outside of these associations. By the close of the nineteenth century, an "old China hand," well-traveled throughout the Qing empire, would observe: "... how scrupulously the Chinese of all classes abstain from desecrating or polluting manuscript or printed paper."[58]

The Cherishing Characters Associations were linked to a popular cult devoted to worshipping a deity thought to determine the outcome of the civil service examinations according to a candidate's accumulation of merits (such as from cherishing characters). Initiated in the Song dynasty and then banned as heterodox by the Ming government in 1488, this cult of the god Wenchang remained very popular with scholars, particularly examination candidates and their fathers. The god's focus of his powers on enabling success in the official examinations restricted his appeal mainly to students and officials, at least until the very late eighteenth or early nineteenth century.[59] In 1801, the god was accepted back into the orthodox imperial pantheon of gods, presumably because the cult's widespread popularity persuaded the government that co-opting it was safer than opposing it. By 1849, on the birthday of this god, "crowds of commoners (*zhongshu fenji*) in droves assembled" at one of his Suzhou shrines in order to burn incense and pay their respects.[60] Thus, by the end of the eighteenth century, scholars no longer had a monopoly on this god, who, in the nineteenth century, is even identified as the deity of commoner occupation groups associated with literacy, such as woodblock carvers and book merchants.[61]

This adoption of literacy as a personal goal and as a set of values by commoners involved in these religious activities suggests three conclusions. Firstly, while some Qing scholars and officials were anxious about the social instability fostered by "the status-changing nature of real literacy in imperial China,"[62] more sought to foster respect for literacy if only to promote orthodox Confucian values and to counter the allure of potentially troublesome religious cults. In addition to establishing and managing these Cherishing Characters Associations and Wenchang shrines, such gentry and scholars opened many charitable schools for commoners in the lower Yangzi delta.[63] Admittedly, the heirs of these donors often chose not to continue their father's charity; yet, such decisions were financial, not ideological. Secondly, the focus in virtually all these discussions of literacy and activities was on the individual and his family. The Wenchang cult and the book worship ritual are centered on scholars as a social group; but the concern of the first case is personal, not group, success, and that of the second is the scholarly book and bibliophile. No concern is expressed for any "imagined national community," the development of an empire-wide written culture, and even the written language as a means for engaging readers and writers into a public, let alone a national, consciousness. The reader, like the members of the Cherishing Characters Association and the Wenchang cult, is to think of his relation with past sages and not with other readers. The ties that might form among participants in these associations and cult could lead to their collective efforts to reform local customs, but nothing political is either intended or desired. Finally, there is no awareness of the impact that success in these efforts to promote literacy — such as the attainment of mass literacy — would have upon the written language and the social order. Such insight would, like nationalism itself, emerge only from the political tragedies of the nineteenth century and the cultural crises of the twentieth century.

Qian Jinren and His Benefactors

All these Qing social, economic, moral, and religious appreciations of literacy, books, and writing could, of course, be held and advocated by a single individual at the same time. What is striking, then, about Qian Jinren's understanding of his literacy and book collecting is how indifferent it was to the economic benefits and perhaps even social status changes that most Chinese expected from the acquisition of literacy. While some skepticism is perhaps warranted about the idealized depiction of Qian presented by our sources, it does seem that examination success, improved status, greater wealth, and a better job held little attraction to him. For forty to fifty years, he read and collected books and yet resolutely remained a shoe repairman. The job held no status: distinguished in Qing times from shoemaking and shoe-selling, the occupation of shoe repairing "was considered base by the masses."[64] Practitioners like Qian suffered demanding routines that kept them walking through neighborhoods in search of uncertain work and waiting to be hailed off the street to repair shoes on request.[65]

> The cobbler … goes his rounds from street to street and announces his presence with the rattle peculiar to his calling. He carries in his basket, on his back, all the implements necessary to this trade; a large piece of leather, more used in mending than in making shoes, a pair of uncouth scissors, a large knife, a stone on which to sharpen it, his wax, thread, needles, brad-awls, and the other implements necessary to his functions.[66]

The itinerant nature of Qian's work possibly explains why he seems never to have married and acquired a family of his own, despite his close identification with Confucian values, like filial piety, that assumed the centrality of family relations in the practice of a moral life.

And, the job paid little, far less than most other skilled work. According to a British visitor to Canton in c. 1870, a shoemaker's monthly wage — and I assume that a shoe repairman like Qian received no more and probably less — was just a third that of a first-class ivory carver's, three-quarters that of a blacksmith's, four-fifths that of a (house) painter's, and the same as that of a skilled embroiderer.[67] In short, he was just one step above the mass of unskilled laborers in status and pay.

Despite these social and economic disadvantages to his employment, Qian proved remarkably reluctant to use his literacy to find a better job or raise his station in life. He did some unspecified work for Suzhou bookstores and temples, and he sometimes responded to requests from neighborhood children, often as many as twenty or thirty, to teach them characters. But, he did so reluctantly, showing little interest in teaching permanently and less in earning an income from it (although he had paid character by character for his own education): "Qian did not ask them about the teaching fee … He did not supervise or punish them but merely held the post as teacher and that is all. Therefore, after a short time they would go away, and Qian practiced shoe repairing as before."[68] In stark contrast to Qian's persistent effort to divorce his learning from his job and source of income stands the more predictable decision of Qian's Suzhou contemporary, Cao Bing. Self-taught like Qian in the Confucian classics, "Cao was by nature simple and rustic. His feet never came into contact with the homes of the titled, and therefore no one in the world knew of him." Yet, Cao's reputed indifference to worldly success did not prevent him from giving up his family job in the clothing trade to pursue a career as a village teacher.[69]

Qian, in contrast, did not actively use his books and book learning to gain admission to higher social circles. He engaged in no book-sharing schemes, made no visits to family collections, took on no literary (*zi*) or personal (*hao*) names in the literati manner, held no parties to discuss his poetry or ideas, and appears not to have indulged in the literati practice of writing colophons into his books.[70] The public success he eventually enjoyed in the eyes of some Suzhou scholars was mainly of their making, not his.

Qian also was no bibliophile. Even though his name is regularly found in twentieth-century books on traditional book collectors, there is no evidence at all that he was a member of any eighteenth-century book-collecting circle or wished to be. He lacked the family pedigree, examination success, and wealth usually required for membership in these groups. Moreover, his book holdings were "tattered" (*po*),[71] consisting of "miscellaneous and old things" arranged disorderly on a white wooden board some three to four feet long, plus "many old books" (*duo gushu*) placed between the walls of his tiny room. Their total of just "10,000 *juan*" was large perhaps for a commoner collector but very small by the standards of the Suzhou collectors of his day. Also, they contained no old or notable edition we know of, except for a Yuan imprint edition of Su Shi's writings.[72]

And, Qian, as his otherwise admiring biographer Wang Jin recognized, was no "thinker":

> In reading books he roughly looked at their general meaning and never could delve into them deeply. But once words moved him, then he tirelessly retained them in his memory.[73]

In a similar vein, Qian's biographer for the prefectural gazetteer of Suzhou observed that Qian skimmed (*liulan*) through a large number of books in a wide range of genres.[74] His main book interests were conventional and orthodox: *The Analects*, the *Xiaojing*, and, less so, some unnamed Daoist writings. The first two texts in particular tended to be learned after a student had mastered one or more of the standard reading primers (though some educators in the Qing found the *Xiaojing* too simple and others found it too difficult for young readers).[75] Qian's Confucian reading seems to have stretched beyond such intermediate fare only tentatively, making him familiar with the oft-quoted twelfth-century neo-Confucian anthology, *Jinsi lu*. His choice of this canonical work of the increasingly rejected Song Learning tradition indicates a commitment to the orthodoxies of all things, the examination curriculum, and a disinterest in Han Learning, then the rage of Suzhou's scholarly circles.[76] In sum, he was learned about a few standard texts and their commentaries, capable of quoting passages from them and perhaps a few more. His functioning library was essentially his memory, and his learning remained that of a man who neither owned nor had access to many books. In the bookish world of eighteenth-century Suzhou, that meant that he would be considered neither learned nor perceptive enough about any of these books to merit plaudits as a "scholar."

Consequently, when Qian's literati admirers spoke of him as "unique (*du*)" and flatteringly called him a "scholar (*shi*)" or "a local scholar in retirement (*chushi*),"[77] what they meant was that he read books, pure and simple, and did not allow the economic concerns of his work to taint his efforts at moral cultivation through reading. They saw his books and literacy as his means to practice spiritual cultivation, to put him in touch with the sages, and to show reverence to their texts. Hence, he often made visits to "burn incense and worship solemnly" at the Suzhou shrine dedicated to Zhou Dunyi (1017–73), the Song founder of the neo-Confucian movement who had "recovered the Way that had not been transmitted since Mencius and passed it on to the brothers Cheng Hao (1032–85) and Cheng Yi [1033–1107]."[78] No wonder that men who saw no reason to admire Qian's book collection or scholarship — but were well aware of the debasement of scholarly ideals in their time — were moved to respect him. His commitment to Confucian learning was exceptional enough to make him an example to more than other artisans. The attention paid to him at his death was thus to honor not so much him as the moral values which he but no longer the typical scholar was seen to embody: diligence, honesty, respect for learning, and a single-minded commitment to reading.

When we examine the writings of Qian's Suzhou literati admirers, however, it is clear that their understandings of the benefits of books and literacy only imperfectly matched what we know of Qian's. Situated towards the opposite end of the social scale from Qian, they enjoyed a type of classical literacy both more comprehensive and intensive than that acquired by Qian. Likewise, their appreciation of literacy and books encompassed all the understandings of literacy and books that we have discussed so far. In their youth, they had studied for the examinations, some proceeding so far that they acquired the provincial or metropolitan degree. When, by middle-age, they had cast aside whatever hopes they had once entertained of a successful official career, men like Peng Shaosheng and Wang Jin stressed other appreciations of literacy than the economic and social, thereby expressing the eclectic nature of their intellectual interests. Along with Qian, they held books and writing in reverence. But, ironically, it was they rather than Qian who became strongly committed to and identified with Suzhou's popular Cherishing Characters Associations and its Wenchang cult for writing and learning. Their sympathy for Qian in his final days would thus derive not from a shared single-minded commitment to Confucian orthodoxies but from their many-sided intellectual commitments and their religious understanding of books and humanity.

Consider the case of the Cherishing Characters Associations. Qian made a living walking the streets of Suzhou but is never linked to any paper-collecting activity for a Cherishing Characters Association. Tattered books he collected for his library and not for burning. Yet, the family of Peng Shaosheng was for generations closely linked to the establishment and operation of such associations, arguably more so than any other Suzhou family over the course of the eighteenth century. His great-grandfather, Peng Dingqiu (1645–1719), wrote what is now the oldest extant essay on the activities suitable for a Cherishing Characters Association (it included a ban on the recycling of used-paper-with-writing for artisan production). The Peng family's devotion to "the cherishing of characters" remained so strong that, in the view of many Chinese, it justified the Yongzheng emperor's unexpected elevation of Peng Shaosheng's father, Peng Qifeng (1701–84), from tenth to top rank in the palace examination of 1727.[79] Later on, in the eighteenth century, Peng Shaosheng continued this family tradition by composing an essay to support the association's fundraising and by donating some fields to it:

> Characters (*zi*) are to give birth, that is to say, they create without limit. To create without limit is the intention of Heaven and is the Way of man. The making of characters is meant to correct virtue, communicate feelings, and in honoring the past look into the future. Therefore, nothing is better than characters for being able to make all under Heaven profit from fine benefits and yet not speak of that which profits. To treasure and cherish [characters] is the intention of Heaven and the Way of man. To destroy and abandon them defies the intention of Heaven and opposes the Way of man. It brings no benefit and does harm.[80]

Peng Shaosheng's insistence that all under Heaven share in the cherishing and creativity of writing was not for him and his family a patch of hollow rhetoric. His great-grandfather, Peng Dingqiu, had, after retiring from office, acquired in the early eighteenth century books of two Wuxi county collectors, the Gus and the Gaos, thereby initiating his family's interest in Confucian scholarship.[81] Peng Shaosheng's father, in the course of a very successful official career, saw to a greater dissemination of books by persuading the Qianlong emperor in 1740 to distribute copies of books recently collected and printed on imperial orders. More importantly, in 1773, he ran for a year an office set up by the court in Suzhou to persuade local collectors to lend rare books to the Qianlong emperor's Four Treasuries project, thereby acquiring over 1,800 titles for the emperor before his project manifested an interest in censorship.[82] And, Peng Shaosheng himself printed a wide variety of texts that he composed, edited, or compiled for distribution.[83]

The Pengs' promotion of literacy was evident also in their worship of the god Wenchang. Their support for this god of the examination-hall students dates to at least the mid-seventeenth century, when they made a major contribution to the reconstruction of a Wenchang shrine in Suzhou city. They again in 1752 made important contributions to the repairs of this shrine. In c. 1775, while denying the validity of Confucian fears that devotion to Wenchang was tainted by its Daoist origins and links, Peng Shaosheng recognized the generous favors that his family had received from this god.[84] Eventually, after the death of his wife and his father, in 1785 he took up permanent residence in the family-supported Wenchang shrine.[85] Wang Jin also showed an interest in the cult, writing an encouraging preface to the text most associated with its god.[86]

This interest of Peng Shaosheng and Wang Jin in not just the preservation but also the distribution of the written and printed word can be traced to their rejection of the academic and examination-linked Confucianism of their time. Both disliked the more narrow interpretations of Zhu Xi's orthodox commentaries used in the examinations. They also showed minimal interest in the Han Learning project then seeking to regain the original meaning of the Confucian classics by restoring their original texts. Instead, they preferred a far more eclectic and inclusive body of thought that blended Confucianism and Buddhism. While they recognized the validity of Zhu Xi's orthodox thought, they gave at least equal preference to the more internal and activist teachings of Wang Yangming. This blending of the two principal schools of neo-Confucian thought can, at least in Peng's case, be traced to the influence of the late Ming scholar-official Gao Panlong (1566–1620). As the teacher of Peng Shaosheng's great-grandfather, Gao had made creative use of Buddhist concepts such as emptiness and isolation that were current in late Ming scholarly circles. He also had supported the teachings of Zhu Xi against the "immoral excesses" of some followers of Wang Yangming. Peng Shaosheng's grandfather, in transmitting this expansive late Ming worldview into the far more empirical and secular intellectual circles of the Qing, earned for himself and his family a reputation for proficiency in Zhu Xi's learning and the activism of Wang Yangming's school.[87] The family continued to support Wang's insistence that moral principles could be found in the human mind and had to be enacted in actual life. Even when discussing the central text of the Wenchang cult, Peng denied any need to look "outside the mind" for the principles of filial piety and loyalty that, in his view, were espoused by this text.[88]

This more personal and internal reading of the Confucian classics was joined by an eclecticism that gave at least equal place to Buddhism. Peng had become interested in Buddhism ever since Wang Jin had discussed it with him in c. 1770. He particularly favored Pure Land Buddhism and its central text, the *Sutra of Infinite Life*

(Wuliang shou jing, aka the Larger Sukāvativyūha). While both surviving versions of this sutra urge all sentient beings to strive to be reborn in the Pure Land, the longer version — the one preferred and chosen by Peng for reprinting in 1775 — emphasizes the central role of good deeds and faith in Amidābha in any sentient being's attainment of enlightenment.[89] Here we have not only a set of beliefs similar to Wang Yingming's core teachings that all men can gain sagehood and that action, not just mental reflection, was essential for the moral life. We also have a social role laid out for Peng as a devout Buddhist layman acting on behalf of the needy and the suffering. Filial piety is basic but so is kindness *(ci).* The resulting openness to the suffering of others is underlined in this sutra's espousal of equality *(pingdeng)* among all sentient beings, both in the intellectual disregard for the conventional distinctions between the mind, Buddhahood, and the mass of sentient beings and in the widespread distribution of the joys of the Pure Land. In 1775, Peng printed his own views of this sutra in two writings that lay out his belief that salvation for all beings lay in compassionate action.[90]

Wang Jin's path to similar views was neither as family based nor as linked to past traditions. His generation was just the third of his family to live in Suzhou, and his father's early death impoverished him, his mother, and his younger brother (for years he was too poor to hire others to copy books).[91] After a particularly slow start at learning to read and memorize, his studies, and especially his proficiency at writing, launched him on a promising career as a Suzhou literatus. But, his efforts to become an official ended mainly in failure, five failures to acquire the provincial degree. His profession of his commitment to writing came in a self-description: "One manifests the Way [or the dharma] by relying on writing *(yinwen jiandao).*"[92] Like Peng, he considered Buddhism and Confucianism closely related bodies of thought, so much so that for him the main route to the Pure Land was the practice of filial piety, and the Buddha was identified with the mind.[93] His faith in Amidābha eventually made him a more pious believer than Peng in Pure Land Buddhism and its *Sutra of Infinite Life.* To him, all sentient beings were originally Buddhas and should regard the Pure Land as their destination.[94] Such inclusiveness is not given an explicit social dimension in Wang's writings, but it suggests an openness that would explain his willingness to write a biography honoring a man he did not know but thought gave meaning to "the manifestation of the Way [Dharma?] through writing."

This range of Confucian and Buddhist sympathies helps to explain the support given to Qian by his literati admirers in his final days. Certainly, the surviving Chinese accounts, even though they disagree about the condition of Qian at the time he was rescued, do stress the care and concern shown to the enfeebled Qian by others. Peng Shaosheng and another of his friends, Xue Qifeng, we read, had spoken often of Qian's admirable qualities to their friends, like the Confucian doctor Wang Bing. So, when Qian was forced by his ulcerous feet to stop working (or was felled by hunger in a famine), Wang Bing won the approval of the other male members of his family to "summon Qian to their house where they treated him with very great courtesy. They then moved him and his books to reside and grow old in their home," under the tireless care of this medical family.[95]

The removal of Qian's books into the Wangs' home, along with their ailing owner, points to the central role that books in general played in the formation of a common ground for Qian and his literati admirers. Peng Shaosheng had suffered the loss of one eye at an early age, Wang Jin been a slow learner until his late teens, Wang Bing had been repeatedly frustrated by disappointments in the examination hall, and Qian Jinren had to overcome poverty and family indifference just to learn his characters.[96] Their sufferings and sacrifices on the way to gaining literacy, whatever its level and type, in no way removed their separate commitments to these books and their awe at what these texts of the Confucian sages and worthies had to teach them for life. These books they revered as sacred receptacles of a moral wisdom that benefited all those who read them.

Yet, it is important to recognize that the Confucian and Buddhist commitments of Qian's admirers had led them to essentially a much more inclusive and learned appreciation of literacy, the book, and learning than that held by Qian. The gap between Qian and these men is perhaps represented by the limited nature of their social interaction. Some of these admirers spoke to Qian only after he had moved into the Wangs' home; others, when they met him, did not converse. Wang Jin himself confessed that he wrote Qian's biography but had seen him only once and had never spoken to him at all. Also, those Suzhou scholars who did speak to him and visit him — such as

Peng Shaosheng and Xue Qifeng — are said, by Suzhou's prefectural gazetteer of 1883, to "have humbled themselves (*zhejie*) to have an association with Qian,"[97] hardly a sign of strong interest and friendship.

Thus, even if Wang Bing did remove an elderly Qian bedded by his ulcerous feet from his room, his rescue of Qian to the Wang family's home was an act of charity, not a sign of this family's acceptance of Qian as a social equal or an expression of interest in his learning. Qian's admission into the ranks of Suzhou's scholars and literati would come only with his death, when he was laid to rest in the literati earth of Tiger Hill on the outskirts of Suzhou. This burial as a scholar may have crowned his life, assuring Qian's reputation of far greater symbolic power in the future than it had enjoyed in his lifetime. But, it cannot be understood as a confirmation of the existence of a social and cultural unity that wove these different types of literacy into a widely shared understanding of literacy and integrated them into a common commitment to book culture. The history of literate men, their literacies and the book in late imperial China was far too complicated and unpredictable to allow for such a boring "happy ending."

Notes

Introduction

1   Wang Jin, *Wang Ziwen lu* (Records of Wang Jin) (XXSKQS ed.), 10.5a–6a; Zhao Erxun, et al., *Qing shi gao* (Draft standard history of the Qing) (Beijing: Zhonghua shuju, 1976–77), 502, pp. 13,882; He Shixi, *Zhongguo lidai yijia chuanlu* (Biographical records of doctors in Chinese history) (Beijing: Renmin weisheng chubanshe, 1991), v. 1, pp. 22–3; and Xu Weixin, "Huqiu you zuoxiejiang mu (Tiger Hill has the grave of a cobbler)," pp. 95–6, in Xu Gangyi, *Qili shantang* (The two-mile-long Mountain Embankment) (Shanghai: Guji, 2003), pp. 95–6.

2   Lu Zhao and Ren Zhaolin, comp., *Hufu zhi* (Gazetteer of Tiger Hill) (1792) (Suzhou: Gu Su xuan chubanshe, 1995), 3, p. 260; most of these charitable graveyards were set up between 1735 and 1743.

3   *Suzhou fuzhi* (Gazetteer of Suzhou Prefecture) (1883), 89.14b–15a; and Xu Gangyi, pp. 95–6.

4   Inoue Susumu, "Zōsho to dokusho (Book collecting and book reading)," *Tōhō gakuhō* (Journal of Oriental Studies) 62 (1990), pp. 425–6.

5   Paul J. Smith, "Family, *Landsmänn*, and Status-Group Affinity in Refugee Mobility Strategies: The Mongol Invasions and the Diaspora of Sichuanese Elites, 1230–1330," *Harvard Journal of Asiatic Studies* 52.2 (1992), pp. 668–72.

6   This topic is well treated in Lucille Chia, *Printing for Profit, The Commercial Publishers of Jianyang, Fujian (11th–17th Centuries)* (Cambridge, MA: Harvard University Asian Center, 2002).

7   In sharp contrast to Jianyang, the lower Yangzi delta could boast of an exceptionally large number of major book collectors, as evident in the numerous recent accounts of Chinese book collectors (e.g., the entries on major Song, Yuan, and Ming collectors in Li Yu'an and Chen Chuanyi, comp., *Zhongguo cangshujia cidian* [Dictionary of Chinese book collectors] [Wuhan: Hubei jiaoyu chubanshe, 1989]).

Chapter 1

1   Zhang Shudong, comp., *Zhang Xiumin yinshua lunwen ji* (Collected essays of Zhang Xiumin on publishing) (Beijing: Yinshua gongye chubanshe, 1988), p. 55.

2   Timothy H. Barrett, "Woodblock Dyeing and Printing: The Innovations of Ms. Liu and Other Evidence," *Bulletin of the School of Oriental and African Studies* 64.2 (June 2001), pp. 240–7. In the West, as Thomas Hobbes observed, such ignorance cloaks the person(s) who invented our alphabet: "The Invention of Printing, though ingenious, compared with the invention of letters, is no great matter. But who was the first that found the use of Letters, is not known" (David McKitterick, *Print, Manuscript and the Search for Order, 1450–1830* [Cambridge: Cambridge University Press, 2003], p. 17).

3   Francis Bacon, *Novum Organum, with Other Parts of the Great Instauration*, trans. and ed. by Peter Urbach and John Gibson (Chicago and La Salle, IL: Open Court, 1994), Bk. 1, aphorism 129, p. 131.

4   Shen Kuo, *Mengxi bitan* (Notes of Shen Kuo) (Hong Kong: Zhonghua shuju, 1975), 18, p. 184; and Ye Mengde, *Shilin yanyu* (Chatter from Ye Mengde) (CSJC ed.), 8, p. 74.

5   Zhang Zexian, *Tangdai gongshang ye* (Industry and commerce in the Tang dynasty) (Beijing: Zhongguo shehui kexue chubanshe, 1995), pp. 201–3; and Seo Tatsuhiko, "Tōdai Chōan toshi no insatsugyō (The publishing industry in Chang'an's Eastern Market in the Tang dynasty)," pp. 200–38, in Tōdai kenkyūkai hokoku shū, *Higashi Ajiashi ni okeru kokka to chiiki* (State and regions in East Asia) (Tokyo: Tōsui shobō, 1999), provides a careful summary of the evidence, both textual and material, on Tang printing, especially in Chang'an. This fine study is now available in English, under the title given above, in *Memoirs of the Tōyō Bunko* (2004), pp. 1–42.

6   Zhang Xiumin, *Zhongguo yinshua shi* (A history of publishing in China) (Shanghai: Renmin chubanshe, 1989), pp. 13–4, 21–2.

7   Li Zhizhong, Zhou Shaochuan, and Zhang Dazao, comp., *Dianchi zhi* (An account of old books) (Shanghai: Renmin chubanshe, 1998; v. 8 of the *Yiwen* set within the 100-volume series *Zhonghua wenhua tongzhi* [Comprehensive account of Chinese culture), pp. 226–7.

8   Tsien, Tsuen-hsuin, *Paper and Printing*, in the series of Joseph Needham, *Science and Civilisation*, v. 5, *Chemistry and Chemical Technology*, pt. I (Cambridge: Cambridge University Press, 1985) [hereafter Tsien], p.149.

9   Timothy H. Barrett, *The Rise and Spread of Printing: A New Account of Religious Factors* (London: School of Oriental and African Studies, University of London, Working Papers in the Study of Religions, 2001), esp. p. 11.

10 Seo, pp. 228–31.

11 Denis Twitchett, *Printing and Publishing in Medieval China* (London: The Wynkyn de Worde Society, 1983), pp. 13–22; and Tsien, pp. 146–54.

12 Tsien, pp. 194–5. Also, Jean-Pierre Drège, "Des effets de l'imprimerie en Chine sous la dynastie des Song," *Journal Asiatique* 282.2 (1994), pp. 409–42, esp. 415, describes this 1947 interview as the first and only detailed discussion of woodblock book production methods in Chinese.

13 Tsien Tsuen-Hsuin (Qian Cunxun), "Zhongguo diaoban yinshua jishu zatan (Miscellaneous talk on the craft of woodblock printing in China)," pp. 139–52, in his *Zhongguo shuji zhimo ji yinshua shi lunwen ji* (Collected essays on Chinese books and publishing history) (Hong Kong: Xianggang zhongwen daxue chubanshe, 1992). A film recently made at Dege Buddist Temple in present Ganzi Tibetan Autonomus Prefecture in western Sichuan Province shows the traditional carving methods used in the past to make 270,000 woodblocks for the Tibetan Buddhist canon (Jun'ichi Nakanishi, "The Dege Printing House and the Local People Who Support It: Hand Printing the Buddhist Canon from Woodblocks," *The Toyota Foundation Occasional Report* 31 [August 2001], pp. 3–6).

14 Ye Shusheng and Yu Minhui, *Ming Qing Jiangnan siren keshu shilüe* (A short history of the private printing of books in Jiangnan in the Ming and Qing) (Hefei: Anhui daxue chubanshe, 2000).

15 Zhao Yushi, *Bintui lu* (Records after the guest has left) (Shanghai: Guji, 1983), 4, p. 44; and, Shen Kuo, 18, p. 178.

16 I.e., Zhang Yanyuan in his *Lidai minghua ji* (Record of famous paintings over the ages) (Robert van Gulik, *Chinese Pictorial Art, as Viewed by the Connoisseur* [Rome: Instituto Italiano per il Medio Estremo Oriente, 1958], pp. 148–ff); and Edward Martinique, *Traditional Chinese Binding* (San Francisco, CA: Chinese Materials Center, 1983), p. 29.

17 Klaas Ruitenbeek, *Carpentry and Building in Late Imperial China: Lu Ban jing, a Study of the Fifteenth-Century Carpenter's Manual* (Leiden: E.J. Brill, 1993), pp. 25–6, 31–2, and 134; also Joseph Needham, *Science and Civilisation in China*, v. 4, *Physics and Physical Engineering*, pt. 3, *Civil Engineering and Nautics* (Cambridge: Cambridge University Press, 1971), pp. 81–4, 128 and 141; and Shen Kuo, 18, p. 177.

18 Su Yijian, *Wenfang sipu* (Four guides on the scholar's study) (CSJC ed.), 4, pp. 52–4; and Sung Ying-hsing, *T'ien-kung k'ai-wu, Chinese Technology in the Seventeenth Century*, trans. E-tu Zen Sun and Shiou-chuan Sun (University Park, PA: The Pennsylvania State University Press, 1966), pp. 223–32.

19 Shen Kuo, 18, p. 184; and, Tsien, pp. 201–11, introduces these sources effectively. See also R.C. Rudolph, *A Chinese Printing Manual, 1776* (Los Angeles, CA: Typophiles, 1954), for a translation of an eighteenth-century Chinese account of making wooden moveable-type for the

imperial court. The survival of such records helps to explain why Chinese accounts of Chinese book technology focus overwhelmingly on the kind of Chinese printing, moveable type, that was least important for virtually all of China's printing history.

20   Li Dengzhai, *Changtan conglu* (A comprehensive record of regular talk) (Weijing tang ed.), 1.13a–b.

21   Bacon, p. 114.

22   William Milne, *A Retrospect of the First Ten Years of the Protestant Mission to China* (Malacca: Anglo-Chinese Press, 1820), pp. 222–87, consisting of Section XVII. On p. 254, Milne says he is writing this passage in 1819; the entire section, however, would not be finished (and published) until 1820 (Robert Morrison, comp., *Memoirs of the Rev. William Milne, D.D.* [Malacca: Mission Press, 1824], p. 85). In the early fourteenth century, the Persian scholar official Rashid-eddin gave an account of Chinese printing, but it is far less detailed than Milne's on technical and economic matters (Edward G. Browne, *A History of Persian Literature Under Tartar Dominion (A.D. 1265–1502)* [Cambridge: Cambridge University Press, 1920], pp. 102–3. About three centuries later, Matteo Ricci wrote a similarly brief account of Chinese printing, one that nowadays is often used by scholars (*China in the Sixteenth Century: The Journals of Matthew Ricci: 1583–1610*, trans. Louis J. Gallagher [New York: Random House, 1942, 1953], pp. 20–1). Tsien's recent accounts in "Zhongguo diaoban" and Tsien, pp. 194–251, are clearly more detailed and informative.

23   Jean-Pierre Drège, "Les aventures de la typographie et les missionnaires protestants en Chine au XIXe siècle," *Journal Asiatique* 280 (1992), pp. 279–305; and "Poirier et Jujubier: La Technique de la Xylographie en Chine," pp. 85–93, in Frédéric Barbier, et al., eds., *Le livre et l'historien: Etudes offertes en l'honneur du Professeur Henri–Jean Martin* (Genèva: Librairie Droz, 1997).

24   Richard Lovett, *The History of the London Missionary Society, 1795–1895* (London: Henry Frowde, 1899), v. 2, p. 431. He also was frustrated by the profusion of dialects: "... when going among the people, in one house the chief part of what was said was understood; in the next, perhaps a half; and in a third not more than a few sentences. In addressing a small company of fifteen or twenty persons, a knowledge of two dialects is in many instances necessary in order to impart instruction with effect to all" (Robert Philip, *The Life and Opinions of the Reverend William Milne, D.D* [London: John Snow, 1840], p. 206).

25   Morrison, pp. 41–2 and 44–5.

26   A. Wylie, *Memorials of Protestant Missionaries to the Chinese: Giving a List of Their Publications, and Obituary Notices of the Deceased* (Shanghai: American Presbyterian Mission Press, 1867; reprt. Taipei: Chengwen Publishing Co., 1967), pp. 12–3. For whatever reason, Milne's biography in the

Dictionary of National Biography (London: Smith and Elder, 1899), v. 38, p. 9, mentions only his work as a shepherd. His own autobiographical memoirs simply refer to this work as service to a family.

27 Philip, p. 264; and Milne, p. 140. The printing workers included the Cantonese Leang A-fa (aka Liang Afa) (1789–1855), who was better known to Westerners as Milne's first convert (Lovett, v. 2, p. 434); his second convert was an assistant of Leang, Kew-Agang (ibid., v. 2, pp. 426–7). Milne also brought from Canton some printing paper and a Chinese language teacher (Milne, p. 140).

28 Wylie, pp. 25, 44. Cecil K. Byrd, *Early Printing in the Straits Settlements, 1806–1858* (Singapore: Singapore National Library, 1970), provides a brief but fascinating account of the early activities of the mission-run Anglo-Chinese Press. Within three months of his arrival in Malacca in 1815, Milne had established this press and printed up its first publication, a periodical. Like most of this press's subsequent publications up to 1842, it was in Chinese and done by woodblock, even though from November 1816 the press also had a printing press recently arrived from Bengal. In June the following year, Medhurst arrived in Malacca and assumed the post of superintendent of all the press's operations (ibid, pp. 9–13).

29 Ching Su, The Printing Presses of the London Missionary Society Among the Chinese (University of London, University College, Ph.D dissertation, 1996), pp. 51 and 119. Milne even had his children study how to read the Chinese language every day (Morrison, p. 116) and had his catechism schools teach the children how to bow in the Chinese manner to their superiors, parents, teachers, and one another (Philip, p. 191). Yet, his own writings show him far from being a blind sinophile (e.g., Milne, p. 280).

30 Ibid, p. 239.

31 Ishii Kendō, *Nishikie no hori to suri* (Tokyo: Geisodō, 1994 reprint of the 1929 original). This book, as the title suggests, is concerned primarily with woodblock illustrations; yet the techniques it describes are, but for the absence of the scribal work, those used for carving and printing from woodblocks. It mentions two earlier Japanese accounts of these techniques: a volume (*ce*) in *[Nihon] Seihin zusetsu* (Pictures and descriptions of Japanese products) (compiled by Ko Eiichi and first printed in 1877) and a brief account in *Bungei ruisan* (Literary arts) (compiled by Sakakibara Yoshino and first printed in 1878) (ibid, p. 2). Both of these texts are of considerable interest but provide far less concrete detail and instruction than Ishii's work, which merits a translation into English in the near future. It should be added that the earliest Chinese illustration of woodblock printing — that is, carving, printing, and binding — that I have found is in the apparently Qing imprint, *Yinzhi wentu zhu* (as reproduced in Luo Shubao, comp.,

Zhongguo gudai yinshua shi tuce [trans. by Chan Sin-wai as *An Illustrated History of Printing in Ancient China*] [Hong Kong: City University of Hong Kong Press, and Beijing: Wenwu, 1998], p. 57).

32 Milne, pp. 223–4. One is tempted to think that this method is linked to the millennia-old, pre-paper practice of writing on strips of bamboo and other kinds of wood.

33 Ibid., p. 223; and Zhang Xiumin, pp. 566–7. William C. Hunter, *Bits of Old China* (London: Kegan, Paul, Trench, and Co., 1885), p. 216, tells of their use, announced by street criers, for every kind of news but political criticism. As elsewhere, he here is writing about mid-nineteenth-century Canton. Roswell Sessoms Britton, *The Chinese Periodical Press, 1800–1912* (Shanghai: Kelly and Walsh, 1933), pp. 4–5, aptly observes of this technique, "Time and cost were saved at the expense of legibility and good appearance."

34 Milne, p. 223.

35 Milne, p. 226. Hunter, p. 213, confirms the preference for pear wood due to "the evenness of its texture and fibre."

36 Ibid., pp. 227–8.

37 Ibid., p. 246.

38 Ibid., pp. 226 and 227.

39 Tsien, pp. 196–200, gives instructive details on the tools and ways to use them. Hunter, p. 214, mentions the use of "a delicate sharp pointed instrument of a triangular form." See also Eugene Cooper, *The Wood-carvers of Hong Kong, Craft Production in the World Capitalist Periphery* (Cambridge: Cambridge University Press, 1980), pp. 36–41, which has interesting comments on carvers' tools. Unfortunately, no knife used for carving woodblocks in the Ming is known to be extant today, but recently made examples survive from Huizhou in Anhui Province and Yangzhou in Jiangsu Province (Miao Yonghe, *Mingdai chuban shi* [A history of Ming publishing] [Nanjing: Jiangsu renmin, 2000], p. 303).

40 William Henry Medhurst, *China: Its State and Prospects, with especial reference to the spread of the gospel* (London: John Snow, 1838), pp. 104–5.

41 The eighteenth-century Jesuit missionary P. du Halde's far more detailed comments on the printer's use of his brushes deserve mention here: "… they have two Brushes, one harder than the other, which are held in the Hand, and which may be used at both ends of the Handles; they dip one a little in the Ink, and rub the Plate with it, but so that it may not be too much nor too little moisten'd; if it was too much, the Letters would be blotch'd; if too little the characters would not print: when the Plate is once in order they can print three or four Sheets without dipping the Brush in the Ink.

The other Brush must pass gently over the Paper, pressing it down a little that it may take up the Ink; this is easily done, because not being dipt in Allum it quickly imbibes it: You must pass the Brush over the

Sheet more or fewer times and press upon it accordingly as there is more or less in upon the Plate; this Brush must be oblong and soft" (P. du Halde, *The General History of China* [London: J. Watts, 1741, 3rd ed.], v. 2, pp. 436–7). The firm brush, according to Hunter, p. 214, is "made of the fibre of cocoa-nut or other wood."

42 Milne, p. 228. Hunter, p. 214, has the printing finished by a specialist writer who brushes onto the foot of each bound volume its title and, if more than one volume, its number. Often, however, the title was written on the volume's cover.

43 Ibid., pp. 228–9. By the Song, all four stages of production and their specialist artisans were specifically identified (Zhang Xiumin, p. 731).

44 Su Ching, p. 108.

45 Yang Shengxin, "Cong *Jisha cang* keyin kan Song Yuan yinshua gongren de jige wenti (From the perspective of printing the *Jisha cang* Buddhist canon, looking at several issues related to Song and Yuan printing workers)," *Zhonghua wenshi luncong* (Collected essays on Chinese literature and history) 1984.1, pp. 41–58, esp. 45–7; and Zhang Xiumin, p. 734 (which also mentions that Buddhist monks were often the carvers of Buddhist sutra woodblocks).

46 Milne, pp. 123 and 252.

47 Ibid., p. 258.

48 The same problem, however, afflicted early nineteenth-century type fonts, as one 1833 advocate of moveable-type printing, Samuel Dyer, admitted: "But [as] successful as our late experiment has proved, there is one serious difficulty attending it; a font in continual use may last, say five or seven years, and then it must be recast; now the difficulty and expense of procuring a new font every seven years, is very great, unless we had the means of casting them in India" (*Chinese Repository*, v. 1 [1833], p. 417).

49 Milne, p. 241.

50 Ibid., pp. 241–2. Up until the end of 1819, Milne's own thirteen titles in Chinese had achieved woodblock runs of from 1,900 to 9,000; his earliest publication, of 1816, in its first print run, had 5,800 copies by 1820. Milne's figures for his publications show first impressions ranging between 700 and 6,000 (this largest run dealt with the evils of gambling) (ibid., pp. 269–71).

51 *Chinese Repository*, v. 14 (1845), p. 129. This piece seems to have been written by Medhurst.

52 The size of Western European imprint runs — estimated at 500 copies in the fifteenth century, 600 in the sixteenth century, and 1,200 to 1,800 for French language books in the seventeenth century — may thus have been considerably smaller than in China, where publishers had to balance harshly contending pressures: "The need to reduce unit costs obviously required a printing run large enough

to be able to spread the fixed expenses—in particular, those for the composition of the text and the engraving of the illustrations—over a large number of copies. Nevertheless, it was important not to print too many copies, thereby tying up for too long a time the capital needed for the purchase of paper, which represented an important expenditure" (Henri-Jean Martin, *The French Book, Religion, Absolutism, and Readership, 1585–1715* [Baltimore, MD: The Johns Hopkins University Press, 1996], p. 3). Quite likely, Chinese printing pressures, thanks to the reliance on woodblocks, were less risky.

53 On the basis of his short stays in Canton and Macao, Milne claims that Chinese "moveable types are commonly made of *wood*. The Canton daily paper called *Yuen-mun-pao* (i.e., A report from the outer gate of the palace,) containing about 500 words, or monosyllables, is printed with these wooden types; but in so clumsy a manner as to be scarcely legible" (Milne, p. 224). He also reports, "With respect to moveable type, the body of the type being prepared, the character is written *inverted*, on the top; this is more difficult work than to write for blocks. After this, the type is fixed in a mortise, by means of two small pieces of wood, joined together by a wedge, and then engraved; after which it is taken out, and the face lightly drawn across a whetstone, to take off any rough edge that the carving instrument may have left" (ibid., p. 226). For a more comprehensive account, including the very scant information on Bi Sheng, see Tsien, pp. 201–22.

54 Yuan Yi, "Qingdai de shuji jiaoyi ji shujia kao (On the book trade and book prices in the Qing dynasty)," *Sichuan tushuguan xuebao* (Journal of Sichuan Library) 1992.1, pp. 73–4. I am grateful to Cynthia J. Brokaw for this reference. Also, the early nineteenth-century American visitor to Canton, W. W. Wood, observed, "The price of books is low, and there are numerous book shops and stalls in all the principal streets" (*Sketches of China* [Philadelphia: Carey and Lea, 1830], p. 124).

55 Martin J. Heijdra, "Technology, Culture, and Economics: Moveable Type Versus Woodblock Printing in East Asia," pp. 223–40 (esp. 230–33 and 236), in Isobe Akira, ed., *Higashi Ajia shuppan bunka kenkyū, niwatazumi* (Research on the Publishing Culture of East Asia—A pool of water in the garden after rain) (Tokyo: Nigensha, 2004). Note that this cost analysis focuses only on different print technologies. Yet, Chinese commercial publishers, anxious to secure customers, would have been aware that their principal competitor in the book market for most if not all of the time we are discussing in this book was the venerable and very cheap "technology" of manuscript copying. Wooden moveable-type printing of very small runs would possibly then have lost much of its attraction to publishers whose customers bought and collected hand copies.

56 With the stereotyping technique, invented in the Netherlands before 1700, printers made a plaster mould of each frame of moveable type. By thus preserving a full face for every page in the book, all the heaviest costs of reprinting by moveable type (i.e., typesetting, editing, and proofreading) were eliminated. By 1839, thanks to technical improvements in France and England, each mould could provide more than 100,000 — and, with care, over 1,000,000 — impressions. For books in constantly high demand, like the Bible, this technique promised huge savings; but it presumed prior use of moveable type (William St Clair, *The Reading Nation in the Romantic Period* [Cambridge: Cambridge University Press, 2004], pp. 183–5).

57 Milne's omission of lithography is understandable. In 1819–20, when Milne was writing in distant Malacca, lithography in Europe was an accepted practice in just one city, Munich. Moreover, until well into the latter half of the nineteenth century, it probably provided no more than half the daily output of the iron platen press of the letter-press printer (in speed it could not compete with the letter-press rotary machines used for mass newspapers throughout the nineteenth century) (Michael Twyman, *Breaking the Mould: the First Hundred Years of Lithography* [London: British Library, 2001], pp. 24 and 45–6).

58 Milne, p. 246.

59 Ibid., pp. 246–9 and 251.

60 Ibid., p. 253. Apt advice on the financing of moveable-type publishing comes from the founder of The Hogarth Press in London: "the road to bankruptcy is paved with overheads—and books which do not sell" (Leonard Woolf, *The Journey, Not the Arrival Matters, An Autobiography of the Years 1939–1969* [London: The Hogarth Press, 1969], p. 110).

61 Morrison, pp. 97–8, n. 8. Milne's stress on the multiplicity of Chinese characters (i.e., viewing them as distinct drawings) is confirmed by the views of a highly experienced expert on printing technology in general and that of lithography in particular: "From Gutenberg's time onwards relief printers have shown a predilection for verbal messages, while intaglio printers, even when working commercially, have tended to concentrate on pictorial and decorative work" (Twyman, p. 63).

62 Milne, pp. 259–60. The same was said, late in the nineteenth century, of blind printers in Beijing: "[The missionary] Mr [William H.] Murray has taught all along [blind] students to do everything for themselves in the preparation of their books, even to the stereotyping, which by a very ingenious contrivance of his own invention, they are able to do so rapidly, and with such accuracy, that anyone of these lads can with ease produce ten pages a day. A blind man in London working with a hand frame could only turn out four or five plates in a day, and the best blind stereotyper in the employment of the British and Foreign Blind

Association who now works with a machine, considers eight pages a good day's work. The Chinese lads work more accurately than their brethern in our own land, and at a far cheaper rate." Constance F. Gordon Cumming, *The Inventor of the Numeral-Type for China* (London: Downey and Co., 1899), p. 42; also, on p. 43, Mr Murray confirms this by saying, "The [blind] boy in Beijing can do with ease in one day double the amount of work which a blind man in England could do with a hand frame and the quality of the work is struck more perfectly."

63   Ricci, p. 21. The early nineteenth-century missionary Charles Gutzlaff even concluded, "For all common work, the Chinese mode of xylography or stereotyping appears to be the cheapest and much to be preferred" (*China Opened* [London: Smith Elder and Co., 1838], v. 2, p. 149). However, see Adriano de las Cortes, S. J., *Le Voyage en Chine d'Adriano de las Cortes, S. J.*, trans. Pascale Girard and Juliette Monbeig (Paris: Chandeigne, 2001), pp. 194–5, for disparaging comments on the "always" low-quality paper and carving of Chinese woodblock imprints that this Jesuit came across in the coastal areas of northeastern Guangdong Province.

64   Milne, p. 240. Hunter, p. 216, confirms this view: "the adroitness of the workmen, and their intelligence, enable them to get through a job with wonderful celerity and neatness."

65   Medhurst, p. 105; and, Wood, p. 214. These two estimates, Milne's "2, 000 copies a day" and Medhurst's 3,000, may well be the source for a British contemporary estimate that "from 2,000 to 3,000 [copies] may be taken off in a day by a single workman" (William B. Langdon, *Ten Thousand Things Relating to China and the Chinese* [London: 1842], p. 163). The arbitrariness of these figures is underlined by Matteo Ricci's late-sixteenth-century estimate for a skilled printer of "as many as fifteen hundred sheets in a single day" (Ricci, p. 21). Note, however, that actual production demands seem to have fallen so low that these ideal estimates, even when we disregard their variations, lose much of their claim to general validity and widespread applicability to past practice. For instance, a modern writer claims just thirty copies were printed for the first impression of an imprint (Tsien, p. 370); Drège (1994), p. 427, mentions 600 to 1,000 copies for a single impression. A very recent set of per-day figures in fact lowers the production level considerably: 100 characters a day (the workers' ancestors did 150 to 200 a day) and 500 sheets (in seven or eight hours), while the carving of a literary collection in 1377 was reportedly done by one man at the rate of 235 characters a day (Miao Yonghe, pp. 305 and 307). Obviously, picking a universally valid figure out of these numbers is at best a pig in a poke.

66   Medhurst, p. 113. Medhurst's carver is reportedly paid sixpence per 100 characters, a page generally containing 500 characters.

67   Ibid., p. 235. The Haechang Temple mentioned here is presumably what in modern Chinese is transcribed as *Haichuang si*, the Buddhist temple that printed so many of the Buddhist imprints in the Morrison Collection at the School of Oriental and African Studies, University of London (Andrew C. West, comp., *Catalogue of the Morrison Collection of Chinese Books* [London: SOAS, University of London, 1998], e.g., pp. 168–208, *passim*). Hunter, p. 216, locates this temple as "opposite the old Factories at Canton" and comments favorably on its woodblock storerooms' "great system and neatness."

68   Milne, pp. 234–5.

69   Ibid., pp. 247–8; and Medhurst, p. 563. The Jesuits in Macao preferred type, since it was easier than woodblocks to conceal from the Chinese police (Drège [1992], p. 284). Medhurst, p. 562, also finds that "the typecutters are very troublesome men, very difficult to keep in order, and should they be prohibited from quitting their native land, our work must come a stand."

70   See the discussion by Samuel Dyer in *Chinese Repository,* v. 2 (Feb. 1834), pp. 477–8.

71   Li Zhizhong, *Jianpu ji* (Collection of essays shouldering the simple) (Beijing: Beijing tushuguan chubanshe, 1998), pp. 321–4.

72   Martinique, p. 38.

73   Miao Yonghe, pp. 310–1, notes that, for each printer, butterfly binding required five binders and stitched printing just three binders.

74   Christian Daniels, "Jūroku—jūnana seki Fukken no chikushi seizō gijutsu—*Tenkō kaibutsu* ni shōjutsu sareta seishi gijutsu no jidai koshō (Bamboo production techniques in sixteenth and seventeenth century Fujian—papermaking techniques as described in detail in the *Tiangong kaiwu*)," *Ajia Africa gengo bunka kenkyū* (Research on the languages and cultures of Asia and Africa) 48–9, bessatsu (1995), pp. 243–79. My discussion here concerns single-color ink printing. Multicolored prints, for which the late Ming is famed, would have required separate applications of a paper sheet to the blocks for each color; the complexity of the operation necessarily drove up the publishing cost.

75   Inoue Susumu, "Zōsho," pp. 424–5.

76   Ibid., p. 424. See also Jonathan M. Bloom, *Paper Before Print, the History and Impact of Paper in the Islamic World* (New Haven, CT: Yale University Press, 2003), pp. 70–1, on the high expense and reputation of Chinese paper in Persia between the tenth and fifteenth centuries.

77   Pan Jixing, *Zhongguo zaozhi zhishu shi gao* (Draft history of the technology of papermaking in China) (Beijing: Wenwu chubanshe, 1979), pp. 110–1, and 114–8.

78   Huang Zongxi, *Mingwen hai* (Great compendium of Ming Dynasty writings) (Beijing: Zhonghua shuju, 1989), v. 1, p. 1,034. For further

information on changes in paper use and prices, see my "The Ascendance of the Imprint in China," pp. 55–104, in Cynthia J. Brokaw and Kai-Wing Chow, eds., *Printing and Book Culture in Late Imperial China* (Berkeley: University of California Press, 2005).

79 Inoue Susumu, *Chūgoku shuppan bunka shi* (A history of publishing culture in China) (Nagoya: Nagoya daigaku shuppankai, 2001), pp. 223–4; Milne, pp. 234 and 251; and Medhurst, pp. 559–60. See Appendix 1.1.

80 Yang Shengxin, p. 42; Zhang Xiumin, pp. 730 and 745; and Miao Yonghe, p. 302.

81 Milne, p. 226.

82 Ibid., p. 223.

83 Frederick W. Mote and Hung-lam Chu, *Calligraphy and the East Asian Book* (Boston, MA: Shambhala, 1989), p. 169. I wish to thank Dr Martin Heijdra for his instructive advice on this point.

84 The delayed shift away from the manuscript model of book was also evident in the West, more so than has often been acknowledged in recent decades. Thus, the comments of Curt Bühler on early Western printing takes on added significance when applied to this key aspect of Chinese woodblock printing: "The student of the earliest printing would be well advised if he viewed the new invention, as the first printers did, as simply another form of writing." As David McKitterick then goes on to say of early Western imprints and manuscripts, "Both were, simply, ways of making books. For the vast majority of printed books very significant changes are, in fact, immediately observable, in (for example, and at a quite basic level) the alignment of type and its more regular spatial organisation into columns. The design of the page had, of course, to be modified by the mechanical limitations of type and of the printing press; but the essential features remained those of books: commonly held properties, appearances and (to a great extent) materials" (McKitterick, pp. 35–7).

85 Takemura Shinichi, *Minchōtai no rekishi* (A history of Ming Dynasty calligraphy for carving) (Tokyo: Shibun kaku shuppansha, 1986), is far from comprehensive; a more recent introduction to the subject is Lin Kunfan, *Genchōtai to Minchōtai no keisei* (The formation of Yuan and Ming Dynasty calligraphy for carving) (Tokyo: Rōbundō, 2002; issued as the August 6, 2002 issue of the typography journal, *Vignette*). Despite their interesting illustrations, neither is a satisfactory treatment of this crucial change in the calligraphic script for printing. See also Miao Yonghe, p. 280; and Qian Yong, *Lüyuan conghua* (Comprehensive talk of Qian Yong) (Beijing: Zhonghua shuju, 1979), v. 1, 12, p. 323, about the use of a squarish brushstroke and its lamentable impact on the quality of the calligraphy used for imprints from the mid-Ming up to the nineteenth century.

86 Lucille Chia, *Printing for Profit*, pp. 11, 39 and 197. This view is at odds with one presented by Wood, p. 123, on the basis of personal observation: "The cost of engraving depends entirely on the size and delicacy of the letter, the price increasing in proportion to the smallness of the type [i.e. carved character]."

87 Ren Zhongqi, "Gushu jiage mantan (Chat on the price of old books)," *Cangshujia* 2 (2000), p. 125.

88 Lothar Ledderose, *Ten Thousand Things, Module and Mass Production in Chinese Art* (Princeton, NJ: Princeton University Press, 2000), pp. 16–8, and 139–61 for moveable-type printing.

89 Lucille Chia's observation on the earlier simplification of script merits mention: "Actually, simplification of the writing and carving of characters for the printing block had occurred far earlier. Even in the Tang, printed ephemera such as cheap calendars used a stripped-down style of characters, and among Jianyang imprints, the characters in Yuan historical fiction in the running illustration format are extremely economical in their execution" (Lucille Chia, "*Mashaben*: Commercial Publishing from the Song Through the Ming," p. 202, in Paul Jakov Smith and Richard von Glahn, eds., *The Song-Yuan-Ming Transition in Chinese History* [Cambridge, MA: Harvard University Asia Center, 2003]). Yet, these Yuan scripts are not as standardized and homogenized as the artisanal characters of the late fifteenth century onwards.

90 Christopher Reed, *Gutenberg in Shanghai, 1850–1950* (Vancouver: University of British Columbia Press, 2004). In the seventeenth century, carvers' knives were said to differ according to region, such as Fujian, Jiangzhe, Nanjing, and Jingde-Huizhou (Zhang Xiumin, p. 534).

91 Miao Yonghe, p. 307.

92 Nagasawa Kikuya, "Kokkō to shuppansha to no kankei (The relation of carvers and publishers)," in *Nagasawa Kikuya chosaku shū* (Collection of the writings of Nagasawa Kikuya) (Tokyo: Kyūko shoin, 1984), v. 3, pp. 215–8.

93 According to Professor Cynthia J. Brokaw, the head of the She County Museum in Huizhou prefecture in southern Anhui Province in 1998 recalled for her that woodblock carvers there before 1950 practiced this kind of division of labor (personal communication from Cynthia J. Brokaw).

94 Sakuma Shigeo, "Mindai no tōki to rekishiteki haikei (Ming ceramics and its historical background)," pp. 145–6, in *Sekai tōki zenshū, Min* (Complete works on world ceramics, the Ming) (Tokyo: Shogakukan, 1976), v. 14, ed. by Fujioka Ryoichi, et al.; and Sung Ying-hsing, pp. 146–54.

95 As can be seen in the knowledgeable comments of Harry Garner, *Chinese Lacquer* (London: Faber and Faber, 1979), p. 134: "A feature of the sixteenth-century wares generally is the use of labour-saving devices in

the carving. The official fifteenth-century wares made great use of the knife in the carving of details ... In the sixteenth century the knife was replaced by the gouge, in which only one stroke was needed, requiring far less skill. The use of the gouge is particularly noticeable in the imperial wares of the sixteenth century."

96 Francesca Bray, *Technology and Society in Ming China (1368–1644)* (Washington, DC: American Historical Association, 2000), p. 65. Of course, some late Ming élite publications showed improved technical skills, but they represent a tiny fraction of the publications then.

97 Yang Shengxin, pp. 41–58; Zhang Xiumin, p. 747; and Inoue, *Chūgoku,* pp. 222–6.

98 As Sören Edgren has noted for the Song, these figures omit the known names of carvers for Buddhist canon editions and thus underestimate the number of knowable names (Sören Edgren, "Southern Song Printing at Hangzhou," *Bulletin of the Museum of Far Eastern Antiquities* 61 [1989], p. 46).

99 Zhang Xiuming, p. 745.

100 Ibid.

101 Ibid., pp. 735, 737–8, and 751–2; Zhang Shudong, pp. 113–7; and, for Hu Mao, n. 143 below.

102 Ming Sun Poon (Pan Mingshen), Books and Printing in Sung China (960–1279) (University of Chicago, Ph.D., 1979), p. 1.

103 Lin Kunfan, pp. 6–17.

104 Edgren, pp. 51–2; and Zhang Xiumin, pp. 733, 746. Some even migrated to Japan (ibid., pp. 742–3).

105 Ibid., p. 733.

106 Qu Mianliang, *Banke zhiyi* (Questions on doubtful points of some woodblock editions) (Ji'nan: Ji Lu shushe, 1987), p. 44; and, Miao Yonghe, p. 316.

107 Inoue, *Chūgoku,* p. 206.

108 Zhang Xiumin, pp. 732 and 742.

109 E.g., Qu Mianliang, *Banke,* p. 58; and Wang Shixing, *Guangzhi yi* (An extensive gazetteer) (Beijing: Zhonghua shuju, 1981), 4, p. 80.

110 Zhang Xiumin, p. 744.

111 Ibid., p. 746.

112 Wang He, *Songdai tushu shilun* (An historical discussion of Song dynasty books) (Nanchang: Baihua zhou wenyi chubanshe, 1999), p. 77.

113 Kitamura Ko, "Gendai Kōshūzō no kakkō ni tsuite (On the carvers of the Hangzhou Buddhist canon in the Yuan dynasty)," *Ryūkoku daigaku ronshū* (Collected articles of Ryūkoku University) 438 (July 1991), pp. 120–36; and Lucille Chia, "Commercial Printing," pp. 319–25.

114 Miao Yonghe, p. 314. It goes without saying that the integration of this labor market and the carved woodblock supplies did not necessarily entail the harmonization of labor costs and book prices, since separate

market niches for different quality publications would have assured considerable variation in prices in these areas, even when they had editions of the same title.

115 Ren Jiyu, ed., *Zhongguo cangshulou* (Chinese libraries) (Shenyang: Liaoning renmin, 2000), v. 1, p. 928.

116 Shen Bang, *Wanshu zaji* (Miscellaneous notes on Beijing) (1593) (Beijing: Guji, 1983), 13, p. 108.

117 Duan Benluo and Zhang Qinfu, *Suzhou shougongye shi* (A history of handicrafts in Suzhou) (Nanjing: Jiangsu guji, 1986), p. 131.

118 Wang Zhaowen, *Guji Song Yuan kangong xingming suoyin* (An index of the names of the carvers of Song and Yuan old books) (Shanghai: Guji, 1990), p. 387; and Miao Yonghe, p. 130.

119 Nagasawa, pp. 215–6; and Michela Bussotti, *Gravures de Hui, Étude du livre illustré chinois (fin du XVIe siècle-première moitié du XVIIe siècle)* (Paris: École Française d'Extrême-Orient, 2001), pp. 284–90, argues persuasively for the coexistence of the two arrangements in at least Changzhou in 1609, the older Song style no longer predominant. Another possibility that Bussotti mentions here is that a single artisan did several pages in succession.

120 Ibid., p. 286.

121 Wang He, p. 30; the daily figure fell to 2,000 in the peak of summer heat or winter cold. Unfortunately, no primary source is indicated here, but these figures, in light of Milne's and Medhurst's figures given above, suggest that, in one day, no fewer than thirteen and as many as twenty-five times more characters could be written than carved by one man over the course of a year.

122 Zhang Xiumin, p. 747. The best-known transcriber of Ming times, Xu Pu of Changzhou of Suzhou, was active from 1570 to 1626 in transcribing no fewer than 384 titles and 2,200-odd chapters. For forty of these fifty-six years, he worked at least part of the time on the Jiaxing edition of the Buddhist canon. These figures support the rough estimate that he wrote, on average, 600 sheets a year; the real figure must be higher, since the list of titles he worked on is incomplete (Li Guoqing, "Shugong Xu Pu shan xie shuban xiaolu [A short note on the transcriber Xu Pu]," *Wenxian* [Documents] 1992.4, p. 143).

123 Li Guoqing, ed., *Mingdai kangong xingming suoyin* (An index of the names of carvers in the Ming dynasty) (Shanghai: Guji, 1998), pp. 551–614, lists 1,300 by name from the late fifteenth to early nineteenth centuries; note that Zhou Wu, *Huipai banhua shi lunji* (Collected essays on the history of woodblock pictures of the Hui school) (Hefei: Anhui renmin, 1984), p. 7, had previously put their number at just 300. For a recent and informative account of Huizhou prints, see Bussotti, especially the discussion of the Huangs on pp. 275–79.

124 Liu Shangheng, *Huizhou keshu yu cangshu* (Book printing and collecting in Huizhou) (Yangzhou: Guangling shushe, 2003), p. 176. Groups of three or five Huangs, after their harvest was in, made the rounds of Huizhou villages with boxes of moveable type, in order to compose and print up pages of genealogical information for the lineages in these villages. They reportedly owned 20,000 to 30,000 type, in three sizes.

125 Kobayashi Hiromitsu, "Min Shin jinbutsu hanga no tokushitsu to hatten shōkyō (The special features of portrait woodblock prints in the Ming and Qing and its development)," pp. 41–9 (esp. 41–3), in *Chūgoku kodai hanga ten* (An exhibition of ancient Chinese woodblock prints) (Machida: Machida shiritsu kokusai hanga bijutsukan, 1988); and Bussotti, p. 280.

126 Liu Shangheng, pp. 176–7.

127 Already in the Yuan, one carver reportedly came from a family of Confucian learning (Zhang Xiumin, p. 742). Also, for the Ming artisans, see Joseph P. McDermott, "The Art of Making a Living in Sixteenth Century China," *Kaikodo Journal V* (Autumn 1997), pp. 73–5.

128 Li Qiao, *Zhongguo hangye shen congbai* (Worship of guild gods in China) (Beijing: Zhongguo huaqiao chuban gongsi, 1990), pp. 146–7.

129 Zhang Xiumin, p. 749. In the Qing, two woodblock carvers who carved their own writings were Qu Jinsheng and Leang A-fa (aka Liang Afa), Milne's first convert to Christianity (ibid.).

130 Qu Mianliang, *Zhongguo guji banke cidian* (A dictionary on the carving of old Chinese books) (Ji'nan: Ji Lu shushe, 1999), pp. 535 and 540.

131 Ibid., pp. 528–9; Qu Mianliang, *Zhongguo*, p. 531; and Zhang Xiumin, p. 748.

132 Ibid., pp. 748–9; and Bussotti, p. 279.

133 Ibid., p. 280; Zhou Wu, p. 24; and Qu Mianliang, *Zhongguo guji*, p. 528.

134 Zhou Wu, pp. 22–3; and Qu Mianliang, *Zhongguo guji*, pp. 521–40, *passim.* One Huang carved books published in Beijing, Fujian, Jiangsu, and Zhejiang (Liu Shangheng, p. 161).

135 Zhou Wu, p. 24.

136 Qu Mianliang, *Zhongguo guji*, p. 529; Zhou Wu, p. 24; Zhang Xiumin, p. 748; and Zhang Shudong, p. 174.

137 Liu Shangheng, p. 184.

138 Kobayashi Hiromitsu, "Min Shin jinbutsu hanga," pp. 41–50 (esp. 41–3).

139 Inoue, *Chūgoku*, pp. 222–6.

140 Niida Noboru, *Chūgoku hōseishi kenkyū, dorei nōdo hō-kazoku sonraku hō* (Studies on the history of Chinese law: slave and serf law and family and village law) (Tokyo: Tokyo daigaku shuppankai, 1962), pp. 780–2; and, Chen Jiru, comp., *Jieyong yunjian* (Numerous notes and forms for successful use) (SKWSSJK ed.), 6.16a.

141 Milne, p. 234; and Medhurst, p. 559.

142 Zhang Xiuming, p. 747.
143 Tang Shunzhi, *Jingquan xiansheng wenji* (Writings of Tang Shunzhi) (SBCK ed.), 12.40b–42a.
144 Hu Yinglin, *Shaoshi shanfang bicong* (Collection of notes by Hu Yinglin) (Shanghai: Zhonghua shuju, 1958), 4, pp. 56 and 58.
145 The image of the carousing, drunken artisan, especially when a woodblock carver, was already evident in the twelfth century, in Hong Mai, *Yijian zhi* (The record of the listener) (Beijing: Zhonghua shuju, 1981), bing, 12, p. 464.
146 Suzhou lishi bowuguan, comp., *Ming Qing Suzhou gongshang ye beike ji* (Collected stone inscriptions on industry and commerce in Suzhou during the Ming and Qing) (Nanjing: Jiangsu renmin, 1981), pp. 89 and 95.
147 McDermott, "The Art of Making a Living," pp. 73–4.
148 Zhang Xiumin, p. 751.
149 Miao Yonghe, pp. 129–30.
150 Zhou Zhaoxiang (1880–1954), *Liuli chang zaji* (Miscellaneous notes about Liuli chang) (Beijing: Beijing Yanshan chubanshe, 1995), p. 79, makes claims of a similar social divide between the calligraphers and stone carvers in post-Song times. He argues that, whereas carvers associated with scholar-officials and understood the principles of calligraphy in the Song and earlier, in later dynasties each group did their work with little interaction. As a consequence, carvers replaced their knives with awls and chisels, at considerable cost to the quality of their work. The carvers then came to occupy the place of clerks and artisans, and scholar officials no longer took them as their companions.
151 Li Guoqing, "Mantan gushu de kegong (Casual talk on carvers of old books)," *Cangshujia* 1 (2000), pp. 123–4. Book illustrators may have been better educated than other printing workers, but we lack the sources to make any reliable generalization on this point.
152 Kobayashi Hiromitsu, *Chūgoku no hanga* (Chinese woodblock illustrations) (Tokyo: Tōshindō, 1995), pp. 121–8; and, Robert E. Hegel, *Reading Illustrated Fiction in Late Imperial China* (Stanford, CA: Stanford University Press, 1998).
153 Li Guoqing, *Jianpu ji*, p. 614, stops the list in the early 1830s. Although this end was artificially imposed, undoubtedly, by Li's reliance on an 1826 genealogy of the Huangs, the destruction of much of Huizhou by the Taiping rebels in the 1850s and 1860s effectively signaled the end of this area's distinctive print culture.

Chapter 2

1 Ji Wenhui and Wang Damei, *Zhongyi guji* (Old books on Chinese medicine) (Shanghai: Shanghai kexue jishu chubanshe, 2000), p. 106.

2   Li Mei, *Ming Qing zhi ji Suzhou zuojiaqun yanjiu* (Studies on the Suzhou group of writers in the Ming-Qing era) (Beijing: Zhongguo shehui kexue yanjiu, 2000), p. 3.

3   Inoue, "Zōsho," p. 428, and *Chūgoku*, p. 181. Inoue's figures, despite my reservations, provide a useful basis for the tabulation now required of other early imprints in other collections of Chinese books.

4   Katsuyama Minoru, "Mindai ni okeru bōkaku bon no shuppan jōkyō ni tsuite—Mindai zenpan no shuppanshū kara miru Kenyō bōkaku bon ni tsuite" (The condition of non-government book publishing in the Ming—non-government printed books, seen in terms of Ming publishing statistics), pp. 83–101, in Isobe, ed., *Higashi Ajia shuppan bunka kenkyū.*

5   Inoue, *Chūgoku*, pp. 139–42.

6   Erik Zürcher, "Buddhism and Education in T'ang Times," p. 55, in Wm. Theodore de Bary and John W. Chaffee, eds., *Neo-Confucian Education: The Formative Stage* (Berkeley: University of California Press, 1989).

7   Zeng Gong, *Zeng Gong ji* (Collected writings of Zeng Gong) (Beijing: Zhonghua shuju, 1984), v. 1, p. 179.

8   Glen Dudbridge, *Lost Books of Medieval China* (London: British Library, 2000) has much on the series of editorial and printing projects at the start of the Song. Also, see Peter Bol, *"This Culture of Ours": Intellectual Transitions in T'ang and Sung China* (Stanford, CA: Stanford University Press, 1992), pp. 152–3.

9   Li Lin, "Bei Song guanke diaoban yishu qiantan (Brief discussion on the craft of woodblock carving of government imprints in the Northern Song)," *Zhongguo yishi zazhi* (Journal of Chinese medical history) 27.3 (1997 July), pp. 148–52 (the Northern Song government printed medical texts for widespread distribution on at least ten occasions); Valerie Hansen, *Negotiating Daily Life in Traditional China, How Ordinary People Used Contracts* (New Haven, CT: Yale University Press, 1995); Inoue, *Chūgoku*, p. 124; and Li Tao, *Xu zizhi tongjian changbian* (Collected data for a continuation of the "Comprehensive Mirror for Aid in Government") (Beijing: Zhonghua shuju, 1980), 102, p. 2,368.

10   Wang Mingqing, *Huichen lu* (Pure talk) (Beijing: Zhonghua shuju, 1961), yuhua, 2, p. 310.

11   E.g., Su Bai, *Tang Song shiqi de diaoban yinshua* (Carving and publishing in the Tang and Song periods) (Beijing: Wenwu chubanshe, 1999), p. 106.

12   Hu Yinglin, 4, p. 60; and Xu Bo, *Biqing* (Distillations of the Notes by Mr Xu) (Fuzhou: Fujian renmin, 1997), 7, p. 239.

13   Pan Mingshen (Ming-sun Poon), "Songdai sijia cangshu kao (On Private Book Collections in the Song Dynasty)," *Huaguo xuebao* (Journal of Sinology) 6 (1971), pp. 215–8; Susan Cherniack, "Book Culture and Textual Transmission in Sung China," *Harvard Journal of Asiatic Studies*

54.1 (1994), p. 33; and Jean-Pierre Drège, *Les bibliothèques en Chine au temps des manuscrits (jusqu'au Xe siècle)* (Paris: École Française d'Extrême-Orient, 1991), pp. 266–8. General consent would seem to be expressed, if less consistently, in Li Ruiliang, *Zhongguo gudai tushu liutong shi* (A History of the Circulation of Books in Pre-Modern China) (Shanghai: Shanghai renmin, 2000), p. 268.

14 The fires that beset the Northern Song's Imperial Library clearly make this comparison difficult, as the destruction of this library in 1015 assured that a fair number of private collectors at least temporarily had more books than did the Imperial Library (Zhang Bangji [d.1109], *Mozhuang manlu* [Casual record of the ink manor] [Beijing: Zhonghua shuju, 2002], v. 5, p. 142). Also, Fan Fengshu, *Zhongguo sijia cangshu shi* [A history of private book collectors in China) (Zhengzhou: Daxiang chubanshe, 2001), pp. 88–9, mentions one collector, Wang Qinchen (1034–1101), whose holdings (43,000 *juan*, excluding his encyclopedias) were said to have been larger than the Imperial Library's at its peak size. But, the peak figures for the latter's holdings in both the Northern and Southern Song are at the top or very close to the top for all book collections then, private as well as public.

15 John H. Winkelman, *The Imperial Library in Southern Sung China, 1127–1279: A Study of the Organization and Operation of the Scholarly Agencies of the Central Government* (in *Transactions of the American Philosophical Society,* n.s. 64.8 [1974]), pp. 10 and 37.

16 Ibid., pp. 8–9 (esp. n. 21) gives 82,384 *juan* for pre-An Lushan Rebellion Tang state libraries. According to Zhou Mi, under Emperor Yuan of the Liang, the court had 140,000 *juan*; under the Sui (589–617), 370,000 *juan* in the Jiace Basilica; and in each of the Tang dynasty's (618–907) two capitals, a total of 70,000 *juan* (Zhou Mi, *Qidong yeyu* [Words of a retired scholar from the east of Qi] [Beijing: Zhonghua shuju, 1983], 12, pp. 216–7). For the Sui and Tang, more detail survives. The Sui court collection reached at least 89,666 *juan*, since that was the number of Sui government scrolls shipped from Yangzhou towards the Tang capital; yet, only ten to twenty percent survived the transfer intact (*Sui shu* [Official history of the Sui dynasty] [Beijing: Zhonghua shuju, 1973], 32, p. 908). For the Tang, important details survive for two court libraries, the Imperial Library and the Library of the Academy of Assembled Worthies (*Jixian yuan*). In c.720, the definitive catalogue of the Tang Imperial Library listed 2,655 works in 48,169 *juan* (i.e., over 6,000 *juan* more than in its 705–06 catalogue). After suffering extensive damage in the An Lushan Rebellion of 755, the library's holdings recovered slowly, so that by 836 its holdings had risen to 54,476 *juan* (David McMullen, *State and Scholars in T'ang China* [Cambridge: Cambridge University Press, 1988], pp. 221–3, and 235–7). The holdings of the Library of the Academy of Assembled Worthies were even greater,

making it the largest collection since at least the Liang court library went up in flames in 555. In 731, it had 89,000 *juan*, mostly newly made copies; but once again it suffered damage during the destruction of the capital in the An Lushan Rebellion and its subsequent growth was greatly curtailed (ibid., p. 222; and Denis Twitchett, *The Writing of Official History under the T'ang* [Cambridge: Cambridge University Press, 1992], p. 26, n. 85).

17   The Imperial Library early on in the Five Dynasties had barely 10,000 *juan* (McMullen, p. 237).

18   Jiang Shaoyu, *Songchao shishi leiyuan* (Classified collection of facts on the Song dynasty) (Shanghai: Guji, 1981), v. 1, p. 393.

19   Ibid.

20   Winkelman, pp. 36, Table 7. Winkelman reminds us that this figure probably contains unprocessed works, duplicates, and extraneous works (ibid.). Yet, even this figure is lower than the 731 figure for the Library of the Academy of Assembled Worthies.

21   Fu Xuanzong and Xie Zhuohua, eds., *Zhongguo cangshu tongshi* (Comprehensive history of Chinese book collecting) (Ningbo: Ningbo chubanshe, 2001), v. 1, pp. 526–7.

22   Ren Jiyu, v. 2, pp. 914–5.

23   Yan Zhitui, *Yanshi jiaxun* (Family instructions of the Yan family) (CSJC ed.), 3, p. 51.

24   Wang Mingqing, qianlu, 1, p. 10. He adds that the books in their collections contained many textual errors.

25   Jean-Pierre Drège, *Les bibliothèques*, pp. 172–3. These figures may be too high: Jiang Yi (747–811) gained fame as a book collector with just 15,000 *juan* in the lower Yangzi delta county of Yixing (Wu Han, *Jiang Zhe cangshujia shilüe* [An abbreviated history of book collectors in Jiangsu and Zhejiang Provinces] [Beijing: Zhonghua shuju, 1981], p. 214). Twitchett, *The Writing of Official History Under the T'ang*, p. 109, tells of the 20,000-*juan* collection of Su Bian that, in the late eighth century, was said to be larger than all collections except for the Imperial Library and the Library of the Academy of Assembled Worthies.

26   Fan Fengshu, pp. 30, 36–7, 46, 57, and 62–82.

27   Inoue, "Zōsho," p. 414.

28   Zhao Zongchuo reportedly had 70,000 *juan* (Hong Mai, *Rongzhai suibi* [Notes of Hong Mai] [Shanghai: Guji, 1978], v. 2, sibi, 13, p. 772), but he acquired many of his books due to his privileged access to government and imperial collections as a member of the imperial clan. Almost as well-connected was the archival official Wang Qinchen who, with his father, Wang Zhu (997–1057), acquired over 43,000 *juan* (Fan Fengshu, pp. 88–9).

29   Ibid., p. 102.

30 Ye Ruibao, comp., *Suzhou cangshu shi* (A history of book collecting in Suzhou) (Nanjing: Jiangsu guji, 2001) [henceforth Ye Ruibao], p. 133.
31 Ibid., pp. 76 and 102; Inoue, "Zōsho," p. 412; and Wu Han, *Jiang Zhe*, pp. 134 and 208.
32 Hu Yinglin, 4, p. 53, explicitly subtracts from his figures the duplicates and randon items of these collections. Li Ruiliang, p. 317, lists a few large Song collections, none more than 40,000 *juan*.
33 Zhou Mi, 12, pp. 217–8, mentions large private collections, each of whose size fell within the range of the Palace Library. Zhou Mi attributes the exceptional size of Chen's library to his transcription of many old books in the Zheng, Fang, Lin, and Wu family libraries in Putian county, Fujian Province. Note also that Chen's catalogue, as it lists books it claims to be extinct, shows clear signs of being the list of not his own books but of books he had seen or heard of (Inoue, *Chūgoku*, p. 173). Thus, the figures here would seem not to merit full belief.
34 Ibid.
35 Hu Yinglin, 1, pp. 17–8.
36 In north China in the thirteenth century, large private collections were very few, but one high official Zhang Shao (1225–88), of Ji'nan in modern Shandong, reportedly acquired a collection with the exceptional size of 80,000 *juan* (Tian Jianping, *Yuandai chuban shi* [A history of publishing in the Yuan dynasty] [Shijiazhuang: Hebei renmin chubanshe, 2003], p. 337).
37 Hu Yinglin, 1, pp. 18–9; Wu Xiaoming, "Mingdai de Shanghai cangshujia (Shanghai book collectors in the Ming)," *Shanghai shifan xueyuan xuebao* (Journal of Shanghai Normal College) 19 (1984.1), p. 102; Li and Chen, p. 106; Ding Shen, *Wulin cangshu lu* (An account of Hangzhou book collectors) (CSJC ed.), zhong, pp. 40–1; Zheng Yuanyu, *Qiao Wu ji* (Collected writings of a sojourner in Wu) (reprint, Taipei: Guoli zhongyang tushuguan, 1970), 10.1b; *Piling zhi* (Changzhou gazetteer) (1484), 22.10a, for the notable collection of the Yixing county native Yue Jun; Inoue, "Zōsho," p. 414; and Fan Fengshu, pp. 138–45, where the 45 collectors with up to 20,000 *juan* accounted for 74 percent of the 61 Yuan collectors whose library size is quantified in our sources.
38 Huang Jin, *Jinhua Huang xiansheng wenji* (Collected writings of Huang Jin) (SBCK ed.), 17.3b, for Lu You of Suzhou; and Lang Ying, *Qi xiu lei gao* (Draft of information compiled in seven categories) (Beijing: Zhonghua shuju, 1961), 40, p. 584, for Sun Daoming of Songjiang.
39 Li and Chen, p. 134.
40 Zheng and Li, p. 30.
41 *Ming shi* (Official history of the Ming dynasty) (Beijing: Zhonghua shuju, 1974), 2, p. 21.
42 Chia, "Commercial Publishing," pp. 302–6, in Smith and von Glahn, eds. *Transition.*

43   Fan Fengshu, pp. 174, 175, 177, and 179. Early Ming literati in Suzhou with "almost 1,000 *juan* of old books" and "several thousand *juan*" are listed as collectors (Ye Ruibao, pp. 144–5).

44   Terada Takanobu, "Shōkō Kishi no Tanseidō ni tsuite (On the Dansheng Hall of the Qi Family of Shaoxing)," pp. 533–48, in *Tōhō gakkai sōritsu yonjū shunen kinen Tōhō gaku shūhen* (Collected essays in honor of the fortieth anniversary of the establishment of the Oriental Studies Association) (Tokyo: Tōhō gaku gakkai, 1987).

45   Inoue, *Chūgoku*, pp. 244–5.

46   Yu Shenxing, *Gushan bizhu* (Brushed notes of Gushan) (Beijing: Zhonghua shuju, 1984), 7, p. 82.

47   Hu Yinglin, 4, pp. 53–4. This view probably exaggerates the role of the dynastic histories.

48   Fan Fengshu, p. 89; and Ren Jiyu, v. 1, p. 766.

49   Inoue, *Chūgoku*, p. 171.

50   Ye Mengde, *Bishu luhua* (Talk recorded when escaping the heat) (CSJC ed.), shang, p. 2.

51   Ren Jiyu, v. 1, pp. 812 and 814.

52   Winkelman, "Imperial Library," p. 32.

53   Inoue, "Zōsho," p. 416. The precise date for this assertion is unclear, but I suspect it refers to sometime in the fifteenth century rather than later on in the dynasty, when the collection declined considerably (see Chapter 4).

54   Ye Ruibao, p. 148.

55   Yang Xunji, *Wuzhong guyu* (Old stories of Suzhou) (Guang baichuan xuehai ed.), 11a–14a; the students successfully resisted these pressures. An imprint shortage may also have lain behind earlier court demands made on Suzhou literati. In 1465, the Suzhou literatus Li Yingzhen was reprimanded for refusing to make a handwritten copy of a Buddhist sutra for the Chenghua emperor, though some others, including Hanlin officials in 1512, obeyed imperial commands to handcopy such sutras (Jiao Hong, *Guochao xianzheng lu* [Record of the dynasty's documents] [Taipei: Xuesheng, 1965], 72.75b; and Shen Defu, *Wanli yehuo bian* [Collected gossip of the Wanli era] [Beijing: Zhonghua shuju, 1955], v. 1, 10, p. 256).

56   Fan Fengshu, pp. 76 (Wang Zhenggong) and 112 (Lou Yue).

57   Inoue, "Zōsho," p. 419.

58   Ye Changchi, 2, p. 159.

59   Niu Shixi, *Kuaiji Niushi shixue lou zhencang shumu* (Catalogue of the books in the rare collection of the library of Mr Niu of Shaoxing), pp. 1,559–70, in Feng Huimin, Li Wanjian, et al., comp. *Mingdai shumu tiba congkan* (Collection of Ming book catalogues and colophons) (Beijing: Shumu wenxian chubanshe, 1994), v. 2. Note, however, that Shang Jun claims that all of Niu's books were handwritten (Fan Fengshu, p. 200).

60 Ye Mengde, *Shilin zhushi Jiankang ji* (Nanjing collection of writings by the retired scholar Ye Mengde) (late Ming ed., Beijing National Library copy), 4.1a–2b.

61 Pan Meiyu, *Songdai cangshujia* (Song dynasty book collectors) (Taipei: Xuehai, 1980), p. 185.

62 Ibid., p. 177. For ten years, this native of Puzhou prefecture in Chengdufu circuit, Liu Yifeng (1110–75), held court appointments, such as the assistant director of the Palace Library, which undoubtedly would have eased his access to the Imperial Library and the rare book collection it had re-established in the mid-twelfth century with many books presented by private collectors in south China; in other words, he probably spent most of his official income on the transcription of books in public collections rather than on buying them in Hangzhou bookstores.

63 Poon, Books and Printing, p. 24. Pan Meiyue, pp. 162–3 and 165 give additional information on the survival of Song imprints in Sichuan during the Southern Song. The widespread destruction of book collections in the Five Dynasties era had left only Sichuan and the lower Yangzi delta as areas with many books at the start of the Song; the early Song government's plunder of Sichuan's libraries only postponed the eventual growth of this area's collections (Jiang Shaoyu, v. 1, p. 393). However, we know very little of these collections, since they suffered greatly from repeated invasions and turmoil there in the last half of the thirteenth century. By the fourteenth century, the flow was definitely reversed, a Sichuanese traveling to the lower Yangzi delta and collecting a vast number of books there within four to five years (Hu Yinglin, 1, p. 17).

64 Chen Zhensun, 5, p. 133.

65 Poon, Books and Printing, pp. 1, 11, and 468–74 (note that both the Northern Song circuits of Liangzhe and Lizhou were divided into eastern and western parts for most of the Southern Song); and Zhang Xiumin, p. 59. Even in the once remote coastal prefectural seat of Chaozhou (in present Guangdong Province), government offices and schools by the thirteenth, or at the latest early fourteenth, century held a total of 10,865 woodblocks (*Chaozhou sanyang tuzhi jigao, Chaozhou sanyang zhi jigao* [Draft gazetteer and maps of Chaozhou, Draft gazetteer of Chaozhou] [Guangzhou: Zhongshan daxue chubanshe, 1989], 10, pp. 55–6).

66 Su Bai, pp. 86–7 (Tables 1, 2, and 3) and 106.

67 Ibid., pp. 84–110, esp. 106. Only in 1622, nearly two centuries after Gutenberg's invention of the printing press, do we have a book catalogue, the Rigault catalogue of the holdings of the French Royal Library, distinguish between manuscript and imprint copies; the practice

would grow from this first occurrence to become regular from the late seventeenth century (McKitterick, pp. 12–5).

68 Yong Rong, et al., comp., *Siku quanshu zongmu tiyao* (Comprehensive list and summary of contents in the four treasuries' complete collection) (Shanghai: Commercial Press, 1933), 37, pp. 4,135–6. Also, see Cherniack, pp. 70–1, on the fate of this text in the Song.

69 Chen Zhensun, 8, p. 237. According to Paul U. Unschuld, *Medicine in China, A History of Pharmaceutics* (Berkeley: University of California Press, 1986), during the Southern Song, the government printed only one new pharmaceutical text, in 1249, and reprinted an 1108 text three times (in 1185, 1195, and 1211). Note how permanent the state's retreat from printing pharmaceutical texts eventually became: "From the seventh century until the end of the Sung [i.e., Song] period, pharmaceutical books were ordered, revised, and published in China with government initiative or support, the only time before the twentieth century that this was to occur. Subsequently, herbals are reported to have been written upon order of the emperor only once during the Ming and once during the Ch'ing period. The works resulting from those later orders, however, were not intended to reach the general public and therefore cannot be considered exceptions to the thesis given above" (pp. 45–6).

70 Yuan Jie, *Qingrong zhushi ji* (Collected writings of Yuan Jie) (CSJC ed.), 22, p. 397.

71 Huang Zhen, *Huangshi richao* (Daily jottings of Huang Zhen) (SKQSZB ed.), 93.1a–2a.

72 Li and Chen, p. 92.

73 Hu Yinglin, 1, p. 17; and Wei Su, *Wei taipu ji* (Collected writings of Wei Su) (reprint, Taipei: Xin wenfeng, 1985), 10.16a–b.

74 Du Fan, *Qingxian ji* (Collected writings of Du Fan) (SKQSZB ed.), 10. 11a. See also my comments in the chapter on economic change during the Song, in the forthcoming *Cambridge History of China* volume on the Song dynasty.

75 Paul J. Smith, "Family, *Landsmänn*, and Status-Group Affinity in Refugee Mobility Strategies: the Mongol Invasions and the Diaspora of Sichuanese Elites, 1230–1330," *Harvard Journal of Asiatic Studies* 52.2 (1992), pp. 668–72. Yet, Lu Shen, *Jintai jiwen* (Record of the Golden Terrace) (CSJC ed.), p. 8, says that at the start of the Ming, Sichuan (*Shu*) still had woodblocks.

76 Shiba Yoshinobu, "The Economy of the Lower Yangzi Delta, 1300–1800" (forthcoming in Joseph P. McDermott, ed., *Commercial Growth and Urban Life in Jiangnan, 1000–1850*); and Richard von Glahn, "Towns and Temples: Market Town Growth and Decline in the Yangzi Delta 1200–1500," pp. 176–211, in Smith and von Glahn, eds. *Transition.*

77 Chia, "Commercial Publishing," pp. 297, and 306, in ibid.

78   Lu Rong, *Shuyuan zaji* (Collection of miscellaneous notes from a vegetable garden) (Beijing: Zhonghua shuju, 1985), 10, pp. 128–9.

79   Gu Yanwu, *Gu Tinglin shiwenji* (Collected prose and poetry of Gu Yanwu) (Beijing: Zhonghua shuju, 1983, 2nd prt.) of 1959 ed.), 2, pp. 31–2.

80   Lu Rong, 4, pp. 39–40.

81   Ōuchi Hakugetsu, *Shina tenseki shidan* (Discussions of the history of the book in China) (Tokyo: Shorinsha, 1944), p. 61.

82   Yang Shiqi, *Dongli xuji* (Continuation of the collected writings of Yang Shiqi) (SKQSZB ed.), 17.15b.

83   Lu Rong, 10, p. 129.

84   Yang Shiqi, *Dongli wenji* (Collected writings of Yang Shiqi) (Beijing: Zhonghua shuju, 1998), 10, p. 143; and Inoue, *Chūgoku*, pp. 212–3.

85   Ye Sheng, *Shuidong riji* (Daily notes of Ye Sheng) (Beijing: Zhonghua shuju, 1980), 20, p. 204; and, Yang Shiqi, *Dongli xuji*, 18.16b.

86   Ye Changchi, *Cangshu jishi, fu fuzheng* (Poems and prose accounts of book collecting, supplemented and corrected), ed. Wang Xinfu (Shanghai: Guji, 1999; published along with Lun Ming, *Xinhai yilai cangshu jishi shi* [Poems and prose accounts of book collecting since 1911]), 2, pp. 117–8.

87   Inoue, *Chūgoku*, pp. 217–8.

88   Yang Shiqi, *Dongli xuji*, 18.13a.

89   Inoue, "Zōsho," pp. 417–8.

90   Ibid., p. 417; and Ye Changchi, 2, p. 136. For another instance of the need to complete a book by matching separate copyings of different incomplete volumes, see also ibid., p. 157.

91   Inoue, "Zōsho," pp. 417–8.

92   Lou Yue, *Gongkui ji* (Collected writings of Lou Yue) (CSJC ed.), heyi, p. 3; and Terada Takanobu, "Shijin no shiteki kyōyō ni tsuite, aruiwa *Shiji tsūkan* no rufu ni tsuite (On scholars' general knowledge of history—or, on the dissemination of the *Zizhi tongjian*)," *Rekishi (Tōhoku daigaku)* (History, Tōhoku University) 82 (1994), pp. 1–17. The blocks of the original 1086 Hangzhou edition seem to have been seized and removed to north China by the Jurchen during their invasion of Hangzhou and the rest of the Yangzi delta in 1129. The Koreans in 1099 asked for a copy (after an initial rejection by the Ministry of Rites, they received a copy, and later as well from the first Ming emperor), the Mongols in 1281 had it translated and printed in Mongolian as written in the Uighur script (the Chinese language version still remained scarce in north China), and the Japanese first printed their own full copy only in 1849 (though they knew of it long before). A mid-thirteenth century Yuan edition's woodblocks were carved near Hangzhou and transferred by the early Ming government to the National University in Nanjing for storage; reprinting in the early Ming seems to have seldom happened.

93   Inoue, "Zōsho," p. 417.
94   Ibid., p. 418; and Inoue, *Chūgoku*, pp. 215–7.
95   Kwang Tsing Wu, "Ming Printing and Printers," *Harvard Journal of Asiatic Studies* 7.3 (February 1943), p. 224; and Ye Changchi, 2, p. 129.
96   Inoue, *Chūgoku*, pp. 215–7. Inoue speculates that the 1514 Jianning edition (mentioned in Chia, *Printing for Profit*, p. 197) may be a reprint. Even if so, other editions soon followed, in 1530, 1534, and 1537.
97   Yang Shiqi, *Dongli xuji*, 17.23a.
98   Ji Shuying, "Xinqin chaoshu de cangshujia Qian Gu fuzi" (Qian Gu and son, book collectors as industrious transcribers), *Lishi wenxian yanjiu* (Studies of historical documents) new series, 2 (1991), p. 76.
99   Gu Yanwu, *Rizhi lu jishi* (Record of daily knowledge, with notes) (Changsha: Yuelu shushe, 1994), 18, pp. 642–3. The *Jiu Tang shu* (Old Tang history), after an initial printing in the early Southern Song, had to wait three centuries for another carving, in 1538, and remained rare until the eighteenth century (Li Ruiliang, p. 272).
100 Cao Rong, *Liutong gushu yue* (Pact for the circulation of old books) (Zhi buzu zhai congshu ed.), 1a.
101 Inoue, "Zōsho," pp. 429–40, provides most of the information in the following section.
102 Inoue, *Chūgoku*, p. 107.
103 Ibid., pp. 134–8.
104 Ibid., p. 131.
105 Ibid., pp. 120–3, 124, 125–6, 128 and 133.
106 Lu Rong, 10, p. 129.
107 Gu Yanwu, *Gu Tinglin shiwen ji*, 2, p. 29.
108 Inoue, *Chūgoku*, pp. 206–7 and 241.
109 Chia, "Commercial Printing," p. 303.
110 Ye Changchi, 2, p. 142.
111 Inoue, "Zōsho," p. 434.
112 Fan Fengshu, pp. 120–7, 163–4, and 251–64. Roughly a quarter of the presently known Ming catalogues, 48, survive.
113 Ōuchi, p. 68.
114 Huang Zongxi, comp., *Ming wenhai*, v. 1, 88, pp. 860–1. Such a view was an extreme expression of literati distaste for commercial, non-Confucian publications that they previously had preferred to dismiss as not worthy of being read — being burnt is not mentioned — by true scholars (e.g., Wu Hai, *Wenguo zhai ji* [Collected writings of the Wenguo Studio] [reprint, Taipei: Xin wenfeng, 1985], 4.1a–2a, in the fourteenth century). Also, see Anne E. McLaren, *Chinese Popular Culture and Ming Chantefables* (Leiden: E.J. Brill, 1998), pp. 1 and 279.
115 Lang Ying, 24, p. 370.
116 Huang Zongxi, *Ming wenhai*, v. 1, 105, p. 1,034. For further information on this key factor in the Ming publishing boom, see Inoue, "Shoshi,"

pp. 323–6 and 328; and Kin Bunkyō, "Tō Hin'in to Minmatsu no shōgyō shuppan (Tang Binyin and commercial publication in the late Ming)," in Arai, pp. 339–85.

117 Han Xifeng and Wang Qingyuan, *Xiaoshuo shufang lu* (A list of private printers of fiction) (Shenyang: Chunfeng wenyi, 1987).

118 Han Xifeng, Mou Renlong, and Wang Qingyuan, comp., *Xiaoshuo shufang lu* (A list of private printers of fiction) (Beijing: Beijing tushuguan chubanshe, 2002).

119 Fan Fengshu, p. 197.

120 Li Bozhong, *Jiangnan de zaoqi gongyehua* (The early period of industrialization in the lower Yangzi delta) (Beijing: Shehui kexue wenxian chubanshe, 2000), p. 181.

121 Inoue, "Zōsho," pp. 426–9. Unfortunately, the figures for Yuan and Ming imprints are available for only one collection, the National Library in Taipei.

122 Inoue, *Chūgoku*, p. 169.

123 Katsuyama, pp. 2–4.

124 Inoue, *Chūgoku*, pp. 159–61 and 204–5.

125 Twitchett, *Printing and Publishing in Medieval China*, p. 64; and Inoue, "Zōsho," pp. 422–7 and "Shoshi," pp. 312–5.

126 Hu Yinglin, 4, p. 57.

127 This figure is based on two sources. Tsien, p. 367, n. c, drawing on the work of Western historians, claims that about 20 million books (representing 10–15,000 different texts or 30–35,000 editions) were printed in Europe between 1450 and 1500. Yet, one of the sources he uses — Lucien Febvre and Henri-Jean Martin, trans. David Gerard, *The Coming of the Book, The Impact of Printing, 1450–1800* (London: Verso Editions, 1984) — after claiming on p. 248 that 20 million books were published during this half-century, accepts on p. 350, n. 343, the possibility of a much lower figure of 12 million. The sixteenth-century figure of 100 million is that found in Michael H. Harris, *History of Libraries in the Western World* (London: The Scarecrow Press, 4th ed., 1995), p. 131. It, too, is based on some speculation and is meant to be a rough figure indicative of a scale of production rather than a precise quantity: "It has been estimated that in the 16th century more than 100, 000 different books were printed in Europe alone, and assuming an average of 1,000 copies each, that would mean a hundred million available to Europeans during the century." The Chinese are not the only fishermen.

128 St Clair, p. 22.

129 James Raven, Helen Small, and Naomi Tadmor, eds., *The Practice and Representation of Reading in England* (Cambridge: Cambridge University Press, 1996), pp. 5 and 7. McKitterick, p. 11, confirms this conclusion with further examples of the persistence of manuscript culture up to

the nineteenth century in parts of the West: "For Hebrew, Greek and music, all requiring type or other printing materials that were not always readily available, or where demand was insufficient to justify them, the manuscript tradition lasted long after the invention of printing. Nineteenth-century Jewish communities in eastern Europe, Italy and Spain all made and used many of their books in manuscript. In Ireland, the manuscript tradition was for many purposes stronger than the printed until the late nineteenth century. In educational communities, whether in Europe or North America, the copying out of texts and habits of note-taking implied a continuing commitment to scribal culture alongside that of printing. Across Europe, news was published in manuscript as well as in print in the seventeenth and eighteenth centuries."

130   Li Bozhong, pp. 172–7.

131   Ōki Yasushi, "Minmatsu Kōnan ni okeru shuppan bunka no kenkyū (Research on the culture of publishing in the Lower Yangzi Delta in the late Ming)," *Hiroshima daigaku bungakubu kiyō* (Journal of the Faculty of Letters of Hiroshima University) 50.1 (Jan. 1991), special issue, pp. 48–61; and Hu Yinglin, 4, p. 57.

132   Chen Dengyuan, *Tianyi ge cangshu kao* (On the Tianyi ge collection) (Nanjing: Jinling daxue Zhongguo wenhua yanjiusuo, 1932), p. 24.

133   Ye Changchi, 2, p. 136; 4, pp. 307 and 353; and Li and Chen, pp. 125–6.

134   Li Xu, *Jie'an laoren manbi* (Casual jottings of old Li Xu) (Beijing: Zhonghua shuju, 1982), 8, p. 334.

135   Hu Yinglin, 4, p. 59; and Inoue, "Zōsho," pp. 419–20.

136   Hu Yinglin, 4, p. 54.

137   Ye Ruibao, p. 210.

138   Ye Changchi, 2, pp. 161–2.

139   Ibid., 2, p. 131. This latter title is said not to have been printed in the Ming, at least up to this date.

140   Ye Ruibao, p. 233.

141   Zheng and Li, p. 42.

142   Xu Bo, *Hongyu lou*, 1.30b.

143   Ibid., 1.13a–b.

144   Zhang Lixing, *Yangyuan xiansheng quanji* (Complete collected writings of Zhang Lixiang) (Beijing: Zhonghua shuju, 2002), v. 2, 20, p. 601. Li Ruiliang, p. 333, claims that, until at least the eighteenth century, the texts of 80 to 90 percent of the 7,000 to 8,000 titles in the *Yongle dadian* survived only in this vast compendium (the three copies of which were kept in only two cities, two in Beijing and one in Nanjing). If so, these books would have remained out of the hands of private collectors, since the collection was off-limits to non-imperial household members and only a few titles leaked out during the Ming.

145 Liu Yucai, "Zhu Yizun yu pushu ting (Zhu Yizun and the Pushu Pavilion)," *Cangshujia* (Book Collector) 2 (2000), p. 43.
146 As conveniently listed in Ren Jiyu, v. 1, p. 129.
147 Li and Chen, p. 90.
148 He Mengchun, *Yanquan He xiansheng Yudong xulu* (Properly ordered writings of He Mengchun) (1584 ed.), 35.10a–b.
149 Gu Yanwu, *Gu Tinglin shiwen ji*, 2, p. 30.
150 Gui Zhuang, *Gui Zhuang ji* (Collected writings of Gui Zhuang) (Shanghai: Guji, 1984), 10, p. 516. His wife reportedly brushed some of these handcopies for him (Wu Qingdi, *Jiaolang cuolu* [Small records from the bamboo corridor] [Beijing: Zhonghua shuju, 1990], pp. 131–2).
151 Wang Wan, *Yaofeng wenchao* (Transcription of the writings of Wang Wan) (SBCK ed.), 15.5b–6b.
152 Sun Dianqi, ed., *Liuli chang xiaozhi* (Short gazetteer of Liuli chang) (Beijing: Guji, 1982), pp. 100–2.
153 James Hayes, "Specialists and Written Materials in the Village World," in David Johnson, Andrew Nathan, and Evelyn Rawski, eds., *Popular Culture in Late Imperial China* (Berkeley: University of California Press, 1985), pp. 78–107.

Chapter 3

1 Fan Fengshu, pp. 159–60; Huang Xingzeng, *Pinshi zhuan* (Biographies of poor scholars) (CSJC ed.), xia, p. 26; Ren Jiyu, v. 2, p. 1,035; and Gu Zhixing, *Zhejiang cangshujia cangshulou* (Book collectors and libraries in Zhejiang) (Hangzhou: Zhejiang renmin, 1987), p. 119.
2 Qi Chengye, *Dansheng tang cangshu yue* (Pacts for the collection of Dansheng Hall) (Shanghai: Gudian wenxue chubanshe, 1957), jushu xun, p. 12; and Fan Fengshu, p. 100.
3 Xu Bo, *Biqing*, 7, p. 242.
4 My discussion here has benefited from a reading of Natalie Zemon Davis, *The Gift in Seventeenth-Century France* (Oxford: Oxford University Press, 2000).
5 Fan Fengshu, pp. 117–20 and 127–8; twice as many collectors, it should be noted, are known to have donated parts of their own collection to the government or allowed it to copy them (ibid., pp. 128–31).
6 Wang He, p. 69.
7 Ren Jiyu, v. 2, pp. 938–9 and 944; and Zhang Xiumin, pp. 402 and 405–6.
8 Ren Jiyu, v. 1, p. 97.
9 E.g., Jiang Naike, *Jiang Naike ji* (Collected writings of Jiang Naike) (Changsha: Yuelin shushe, 1997), pp. 382–3; and *Huangshan zhi dingben* (Gazetteer of Yellow Mountain, fixed edition) (1686 pref.), 3, yiwenzhi, shang, 21a–b.

10 Fu and Xie, v. 1, pp. 360–76; and Ren Jiyu, v. 1, p. 771.
11 Fan Fengshu, p. 193; and Ren Jiyu, v. 2, p. 961. The family's retention of at least some of Ye's books required a strenuous effort by a grandson (Zheng and Li, p. 31; and Ye Changchi, 2, pp. 116–7).
12 Ibid., v. 2, p. 963.
13 Ibid., v. 2, p. 983.
14 Fan Fengshu, p. 223.
15 Ren Jiyu, v. 2, p. 1,059.
16 As related in Liu, Song, and Zheng, pp. 58–363.
17 E.g., Zhou Mi, 12, p. 216; and personal interview with Ren Guiquan (Shaoxing, September 2004). Xu Bo, *Biqing*, 7, p. 240; and Liu Yucai, "Zhu Yizun yu pushu ting (Zhu Yizun and the Pushu Pavilion)," *Cangshujia* 2 (2000), p. 44.
18 Gui Youguang, *Gui Youguang quanji* (Collection of the complete writings of Gui Youguang) (Hong Kong: Guangjie, 1959), 25, p. 308.
19 Fan Jingzhong, "Cangshu mingyin ji (Inscriptions on collectors' seals)," *Cangshujia* 3 (2001), p. 150. For a case of a collector forced by his financial circumstances to sell books, see Zhang Huibian, p. 375.
20 Xu Bo, *Hongyu lou tiba* (Colophons in the collection of Xu Bo), in Feng Huiming, Li Wanjian, et al., v. 2, 1.36b.
21 Fan Fengshu, p. 152.
22 Kong Qi, *Zhizheng zhiji* (A frank account of the Zhizheng [1341–67] reign era) (Shanghai: Guji, 1987), 2, pp. 39–40.
23 Gu Qiyuan, *Kezuo zhuiyu* (Superfluous talk from the guest's seat) (Beijing: Zhonghua shuju, 1987), 8, p. 253.
24 Wang Shizhen, *Yanzhou shanren xugao* (A draft of the Continuation of the writings of Wang Shizhen) (Taipei: Wenhai chubanshe, 1974), 164.5a. He also tells of the damage the heirs do to books when they divide them up as part of the family's estate.
25 Li Xu, 5, pp. 200–1; and Fan Fengshu, p. 196. This story is reminiscent of the fate of the famous medieval English collector Richard de Bury: he "was a heavy debtor, and as he lay dying, his servants stole all his moveable goods [including his books] and left him naked on his bed save for an undershirt which a lackey had thrown over him" (Ernest A. Savage, *Old English Libraries, the Making, Collection, and Use of Books During the Middle Ages* [London: Methuen and Co., Ltd., 1911], p. 179).
26 Ye Ruibao, p. 220. Likewise, Gui Zining, a son of the influential Suzhou writer Gui Youguang, sold off to a book merchant his father's unpublished writings for publication; he later recovered not these manuscripts but the woodblocks carved with these texts, to control and profit from all subsequent publication of these works of his father (ibid., p. 208).
27 Fan Fengshu, p. 237.
28 Ye Ruibao, p. 233.

29 Huang Zongxi, comp., *Ming wenhai*, 479, p. 5,158.
30 Toyama Gunji, *Chūgoku no sho to hito* (Calligraphy and men in China) (Osaka: Sōgensha, 1971), pp. 238–9. Xiang's book collection, however, seems to have survived until it was plundered by Wang Liushui and his numerous underlings during the Manchu invasion of the delta in the mid-seventeenth century (Fan Fengshu, pp. 212–3).
31 Ibid., 2, p. 100.
32 Li and Chen, p. 119.
33 Fan Jingzhong, p. 150. He is quoting here the major Huzhou painter and collector Zhao Mengfu (1254–1322).
34 Ibid., p. 152.
35 Wang Mingqing, houlu, 7, pp. 173–4. Lu You's story about this misfortune, though slightly different, underlines the family's attachment to its book collection: when the father, Wang Xingzhi, died, Qin Xi, a son of the notorious prime minister Qin Gui [in 1147], took advantage of his father's position to inform the prefecture by a handwritten note that he wanted to take over this book collection and would be willing to have an official title conferred on the son(s?). The son, Wang Lianqing [the elder brother of Wang Mingqing], tearfully resisted, [saying], "I wish to protect it to the death and do not wish to be made an official." The prefect then pressured and enticed him with [talk of] disaster and good fortune, but he listened to none of this. Qin Xi still could not snatch it and stopped" (Lu You, *Laoxue an biji* [Notes of the hut of old learning] [Beijing: Zhonghua shuju, 1979], 2, p. 20).
36 Gu Yanwu, *Gu Tinglin shiwen ji*, 2, pp. 31–2; and Inoue Susumu, "Chō shi *Ko Teirin sensei nenpyō fukusei* (A supplement to the *Chronicle of Gu Yanwu's Life* compiled by Zhang Mu)," p. 431, n. 1, in Iwami Hiroshi and Taniguchi Kikuo, eds., *Minmatsu Shinshū ki no kenkyū* (Studies on the late Ming and early Qing) (Kyoto: Kyoto daigaku jimbun kagaku kenkyūjo, 1989).
37 Inoue, *Chūgoku*, p. 109.
38 Huang Zhen, 70.18b; and Fang Hui, comp., *Yingkui lüsui* (Collection of Tang and Song regulated verse) (SKQSZB ed.), 20.49a.
39 Wing-tsit Chan, *Chu Hsi, New Texts* (Honolulu: University of Hawaii Press, 1989), p. 78.
40 Zhu Xi, *Huian xiansheng Zhu Wengong wenji* (Collected writings of Zhu Xi) (SBCK ed.), 18.17a–32a, and 19.1–27a.
41 Ōuchi, pp. 62–3; K.T. Wu, pp. 249–50; Wang He, pp. 73–7; and Ye Dehui, *Shulin qinghua* (Pure talk on books) (Beijing: Zhonghua shuju, 1957; 4th print., 1999), 7, p. 180.
42 Lucille Chia, *Printing for Profit*, p. 183; also Lu Shen, p. 8, where the quality of their printing is criticized as inferior to that of books from commercial establishments.

43   Hu Yinglin, 4, p. 54. Lest the practice seem uniquely Chinese, it is useful to note the medieval English and French practice of presenting books for favors (Savage, pp. 180–1; and Davis, *passim*).

44   Gu Yanwu, *Rizhi lu jishi*, 18, p. 644.

45   Xu Bo, *Biqing*, 7, p. 242.

46   Ding Shen, zhong, p. 50.

47   Zhao Ruzhen, *Guwan zhinan quanbian* (Complete text of a manual for antiquities) (Beijing: Beijing chubanshe, 1995), p. 12. Such gifts were doubtless far more defensible "bribes" than money gifts and could more easily survive any government campaign to do away with corruption. Also, many officials collected books and artwork, often exchanging and dealing in them to improve their holdings; and, many booksellers commonly presented their clients with gifts, particularly when visiting them to show their latest offerings (Ren Jiyu, v. 1, p. 253).

48   Inoue, *Chūgoku*, pp. 210–4.

49   E.g., Yang Shiqi, *Dongli xuji*, 17.15a–b. Two titles were purchased by personally seeking out their holders, a villager and a servant (ibid., 17. 7b and 12b).

50   Inoue, *Chūgoku*, p. 211, mentions two; three others are found in Yang Shiqi, *Dongli xuji*, 17.15a–b, 19.3a, and 20.2a.

51   Ibid., 17.3b, 4a, 5a, 5b, 8a, 13a, 19a, 23b–24a; 18.24b, 25a, 30b; and 19.13b.

52   Ibid., 18.5a.

53   Ibid., 16.1a–ff.

54   Inoue, *Chūgoku*, p. 214.

55   Yang Shiqi, *Dongli xu ji*, 17.25b.

56   Ibid., 17.23b–24a and 18.15b.

57   Ibid., 19.1a–b.

58   Ibid., 17.6a.

59   Ibid., 16.16a.

60   Ibid., 17.1b–2a. Here he explains that only after moving to Wuhan did he acquire the full text, since "when I was young, it was very hard to get books."

61   Ibid., 16.21b.

62   Ibid., 16.14b–15a.

63   Ibid., 17.12a–b and 19b–21a.

64   Ibid., 18.5b and 13b–14a.

65   Ibid., 17.15b. Also, Xu Bo, *Biqing*, 7, pp. 238–9.

66   Yang Shiqi, *Dongli xuji*, 19.4a, and 15a.

67   Ibid., 17.13a.

68   Ibid., 17.20b–21a.

69   Ibid., 17.23a–b. His copy of the *Shiji* was completed only after receiving unexpected help from an official friend (ibid., 17.18b–19a).

70 The experience of a contemporary, the similarly well-placed high scholar-official and bibliophile Chen Ji (1364–1457), would appear to support this conclusion, as Chen is said to "have bought very many books throughout his life" (Ye Ruibao, p. 147).

71 Xie Zhaozhe, 13, pp. 379–80; Xu Bo, *Boqing*, 7, pp. 238–9, 240; and Gu Qiyuan, 8, p. 253.

72 Anon., *Daoshan qinghua* (Pure talk from Daoshan) (CSJC ed.), p. 6. One thirteenth-century book peddler's catalogue was headed by a preface written by a well-known literatus (Xu Fei, *Xianchou ji* [Collection of an offering of meagre writings] [CSJC ed.], p. 4).

73 Pan Meiyue, pp. 14–7.

74 Fan Fengshu, pp. 251–63. Fewer than half were published, usually only in the twentieth century.

75 Chen Zhensun, *Zhizhai shulu jieti* (Book catalogue of Chen Zhensun, with bibliographic explanations) (Shanghai: Guji, 1987), pp. 1 and 3.

76 Huang Yuji, *Qianqing tang shumu* (Book catalogue of the Hall of a Hundred Thousand Acres) (Shanghai: Guji, 1990), p. 3.

77 Pan Mingrong, "Shuyu efeng shiyu Nan Song kao (On the beginning in the Southern Song of bad practices in the book business)," *Xianggang zhongwen daxue Zhongguo wenhua yanjiusuo xuebao* (Journal of the Institute of Chinese Culture of the Chinese University of Hong Kong) 12 (1981), pp. 271–6; Ye Quan, *Xianbo bian* (Extensive and worthy collection) in *Mingshi ziliao congkan* (Collection of Ming history sources), v. 1 (Nanjing: Jiangsu renmin, 1981), p. 165, on fake products in Nanjing, Beijing, and Suzhou; and on the case of the faker Feng Fang, Gu Zhixing, *Zhejiang cangshujia*, p. 98. For private publishing in the Ming and Qing, see Ye Shusheng and Yu Jinghui, *Ming Qing Jiangnan siren keshu shilue*. Hu Yinglin, 32, sibu zhenghua, xia, p. 423, noted that counterfeit books were most numerous, in descending order, among philosophical writings (especially Daoist and various texts of military schools), then the Confucian canon (especially the *Yijing* [Book of Changes] and divination texts), next history (especially historical accounts and miscellaneous stories), and, least of all, literary collections. Presumably, this order reflected the relative demand for these books, their market value, and the reading matter of sixteenth-century literati (but for fiction). Wu Han, "Hu Yinglin nianpu (Chronology of Hu Yinglin)," in Beijing shi lishi xuehui, comp., *Wu Han shixue lunzuo xuanji* (Selection of historical writings by Wu Han) (Beijing: Renmin, 1984), v. 1, pp. 401–4, has much interesting information on fake books.

78 Xu Fei, p. 4.

79 Chen Xuewen, *Ming Qing shiqi Hang Jia Hu shizhen shi yanjiu* (Research on the history of markets and market towns in Hangzhou, Jiaxing, and Huzhou in the Ming and Qing periods) (Beijing: Qunyan chubanshe, 1993), pp. 301–5; and Ye Changchi, 6, pp. 604–5.

80   Li Xu, 3, pp. 106–7. These stores probably provided a wide variety of related services, including the sale of stationery (Inoue, *Chūgoku,* p. 146, for the Song). Contrast this early date in China with Benjamin Franklin's complaint that, in 1725, London had no book-renting facility (St Clair, p. 239).

81   *Qiongzhou fuzhi* (Gazetteer of Qiongzhou prefecture) (1619), 11.26b.

82   Ibid., 11.26b–29b; and Yu Zhi, *Deyi lu* (A record of attaining unity) (1869 ed.; reprt., Taipei: Huawen shuju, 1968), 11.1.5b–6a.

83   Murakami Kōichi, "Chūgoku no shoseki ryūtsū to kaeshihonya (2) (Book circulation and lending libraries in China, pt. 2)," *Nagoya daigaku bungakubu kenkyū ronshū* (Collection of research essays at the Faculty of the Arts at Nagoya University) 106 (1990), pp. 229–43. These women seem to have been able to "read" these books by reading aloud the characters they recognized in order to help them remember all the lyrics of particularly popular tunes. Li Ensoku, "Chōsen goki no seisatsu (Lending libraries in the late Chōsen period)," paper presented at the Third International Conference on Publishing Culture in East Asia, Sendai, November 2003, shows that the principal clientele for Korean lending libraries, from their appearance in the eighteenth century, also was female readers, especially for books of fictional stories that were written in Han'gŭl script and presented in manuscript form.

84   *Chinese Repository* 4 (1835–36), p. 190.

85   Xu Yang, "Shupu shuo (Talk on bookstores)," *Cangshujia* 5 (2002), pp. 168–78, esp. 169–71.

86   Inoue, *Chūgoku,* p. 146.

87   Ibid., pp. 78–9 and 148–9. Note that, in Kaifeng, many bookstalls opened only at the periodic market, held every six days, at the large Buddhist temple, the Xiangguo si. Just outside the east gate were specialized bookshops (ibid. *Chūgoku,* p. 145; and Xiung Boli, *Xiangguo si kao* [A study of Xiangguo Temple] [Henan: Zhongzhou guji chubanshe, 1985], pp. 90–2).

88   Inoue, *Chūgoku,* pp. 110–1, 130. In 1072, the Japanese monk Jōjin, who visited China in the late eleventh century, reports buying Buddhist and non-Buddhist books at the entrance to a Buddhist temple in present-day northern Jiangsu Province (ibid., p. 111).

89   Wang He, pp. 80–3; Gu Zhixing, comp., *Zhejiang chuban shi yanjiu, Zhong Tang Wudai Liang Song shiqi* (Research on the publishing history of Zhejiang, in the mid-Tang, the Five Dynasties, and the Northern and Southern Song periods) (Hangzhou: Zhejiang renmin, 1991), pp. 16–7; and *Nan Song Jingcheng Hangzhou* (Hangzhou, the capital city of the Southern Song) (Hangzhou: Zhejiang renmin, 1988; v. 4 of the *Hangzhou lishi congbian*), pp. 124–7. As late as 1948, it was reported, "many of the larger book stores in China are also printing offices" (Rudolph, p. xi).

90 Inoue, *Chūgoku*, p. 209; and Ye Changchi, 3, pp. 309 and 311.
91 Xie Zhaozhe, 13, p. 265; and Ren Jiyu, v. 1, p. 245. In the late Ming, a major collector like Qian Qianyi might buy other collectors' entire holdings from such visiting book merchants (Ye Changchi, 4, p. 335); in the nineteenth century, the collection that Sir Thomas Wade acquired in China between 1842 and 1882 was, according to Herbert Giles, "not bought off-hand in the market—such a collection indeed would never come into the market ..." (Herbert A. Giles, *China and the Chinese* [New York: Columbia University Press, 1902], p. 39). I take Giles's remark to mean that book dealers delivered to Wade in the British Consulate the books they had found at his request or they wished to introduce to him for sale. Either way, he did not acquire in a bookstore a sizeable portion of his collection in one purchase.
92 Inoue, *Chūgoku*, p. 148.
93 *Songjiang fuzhi* (Gazetteer of Songjiang prefecture) (1817), 30.10b.
94 Inoue, *Chūgoku*, p. 234.
95 Ibid., pp. 234–5; and p. 48 n40 above.
96 Inoue, "Shoshi," pp. 316–7; and Wu Xiaoming, pp. 102–3.
97 Zhang Xiumin, pp. 343–8, 365–6, 369–72. See also Shen Zhenhui, "Mingdai Jiang Zhe diqu de shangpin jingji yu cangpin shichang (The commodity economy and the commercial market in the Jiangsu and Zhejiang area in the Ming dynasty)," *Wenhua yichan yanjiu jikan* (Seasonal journal of research on cultural heritage), 3 (2003), pp. 282–8. Ye Ruibao, "Suzhou shufang keshu kao" (On commercial publishing houses in Suzhou), *Jiangsu chubanshi* 1992.3, pp. 78–149, lists thirty-one pre-1600 Ming commercial publishing houses and another ninety-six in the next forty-five years. Between 1601 and 1610 alone, forty-one new publishing houses appeared. However, most appear to have been only irregularly active.
98 Inoue, "Shoshi," pp. 316–9. Jiang Jinghuan, 13a, tells of a store for old books in Suzhou to the right of the City God Shrine in the city's center in the late Ming. In early seventeenth-century Nanchang, two book merchants paid no attention to recent commercial publications. They made a living by specializing solely in old books, which they acquired from large, old families in the area (Inoue, *Chūgoku*, pp. 245–6).
99 Wu Han, "Hu Yinglin," is the best study we presently have of Hu's life and bibliophilia. Also, Ren Jiyu, v. 2, pp. 1,087–92, is useful.
100 Hu's inclusion of several thousand *juan* of Buddhist and Daoist texts (attached to the end of his catalogue as a distinct category of books along with encyclopedias and fake old books, a topic which fascinated him) marked Hu off from the more conventional collectors of his time (Ren Jiyu, v. 2, pp. 1,091–2).
101 In 1588, obeying his father's order to take the metropolitan exams, Hu

went as far north as Hangzhou, before he fell ill and had to return home (Wu Han, "Hu Yinglin," p. 406).

102 Xie Zhaozhe, 13, p. 265, relates how Hu outfoxed the ignorant heirs of a major local collector to purchase a sizeable collection very cheaply, one further sign that this master of the sixteenth-century book trade quite likely dealt in valuable rare books in some capacity.

103 Ren Jiyu, v. 2, pp. 1,088–9.

104 Hu Yinglin, 4, pp. 65–ff. Hu's underestimate of the production level of Fujian imprints seems doubly odd due to their reputed significance in his own collection.

105 Fu Xuanzong, v. 1, p. 523; and n. 87 above.

106 Lu Shen, p. 7. According to Lu Shen, only Suzhou book artisans were even slightly up to past standards of book production (ibid.). By the early seventeenth century, Hangzhou's neighboring prefecture of Huzhou would replace it as a production, yet not a distribution, center of quality imprints (Chen Wenxue, pp. 303–4).

107 Ji Shuying, "Tantan Ming keben ji kegong — fu Mingdai zhongqi Suzhou diqu kegong biao" (A discussion of Ming woodblock imprints and woodblock carvers in the Suzhou area in the mid-Ming), *Wenxian* 7 (1981.1), pp. 211–31. Yet, Ye Ruibao, "Suzhou shufang," pp. 85–94, lists just twenty-seven (plus five for which we first have record of a publication in 1600).

108 Inoue, *Chūgoku*, p. 251.

109 Hu's estimate has been effectively contested by Lucille Chia, who argues for considerable exchange between Nanjing and Jianyang at all levels of book production and distribution (Lucille Chia, "Of Three Mountains Street: The Commercial Publishers of Ming Nanjing," pp. 107–51, in Brokaw and Chow, eds., *Printing and Book Culture*).

110 Exactly how far they went up the Yangzi Valley at this time is not clear. In the late eighteenth century, Hong Liangji, upon taking up an appointment in Guizhou Province, noted the absence of books and ordered the purchase in the delta (*Jiang Zhe*) of numerous well-known titles, including the fourteen classics, the twenty-one dynastic histories, the *Wenxuan* and the *Zizhi tongjian* (Hong Liangji, *Beijiang shihua* [Talks on poetry from the north window] [CSJC ed.], 5, p. 61).

111 Zhou Lianggong, *Shuying* (Book notes) (Shanghai: Guji, 1981), 1, p. 8.

112 Inoue, *Chūgoku*, p. 243.

113 The development of insights along these lines, such as found in Chia, "Three Mountains Street," will eventually allow some solid generalizations on the practices of the book trade. It is worth noting that the discussion of title figures and availability in the previous chapter proceeds, perhaps mistakenly, on the assumption of an open market working solely in response to perceived needs rather than according to

private agreements reached by publishers on who could print what title when and where. The practice of such agreements in the Sibao area of southwestern Fujian in the Qing period (personal communication from Cynthia J. Brokaw) suggests a similar practice may have existed among the commercial publishers of a particular region in earlier times. Clearly, more work needs to be done on this key aspect of the book trade.

114 Huang Jin, 17.3b; and Lang Ying, 40, p. 584.

115 According to Zhang Xiumin, the fame of most top graduands in the Ming was hollow, as only two of them, Yang Shen and Jiao Hong, proved to be learned. The great mid-Ming thinker, Wang Yangming, acquired just the metropolitan degree, whereas his father ranked as a top graduand and never matched his son in learning and insight (Zhang Xiumin, "Mingdai Beijing de keshu [Printing books in Ming dynasty Beijing]," in Zhang Shudong, p. 156).

116 Inoue, *Chūgoku*, p. 252–3. Also, the metropolitan degree holder Chen Renxi published ten to twenty titles of old books and unorthodox books of exceptional contemporary interest (e.g., the works of Li Zhi) (ibid., p. 254).

117 Ibid., pp. 255–61.

118 Zheng Zhenduo, *Chatuben Zhongguo wenxue shi* (A literary history of China) (2), v. 9 in *Zheng Zhenduo quanji* (Complete collected writings of Zheng Zhenduo) (Beijing: Huashan wenyi chubanshe, 1998), p. 354.

119 Ai Nanying, *Tian yongzi ji* (Collected writings of a Heavenly Hired Hand) (1699 ed.; reprt., Taipei: Yiwen chubanshe, 1980), esp. 4.63a–64a and attached life-chronology.

120 Wen Zhengming, *Wen Zhengming ji* (Collected writings of Wen Zhengming) (Shanghai: Guji, 1987), pp. 584–5.

121 Benjamin A. Elman, *A Cultural History of Civil Examinations in Late Imperial China* (Berkeley: University of California Press, 2002), p. 661, Table 3.3.

122 *Suzhou zhuangyuan* (The top graduands of Suzhou) (Shanghai: Shanghai shehui kexue yuan chubanshe, 1993), *passim.*

123 Sawada Masahiro, "Ban Min bunjin no kumon — sakubun irai no taiei ni miru (The painful melancholy of late Ming literati — as seen in the response to being dependent on writing [for a living]," *Daitō bunka daigaku kangaku kaishi* (Great East Asian Culture University, Sinological studies) 26 (March 1987), pp. 41–55.

124 McDermott, "The Art of Making a Living," pp. 63–81; and Fan Fengshu, pp. 242–51, conveniently discusses ten collector-publishers for the late Ming.

125 For exceptions to this generalization, see Dorothy Ko, *Teachers of the Inner Chambers* (Stanford, CA: Stanford University Press, 1994).

126 Hu Yinglin, 4, p. 64.

127 Ye Changchi, 3, p. 274.

128 It is worth noting that, even as late as the Romantic period, a highly regarded poet like Wordsworth (for the far more popular Byron, it was different) found it hard to make a living as a writer. Earning from his writing no more than £5 a week for most of his adult life, "he could not have easily afforded to buy his own books" (St Clair, p. 202).

129 Anon., *Daoshan qinghua*, p. 6.

130 Wang He, pp. 79–80.

131 Wing-tsit Chan, pp. 77–81; Gao Lingyin, *Zhu Xi shiji kao* (Facts about the life of Zhu Xi) (Shanghai: Renmin, 1987), pp. 30–1; and Zhu Xi, *Zhuzi daquan* (Complete writings of Zhu Xi) (SBBY ed.), bieji, 5.4a.

132 Ibid., 18.17a–32a. For a seventeenth-century literatus who established his own bookstore (which his descendants continued to run), see Jonathan D. Spence, *Treason by the Book* (New York: Penguin Books, 2001), p. 55.

133 Inoue, *Chūgoku*, pp. 154 and 350 (n. 51).

134 Gu Zhixing, *Zhejiang chubanshi*, pp. 164–92 and 194–206. How different this attitude was from the judgment of Denis Diderot: "I have come close to practicing both professions, bookseller as well as author; I have written, and I have on several occasions printed works on my own account; and I can assure in passing that nothing accords less well with the active life of the businessman than the sedentary life of the man of letters. Incapable as we are of an endless round of petty chores, out of a hundred authors who would like to retail their own works, ninety-nine would suffer and be disgusted by it" (Roger Chartier, "Property and Privilege in the Republic of Letters," *Daedalus* 131.2 [Spring 2002], pp. 60–6, esp. 64).

135 Ding Shen, zhong, pp. 34–5.

136 Fan Fengshu, p. 158; and Ye Ruibao, p. 137. For other information on Song literati publishers, see Gu Zhixing, *Zhejiang chuban shi*, pp. 31–8, 157–60, 163–92, and 192–206; and Wang He, pp. 94–104. Ibid., p. 95, says that family-based publishers commonly concentrated on printing the collected writings of literati and dynastic histories and neglected practical or technical works; but, this apparent preference may simply reflect the arbitrary survival rate of their different types of publication.

137 Ōuchi, p. 78, mentions Qing scholars' criticism that Mao's textual collating was sloppy and based on Song and Yuan editions riddled with errors.

138 Miao Yonghe, pp. 124–30. Yet, see the ratio of three printers, twenty-four carvers, three binders, and an unknown number of scribes in the production of a woodblock imprint in Wuxi in the early sixteenth century (Ji Shuying, "Tantan banke zhong de kegong wenti [Discussion of issues about woodblock carvers]," *Wenwu* [Cultural objects] 1959.3, pp. 4–10, esp. 5).

139 Ren Jiyu, v. 2, pp. 1,127–30; Miao Yonghe, pp. 111–32; and Inoue, *Chūgoku*, p. 251.

140 Ōki Yasushi, "Sanjin Shin Kijū to sono shuppan katsudō (Chen Jiru and his publication activities)," pp. 1,233–52, in *Yamane Yukio kyojū taikyū kinen Mindai ronsō* (Collection of essays on the Ming dynasty, a festschrift upon the retirement of Professor Yamane Yukio) (Tokyo: Kyūko shoin, 1990), v. 2.

141 Another boss editor, Tang Binyin, showed how this kind of publication flourished in political and practical matters. A native of Jiangxi Province, he graduated top graduand in the palace examination of 1596 and advanced rapidly in Beijing political circles. As he rose principally through his reputation for knowledge of examination topics and literary skills, he often examined students at all levels, especially at the metropolitan exams. Soon, the offices of Beijing ministries were full of young ambitious men who considered him their patron and their teacher, and Tang's influence stretched wide enough not only to win fierce battles in the political wars of the early seventeenth-century court but also to attract enemies. Thought to be guilty of both passing an unworthy disciple in the metropolitan examination and trying to force a student's wife to become his concubine, he was then forced to leave the frontlines of Beijing politics. His solution, even as he retreated first to the Yangzi delta and then to southern Anhui, was to create men who considered him their disciples in the examination system. By relying on friends in political, Buddhist, and publishing circles, he had at least thirty-nine titles put out under his name from 1614 to 1629. All this editing work, once again, was farmed out to his numerous disciples; some of them were examination failures happy to be in proximity to his name, but others were highly successful officials still beholden to the man who had passed them and in some cases the man who had taught them how to pass over the examination hurdles. Tang's seemingly soiled reputation and extended retirement did little to reduce student demand for his exam manuals, which were said to earn ten times more than rival publications by other authors. Kin Bunkyō, "Tō Hinin to Minmatsu no shōgyo shuppan (Tang Binyin and late Ming commercial publishing)," pp. 339–85, in Arai, *Chūka no bunjin seikatsu*.

142 Jiang Jinghuan, *Wuzhong cangshu xianzhe kaolue* (Suzhou: Suzhou tushuguan, 1935), 8b.

143 Li and Chen, p. 142. Two other Suzhou collectors of books of medical prescriptions were Lu Guan (1298–1362) and Jiang Chu (1544–?) (Ye Ruibao, pp. 137 and 228–9).

144 Ye Changchi, 7, pp. 737–9; and, e.g., Du Xinfu, 5.4b.

145 Ye Changchi, 7, pp. 737–9; and Hu Yinglin, 4, pp. 65–6. This kind of "lending library" probably was more common than our scant sources suggest.

146 See Gui's appreciative comments in his *Zhenchuan xiansheng ji* (Collected writings of Gui Youguang) (Shanghai: Guji, 1981), 9, pp. 208–9; and Huang Yuji, comp., *Qianqing tang shumu* (Catalogue of the Hall of a Thousand Acres) (Shanghai: Guji, 1990), p. 611.

147 Wang Shizhen, 72.15b. A generation later, the celebrated Shaoxing collector Qi Chengye noted the existence of such a link when he observed, "Just as an old medicine seller will talk of medical skills in his old age, so will many elderly book merchants often talk of letters. After all, if you are close to vermilion seal ink and black ink for writings, you will be forced to understand things" (Qi Chengye, Cangshu xunlüe, p.16).

148 Yang Shiqi, *Dongli xuji*, 18.6a.

149 Jiang Jinghuan, 22a. Also, Luo Jizu, *Fengchuang zuoyu* (Trivial talk at the maple window) (Beijing: Zhonghua shuju, 1984), pp. 146–8. Qian's descendant took up the same job; though knowledgeable, he was judged not up to his father's ability (ibid., p. 148).

150 Langdon, p. 50.

151 Sun Dianqi, pp. 100–2. The presence of Jiangxi merchants in Liuli chang would remain strong from the mid-eighteenth century to the early twentieth, when the civil service examinations ended; a book merchant group from Jiangxi (probably mainly Jinxi county) is mentioned for eighteenth- and nineteenth-century Liuli chang on ibid., pp. 16 and 48.

152 A useful, if incomplete, chronology of his life is found in Ichihara Kōkichi, "Xu Bo nenpyō koraku (A chronology of Xu Bo)," pp. 635–50, in *Iriya kyōju Ogawa kyōju taikyū kinen Chūgoku bungaku gogaku ronshū* (Collected essays on Chinese literature and language, a festschrift for Professors Iriya and Ogawa) (Kyoto: Chikuma shobō, 1974).

153 Xie Zhaozhe, 13, p. 267.

154 I.e., 1592, 1595, 1601 (Ye Changchi, 3, p. 294; and Zhang Huibian, p. 352). Yet, he also is reported as book hunting in Suzhou in 1598 (Ye Changchi, 3, p. 295), in Nanjing in 1606 (Zhang Huibian, p. 339), and in 1609 and 1638 in Suzhou (Ye Changchi, 3, p. 312; and Zhang Huibian, p. 410).

155 Xu Bo, *Hongyu lou*, 1.6a, 12a (where he bought a 200-year-old manuscript at an old store) and 48b.

156 Ibid., 1.2b, 3a, 3a–b, 8a, 12a, 12b, 18b–19a, 27b, 36b and 41b; and Ye Changchi, 4, p. 399.

157 Xu Bo, *Hongyu lou*, 1.26b–27a, 27b–28a and 44a.

158 Fu and Xie, v. 1, p. 365.

159 Ichihara, p. 642.

160 This preference did not prevent him from doing editorial work, as when he compiled the collected writings of the Wuxi scholar-official Pu Yuan, who visited Fujian in the early Ming; it is not clear what remuneration, if any, was received (Zhang Huibian, p. 552).

161 Fu and Xie, v. 1, p. 634.
162 Zhang Huibian, p. 399.

Chapter 4

1 Robert Darnton, "What is the History of Books?," *Daedalus* 111.3 (1982), pp. 65–83; and Thomas R. Adams and Nicolas Barker, "A New Model for the Study of the Book," pp. 5–43, in Nicolas Barker, ed., *A Potencie of Life: Books in Society* (London: British Library, 1993).

2 Paul U. Unschuld, p. 55; Gu Tingchen, *(Kunshan Gu gong) Yiyan lun bingfang* (Medical discussions and prescriptions on the eye by Mr Gu of Kunshan) (1540 postface; Korean imprint in Naikaku bunko), 1b; John Kieschnick, *The Impact of Buddhism on Chinese Material Culture* (Princeton, NJ: Princeton University Press, 2003), pp. 184–5; and Cynthia J. Brokaw, *The Ledgers of Merit and Demerit, Social Change and Moral Order in Late Imperial China* (Princeton, NJ: Princeton University Press, 1991), pp. 216–7, 220–1, and 224. Xu Bo, *Hongyu lou*, 1.10a–b, relates the case of the late Ming Fuzhou publisher who deliberately left the recarved woodblocks to a Song gazetteer in a Chan temple, lest they be secreted away in a family school. He instructed the head of the temple not only to protect them but to print up a copy for interested parties. This donation, as Xu Bo recognizes, is reminiscent of the deposit by the late Tang poet Bai Juyi of copies of his complete writings in three temples (as opposed to copies given to just two relations), on the condition that they agree not to let them leave the temple precincts and not to be loaned to anyone from outside their walls (ibid.; Inoue, *Chūgoku*, pp. 102–3).

3 Winkelman, pp. 9–10; and Thomas Lee, *Government Education and Examinations in Sung China* (Hong Kong: The Chinese University Press, 1985), pp. 111–2.

4 Daoshan xiansheng, p. 6. Also, Xu Fei, p. 4, has a preface written for a bookseller's book catalogue, presumably listing his books for sale. Many book catalogues, I suspect, were compiled by the owners of the books, at least in part to instruct heirs on exactly what books they had inherited; they presumably would then be used to sell off the collection (e.g., Ye Changchi, 3, p. 281, for the late Ming Fukienese Chen Di). All parties would then have considered such a catalogue a part of the collector's will.

5 Note that my discussion here ignores two major kinds of imprint significant in the late Ming publishing boom — entertainment literature and examination manuals — to focus more on academic kinds of learning. Thus, the practices I describe may not have been relevant for these types of literary publications.

6 E.g., Marc Fumaroli, "The Republic of Letters," *Diogenes* 143 (Fall 1988), pp. 129–52.

7   See the perceptive comments on the gradual growth of this understanding in early Chinese history in Michael Nylan, "Calligraphy, the Sacred Text and Test of Culture," pp. 16–77, in Cary Y. Liu, Dora C.Y. Ching, and Judith G. Smith, eds., *Character and Context in Chinese Calligraphy* (Princeton, NJ: The Museum of Art, Princeton University, 1999).

8   Cao Xuequan, *Shicang wengao* (Draft of the writings of Cao Xuequan), in *Cao Dali ji* (Ming imprint in Naikaku bunko), 10th ce, 17a–18a; and Ye Changchi, 3, pp. 271–2.

9   Li Xibi and Zhang Jiaohua, eds., *Zhongguo gudai cangshu yu jindai tushuguan shiliao, Chunqiu zhi Wusi qianhou* (Book collecting in ancient China and historical sources on libraries in modern times, from the Spring and Autumn Period to the period of the May Fourth Movement) [Beijing: Zhonghua shuju, 1982], pp. 47–52; Li and Chen, pp. 211–2; R. Kent Guy, *The Emperor's Four Treasuries, Scholars and the State in the Late Ch'ien-lung Era* (Cambridge, MA: Council on East Asian Studies, Harvard University, 1987), pp. 59–60; and Benjamin A. Elman, *From Philosophy to Philology, Intellectual and Social Aspects of Change in Late Imperial China* (Cambridge, MA: Council on East Asian Studies, Harvard University, 1984), p. 154.

10 Liu Mo, "Qingdai cangshujia sanzhuan (Three biographies of Qing collectors)," *Cangshujia* 3 (2001), pp. 70–1. Zhou collected 50,000 *juan* by purchasing through book merchants the book collections of some old families (ibid., p. 70). Also, he received a friend's entire collection. But before his death, he started selling off some of these books, and his heirs then completed the dispersal.

11 Yuan Yi, "Shilun Zhongguo gudai minjian jieshu huodong (Trial discussion of book-lending activities among people in ancient China)," in Huang Jianguo and Gao Yaoxin, eds., *Zhongguo cangshulou yanjiu* (Research on Chinese libraries) (Beijing: Zhonghua shuju, 1999), pp. 360–85, claims it is very easy to draw up "a very long blacklist" (*changchang de "hei ming dan"*) (p. 363) of those who did not loan their books.

12 On Song censorship, see Niida Noboru, "*Keigen jōhō jirei* to Sōdai no shuppanhō (The *Qingyuan Era Laws and Regulations* and publishing laws in the Song dynasty)" and "*Sōkaiyō* to Sōdai no shuppanhō (The *Song huiyao* and publishing laws in the Song dynasty)," in his *Chūgoku hōsei shi kenkyū, v.4, hō to shūkan, hō to dōtoku*, pp. 445–65 and 466–91. Such laws were not enforced uniformly in the Song, and by the Ming no longer existed. Yet, the early Ming purges of officials and punishment of large landholding families in the lower Yangzi delta were not readily forgotten; witness the Suzhou author who, in 1540, burned his manuscript out of fear that the essays had deeply offended some suspicious local officials (Zhang Huibian, p. 209).

13 Eva Hanebutt-Benz, Dagmar Glass, and Geoffrey Roper, eds., *Middle Eastern Languages and the Print Revolution, a Cross Cultural Encounter* (Westholfen: WVA-Verlag Skulima, 2002), p. 56. The history of printing in the Middle East, as already noted, is greatly complicated by the use of various languages by various peoples; the first use of moveable-type printing for Arabic books there was achieved in 1610 by the Bishop of Damascus in northern Lebanon, but widespread use of this technology by Islamic Arabs for Arabic texts came only two centuries later (ibid., p. 177).

14 Johannes Pedersen, *The Arabic Book* (Princeton, NJ: Princeton University Press, 1984), esp. pp. 114–21; and Bloom, pp. 116–22, for a partial defense of the very high book figures attributed to these large collections. My experience with Chinese figures for Chinese book collections leaves me seriously skeptical of these numbers, although these Arabic libraries were in all likelihood far larger than their European counterparts at this time. More persuasively, Bloom writes of the establishment of the first public book collections in Iraq in the second half of the eighth century and the formation there as well as in Mosul, Basra, Hormuz, and Ravy of other libraries open to all scholars of all countries in the ninth century. Other large libraries were established in Cairo, and in the late tenth century in Córdoba.

15 Guglielmo Cavallo, "Between Volumen and Codex: Reading in the Roman World," p. 70, in Guglielmo Cavallo and Roger Chartier, eds., *A History of Reading in the West* (Amherst: University of Massachusetts Press, 1999).

16 Robert Bonfill, "Reading in the Jewish Communities of Western Europe in the Middle Ages," pp. 162–6, in Cavallo and Chartier. Also, a twelfth-century Jewish text, *Book of the Pious*, instructs, "If A has two sons, one of whom is averse to lending his books and the other does so willingly, the father should have no doubt in leaving all his library to the second son, even if he be the younger" (James Westfall Thompson, *The Medieval Library* [New York: Hafner Publishing Company, 1957; reprt. of the 1939 ed. from the University of Chicago Press], p. 345).

17 Montague Rhodes James, *The Ancient Libraries of Canterbury and Dover* (Cambridge: Cambridge University Press, 1903), p. xlv, on the English practice in the thirteenth and fourteenth centuries; and, Savage, pp. 115–6, on a library in Worcester Cathedral which during the second half of the fifteenth century in England was open to the literate laity, or "the public," for four hours every weekday.

18 Thompson, pp. 627–8. Some interlibrary loans were made to monasteries even in other countries.

19 Ibid., p. 637; and, Jacqueline Hamesse, "The Scholastic Model of Reading," pp. 103–19, in Cavallo and Chartier.

20   In fourteenth century Paris poor students could borrow lecture-related books from the Cathedral of Notre Dame and, when backed by security deposit, from the Sorbonne (Paul Saenger, "Reading in the Later Middle Ages," p. 133, in Cavallo and Chartier). Yet, Savage, pp. 168–9, has much of interest about the protective practices of medieval Oxford colleges: the multiple locks to their libraries and book chests, the separate holders of their keys, and the punishments, including loss of fellowship, awaiting any violator of their highly restrictive rules on access to and circulation of books.

21   Berthold L. Ullman and Philip A Stadter, *The Public Library of Renaissance Florence, Niccolò Niccoli, Cosimo de' Medici and the Library of San Marco* (Padova: Editrice Antenore, 1972).

22   Claude Jolly, et al., *Histoire des bibliothèques françaises, v. 2, Les bibliothèques sous l'Ancien Régime, 1530–1789* (Paris: Promodis, 1988), pp. 391–411 (the author here, Louis Desgraves, notes the establishment of a parish library in c.1429 in Sélestat in Alsace, and then from the mid-sixteenth century the opening elsewhere in France of book collections to professional or interested parties); Thompson, pp. 551–2, 555–6, 559, and 562–7 (on the Vatican Library); and, Anthony Grafton, *Rome Reborn: The Vatican Library and Renaissance Culture* (Washington, D.C.: Library of Congress, and New Haven: Yale University Press, 1993), p. 38.

23   Ibid, pp. 39, 42. McKitterick, p. 17, notes, however, that most Italian book collectors were reluctant to share their holdings, due to a concern for secrecy as much as for their books' safety.

24   Peter Burke, *A Social History of Knowledge: From Gutenberg to Diderot* (Cambridge: Polity Press, 2000), p. 178; Jonathan Israel, *Radical Enlightenment, Philosophy and the Making of Modernity, 1650–1750* (Oxford: Oxford University Press, 2001), p. 121; and, Jolly, v. 2, p. xii.

25   Hilde de Ridder-Symoens, "Management and Resources," pp. 155–209 (especially 195, 201), in Hilde de Ridder-Symoens, ed., *A History of the University in Europe, v. 2, Universities in Early Modern Europe (1500–1800)* (Cambridge: Cambridge University Press, 1996).

26   Reinhard Wittmann, "Was There a Reading Revolution at the End of the Eighteenth Century?," p. 306, in Cavallo and Chartier.

27   Ian Philip, *The Bodleian Library in the Seventeenth and Eighteenth Centuries* (Oxford: Clarendon Press, 1983), p. 64. In 1645 the university's leaders may have had political sympathy for the beleaguered Charles I, but they did not prevent the head of the Bodleian from thwarting their monarch's efforts to borrow the Bodleian's copy of Théodore Agrippa d'Aubigné's *Histoire universelle*; the same librarian denied a similar request, transmitted by Cromwell, from the Portuguese ambassador.

28   Philip, p. 36. As a rule, only under special terms were undergraduates admitted to the Bodleian's reading room. Even then, these privileged "undergraduates and all graduates of inferior order" were obliged, in

1613, to surrender any book they were reading when it was wanted by a senior member of the university and to defer to the passage of these superiors alongside bookcases and benches (ibid., p. 34).

29 Elisabeth Leedham-Green, "University Libraries and Book Sellers," pp. 316–53, in Lotte Hellinga and J. B. Trapp, eds., *The Cambridge History of the Book in Britain, v. 3, 1400–1547* (Cambridge: Cambridge University Press, 2002), pp. 319–27; and, *The Eagle* (St John's College, Cambridge), XXIV, no. 10 (March 1903), pp. 11–7. The situation in the Cambridge University Library was similarly restrictive. Its head in 1581–83 was expected to lock up all history and mathematics books, report to the university head all necessary repairs to chains, clasps, and bosses on the books, and restrict readers to a total at any time of just 10 masters of arts, bachelors of law or physic or persons of higher degree: "none of them [are to] tarrie at one booke above an houre at one tyme if enye other shall desire to vse the sayde booke." No book was borrowable without special permission from the university and then only "under payne of foreitture of triple valew of enye booke or instrumente lente or alienated ..." (J. C. T. Oates, "The Libraries of Cambridge, 1570–1700," pp. 213–35 [esp. 227–8], in Francis Wormald and C. E. Wright, eds., *The English Library Before 1700* [London: University of London, The Athlone Press, 1958]). In 1659 the Library's new rules let just books of common use be borrowed, but only "under caution of twice its value, to be deposited in a special chest under several keys, and manuscripts and other books of special importance to be lent out only with the consent of the Regent House and upon sufficient security or caution. No one of lower degree than Master of Arts of Bachelor of Law or Physic was to be admitted ..." Strangers were only to be admitted to use the Library if someone himself qualified to use it were willing to "be engaged for them, that the university receyve nor damage thereby." In 1675 strangers were said to gain admission only with permission of the university's head; enforcement was on some other points less rigorous. Books went astray, but admission was further restricted to only M.A. degree holders resident at the university and those expressly permitted by the head of the university. It must be said, nonetheless, that these rules fell all too easily into neglect (J. C. T. Oates, *Cambridge University Library, a History: From the Beginnings to the Copyright Act of Queen Anne* [Cambridge: Cambridge University Press, 1986], pp. 82, 122, 295–7, 300, 457, and 458–9).

30 Simone Balayé, *La Bibliothèque Nationale des origins à 1800* (Genève: Librairie Droz, 1988), pp. 70, 229; and, Jolly, v. 2, passim, esp. p. 143 on the Mazarine.

31 Ibid., v. 2, pp. 213, 224 and 226; and, Peter Burke, "Erasmus and the Republic of Letters," *European Review* 7.1 (1999), p. 10.

32   Burke, *A Social History of Knowledge*, p. 178; and, Dominique Varry, "Libraries," pp. 401–2, in Alan C. Kors, ed., *Encyclopedia of the Enlightenment* (Oxford: Oxford University Press, 2003).

33   Ibid., p. 402; Jolly, v. 2, pp. 391–411.

34   David M. Wilson, *The British Museum: A History* (London: British Museum Press, 2002), pp. 35–40.

35   St Clair, p. 237.

36   Lisa Jardine, *Worldly Goods: A New History of the Renaissance* (London: Macmillan, 1996), p. 154: "A remarkable amount of fifteenth and sixteenth-century correspondence between scholars in what was increasingly widely known as the 'republic of letters' (the global village of intellectual pursuits) was taken up with tracking down and obtaining published works hot off the printing press." See also David S. Lux and Harold J. Cook, "Closed Circles or Open Networks? Commenting at a Distance During the Scientific Revolution," *History of Science* 36.2 (1998), pp. 172–211.

37   G. D. Hobson, "'Et Amicorum'," *The Library* 5th series, 4.2 (September 1949), pp. 87–99.

38   Sir Robert Cotton provided access to his books to all those with a legitimate claim to see them. When his next two successors, from 1631 to 1707, imposed more restrictions, they did no more than oblige borrowers to sign a note confirming their loan of any book from the collection (Colin G. C. Tite, *The Manuscript Library of Sir Robert Cotton* [London: The British Library, 1994], pp. 20, 25–6, and 110–1). Sir Robert, it appears, pilfered manuscripts from an Oxford college and other collectors (ibid., pp. 106–7), suggesting that he had access to their libraries without strict controls but could not properly borrow from them. Also, see St Clair, p. 237.

39   Burke, *A Social History of Knowledge*, pp. 35, and 39–48. Yet, Roy Porter, "The Scientific Revolution and Universities," pp. 531–62, in Hilde de Ridder-Symoens, v. 2, gives a more favorable assessment of intellectual life inside Western universities in the seventeenth and eighteenth centuries.

40   L. W. B. Brockliss, *Calvet's Web, Enlightenment and the Republic of Letters in Eighteenth-Century France* (Oxford: Oxford University Press, 2002), pp. 312–23; and, Dena Goodman, *The Republic of Letters: A Cultural History of the French Enlightenment* (Ithaca: Cornell University Press, 1994).

41   Henri-Jean Martin, *Print, Power, and People in 17th Century France*, trans. David Gerard (London: Scarecrow Press, 1993), p. 608; and, Louis Desgraves, "Vers la bibliothèque publique," pp. 391–413, in Jolly, v. 2.

42   Paul Lodge, ed., *Leibnitz and His Correspondents* (Cambridge: Cambridge University Press, 2004), esp. p. 1. Descartes, to cite another example, has left over 500 letters, in what is thought to be only a small portion of his actual correspondence. Even a manic collector like Thomas Phillipps

regularly shared his collection with fellow antiquarians and scholars (A. N. L. Munby, *Portrait of an Obsession: The Life of Sir Thomas Phillipps, the World's Greatest Book Collector*, adapted by Nicolas Barker [London: Constable, 1967], pp. 249–50).

43 Varry, p. 402.

44 Wittmann, pp. 306–12; and Jonathan Rose, *The Intellectual Life of the British Working Classes* (New Haven: Yale University Press, 2001).

45 As argued very forcefully in William St Clair's *magnum opus, The Reading Nation in the Romantic Period.*

46 Fu and Xie, v. 1, p. 526–7.

47 Ibid., v. 1, pp. 337–8. It should go without saying that few if any women received such privileged access to any government library.

48 Stephen H. West, "Text and Ideology: Ming Editors and Northern Drama," pp. 343–44, in Smith and von Glahn, eds., *Transition.*

49 Fu and Xie, v. 1, pp. 532–33 and 538.

50 Ibid., pp. 540–1; and Shen Defu, v. 2, 25, p. 637. The surviving parts of this second copy were kept in the Hanlin Academy during the Qing dynasty.

51 Little relevant information seems to survive on the management of similar court libraries in the Jin, Liao, and Yuan dynasties. The best, if short, discussion is Fu and Xie, v. 1, pp. 417–19, 449–52, and 464–70.

52 Ibid., v. 1, pp. 337–8. Fan Jingzhong, "Cangshu mingyin ji,"*Cangshujia* 3 (2001), pp. 147–8, mentions that borrowers of government books in the Institute for the Veneration of Literature of the Directorate of Education were expected "to love and protect them." Those in charge of the books were not allowed to accept them back if damaged in any way.

53 Chen Shidao, *Houshan zhushi wenji* (Collected writings of Chen Shidao) (Shanghai: Guji, 1984), v. 2, 11.9b–10a, tells of rising book prices at this directorate, towards the end of the Northern Song. A similar case occurred in the early Ming, when Yang Shiqi, through a kinship tie, had a copy printed for himself from the National University woodblocks (Yang Shiqi, *Dongli xuji,* 17.17a). These arrangements were superior to those of the Five Dynasties, when imprints of the classics printed at the Directorate of Education were available only through purchase or as gifts to high officials, one of whom proceeded to make much money from his sale of these books (Inoue, *Chūgoku,* p. 109).

54 Lee, pp. 111–2; Fan Jingzhong, pp. 143–4; and Ōuchi, p. 40.

55 Ibid.

56 Ibid., pp. 40–1 and 56–7 (which discusses funds that schools in the Yuan acquired from rent on their landholdings [*xuetian*] and then used to print books on their own with government permission); Inoue, "Zōsho," pp. 427–8; and Lu Shen, p. 8. Ming schools lacked such funds for publishing.

57 Fan Fengshu, pp. 95–6; and Fu and Xie, v. 1, p. 812.
58 Li Tao, 193, p. 4,666.
59 Ibid., 194, p. 4,699.
60 Inoue, *Chūgoku*, pp. 164–5; and Jiang Shaoyu, v. 1, p. 397.
61 Fu and Xie, v. 1, pp. 306–9.
62 Jiang Shaoyu, v. 1, p. 401.
63 Chen Kui, *Nan Song guange lu, xulu* (An account, with an anonymous supplement, of the Southern Song Imperial Library and associated scholarly agencies of the government) (Beijing: Zhonghua shuju, 1998), pp. 21, 22, 175, and 191–2; and Cheng Zhu, *Lintai gushi jiaozheng* (Stories of the Palace Library, a collated edition) (Beijing: Zhonghua shuju, 2000), pp. 270, 274, and 276–7; and Fu and Xie, v. 1, pp. 338–40.
64 Chen Kui, p. 21.
65 Ibid., pp. 22 and (*xulu*) 175.
66 Ibid.
67 Kong Dingchen, *Dongyuan lu* (Record of the eastern plain) (CSJC ed.), p. 17.
68 Chen Kui, *xulu*, p. 175.
69 Ibid., *xulu*, pp. 191–2.
70 Li and Chen, p. 117.
71 Gu Qiyun, p. 193.
72 Yu Jideng, *Diangu jiwen* (Record of quotations) (Beijing: Zhonghua shuju, 1981), 16, p. 284; and Fu and Xie, v. 1, p. 537.
73 Shen Defu, v. 1, 1, p. 28; and Matsumi Hiromichi, *Toshokan to kanseki* (Libraries and Chinese books) (Tokyo: Meisei daigaku, 1989), p. 212. Qiu Jun, in 1493, claimed that not even ten percent of the books originally stored in the Cabinet Library survived. A subsequent check in 1515 revealed big gaps in the Grand Secretary and Eastern Pavilion collections. Officials working there had walked off with many of the books (ibid., pp. 211–2).
74 Wang Meiying, "Shilun Mingdai siren cangshu (On private book collections in the Ming dynasty)," *Wuhan daxue xuebao (zhexue shehui kexue ban)* (Journal of Wuhan University [Philosophy and Social Sciences Edition]), 1994.4, p. 117. Another explanation attributes the problem to the 1380 decision to put the library under the administration of the Hanlin Academy, whose members, enjoying a far higher official rank than that of the library's reduced staff, abused their powers and rifled the library with impunity (Fu and Xie, v. 1, p. 526).
75 Sun Nengchuan and Zhang Xuan, *Neige cangshu mulu* (Catalogue of the Grand Secretariat collection) (Shiyuan congshu ed.), 1a.
76 Zheng and Li, p. 63; and Ye Changchi, 3, p. 269.
77 Zheng and Li, p. 63.
78 Wang Kentang, *Yugang zhai bizhu* (Notes of Wang Kentang) (pref. 1602), 2.43a–44a.

79 E.g., Xie Zhaozhe, v. 2, 13, p. 379; and Yu Shenxing, 7, p. 82; and Shen Defu, v. 1, p. 28. It is worth recalling here one modern historian's judicious comment on the fate of books in sixteenth-century England: "For many years after the Dissolution [of the monasteries] books were thought to be safer in private hands than in institutional libraries, so that men bequeathed their books not to the universities or to colleges but to their friends or to be distributed among poorer scholars" (Oates, *Cambridge University Library*, pp. 85–6). The small number of books in these libraries indicates as much the private book collectors' lack of trust in such institutions as these institutions' lack of books.

80 Xie Zuozhe, v. 2, 13, p. 379; and Shen Defu, v. 1, 1, p. 28.

81 Liu Ruoyu, *Zhuozhong zhi*, as mentioned in Xiang Gongan, "Mingdai jingguang ben qianxi," *Gugong bowuyuan yuekan* (Palace Museum monthly) 28 (1985.2), pp. 41–5, esp. 42. It is worth noting that the early Qing regulations were far more strictly enforced: in 1685, the Hanlin Academy scholar Zhu Yizun was demoted on the charge of bringing copyists into the Hanlin Academy to transcribe official records for him (Arthur Hummel, ed., *Eminent Chinese of the Ch'ing Period* [Washington, DC: United States Government Printing Office, 1943], p. 183). By the late nineteenth century, however, prolonged neglect, theft by scholars during the annual airing of the books, and misuse of carved woodblocks as kindle wood greatly reduced the holding of books and woodblocks in the Hall of Military Glory (*Wuying dian*) in the imperial palace (Luo Jizu, p. 141).

82 Ye Changchi, 2, p. 100.

83 Ibid., 2, pp. 98–9.

84 Yu Li, "Social Change during the Ming-Qing Transition and the Decline of Sichuan's Classical Learning in the Early Qing," *Late Imperial China* 19.1 (June 1998), pp. 26–55, esp. 34.

85 Qian Qianyi, *Muzhai yuxue ji* (Collected writings of Qian Qianyi) (Shanghai: Guji, 1996), v. 2, 26, pp. 994–6.

86 Xie Zhaozhe, v. 1, 13, p. 265.

87 Timothy Brook, "Edifying Knowledge: The Building of School Libraries in Ming China," *Late Imperial China* 17.1 (June 1996), pp. 93–119, esp. 94.

88 Wei Su, 10.16a–b.

89 Timothy Brook, "Communications and Commerce," pp. 667–70, in Denis Twitchett and Frederick W. Mote, eds., *Cambridge History of China*, v. 8, *The Ming Dynasty, 1368–1644, part 2* (Cambridge: Cambridge University Press, 1998).

90 E.g., *Songjiang fuzhi* (Gazetteer of Songjiang prefecture) (1817), 30.10b.

91 Brook, "Edifying Knowledge," pp. 109–10.

92 Ye Dehui, *Shulin qinghua*, 8, pp. 222–4.

93 Fan Fengshu, pp. 60, 137, 166, and 269.

94 The big exception here was the *Yongle dadian*, but it was off-limits to all officials and had minimal impact on learning at court or elsewhere during the Ming.
95 Wang Mingqing, houlu, pp. 309–10. Wang here helps to lay the basis for mistaken claims by some later Chinese writers that this printing of the Confucian classics represented the discovery of printing.
96 Pan Meiyue, p. 131.
97 Huang Zongxi, *Huang Zongxi quanji* (Complete collection of the writings of Huang Zongxi) (Hangzhou: Zhejiang guji, 1985), v. 1, p. 389.
98 Li and Chen, pp. 135–6 and 154.
99 Ye Changchi, 3, p. 254.
100 Ibid., 2, p. 117.
101 Xie Zhaozhe, v. 2, 13, p. 381; and Gu Zhixing, *Zhejiang cangshujia*, p. 119.
102 Ye Changchi, 1, pp. 48–50.
103 Cai Peiling, *Fanshi Tianyi ge yanjiu* (Research on the Tianyi ge of the Fan family) (Taipei: Han Mei tushuguan yuxian gongsi, 1991), is the best account so far of the history of this famous collection.
104 Chen Dengyuan, *Tianyi ge cangshu kao* (A study of the Tianyi ge collection) (Nanjing: Jinling daxue Zhongguo wenhua yanjiusuo, 1932), pp. 24–7; and Liu Hecheng, Song Luxia, and Zheng Ning, *Cangshu shijia* (Families with inherited book collections) (Shanghai: Renmin, 2002), p. 65.
105 Chen Dengyuan, pp. 35–6.
106 Luo Zhaoping, *Tianyi ge congtan* (Collection of talks on Tianyi ge) (Beijing: Zhonghua shuju, 1993), pp. 34–5.
107 Li Zhizhong, et al., p. 357.
108 Luo Zhaoping, pp. 68–9.
109 Liu Hecheng, pp. 71–2; Huang Yuji, leishu lei, p. 400; and Cai Peiling, pp. 222–3.
110 Chen Dengyuan, p. 37. So did at least two other private collectors in Ningbo (Ren Jiyu, v. 1, p. 128).
111 Elman, *From Philosophy to Philology*, pp. 158–9.
112 Luo Zhaoping, pp. 41–6.
113 Chen Dengyuan, pp. 33–4.
114 Wang Mou, *Yeke congshu* (Collected writings by a rustic guest) (Shanghai: Guji, 1991), 11, p. 160. The proverb dates, it appears, from before the third century.
115 Zhou Hui, *Qingbo zazhi* (Notes by one who lives near the gate of Qingbo) (CSJC ed.), 4, p. 29.
116 Wu Xiaoming, "Mingdai de Shanghai cangshujia (Shanghai book collectors in the Ming dynasty)," *Shanghai shifan xueyuan xuebao* (Journal of Shanghai Normal College) 19 (1984.1), p. 104; Ōki Yasushi, p. 10; and Wu Han, *Jiang Zhe*, p. 159.

117 Ibid., p. 217.

118 Fan Jingzhong, p. 148.

119 Deng Zhicheng, *Gudong suoji quanbian* (A complete compilation of trifling records on curios) (Beijing: Beijing chubanshe, 1996), 3, p. 85. This comparison of bookselling heirs to beasts was far from new (e.g., Zhao Mengfu of the Yuan claimed that any descendant of his who sold his books was worse than a bird or a beast [Fan Jingzhong, p. 146]).

120 Wang Kentang, 3.5a.

121 Yuan Yi, p. 364.

122 Chen Hongxu, *Shizhuang xiansheng ji* (Collected writings of Chen Hongzhu) (SKQSCMCS, bubian), 6.4b–5a; and Ren Jiyu, v. 1, p. 129.

123 Ye Changchi, 3, p. 256. Qian Qianyi acquired all Zhao Qimei's books upon Zhao's death (Li and Chen, p. 148).

124 Wu Han, *Jiang Zhe*, p. 220; and Ye Ruibao, p. 248.

125 Zheng and Li, pp. 59, 78; Li and Zhang, p. 33; Ren Jiyu, v. 1, pp. 129–30; and Zhang Huibian, pp. 444 and 452.

126 Ye Changchi, 4, p. 399; and Zheng and Li, pp. 77–8. Qian reportedly said, "Heaven can burn the books in my house, but cannot burn the books in my stomach" (ibid., p. 79). Qian's library, however, had previously suffered serious damage during the Manchu army's conquest of Changshu county seat, where his library was stored. As Ye Ruibao, p. 248, noted, Qian and later commentators, for political reasons, preferred to attribute the destruction of the library to the clumsy servant than to the reigning dynasty's troops.

127 Gui Zhuang, v. 2, p. 494. See also Zheng and Li, p. 64, for similar sentiments expressed by Xie Zuozhe.

128 E.g., Yuan Yi, pp. 368–77.

129 Zhao Lingzhi, *Houzheng lu* (A record of fine dishes with meat and vegetables) (CSJC ed.), 7, p. 63.

130 Yang Shiqi, 17.11b.

131 Wang Kentang, *Yugang zhai*, 3.5a. The well-known Suzhou literatus He Dacheng (1574–1633) kept a borrowed copy of *Yutai ji* (Collection of the jade terrace) for twenty years (Ye Ruibao, p. 219).

132 Xu Xianqing, *Xu Yuncun yimou* (Examples for posterity prescribed by Xu Xianqing) (CSJC ed.), p. 9.

133 Gu Zhixing, *Zhejiang cangshujia*, pp. 168–9.

134 Burnett Hillman Streeter, *The Chained Library* (London: Macmillan, 1931), p. 3.

135 Holbrook Jackson, *The Anatomy of Bibliomania* (London: The Soncino Press, 1932), pp. 446–7, 460, 467, and 469. Another medieval Bodleian book bears the written warning: "He that steals this book / Shall be hanged on a hooke./ He that this book stelle wolde, / Sone be his herte colde. / That it may so be, / Seith Amen for charite" (ibid., p. 469). Ian Philip, pp. 5 and 93. William Dunn Macray, *Annals of the Bodleian*

Library, Oxford (Oxford: Clarendon Press, 1890, 2nd ed.), pp. 6–13, mentions the figure of c.600 manuscripts donated between 1439 and 1444, but many promised manuscripts seem never to have arrived. Streeter, pp. 234–9, for the retention of chains on 5,717 books in the library of Queen's College, Oxford, until 1781. Macray, p. 121, n. 1, dates the end of chaining in the Bodleian to 1761, but Arthur Waley, *The Secret History of the Mongols* (London: George Allen and Unwin, 1963), p. 19, mentions the use of a chain for a very rare Persian text, the *Vendidad*, on January 17, 1762.

136 Dominique Varry, et al., *Histoire des bibliothèques françaises, v. 3, Les bibliothèques de la Revolution et du XIXe siècle* (Paris: Promodis, 1991), pp. 267–70, for a succinct account of this scandal.

137 Ye Changchi, 3, pp. 272–3.

138 Elman, *A Cultural History of Civil Examinations*, pp. 260–70; and Jonathan D. Spence, *The Memory Palace of Matteo Ricci* (London: Faber and Faber, 1985).

139 Joanna F. Handlin, *Action in Late Ming Thought, The Reorientation of Lü Kun and Other Scholar Officials* (Berkeley: University of California Press, 1983), esp. pp. 74–7 and 84–8; and Wm. Theodore de Bary, "Individualism and Humanitarianism in Late Ming Thought," pp. 145–248, in Wm. Theodore de Bary, ed., *Self and Society in Ming Thought* (New York: Columbia University Press, 1970).

140 Gui Zhuang, v. 2, p. 494. See also Zheng and Li, p. 64, for similar sentiments expressed by Xie Zhaozhe.

141 Kristopher Schipper, "Vernacular and Classical Ritual in Taoism," *Journal of Asian Studies* 45 (1985), pp. 21–57; Cooper, pp. 23–4; Isabelle Robinet, *Taoism, Growth of a Religion* (Stanford, CA: Stanford University Press, 1997), pp. 126–8; Kieschnick, p. 184; and William Eamon, "From the Secrets of Nature to Public Knowledge," pp. 333–65, in David C. Lindberg and Robert S. Westman, eds., *Reappraisals of the Scientific Revolution* (Cambridge: Cambridge University Press, 1990).

142 Gu Zhixing, *Zhejiang cangshujia*, pp. 128–30; L. Carrington Goodrich and Fang Chaoying, eds., *Dictionary of Ming Biography* (New York: Columbia University Press, 1976), pp. 622–4 and 1,355–6; and Hummel, pp. 565–66.

143 Fan Fengshu, pp. 168–87. Another estimate, in Fu and Xie, v. 1, pp. 559–60, roughly doubles this figure to eighty percent, Jiangsu and Zhejiang Provinces along with Shanghai accounting for 275 of the 358 "famous Ming book collectors" listed in Wang He, ed., *Zhongguo lidai cangshujia zidian* (Dictionary of book collectors in Chinese dynasties) (Shanghai: Tongji daxue chubanshe, 1991). Fan's figure thus can probably serve as a minimal estimate.

144 Yuan Tongli, "Qingdai sijia cangshu gailüe" (Brief account of four private book collectors in the Qing dynasty), *Tushuguan xue jikan* (Journal of Library Science) 1.1 (1926), p. 31.

145 An example of such a club publication is Wang Guangmei, *Bailu she cao* (Draft writings of the White Deer Association) (Ming imprint, in the Naikaku bunko), published by a literary association in Wenzhou in coastal Zhejiang.

Chapter 5

1 Inoue, "Soshi," pp. 316–7; and Wu Xiaomin, pp. 102–3.

2 Jiang Jinghuan, 9a–b, tells of one Ming collector, Zhu Liangyu, paying a fellow Suzhou collector, Yuan Yi, 50 ounces of silver for allowing Zhu's servant to handcopy a book for him during several tens of visits made over the course of half a year. The Shandong collector Li Wenzao sent an expensive fur coat to a book dealer to gain permission to copy a book that this dealer was trying to conceal from others (Li Yonghui, "Beifang zhi puxue, Lingnan zhi xunli [Simple learning of the north, obliging clerks in the far south]," *Cangshujia* 3 [2001], p. 76).

3 Ren Jiyu, v. 2, p. 766 and 769.

4 Li and Chen, p. 92. Zhao provided access to students in local schools and set up a collection for guest readers (ibid.). Also, Lü Zujian, comp., *Ou gong benmo* (Basic and incidental writings of Ouyang Xiu) (1212 carving, Yuan dynasty printing; copy in Seikadō bunko), 1.1a, on how the young Ouyang Xiu acquired some learning by borrowing books from other villagers.

5 Yang Shiqi, 18.11a.

6 Zheng and Li, pp. 58–60; and Li and Chen, p. 145. Li Ruyi's reputation, however, was not perfect, as he reportedly borrowed a book (apparently a manuscript) from the Suzhou collector Qian Yunzhi and returned him only a handcopy he had made, keeping the original book for himself (Ji Shuying, p. 78).

7 Jiao Hong, *Jiaoshi bicheng xuji* (Continuation of the collected notes of Mr Jiao) (Shanghai: Guji, 1980), 7, p. 379; and Joseph McDermott, "The Ascendance of the Imprint in Late Imperial Chinese Culture," pp. 55–104 (esp. 76 and 80) in Brokaw and Chow, eds., *Printing and Book Culture*. Note that some books remained costly, presumably because of their fine carving and paper. Such costs, as well as regional price differences, help to explain why in the late sixteenth century a successful official from Songjiang prefecture spent more money for a new edition of Su Shi's writings than for a young bondservant. The price of an imprint copy of the *Wenxuan* that he also bought is estimated to have come to more than the cost of five horses, or six oxen, or ten young bondservants. Many literate Chinese anxious to be collectors or even scholars would have lacked the funds to acquire such books (Miao Yonghe, pp. 398–400).

8 Chao Gongwu, pp. 1,264–5. Other Song examples include Song Shou's acquisition of bequests from his friend Bi Shian and his mother's sonless father (Ren Jiyu, v. 1, pp. 764–5; and Fan Fengshu, p. 86).

9   Liu Yucai, p. 43.
10 Linda A. Walton, *Academies and Society in Southern Sung China* (Honolulu: University of Hawai'i Press, 1999), pp. 129, 136–7 and 141.
11 Ren Jiyu, v. 1, p. 796.
12 Zhang Jinwu, comp., *Jin wen zui* (The best of Jin dynasty writings) (Beijing: Zhonghua shuju, 1990), shang, 28, p. 385.
13 Qiao Pingnan, "Sōdai no shoin seido ni tsuite (On the system of academies in the Song dynasty)," *Teizukayama daigaku ronshū* (Collected writings of Teizukayama University) 14 (April 1977), pp. 64–89.
14 The late Ming collector Chen Yujiao, quoting a famous Tang dynasty set of family instructions, advised his heirs to keep three copies of a book: one with fine paper and ink to be stored up, a second to be seen, and a third to be inherited by the heirs (Fan Jingzhong, p. 145). I have excluded those cases of the owner loaning a book for a charge, even at an annual rate of interest (cf., Chapter 3's discussion of Tong Pei).
15 Wang Shizhen, 175.19b.
16 Li and Chen, p. 141; Ye Changchi, 3, pp. 257 and 282; Xu Bo, *Hongyu lou*, 1.16a–b; and Zhang Huibian, pp. 409 and 413.
17 Ye Ruibao, pp. 235 and 251.
18 Li and Zhang, p. 37. Huang Zongxi, it should be noted, seems to have loaned out his books to friends and to have had copies made for them (Luo Yusong and Xiao Linlai, "Huang Zongxi cangshu kao [On the collection of Huang Zongxi]," *Huadong shifan daxue xuebao* [Journal of East Normal China University] 30 [1980.4], pp. 85–9), even though not all his acquaintances were willing to show him their prized collections (Ye Changchi, 3, p. 301).
19 *Tandu xiaoli Huangshi zongpu* (Genealogy of the Huang family of Xiaoli of Tandu) (1731 pref.), 4.8a.
20 Chao Gongwu, pp. 1,253–4; and Fan Fengshu, p. 85.
21 Ibid., p. 200.
22 Sawada Masahiro, "Mindai Soshū Bunshi no konseki — Gochū bun'en kōsatsu e no tegakari (Marriage ties of the Wen Family in Suzhou — some clues for the investigation of literary circles in Suzhou)," *Daitō bunka daigaku kiyō* (Journal of the University of Greater East Asian Culture) (Jimbun kagaku) 22 (March 1984), pp. 55–71; Chen Guanzhi, *Mingdai de Suzhou cangshu* (Taipei: Mingshi yanjiu xiaozu, 2002), pp. 138–45; and Marc F. Wilson and Kwan S. Wong, *Friends of Wen Cheng-ming, a View from the Crawford Collection* (New York: China Institute in America, 1974), pp. 20–1, has some perceptive remarks on the exclusivity of this circle.
23 Joseph P. McDermott, "Friendship and Its Friends," pp. 67–96, in *Family Process and Political Process in Modern Chinese History* (Nankang: Institute of Modern History, Academia Sinica, 1992), v. 1.
24 Ye Ruibao, p. 232.

25 Xie Guozhen, *Ming Qing zhi ji dangshe yundong kao* (A study of the activities of political factions and societies in the Ming and Qing) (Beijing: Zhonghua shuju, 1982), *passim.*
26 Ren Jiyu, v. 1, pp. 773 and 781; and Fan Fengshu, p. 96.
27 Li and Chen, pp. 125–6; and Jiang Jinghuan, 6a.
28 Gu Yanwu, *Gu Tinglin shiwenji*, p. 221; and Zhang Huijian, p. 640.
29 Yuan Mei, *Yuan Mei quanji* (Complete collected writings of Yuan Mei) (Nanjing: Jiangsu guji, 1993), v. 2, pp. 378–9.
30 Ōuchi, p. 147.
31 Li Yonghui, p. 76.
32 Wang Mingqing, houlu, 7, p. 171.
33 Ren Jiyu, v. 1, p. 813.
34 Ibid., v. 2, pp. 973–4, 989–90, 1038, 1064, 1065 and 1081; Li and Chen, p. 118; and Jiang Jinghuan, 7b.
35 Ibid., 5b.
36 Ye Ruibao, pp. 171, 173, 178 and 214.
37 Li and Chen, pp. 156–7. Another such threesome seems to include Feng Shu, Ye Shulian, and Zhang Gongduan, who borrowed one another's books for copying (Jiang Jinghuan, 13a).
38 Li and Zhang, pp. 37–8; and Li and Chen, p. 149. Xu Ke, *Qingpai leichao* (Notes on types of information from the Qing) (Beijing: Zhonghua shuju, 1986), v. 9, p. 4,213, gives the names of eight of them.
39 Ren Jiyu, v. 1, p. 769.
40 Ibid., v. 1, p. 814.
41 Qi Chengye, p. 4. Qi Chengye also had a seal with a legend that underlined his wish to keep the collection intact: "My descendants are to preserve this [book] permanently" (Ye Changchi, 3, p. 278).
42 Terada Takanobu, "Shōko," p. 544.
43 Wang Shizhen, *Chibei outan* (Accidental talk north of the pond) (Beijing: Zhonghua shuju, 1982), v. 2, 13, p. 318.
44 Fan Fengshu, pp. 86, 88, and 95; and Ren Jiyu, v. 1, pp. 772–3 and 812, and v. 2, p. 1,063.
45 *Song shi* (Dynastic history of the Song) (Beijing: Zhonghua shuju, 1979), 291, pp. 9,736–7, and 294, pp. 9,817; and Fan Fengshu, pp. 86–9.
46 *Song shi*, 291, p. 9,737. Song's family collection earned such a reputation for allowing borrowing that many scholar-officials are said to have chosen to live near it, thus driving up the price of houses in the neighborhood. Song's paternal grandfather had inherited the library of his sonless maternal grandfather, Yang Hui. Since he also for some time served with his own son (i.e., Song Minqiu's father) in the court's academies and institutes, they obtained, for free, two copies of each imprint the emperor bestowed on officials in these institutions (Fan Fengshu, pp. 86–9; and Song Jijiao, comp., *Dongjing zhi lüe* (Summary record of Kaifeng) [Kaifeng: Henan daxue chubanshe, 1999], p. 395).

47   Tian Jianping, p. 347.
48   See, for example, Niida Noboru, "Gen Min jidai no mura no keiyaku to kosaku shōsho nadō (3) (Village contracts and tenancy documents, etc., of the Yuan and Ming dynasties)," pp. 671–93, in *Chūgoku hōseishi kenkyū, hō to shūkan, hō to dōtoku.*
49   Wang Shizhen, *Yanzhou shanren xugao,* 175.19b.
50   Zhang Huibian, p. 409. Li and Chen, p. 142, includes Feng Mengzhen in this pact, but Feng died in 1595, over a decade before the pact was agreed to.
51   Ibid., p. 153; and Wang Meiying, p. 118.
52   Jiang Jinghuan, 13a; Ye Changchi, 4, pp. 370–1; and Wu Han, p. 180.
53   *Qing shi gao* (Draft of the history of the Qing) (Beijing: Zhonghua shuju, 1977), 484, pp. 13, 326–7; Ye Changchi, 3, p. 354; *Jiaxing fuzhi* (Gazetteer of Jiaxing prefecture) (1872), 52.49a–b; and Xie Zhengguang, *Qingchu shiwen yu shiren jiaoyu kao* (An examination of early Qing poetry and prose and exchanges and travels among scholars) (Nanjing: Nanjing daxue chubanshe, 2001), pp. 181–300, for an extended discussion of Cao's relations with Gu Yanwu and other mid-seventeenth century scholars.
54   Cao's estimates of the loss are fifty to sixty percent of all the books (i.e., book titles) listed in ten-odd catalogues compiled since the Song, and seventy to eighty percent of "past men's poems and writings" (Ye Changchi, 3, pp. 352 and 354). These figures would seem to include both manuscripts and imprints. Though clearly guesswork, they capture well the deep sense of loss that prompted Cao and others of his generation to break with the exclusive practices of earlier generations in order to preserve the all too little that had survived.
55   Li and Zhang, pp. 31–2. Note that Ye Changchi, 3, p. 353, claims that Cao made this pact with a friend, and each of them searched for others to copy the books each wanted to read.
56   Ibid., 3, p. 354.
57   Gu Zhixing, *Zhejiang cangshujia,* p. 168; and Li and Chen, p. 179 (Lu Liao also exchanged books for copying with He Zhuo and Gu Weiyue).
58   Fan Fengshu, pp. 186 and 223–4; and Zhang Huijian, pp. 584, 627, and 640. The first Ding known to have "delighted in reading books" lived in the second half of the fifteenth century (*Jiangpu xianzhi* [Gazetteer of Jiangpu county] [1579], 12.6b–7a), so the Ding book collection presumably dated to the fifteenth century, a century after they had first become known for their medical skill.
59   Huang Yuji, pp. 380, 383 and 384. Ding Yi received the longest biography of any doctor-author named in this section; Fan Fengshu, p. 186 and 223–4; and Zhang Huijian, pp. 584, 627, and 640. The first Ding known to have "delighted in reading books" lived in the second half of the fifteenth century (*Jiangpu xianzhi* [Gazetteer of Jiangpu county] [1579],

12.6b–7a), so the Ding book collection presumably dated to the fifteenth century, a century after they had first become known for their medical skill.

60 Li Jingwei, et al., *Zhongyi renwu cidian* (Biographical dictionary of Chinese medicine) (Shanghai: Shanghai cishu chubanshe, 1988), pp. 1–4; and Ding Xiongfei, *Guren zhujia xiang fa* (Ways the ancients had of living at home and in their local district) (Tanji congshu ed.), 2a–b.

61 *Jiangpu xianzhi,* 8.30b.

62 Ibid., 8.30b.

63 Ding Xiongfei, *Guren jiazhu xiang fa,* 1a and 3a–b.

64 Li and Zhang, pp. 46–47.

65 Ren Jiyu, v. 2, pp. 1,101–10; and Li and Chen, pp. 147 and 172.

66 Huang Zongxi, *Huang Zongxi quanji,* v. 1, p. 363; and Ye Changchi, 3, pp. 264–5.

67 Li and Chen, pp. 147 and 172.

68 Zhang Huijian, pp. 627 and 640; Fan Fengshu, pp. 223–4; and Xu Bo, *Xushi biqing* (Distillations of the notes of Mr Xu) (Taipei: Xuesheng shuju, 1971), modern preface by Liu Zhaoyou, p. 1.

69 Zheng and Li, pp. 84–6; and Ye Changchi, 3, p. 264.

70 Zhang Huijian, p. 660.

71 Li and Zhang, pp. 45–7.

72 Xie Guochen, pp. 1–80; and Frederic Wakeman, *The Great Enterprise* (Berkeley: University of California Press, 1985), v. 2, p. 941.

73 As described in Elman, *From Philosophy to Philology.*

74 For the contrasting evolution of reading societies into public libraries in England, see St. Clair, pp. 246–ff.

75 Xu Chunfu, *Yiti tangzhai renyihui lu,* p. 1,197, in his *Gujin yitong daquan* (Comprehensive and unified collection of past and present medical knowledge) (Hefei: Anhui kexue jishu chubanshe, 1995). Two brief modern studies of this topic by Xiang Changsheng are "Woguo lishi shang zuizao de yixue zuzhi—"zhairen yihui (The earliest medical organization in our country's history—the Zhairen Medical Association)," *Zhonghua yishi zazhi* (Journal on Chinese medical history) 11.3 (1981), pp. 144–6, and "Woguo zuizao de yixue duan Yiti tang zhairen yihui (Our country's earliest medical group, the Yiti Hall's Zhairen Medical Association)," *Zhongguo keji shiliao* (Historical sources on Chinese medicine), 12.3 (1991), pp. 61–9.

76 Xu Chunfu, pp. 1,184–5.

77 Ibid., pp. 1,195–6. These shamans in the north, he says, are often female; those in the south are, by implication, often male.

78 Ibid., p. 1,191.

79 Ibid., pp. 1,189 and 1,190.

80 Ibid., p. 1,192.

81 Willard J. Peterson, "Fang I-chih: Western Learning and the 'Investigation of Things,'" pp. 370–411, in Wm. Theodore de Bary, ed., *The Unfolding of Neo-Confucianism* (New York: Columbia University Press, 1975).

82 John D. Young, *Confucianism and Christianity, The First Encounter* (Hong Kong: Hong Kong University Press, 1983), pp. 47–8. In particular, see Xu Guangqi, *Xu Guangqi ji* (Collected writings of Xu Guanqi) (Shanghai: Guji, 1984), v. 2, 11, pp. 505–8, for a discussion of the importance of *gong* to Xu, although here he does not relate it to Christianity. For a more nuanced interpretation, see Willard Peterson, "Why Did They Become Christians? Yang T'ing-yün, Li Chih-tsao, and Hsü Kuang-ch'i," pp. 129–52 (esp. 142), in Charles E. Ronan, S.J. and Bonnie B.C. Oh, eds., *East Meets West, The Jesuits in China, 1582–1773* (Chicago, IL: Loyola University Press, 1988).

83 Jacques Gernet, *China and the Christian Impact* (Cambridge: Cambridge University Press, 1985), p. 251, n. 22. Gernet goes on to say, "[The Jesuits'] teaching always remained in conformity with that purveyed in their colleges in Coimbra and Rome. Neither Copernicus nor Galileo were [*sic*] really legitimated in China."

84 Young, pp. 85–91.

85 Gu Jiegang, *Suzhou shizhi biji* (Notes for a historical treatise on Suzhou) (Nanjing: Jiangsu guji, 1987), pp. 185–6.

86 Liao Yan, *Ershiqi song tang ji* (Collected writings of the Hall of 27 Pines) (Taipei: Zhongyang yanjiu yuan, 1995), v. 9, pp. 383–4.

87 Cynthia J. Brokaw, "On the History of the Book in China," pp. 3–54, esp. 30, in Brokaw and Chow, eds, *Printing and Book Culture in Late Imperial China.*

88 Li Guojun, comp., *Qingdai qianqi jiaoyu lunzhuo xuan* (Selections of writings about education in the Early Qing) (Beijing: Renmin jiaoyu chubanshe, 1990), v. 3, p. 456, quoting Zhang Haishan (1781–1831) of Wujiang county in Suzhou prefecture. The availability of Song writings in the book market doubtless reflects the predominance (and presumably high prices) of Han learning scholarship at this time.

89 Alexander Woodside, "The Divorce between the Political Center and Educational Creativity in Late Imperial China," pp. 458–92 (esp. 464), in Benjamin A. Elman and Alexander Woodside, eds., *Education and Society in Late Imperial China, 1600–1900* (Berkeley: University of California Press, 1994); and Elman, *From Philosophy to Philology*, p. 203.

90 Wu Han, *Jiang Zhe*, p. 19; Ren Jiyu, v. 2, pp. 1,399–1,400; and Hummel, pp. 182–5.

91 Nancy Lee Swann, "Seven Intimate Library Owners," *Harvard Journal of Asiatic Studies* 1 (1936), pp. 363–90. Swann, even though she stresses the practice of shared reading and loaning, also mentions the unwillingness of several collectors to loan their books (pp. 374, 381 and 383).

92 Zhong Weixing, Wu Yongan and Ceng Kang, eds., *Tieqin tongqian lou yanjiu wenxian ji* (Collection of documents and research on the Tieqin tongqian library) (Shanghai: Guji, 1997), pp. 111–2. Note that the nineteenth-century gentry's efforts to open their collections to others could succumb to the old problems of poor management and theft (Li Xuemei, *Zhongguo jindai cangshu wenhua* [Book collecting culture in China in the modern period] [Beijing: Xiandai chubanshe, 1999], p. 38). Nonetheless, in some regions outside of the Yangzi delta, the sheer abundance of imprints seems to have eased matters greatly. For instance, about twenty families established a book-lending club in 1872 in the isolated Zhejiang county of Rui'an: "Since the county had few book collectors, it was not easy to borrow books unless you were an old friend of these collectors." Each of these readers thus contributed 15 cash to fund the purchase of books, which each member then could borrow. Later, the club purchased some two *mou* of land, which it used along with an adjoining temple to set up a school that would hold the library and make it public to the county. Further details of this arrangement seem unknown, but the club lasted over twenty years (ibid., p. 33).

93 Elman, *From Philosophy to Philology*, p. 104.

94 Guy, pp. 93–5.

95 Elman, *From Philosophy to Philology*, p. 159.

96 As adapted from Guy, p. 105. See also Ye Dehui, 8, p. 224.

97 Elman, *From Philosophy to Philology*, pp. 100–12.

98 Alexander Woodside, "State, Scholars, and Orthodoxy: The Ch'ing Academies, 1736–1839," pp. 158–84, esp. 175, in Kwang-ching Liu, ed., *Orthodoxy in Late Imperial China* (Berkeley: University of California Press, 1990).

99 Ren Jiyu, v. 1, p. 126.

100 Gu Jiegang, p. 186.

101 Chen Zhan, *Huang Peilie nianpu* (A chronology of the life of Huang Peilie) (Beijing: Xinhua shuju, 1988), *passim*.

102 Yao Boyue, *Huang Peilie pingzhuan* (An evaluative biography of Huang Peilie) (Nanjing: Nanjing daxue chubanshe, 1998), pp. 83–112, esp. 84–6.

103 Ren Jiyu, v. 1, pp. 133–4.

104 Ibid., v. 1, p. 130.

105 Philip Short, *Mao, A Life* (London: Hodder and Stoughton, 1999), pp. 83–4.

Chapter 6

1 Alexander Woodside and Benjamin A. Elman, "Afterward: The Expansion of Education in Ch'ing China," p. 530, in Elman and Woodside, eds., *Education and Society in Late Imperial China, 1600–1900*.

2   Hayes, pp. 76 and 92–111; and Wilt Idema, review of Rawski, *Education and Popular Literacy in Ch'ing China* (Ann Arbor: University of Michigan Press, 1979), in *T'oung Pao* LXVI.4–5 (1980), pp. 314–24, esp. 323. In Hayes's experienced judgment, these men did much to transmit the written traditions of imperial China into the life of illiterate villagers, by providing them with services that they the literate had learned about from books.

3   *Songjiang fuzhi* (Gazetteer of Songjiang prefecture) (1629), 7.2b (quoting Xu Kechang, a mid-twelfth century native of the Shanghai area) and 5b.

4   John Henry Gray, *China, A History of the Laws, Manners, and Customs of the People* (London: Macmillan and Co., 1878), v. 1, p. 167, notes a literacy divide along north-south lines among females in China, whereby female education was almost entirely neglected in the north but numerous boarding establishments and private tutors educated women in the south.

5   Zhang Shizai, *Kezi suibi* (Notes on instructing children) (Shanghai: Wenduanlou shuju, 1918; reprt. of 1873 ed. of an original 1745 publication), 6.8a. Yet, Edward Joshua Dukes, *Everyday in China, Scenes along River and Road in Fuh-kien* (London: The Religious Tract Society, 1885), p. 164, claims "In the northern provinces ... the proportion of readers is larger than in the south," a view that probably would not win the consent of most social historians of China today.

6   Idema, p. 322.

7   Zhang Zhitong, *Zhang Zhitong wenji, v. 4, Chuantong yuwen jiaoxue yanjiu* (The collected writings of Zhang Zhitong, v. 4, Studies of traditional language teaching) (Guangzhou: Guangdong jiaoyu chubanshe, 1991), pp. 19–56; and, in contemporary China, Glen Peterson, *The Power of Words, Literacy and Revolution in South China, 1949–1965* (Vancouver: University of British Columbia Press, 1997), pp. 50–1.

8   Alexander Woodside, "Real and Imagined Continuities in the Chinese Struggle for Literacy," pp. 22–45 (esp. 22 and 31), in Ruth Hayhoe, ed., *Education and Modernization, the Chinese Experience* (Oxford: Pergamon Press, 1992).

9   Rawski, *Education and Popular Literacy*, p. 23; Nakamura Tetsuo, "Kakyo taisei no hōkai (The collapse of the Chinese examination system)," pp. 115–43, in Nozawa Yutaka and Tanaka Masatoshi, eds., *Kōza Chūgoku kingendai shi* (Modern and contemporary Chinese history lectures), v. 3 (Tokyo: Tokyo daigaku shuppankai, 1978); Medhurst, pp. 171 and 178; and *Chinese Repository* 2 (1833), p. 252, and 6.5 (Sept. 1837), pp. 229–44.

10 Rawski, *Education and Popular Literacy*, p. 140; and Idema, p. 321.

11 Philip A. Kuhn, *Origins of the Modern Chinese State* (Stanford, CA: Stanford University Press, 2002), pp. 14–5.

12 Elman, *A Cultural History of Civil Examinations*, p. 247: "Although the civil service competition was theoretically open to all, its content linguistically excluded over 90% of China's people from even the first step on the ladder to success." F.W. Mote, "China's Past in the Study of China Today — Some Comments on the Recent Work of Richard Solomon," *Journal of Asian Studies* 32.1 (1972), pp. 107–20, puts the minimal adult male figure at no less than ten percent, since roughly that percentage took the examinations in the nineteenth century. W. A. P. Martin, *Hanlin Papers, or Essays on the Intellectual Life of the Chinese* (London: Trübner and Co., 1880), p. 98, puts the classically literate at just five percent of adult males.

13 Rawski, *Education and Popular Literacy*, p. 2.

14 Ibid., pp. 97–8.

15 Dukes, pp. 163–4 and 165–6, as in Rawski, *Education and Popular Literacy*, pp. 2–3. In the twentieth century, confirmation of the difference between official estimates of literacy and the real book-reading literacy described by Martin and Dukes comes in an account of a Yunnan village in 1938 by Cornelius Osgood, *Village Life in Old China* (New York: Ronald Press, 1963), pp. 95–6. Of the 126 village people judged literate, only a few could read the average book, and most knew relatively few characters.

16 David Johnson, "Communication, Class, and Consciousness in Late Imperial China," pp. 34–72, in Johnson, Nathan, and Rawski. It is probably valid to say that Chinese, more aware of the difficulties of such an endeavor, traditionally tended to focus on the individual's level of literary ability and indeed preferred to judge learning and character by examining that individual's calligraphy, not the number of characters he could identify or reproduce.

17 De Bary, "Individualism and Humanitarianism in Late Ming Thought," pp. 145–248 (esp. 168), in de Bary, ed., *Self and Society in Ming Thought*.

18 Patricia Buckley Ebrey, trans. and introd., *Family and Property in Sung China, Yuan Ts'ai's "Precepts for Social Life"* (Princeton, NJ: Princeton University Press, 1984), pp. 267–8.

19 Chen Que, *Chen Que ji* (Collected writings of Chen Que) (Beijing: Zhonghua shuju, 1979), 5, pp. 158–9, and Yu Yingshi, *Shi yu Zhongguo wenhua* (Scholars and Chinese culture) (Shanghai: Shanghai renmin, 1987), pp. 521–79. Tang Zhen, *Qianshu* (A book to be hidden) (Beijing: Xinhua shuju, 1984, 4th printing), shangbian, xia, p. 91, tells of his working in Suzhou as a merchant and then as a broker despite others' criticism that these jobs were demeaning.

20 Ho Ping-ti, *The Ladder of Success in Imperial China* (New York: Wiley and Sons, 1962), pp. 36–7 and 122–4.

21 Li Guojun, *Qingdai qianqi jiaoyu lunzhu xuan* (A selection of early Qing writings on education) (Beijing: Renmin jiaoyu chubanshe, 1990), v. 3,

p. 446, in a passage written by the Nanjing scholar Guan Tong (1780–1831). In response to complaints about such mispractice, the government, in 1793 and 1812, issued statutes that banned degree holders from working also as bookkeepers, irrigation project clerks, brokers, and even yamen runners (Ho Ping-ti, p. 37).

22   Ye Changchi, 4, pp. 742–4; and Luo Jizu, pp. 146–8.

23   Qu Zhongrong, *Qu Dafu xiansheng ziding nianpu* (A chronological autobiography of Qu Zhongrong) (Jiaye tang congshu ed. in the Republican era; reprt., Beijing: Beijing tushuguan, 1999), 61a–b.

24   Huang Jin, 17.3b; and Lang Ying, 40, p. 584.

25   Fan Fengshu, p. 212.

26   As mentioned here, the existence of Huizhou merchant collectors in the Ming may represent an exception to this general statement. They usually came from large lineages with some degree holders.

27   Ye Changchi, 4, pp. 444–7; and Ye Ruibao, p. 346. The Yangzhou- and Hangzhou-based merchant collectors, like the Ma brothers, are other important representatives of this cultural change (Ginger Cheng-chi Hsü, *A Bushel of Pearls, Painting for Sale in Eighteenth–Century Yangchow* [Stanford, CA: Stanford University Press, 2001], pp. 24–7).

28   My copy of this book is a one-volume (*ce*) imprint, published in 1941 in 3,000 copies (*bu*) for wide distribution by a Shanghai merchant identified merely as Wusheng (Aware of Sound). This book has a preface written in 1694 at Wencheng Academy in Henan; when and how it reached the lower Yangzi delta is not clear. The passages discussed and translated here are found on pages 8a–12a.

29   Daniel K. Gardner, *Chu Hsi, Learning to Be a Sage* (Berkeley: University of California Press, 1990), pp. 128–9.

30   Guan Huai, *Shilin huixun* (Collected instructions from scholars) (pref. 1789) (SKWSSJK ed.), 1, jingye, 10b.

31   Cynthia J. Brokaw, *The Ledgers of Merit and Demerit, Social Change and Moral Order in Later Imperial China* (Princeton, NJ: Princeton University Press, 1991), pp. 157–228.

32   E.g., Philip Kuhn, "Chinese Conceptions of Social Stratification," pp. 16–28, in James E. Watson, ed., *Social Stratification and Socialism in Contemporary China* (Cambridge: Cambridge University Press, 1984).

33   Gui Zhuang, v. 2, 10, p. 515, tells a remarkable story about an illiterate great-grandson of the deceased Grand Secretary Xu Jie, who was appointed to an office, thanks to holding a hereditary privilege. When his wife — who had handled all his official papers and correspondence — died, his servant told him to retire "now that you cannot work as an official." He followed the advice.

34   Donald Sutton, "Shamanism in the Eyes of the Ming and Qing Elites," p. 227, in Kwang-Ching Liu and Richard Shek, eds., *Heterodoxy in Late Imperial China* (Honolulu: University of Hawai'i Press, 2004). Apropos

of this, Woodside, "Real and Imagined Continuities," p. 32, writes of a famous Qing scholar who lamented the decline of student literacy level, from knowing over 10,000 words in the Tang to knowing about 2,000 words in the late eighteenth century: "The object of literacy theory for Sun [Xingyuan] and others like him was not to discover how many words peasant children could comfortably learn in season schools. It was how to regain for the elite the world-conquering esoteric literacy by which some sort of moral refeudalization of Chinese life might be attempted."

35 Zhang Xikong, *Jiaxun* (Family Instructions), 18.7b (in Tanji congshu ed.).
36 Zhang Shizai, 3.13a, quoting Zhu Yongjun.
37 Zhang Xuan, *Kuanyuan zashuo* (Miscellaneous talk), shang, 15a–b.
38 Guan Huai, 1, jingye, 11a.
39 Zhang Shizai, 5.2a.
40 Zhang Xikong, 18.7a.
41 Zhang Shizai, 5.10a.
42 Ibid., 5.10b, after saying that his family had continued their unbroken tradition of reading books right up to his passing of the exams and his admission into the Hanlin Academy.
43 Zhang Shizai, 4.11a.
44 Zhang Lixiang, v. 3, 48, p. 1,375.
45 Sun Qingceng, *Cangshu jiyao* (Essentials of notes on book collecting) (Shanghai: Gudian wenxue, 1957), pp. 33–4.
46 Ibid., p. 34.
47 Kai-wing Chow, *The Rise of Confucian Ritualism in Late Imperial China, Ethics, Classics, and Lineage Discourse* (Stanford, CA: Stanford University Press, 1984).
48 Kim Hongnam, *The Life of a Patron, Zhou Lianggong (1612–1672) and the Painters of Seventeenth-century China* (New York: China Institute in America, 1996), p. 71; and Qu Zhongrong, 16a.
49 Chen Zhan, pp. 116, 118, 122, 131, 141, and 145; Yuan Yixin, comp., *Suzhou gucheng Pingjiang lishi jiequ* (The historical neighborhood of Pingjiang within the old city wall of Suzhou) (Shanghai: Sanlian shudian, 2004), p. 179; and Ye Changchi, 5, pp. 574–5, for sources that date the rituals to annual occasions between 1801 and 1811 and then in 1816.
50 Hummel, *Eminent Chinese*, pp. 340–1; and Ren Jiyu, v. 1, p. 242.
51 Liu Hecheng, et al., p. 284.
52 Tsien, p. 109, esp. n.d.
53 Liang Qizi (aka Angela Ki Che Leung), *Shishan yu jiaohua — Ming Qing de cishan zuzhi* (Good deeds and indoctrination — philanthropic organizations in the Ming and Qing) (Shijiazhuang: Hebei jiaoyu chubanshe, 2001), pp. 172–203.

54 *Xuzuan Huaiguan tongzhi* (Continuation of the unified gazetteer of Huaiguan) (1816), 9.18b, mentions also the practice of burial of the ashes in pure earth; the origin of this option is unfortunately not dated.

55 Susan Naquin, *Millenarian Rebellion in China, The Eight Trigrams Uprising of 1813* (New Haven, CT: Yale University Press, 1976), pp. 20–1.

56 The dominance of the Confucian scholars in these organizations did not prevent many of their headquarters from remaining in Buddhist temples, Daoist shrines, or even cult shrines (e.g., *Wujin Yanghu xianzhi* [Gazetteer of Yanghu county in Wujin] [1879], 3.12b–13a).

57 Yu Zhi, *Deyi lu*, 12.1a–b. A local official even prevented the potters in Jingdezhen, at least for a while, from writing characters onto the base of their bowls.

58 E. H. Parker, *Chinese Customs* (Shanghai: Kelley and Walsh, Ltd., 1899), p. 35.

59 Liang, pp. 192–200; and Sakai Tadao, *Chūgoku zensho no kenkyū.* (Studies of Chinese morality books) (Tokyo: 1960), pp. 430–1.

60 Yuan Jinglan, *Wujun suihua jili* (Record of annual festivities in Suzhou) (Nanjing: Jiangsu guji, 1998), 2, p. 63. A slightly earlier description of the same festivities in Suzhou in the 1820s stresses the inclusion of the poor but not explicitly the commoners (Gu Lu, *Qingjia lu* [A clear and delightful record] [Nanjing: Jiangsu guji, 1986], 2, pp. 48–9; and Terry L. Kleeman, *A God's Own Tale, The Book of Transformations of Wenchang, the Divine of Zitong* [Albany: State University of New York Press, 1994], p. 81).

61 Li Qiao, *Zhongguo hangye shen chongbai* (Worship of occupation deities in China) (Beijing: Zhongguo huaqiao chubanshe, 1990), pp. 144–7.

62 Woodside, "Real and Imagined Continuities," pp. 32–8.

63 Angela Ki Che Leung, "Elementary Education in the Lower Yangtze Region in the Seventeenth and Eighteenth Centuries," pp. 381–416, in Elman and Woodside, eds., *Education and Society in Late Imperial China, 1600–1900.*

64 Rev. R. H. Cobbold, *Pictures of the Chinese, Drawn by Themselves* (London: John Murray, 1860), p. 191; and Gu Lu, *Tongqiao yizhao lu* (Record of leaning on an oar at Paulownia Tree Bridge) (Shanghai: Guji, 1981), 5, p. 73. In theory, the baseness of this job might be linked to its leatherwork, as Qian, like his foster parents, was labeled a leather worker (*gongpijia*). Yet, leather workers in China seem not to have suffered the institutionalized social discrimination or ostracism evident in much of the rest of East Asia (Anders Hansson, *Chinese Outcasts, Discrimination and Emancipation in Late Imperial China* [Brill: Leiden, 1996], pp. 51 and 176).

65 Rudolf P. Hummel, *China at Work* (Cambridge, MA: MIT Press, 1969; reprt. of 1937 ed.), pp. 204–5, 212, 216, and 218 reports on the pre-industrial working conditions he observed in the Yangzi Valley and the rest of central China in the 1920s. See William Alexander and George Henry Mason, *Views of 18th Century China, Costumes: History: Customs*

(London: Studio Editions, 1988; reprt. of each author's separate *The Costume of China*, 1804 and 1805 respectively), pp. 78–9 for comments and a true-to-life portrait of a shoemaker in the suburbs of Canton that confirms Hummel's portrait of the shoe-repairman, even though the region they described is different.

66 Cobbold, pp. 196–7. The rain shoe is "made altogether of leather, and is raised at least half-an-inch from the ground by iron pegs, which look very like the large stud-nails on the doors of churches. The poorer classes, in wet weather, often use a shoe with an inch-thick-sole of wood, well deserving the name of our exploded clog. As only the sole is of wood, and the upper part of some soft material, this is greatly preferable to the wooden shoes of the Dutch sailors." (ibid., p. 195).

67 John Thomson, *The Straits of Malacca, Indo-China, and China; or, Ten Years' Travels, Adventures, and Residence Abroad* (New York: Harpers and Brothers, 1875), p. 252.

68 Wang Jin, 10.5b.

69 *Wu xianzhi* (Gazetteer of Wu county) (1933), 68, shang. 24a–b.

70 In the one book from his collection that is known to survive, he merely embossed three seal legends, in the manner of Chinese artisan painters who adorned their paintings with seals but not with poems or any writing other than perhaps an occasional signature (Ye Ruibao, p. 362). It is tempting to think that Qian resorted to the seals partly because he was gifted at neither calligraphy nor composition.

71 *Suzhou fuzhi*, 89.14a.

72 Ye Ruibao, p. 362. This imprint ended up in the famous Jiaye tang collection formed in the late Qing and early Republican years by a silk merchant from Nancun town in Huzhou prefecture. As Ye Ruibao notes, Su Shi's writings were one of the most popular and frequent literati publications from the late eleventh to mid-sixteenth centuries. See also Zhu Shangshu, *Songren bieji xulu* (Appraisal and record of the collected writings of Song persons) (Beijing: Zhonghua shuju, 1999), v. 1, pp. 401–68, with a discussion of Qian's particular title on pp. 434–50 and specific imprint edition on pp. 446–8.

73 Wang Jin, 10.5b.

74 *Suzhou fuzhi* (1883), 89.14b. The binome *liulan* can also mean "widely look at," but examples in Luo Zhufeng, et al., eds., *Hanyu da cidian* (Shanghai: Hanyu da cidian chubanshe, 1990), v. 5, p. 1278, indicate the suitability of the translation given above. Either translation, however, implies that Qian was a shallow reader (the Chinese term for which, *liulan*, is a perfect homonym for the binome in this Suzhou gazetteer biography).

75 Leung, "Elementary Education" pp. 394–5, in Elman and Woodside, eds., *Education and Society in Late Imperial China, 1600–1900*.

76 It is conceivable that he bought some of his books by Song writers, since the fall of Song learning from scholarly grace in the eighteenth century had made Song writings "extremely cheap" in Suzhou by the close of the century (Li Guojun, v. 3, p. 456).

77 Wang Jin, 10.5b; Gu Lu, *Tongqiao*, 5, p. 73; and *Suzhou fuzhi* (1883), 89.14a.

78 Wang Jin, 10.5b; and Bol, p. 28.

79 Elman, *A Cultural History of Civil Examinations*, p. 318; and Liang, pp. 180–1.

80 Peng Shaosheng, *Erlin ju ji* (Collected writings of the Two Groves) (XXSKQS ed.), 7.9b–10a.

81 Zhu'an, *Renwu fengsu zhidu congtan* (Collection of chats on historical figures, customs, and institutions) (Shanghai: Shanghai shudian, 1988), p. 250.

82 Ye Ruibao, pp. 355–6; and Guy, pp. 162–3.

83 E.g., Makita Teiryō, "Koji Bukkyō ni okeru Hō Saisei no chii (The place of Peng Jiqing [aka Peng Shaosheng] in lay Buddhism)," pp. 231–52, esp. 244–5, in his *Kinsei Chūgoku Bukkyō shi kenkyū* (Research on the history of Buddhism in early modern China) (Kyoto: Heirakuji shoten, 1957); and West, *Catalogue of the Morrison Collection of Chinese Books*, pp. 44 and 175.

84 Peng Shaosheng, 10.1a–2a.

85 Jiang Hong, Zhu Zinan, et al., *Suzhou cidian* (Dictionary of Suzhou) (Suzhou: Suzhou daxue chubanshe, 1999), pp. 1,142–3; and Makita, p. 241.

86 Wang Jin, 2.4a–5a.

87 Lu Baoqian, *Qingdai sixiang shi* (A history of Qing dynasty thought) (Taibei: Guangwen shuju, 1983), pp. 197–220, has much of interest on Peng and his circle's interest in Buddhism. Lu stresses the influence of Zhu Xi, rather than Wang Yangming, on the thought of Peng Shaosheng; by contrast, and in my view correctly, Hummel, *Eminent Chinese*, pp. 617–8, draws a descent line of intellectual influence from Wang to the Peng family via Gao Panlong and Tang Pin (1627–87). See also Peng Shaosheng, 22.13b–14a, for Peng's own discussion of his and Wang Jin's efforts to continue the efforts to combine late Ming Buddhism and Confucianism.

88 Peng Shaosheng, 9.9b–10a, for views confirmed by Kleeman, pp. 51–6.

89 Stanley Weinstein, *Buddhism Under the T'ang* (Cambridge: Cambridge University Press, 1984), p. 67; and Kenneth K. S. Ch'en, *Buddhism in China, A Historical Survey* (Princeton, NJ: Princeton University Press, 1964), p. 338; and Makita, pp. 244 and 249.

90 Ibid., p. 244.

91 Wang Jin, 6.15a; Peng Shaosheng, 22.14a–b; and *Suzhou fuzhi* (1883), 83.18a–b.

92 Peng Shaosheng, 22.15a.
93 Lu Baoqian, pp. 201 and 212.
94 Wang Jin, 2.3a–4a.
95 Xu Weixin, p. 96.
96 Peng Shaosheng, 22.14a–b and 16b.
97 Xu Weixin, p. 96.

Bibliographical Notes on Studies Useful for the Writing of This Book

Over the past two millennia, Chinese bibliographers have repeatedly demonstrated a high level of competence in understanding the origins and history of their books. They have compiled detailed catalogues for both private and governmental book collections, with admirable precision. They have made comprehensive regional surveys of book titles, that have greatly facilitated research on local history. They have developed remarkable skill at discerning subtle differences in paper, ink, and carving techniques, thereby revealing the complex history of textual and technical transmission in Chinese book history. In many ways, these scholarly traditions reached their peak in the late nineteenth and early twentieth centuries, the very time when these and other Chinese cultural traditions were perceived to be facing unprecedented threats from inside and outside the country. Classic works on Chinese book history written then, such as Ye Dehui's 葉德暉 *Shulin qinghua, fu shulin yuhua* 書林清話, 付書林餘話 (Beijing: Zhonghua shuju, 1957; 4th printing, 1999), may have been researched without all the library facilities that modern scholars take for granted. But they remain today, a full century after their first publication, important first-call reference works for all serious students of Chinese book history. Fortunately, they have been repeatedly reprinted in East Asia.

Today, the continuation of such scholarly traditions and command of the bibliographical record is evident in Chinese journals like *Wenxian* 文獻 and *Wenshi* 文史 as well as in the printed catalogues of modern libraries. These modern rare-book catalogues now number over fifty. The most comprehensive Chinese examples include those for major individual libraries, especially the National Library 國家圖書館 (formerly known as the Beijing Library 北京圖書館) with its *Beijing tushuguan guji shanben shumu* 北京圖書館古籍善本書目 (Beijing: Shumu wenxian, 1989), 5 vols., and for a nationwide consortium of 781 libraries with the *Zhongguo guji shanben shumu* 中國古籍善本書目 (Shanghai: Guji, 1986–). A seven-volume update of this catalogue, with 15 percent more entries, more information on each entry, and corrections, is Weng Lianxi 翁連溪, *Zhongguo guji shanben zongmu* 中國古籍善本總目 (Beijing: Xianzhuang shuju, 2005). Drawing upon centuries of solid bibliographical study, these catalogues have laid the basis for much future bibliographical research on imprint and manuscript transmission in East Asian history. In Taiwan, similar work has been done for the rare books in the National Library 國家圖書館 and other libraries in the *Taiwan gongcang shanben shuming suoyin* 臺灣公藏善本書名索引 (Taibei: Guoli zhongyang tushuguan, 1971). In Japan, the pre-World War II catalogue for Seikadō bunko's 靜嘉堂文庫 collection of Chinese books, *Seikadō bunko kanseki bunrui mokuroku* 靜嘉堂文庫漢籍分類目錄 (Tokyo, 1930), has been extended by detailed studies of its Song and Yuan imprints in *Seikadō bunko Sō-Gen han zuroku* 靜嘉堂文庫宋元版圖錄 (Tokyo: Kyūko shoin, 1992; 2 vols.). Unfortunately, little systematic work beyond a printed catalogue has been done on the rare Ming editions in two other important Tokyo collections, those of the Sonkeikaku bunko 尊經閣文庫 with the *Sonkeikaku bunko kanseki bunrui mokuroku* 尊經閣文庫漢籍分類目錄 (Tokyo, 1934 and 1935) and the Naikaku bunko 內閣文庫 with the *Naikaku bunko kanseki bunrui mokuroku* 內閣文庫漢籍分類目錄 (Tokyo, 1956; rev. ed., 1971). In the West, the Harvard-Yenching Institute has recently had a highly professional catalogue of its own rare books compiled by its rare-book librarian, Shen Jin 沈津, the *Meiguo Hefo daxue Hefo Yanjing tushuguan zhongwen shanben shuzhi* 美國哈佛大學和哈佛燕京圖書館中文善本書志 (Shanghai: Shanghai cishu chubanshe, 1999).

Advances in technology now promise to make possible a comprehensive online list of rare and old Chinese books surviving in China, the other countries of East Asia, and the rest of the world. The Chinese Rare Books Project, based at the Gest Library of East Asian Books at Princeton University and under the leadership of Sören Edgren, aims to compile a complete as possible bibliographical record for each individual rare book outside and inside China and to make the records available on-line. Its notable progress over the past decade and a half promises to provide a "great leap forward" for Chinese book studies, and one looks forward to the success of this and similarly comprehensive projects for cataloguing and dispensing digital information on East Asian language collections. It is clear that such data will be indispensable for future studies of Chinese bibliography and book history.

In the past century, as Western and Chinese scholars learned of the other culture's separate accomplishments, they have often focused their research on the origin of printing in China, especially the printing technology for woodblocks and moveable type. Thomas Carter's path-breaking *The Invention of Printing in China and Its Spread Westward* (New York: Columbia University Press, 1925; second rev. ed., L. C. Goodrich ed., New York: Ronald Press, 1955) made a major advance in our common understanding of pre-Gutenberg printing. Although published nearly a century ago, it contains a fair amount of information still essential to the discussion of the technical features of these inventions. Equally impressive is Paul Pelliot's *Les débuts de l'imprimerie en Chine* (Paris: Imprimerie national, 1953), a work with many suggestive comments that still await careful investigation. More up-to-date and comprehensive is Tsien Tsuen-hsuin's magnum opus, in Joseph Needham's famous series, *Science and Civilisation in China, Chemistry and Chemical Technology, V, Part 1: Paper and Printing* (Cambridge: Cambridge University Press, 1985). The synthesis of a lifetime of research and experience with Chinese books, this volume belies its title by being far more than a discussion of printing technology. It treats everything from wallpaper and the ceremonial uses of paper to ink-making methods and the format and binding of Chinese books. Perhaps the facet of woodblock printing least treated in this admirable book is calligraphy; for knowledgeable discussions of its role in Chinese printing one can safely turn to Frederick W. Mote and Hung-lam Chu, *Calligraphy and the East Asian Book* (Boston, MA: Shambhala, Inc., 1989). For a detailed photographic record of the repair and binding of old books, one can do no better than consult Du Weisheng 杜偉生, *Zhongguo guji xiufu yu zhuangbiao jishu tujie* 中國古籍修復與裝裱技術圖解 (Beijing: Beijing tushuguan chubanshe, 2003).

Detailed historical information on a great variety of technical features of woodblock book production can be acquired from the comprehensive volume compiled by Qu Mianliang 瞿冕良, *Zhongguo guji banke cidian* 中國古籍版刻辭典 (Ji'nan: Ji Lu shushe, 1999). The most complete lists of known woodblock workers (mainly the carvers) in the Song, Yuan, and Ming dynasties are found in Wang Zhaowen

王肇文, comp., *Guji Song Yuan kangong xingming suoyin* 古籍宋元刊
工姓名索引 (Shanghai: Guji, 1990) and Li Guoqing 李國慶, comp.,
Mingdai kangong xingming suoyin 明代刊工姓名索引 (Shanghai: Guji,
1998). These works, the result of many decades of hard work by
bibliographers in East Asia, bring together details that separately have
limited use but together constitute a mine of basic information on
the various individuals involved in the production of imprints during
these dynasties. Being virtually complete lists of what we can know
of the names of book workers, they are essential aids for the
reconstitution of early printing activities and thus will long remain
important contributions to Chinese book studies. Likewise, no
dictionary of printmaking terms rivals David Barker's *An English-
Chinese Glossary of Printmaking Terms* (Belfast: University of Ulster Press,
1995).

In the past few decades, a large number of surveys of Chinese
printing history have been published. Of these, Zhang Xiumin's 張
秀民 landmark *Zhongguo yinshua shi* 中國印刷史 (Shanghai: Renmin,
1989) stands out for the breadth and depth of its learning. Few
surveys in this field contain as much information on as wide a range
of topics as this volume, which clearly is the lifework of a distinguished
scholar. One novel survey of printing is Yang Shengxin's 楊繩信
Zhongguo banke zonglu 中國版刻總錄 (Xianyang: Shaanxi renmin,
1987), a pioneering effort to list the titles published in all dynasties
from the Tang to the end of the Qing. Listed, in order, by dynasty,
type of publishing house, number of character strokes in the first
character of the name of the publishing house, and then date of
publication, the titles here constitute a record of pre-1912
publications in three catalogues of the National Library, eleven other
major libraries, and three previously published lists or studies.
Inadequate in the digital world of today, it remains nonetheless the
only printed piece of bibliographical research that tries to give some
overall chronological order to the printing record of the entire
empire.

Outside of China, Japan has long been a center of bibliographical
research, and its scholars frequently proficient in their study of
Chinese books. From the 1930s up to the 1970s, the noted bibliophile
Nagasawa Kikuya 長澤規矩也 studied virtually all periods of Chinese-
language book production in China and Japan, and his ten volumes
of detailed bibliographical studies, *Nagasawa Kikuya chosaku shū* 長

澤規矩也著作集 (Tokyo: Kyūko shoin, 1984), are of use to both the book collector and the social historian. Another comprehensive collection of mainly Japanese language studies of Chinese books is the recent conference volume *Higashi Ajia shuppan bunka kenkyū, niwatazumi* 東アジア出版文化研究, にはたずみ edited by Isobe Akira 磯部彰 (Tokyo: Nigensha, 2004); its twenty-six articles in Japanese, Chinese, and English cover all periods from the Tang to the twentieth century, in a splendid demonstration of how wide-ranging and international the study of Chinese books has become in the past two decades.

For single-author surveys in Japanese, a useful, if little known, account of Chinese book history is Ōuchi Hakugetsu 大内白月, *Shina tenseki shitan* 支那典籍史談 (Tokyo: Shorinsha, 1944); the range of sources it draws on, remarkable for its time, remains impressive. But, the most significant Japanese survey is unquestionably Inoue Susumu's 井上進 *Chūgoku shuppan bunka shi* 中國出版文化史 (Nagoya: Nagoya daigaku shuppankai, 2002), a brilliant account of Chinese book culture from the Zhou dynasty to the start of the Qing dynasty. It principally is interested in how the imprint replaced the manuscript in élite reading circles over the course of the Song, Yuan, and Ming dynasties. But, Inoue's command of the sources, the insights of his treatment of both old and new topics, and the broad range of issues he addresses make this book essential reading for anyone even marginally interested in Chinese printing culture and intellectual life during these centuries. A fine introduction to the findings can be found in Cynthia J. Brokaw's insightful review of this book, in the *International Journal of Asian Studies* 2.1 (January 2005), pp. 135–65. One finishes this all too short volume, hoping only that Inoue will someday complete this survey with a companion volume on Qing publications.

Thanks in part to the stimulation of such fine general surveys, our expanding knowledge about printing and publications has naturally led to greater research specialization, usually by dynasty and region. For the early history of printing, one can turn to two notable Chinese collections of essays, Su Bai's 宿白 *Tang Song shiqi de diaoban yinshua* 唐宋時期的雕版印刷 (Beijing: Wenwu chubanshe, 1999) and Li Zhizhong's 李致忠 *Jianpu ji* 肩樸集 (Beijing: Beijing tushuguan chubanshe, 1998). In the past few decades, Western scholars, perhaps under influence from the seminal studies by Carter and Pelliot, have continued to make important contributions to the very early years of Chinese printing. Two decades ago, Denis Twitchett's survey of Tang and Song printing deftly introduced much Chinese and Japanese work previously not discussed in Western-language studies in his *Printing and Publishing in Medieval China* (London: The Wynkyn de Worde Society, 1983). His astute assessments and breadth of concerns make this book important to those interested in particularly the first six centuries of book production in China. In the past decade, Timothy Barrett has published a series of interesting papers, most notably "The Rise and Spread of Printing: A New Account of Religious Factors" (London: School of Oriental and African Studies, University of London, Working Papers in the Study of Religions, 2001), that address various dimensions of the origins of printing in China. His work often focuses on the origin and development of woodblock printing in China from a variety of angles, including religion and handicraft production, that most scholars have neglected, and thus is particularly instructive about the uses of printing for media other than books (e.g., charms, textiles, and paper money). Also available in English is a fine article by the Japanese scholar Seo Tatsuhiko, "The Printing Industry in Chang'an's Eastern Market," *Memoirs of the Tōyō Bunko* (2004), pp. 1–42. This essay is the first portion of what promises to be an important account of books and other materials printed in this Tang dynasty capital; it also provides a fine overview of printed materials that survive elsewhere in pre-Song East Asia.

Useful dynasty-wide surveys of publishing are Wang He's 王河 *Songdai tushu shilun* 宋代圖書史論 (Nanchang: Baihua zhou wenyi chubanshe, 1999) for the Song, Tian Jianping's 田建平 *Yuandai chuban kao* 元代出版考 (Shijiazhuang: Hebei chubanshe, 2003) for the Yuan, and Miao Yonghe's 繆詠和 *Mingdai chuban shi gao* 明代出版史稿 (Nanjing: Jiangsu renmin, 2000) for the Ming. Each of these volumes brings together past research and introduces topics (e.g., Daoist and Buddhist printing, printing in foreign languages, impact on foreign countries, and changes in binding) that have all too often been neglected in ordinary accounts of Chinese printing.

More detailed work on publishing activities during these dynasties has in recent years focused on local regions, usually provinces or prefectures. The most notable regional account in Chinese for the early period, *Zhejiang chuban shi yanjiu* 浙江出版史研究 (Hangzhou:

Zhejiang renmin, 1991) by Gu Zhixing 顧志興, covers Zhejiang Province from the ninth to the thirteenth centuries. Li Zhizhong's *Song banshu xulu* 宋版書敘錄 (Beijing: Beijing tushuguan chubanshe, 1994) gives a noted bibliographer's detailed description of sixty Song imprints, most of them stored in the National Library in Beijing. A wide-ranging Western account of Hangzhou printing in the twelfth and thirteenth centuries, and the best in any language, is Sören Edgren, "Southern Song Printing at Hangzhou," *Bulletin of the Museum of Far Eastern Antiquities* 61 (1989), pp. 1–212. Shanxi Province's publishing record from the Song (and on up to the twentieth century) is found, with some commentary, in Li Jinlin 李晉林 and Chang Yinting 腸引婷, comps., *Shanxi guji yinshua chuban shi zhi* 山西古籍印刷出版史志 (Beijing: Zhongyang bianyi chubanshe, 2000). For Lucille Chia's important studies of Fujian publishing in the Song (as well as the Yuan and Ming), see the comments below.

For the Ming, the list of both general surveys and detailed regional studies is far greater. The most comprehensive, if still incomplete, list of Ming imprint titles remains Du Xinfu's 杜信孚 *Mingdai banke zonglu* 明代版刻總錄 (Yangzhou: Jiangsu Guangling guji keyinshe, 1983), and the most informative Ming account of book distribution and purchase is the series of notes in Hu Yinglin's 胡應麟 *Shaoshi shanfang bicong* 少室山方筆叢 (Shanghai: Zhonghua shuju, 1958) that I have repeatedly used in this book. In the past two decades, the writings of two Japanese scholars, Ōki Yasushi 大木康 and Inoue Susumu, have attracted much attention. In 1991, Ōki's long study "Minmatsu Kōnan ni okeru shuppan bunka no kenkyū 明末江南における出版文化の研究," *Hiroshima daigaku bungakubu kiyō* 廣島大學文學部紀要 50.1 (January 1991), special issue, pp. 1–176, opened up the discussion of a wide variety of topics and stimulated both Japanese and non-Japanese scholars of Ming culture to carry out similar work. His findings in this and several subsequent articles have been conveniently assembled in the volume *Minmatsu Kōnan no shuppan bunka* 明末江南の出版文化 (Tokyo: Kenbun shuppansha, 2004). Also, Inoue Susumu, while laying the basis for his general survey of 2002, wrote seminal studies of Ming printing, notably "Zōsho to dokusho 藏書と讀書," *Tōhō gakuhō* 東方學報 62 (1990), pp. 409–45, and "Shoshi · shoko · bunjin 書肆 · 書賈 · 文人," pp. 304–38, in Arai Ken 荒井健, ed., *Chūka bunjin no seikatsu* 中華文人の生活 (Tokyo: Heibonsha, 1994). These essays, although many of their findings were later used in their author's book, contain important information found nowhere else and still merit careful reading.

For long, the sole study in English on Ming printing was Kwang Tsing Wu's "Ming Printing and Printers," *Harvard Journal of Asiatic Studies* 7.3 (February 1943), pp. 203–60. Fortunately, a spate of new publications has begun to change this situation. A conference volume edited by Cynthia J. Brokaw and Kai-wing Chow — *Printing and Book Culture in Late Imperial China* (Berekely: University of California Press, 2005) — contains many examples of fine research on the social history of the book during the Ming and Qing dynasties. Nanjing publishing houses, printing practices for novels and drama, the range of bestsellers, and the printing of Manchu language books in Beijing are just a few of the topics introduced in a book that promises to set the agenda for research in the field for the next generation or two.

Publishing practices in different regions or prefectures during the Ming have benefited from close study. Most recently (too recently to include the findings in this book), Kai-wing Chow's *Publishing, Culture, and Power in Early Modern China* (Stanford, CA: Stanford University Press, 2004) brings together a considerable amount of information on late Ming and early Qing book culture in the lower Yangzi delta, especially on the publishing and writing circles. This book is particularly useful for its account of the formation and operations of a commercial imprint culture among late Ming literati in the lower Yangzi delta. More detailed studies, by prefecture, include several essays by Ye Ruibao 葉瑞寶 on Suzhou prefecture, most notably his milestone account of commercial publishing houses in "Suzhou shufang keshu kao 蘇州書房刻書考," *Jiangsu chubanshi* 江蘇出版史 1992.3, pp. 78–149. To complete the picture for Suzhou, Cao Zhengyuan 曹正元 offers an overview of government publishing agencies in "Suzhou guanjia keshu kaolüe 蘇州官家刻書考略," *Jiangsu chubanshi*, 1992.3, pp. 44–61. Ellen Widmer focuses on one Hangzhou and Suzhou publishing house, adopting an approach that promises to become more popular in the coming years, in her essay, "The Huangduzhai of Hangzhou and Suzhou: A Study in Seventeenth Century Publishing," *Harvard Journal of Asiatic Studies* 56.1 (June 1996), pp. 77–122. The southern Anhui prefecture of Huizhou has also attracted much attention for its printing traditions. Books introducing and discussing its local publishing practices and publishing houses include Liu Shangheng 劉尚恒's *Huizhou keshu yu cangshu* 徽州刻書與藏書 (Yangzhou: Guangling shushe, 2003) and, more helpfully and comprehensively, Michela Bussotti's *Gravures de Hui, Étude du livre illustré chinois (de la fin du XVIe siècle à la première moitié du XVIIe siècle)* (Paris: École française d'Extrême Orient, 2001). For Fujian Province, there is the useful volume *Fujian gudai keshu* 福建古代刻書 (Fuzhou: Fujian renmin, 1997) by Xie Shuishun 謝水順 and Li Ting 李鋌. This chronological survey of printing activities at a variety of Fujian printing sites ranges over nearly 1,000 years, from the early Song to the end of the Qing, with an emphasis on the northern Fujian area of Jianyang from the Song through the Ming. In recent years, two American scholars, Lucille Chia and Cynthia J. Brokaw, have made invaluable contributions to our understanding of Fujian's printing history by taking advantage of recent improvements in research conditions in China for library work on rare books and for field research at former publishing sites. In thus attaining a comprehensive command of the extant bibliographic record as well as an intimate knowledge of local book printing cultures, these scholars have sidestepped many of the deficiencies of the manuscript and imprint record on Fujian printing that had thwarted previous efforts to write its book history from the perspective of the social and economic historian. In doing so, they have helped to shift scholars' interest away from questions of printing technology, so difficult to study in China due to a shortage of sources, to issues of book distribution, reading taste, and reading practices.

Chia's *Printing for Profit, the Commercial Publishers of Jianyang, Fujian (11th–17th Centuries)* (Cambridge, MA: Harvard University Asia Center, 2002) is a milestone in the study of Song printing. Written with an unrivalled command of the surviving imprints from this center of "popular book publishing," it is the first Western-language book dedicated to the study of a Chinese book-producing region. Her thoroughness, aided by keen historical analysis, allows her to draw conclusions beyond the capacity of earlier historians of Song publishing. Working within a field of study that all too often veers between excessive detail and unfounded generalizations, she has been able to acquire a virtually global command of the basic data about this region's publishing history as well as write insightfully about it. Some of her findings are summarized in her essay, "*Mashaben*: Commercial Publishing in Jianyang from the Song to the Ming," pp. 284–328, in Paul Jakov Smith and Richard von Glahn, eds., *The Sung-Yuan-Ming Transition in Chinese History* (Cambridge, MA: Harvard University Asia Center, 2003).

For a rural district at the opposite end of Fujian, Cynthia J. Brokaw has carried out path-breaking field work and library research for her detailed study, *Commerce and Culture in the Sibao Book Trade* (Cambridge, MA: Harvard University Asia Center, forthcoming), a striking account of book publishing and book distribution activities in the Sibao region of Fujian and in the interior of Guangdong, Guangxi, and southern Jiangxi Provinces from the late sixteenth to the mid-twentieth centuries. The findings of her book promise to shape discussions of Qing and Republican "popular" and regional publishing for the next generation as well as to highlight the necessity of field research for the productive study of regional book culture.

One important aspect of Ming printing, single sheet prints either in black or multicolored ink, is well represented in the best single-volume collection of Chinese prints, *Chūgoku kodai hanga ten* 中國古代版畫展 (Machida: Machida shiritsu kokusai hanga bijutsukan, 1988). The fine study of Chinese prints by Kobayashi Hiromitsu 小林宏光, *Chūgoku no hanga* 中國の版畫 (Tokyo: Tōshindō, 1995) is instructive reading for all researchers of the Chinese book, not just the art historians.

For Qing publishing, Cynthia J. Brokaw's forthcoming volume on Sibao, mentioned above, along with the volume she has edited with Kai-wing Chow, are the major Western studies. Chinese and Japanese surveys, partly because of their concentration on high-quality productions and rare editions, usually downplay the significance of printing in this period. Their study has often concentrated on the role of government censorship, and among a host of fine studies on this topic Okamoto Sae's 岡本さえ *Shindai kinsho no kenkyū* 清代禁書の研究 (Tokyo: Tokyo daigaku shuppankai, 1996) stands out for its grasp of the sources and depth of insight. Timothy Brook's article, "Censorship in Eighteenth Century China: A View from the Book Trade," *Canadian Journal of History* 22.2 (August 1988), pp. 177–96, gets behind the Qing sources' usually superficial accounts of the book trade and government censorship to explore their operations in some detail (this study has been revised, with some material on Ming government censorship, for inclusion in his *The Chinese State in Ming Society* [London: Routledge Curzon, 2005]). Qing fiction is well treated in Robert Hegel's *Reading Illustrated Fiction in*

Late Imperial China (Stanford, CA: Stanford University Press, 1998). For local book culture in the Qing, so far the most detailed Chinese language account is Sun Dianqi's 孫殿起 *Liuli chang xiaozhi* 琉璃廠小志 (Beijing: Guji, 1982), largely a collection of Chinese sources on Beijing's famous book quarter of Liuli chang.

Book collecting has been a persistently self-defining activity of Chinese intellectuals for over two millennia. Recently, after several decades of largely government-enforced somnolence in the latter half of the twentieth century, it has revived, as if with a vengeance. Numerous books on the topic have been republished, most notably Ye Changchi's 葉昌熾 (1847–1917) *Cangshu jishi shi* 藏書紀事詩 (orig. 1909; Shanghai: Guji, 1999), an extremely rich collection of biographical information about more than 100 collectors from the tenth to the early twentieth centuries (this edition's accompanying study of 155 book collectors in the Republican era is Lun Ming 倫明, *Xinhai yilai cangshu jishi shi* 辛亥以來藏書紀事詩). Ye's handy compendium is often the most reliable and informative book on Chinese book collectors, a labor of love that all students of the subject turn to regularly with gratitude. Some important sources on Chinese libraries are conveniently collected in Li Xibi 李希泌 and Zhang Jiaohua 張椒華, *Zhongguo gudai cangshu yu jindai tushuguan shiliao (Chunqiu zhi wusi qianhou* 中國古代藏書與近代圖書館史料（春秋至五四前後）(Beijing: Zhonghua shuju, 1982).

Chinese treatments of private libraries invariably focus on their founders and owners. A short, and surprisingly, useful example of this kind of biographical dictionary of book collectors is Li Yu'an 李玉安 and Chen Chuanyi's 陳傳藝 *Zhongguo cangshujia cidian* 中國藏書家辭典 (Wuhan: Hubei jiaoyu chubanshe, 1989). Covering all periods from the Qin dynasty (221–202 BCE) up to the late twentieth century, it transcends the practice, all too common in the Chinese publishing world, of merely rephrasing the entries in previously printed biographical dictionaries. Two recent and interesting studies of Chinese book collectors and book collecting are Fu Xuancong 傅璿琮 and Xie Zhuohua's 謝灼華 *Zhongguo cangshu tongshi* 中國藏書通史 (Ningbo: Ningbo chubanshe, 2001) in two volumes, and Ren Jiyu's 任繼愈 edited three-volume survey *Zhongguo cangshulou* 中國藏書樓 (Shenyang: Liaoning renmin, 2000). Along with Fan Fengshu's 毓風書 *Zhongguo sijia cangshu shi* 中國私家藏書史 (Zhengzhou: Daxiang chubanshe, 2001), these multi-volume accounts do more than provide detailed comprehensive surveys of each dynasty's major and minor collectors. They also engage in the first Chinese-language discussion of such subjects as the relation of collectors and merchants, a study of the imperial princes, and even a list of the private libraries that suffered from the Wakō invasions of the sixteenth century and the turmoil of the Ming-Qing transition in the seventeenth century. The warm reception accorded these works as well as the popularity of the new periodical *Cangshujia* 藏書家 (Book Collector) (April 1999–) are welcome signs that Chinese bibliophiles and book scholars will continue to carry out imaginative work in the future.

Government collections are well treated for the Song dynasty in modern editions of basic primary sources like Chen Kui 陳騤, *Nan Song guange lu* 南宋館閣錄 and Anonymous, *Xulu* 續錄 (Beijing: Zhonghua shuju, 1998) and Cheng Zhu 程俱, *Lintai gushi jiaozheng* 麟台故事校證 (Beijing: Zhonghua shuju, 2000). John H. Winkelman, *The Imperial Library in Southern Sung China, 1127–1279* (Philadelphia, PA: American Philosophical Society, 1974; *Transactions of the American Philosophical Society*, n.s. 64.8) remains the best study of the holdings of Song government libraries and history. For the Ming, we have Gu Liren's 顧力仁 account of the Yongle dadian, *Yongle dadian ji qi jiyishu yanjiu* 永樂大典及其輯佚書研究 (Taipei: Wenshizhe chubanshe, 1985); and, for the Imperial Library, the accounts found in Ren Jiyu, v. 1, and Fu and Xie, v. 1, are presently the most complete.

Important private book collectors from the Song are usefully introduced in Pan Meiyue's 潘美月 *Songdai cangshujia kao* 宋代藏書家考 (Taipei: Xuehai chubanshe, 1980); unfortunately, no similar survey is yet available for the collectors of any of the subsequent dynasties. In general, detailed study of separate collections has only just begun. Two extant Song catalogues — Chao Gongwu 晁公武, *Qunzhai dushu zhi jiaozheng* 群齋讀書志校證 (Shanghai: Guji, 1990) and Chen Zhensun 陳振孫, *Zhizhai shulu jieti* 直齋書錄解題 (CSJC ed.; and Shanghai: Guji, 1987) — are available in fine modern editions; a recent study of Chao Gongwu and his family by Liu Huanyang 劉煥陽, *Songdai Chaoshi jiazu ji qi wenxian yanjiu* 宋代晁氏家族及其文獻研究 (Ji'nan: Ji Lu shushe, 2004) introduces much information about their collecting activities. Extant catalogues of private Ming collections, along with some of the colophons of their owners, have been conveniently assembled in the two volumes of Feng Huimin 馮惠民 and Li Wanjian's 李萬鍵 *Mingdai shumu tiba zongkan*

明代書目題跋總刊 (Beijing: Shumu wenxian chubanshe, 1994). Unfortunately, this last title does not contain the informative colophons written into his books by the most important private collector of the first half of the fifteenth century, Yang Shiqi 楊士奇; one must look for them instead in his *Dongli xu ji* 東里續集 (SKCSZB ed.).

The Tianyi ge Library of the Fan family of Ningbo has attracted more scholarly attention than any other private library, primarily because of its status as China's oldest standing library and surviving private collection. Perhaps the richest collection of information on this library and collection is Cai Peiling's 蔡佩玲 *Fanshi Tianyi ge yanjiu* 毓氏天一閣研究 (Taipei: Han Mei tushu yuxian gongsi, 1991), but the library has its own excellent website (tianyige.com.cn) with a wealth of research articles, photographs, and announcements. The Fan family and twelve other Ming and Qing family book collectors are the subject of the informative *Cangshu shijia* 藏書世家 (Shanghai: Shanghai renmin, 2002) by Liu Hecheng 柳和城, *et al.* A useful collection of sources and commentary on the famous Qing and early Republican collection, the Tieqin tongjian library 鐵琴銅劍樓 of the Qu 瞿 family of Changshu county in Suzhou, is Zhong Weixing 仲偉行, et al., *Tieqin tongjian lou yanjiu wenxian ji* 鐵琴銅劍樓研究文獻集 (Shanghai: Guji, 1997).

Studies of regional traditions of book collectors have long been of interest to Chinese scholars. In the first half of the twentieth century, before the outbreak of World War II, Hangzhou prefecture was studied by Ding Shen 丁申 in his *Wulin cangshu lu* 武林藏書錄 (CSJC ed.; Shanghai: Gudian wenxue chubanshe, 1957), Suzhou prefecture by Jiang Jinghuan 蔣鏡寰 in his *Wuzhong xianzhe cangshu kaolüe* 吳中賢哲藏書考略 (Suzhou: Suzhou tushuguan, 1937), Huzhou prefecture by Zheng Yuanqing 鄭元慶 in the *Wuxing cangshu lu* 吳興藏書錄 (Shanghai: Gudian wenxue chubanshe, 1957), Zhejiang Province by Gu Zhixing 顧志興 in his *Zhejiang cangshujia cangshulou* 浙江藏書家藏書樓 (Hangzhou: Zhejiang renmin, 1987), and both Jiangsu and Zhejiang Provinces by Wu Han 吳晗 in his *Jiang Zhe cangshujia* 江浙藏書家 (Beijing: Zhonghua shuju, 1981). More recently, information on the history of book collecting in Suzhou has been compiled in an exemplary manner by Ye Ruibao 葉瑞寶 in *Suzhou cangshu shi* 蘇州藏書史 (Nanjing: Jiangsu guji chubanshe, 2001); the emphasis is on private collectors (making unusually fine

276 Bibliographical Notes

use of the colophons of book collectors), but this volume also exceptionally includes information on Buddhist temple and government school collections. A useful encyclopedia of, among other things, reading and publishing information from Jiangsu Province is conveniently arranged in chronological order in Zhang Huijian's 張慧劍 compilation, *Ming Qing Jiangsu wenren nianbiao* 明清江蘇文人年表 (Shanghai: Guji, 1986).

And, for those interested in a book-by-book (i.e., price-by-price) account of how a wealthy Tianjin businessman built up his collection right into the 1960s, we can do no better than Li Guoqing's chronology of the book-collecting activities of Zhou Shutao 周叔弢 (aka Zhou Mingyang and the father of the noted Beijing University historian Zhou Yiliang 周一良), *Taoweng cangshu nianpu* 弢翁藏書年譜 (Hefei: Huangshan shushe, 2000). The publication of such a book provides ample evidence that, in the highly commercial-minded China of today, the traditional interest in books and book collecting is certainly thriving. Though less central to élite culture than it was a century ago, it continues to flourish in some urban circles and supports an extensive social network that merits attention from students of Chinese culture, present as well as past.

Western-language studies of the history of Chinese book collecting, and by extension the transmission of Chinese texts, remain unfortunately few. Recently, Glen Dudbridge's *Lost Books of Medieval China* (London: British Museum, 2000) interestingly describes the losses that China's written and printed heritage suffered over the first millennium of its imperial history. Jean-Pierre Drège's *Les bibliothèques en Chine au temps des manuscrits (jusqu'au Xe siècle)* (Paris: École française d'Extrême-Orient, 1991) covers an impressive range of sources to depict the development of government, monastic, and individual libraries up to the tenth century. For the Song period, Piet van der Loon's *Taoist Books in the Libraries of the Sung Period* (London: Ithaca Press, 1984) provides a unique introduction to Daoist institutional libraries, some of which in the Southern Song held large collections of religious texts handcopied or printed with Sung imperial support. For an overview of the major developments in book collecting during the entire Qing period, one has to go back seven decades to Tan Cho-yüan's introduction of the topic in his still useful work, *The Development of Chinese Libraries under the Ch'ing Dynasty, 1644–1911* (Shanghai: Commercial Press, 1935). For the seventeenth and eighteenth centuries, Benjamin Elman's *From Philosophy to Philology, Intellectual and Social Aspects of Change in Late Imperial China* (Cambridge: Council on East Asian Studies, Harvard University, 1984; second revised ed., Los Angeles: UCLA Asian Pacific Monograph Series, 2001) and R. Kent Guy, *The Emperor's Four Treasuries, Scholars and the State in the Late Ch'ien-lung Era* (Cambridge, MA: Council on East Asian Studies, Harvard University, 1987) remain important studies of the role of private book collections in the social and political history of this dynasty.

Libraries and collectors in Western countries, of course, have shown interest in Chinese books for at least four centuries. Two fine efforts to introduce some of these riches are Sören Edgren, *et al.*, *Chinese Rare Books in American Collections* (New York: China House Gallery, Chinese Institute in America, 1984), and Monique Cohen and Nathalie Monnet, eds., *Impressions de Chine* (Paris: Bibliothèque Nationale, 1992). The first provides learned commentary to the history of some valuable examples of the élite tradition of book publishing and collecting inside China, and the latter includes informed descriptions and excellent plates for a wide variety of imprints produced in China, including some done in collaboration with Jesuits and other Westerners.

Literacy in China is a historical topic that Westerners have discussed in greater detail than have East Asians. Evelyn Rawski's *Education and Popular Literacy in Ch'ing China* (Ann Arbor: University of Michigan Press, 1979) is a pioneering and provocative study that brings together much important information on the topic from nineteenth- and twentieth-century sources, Chinese as well as Western. Her high estimate of Qing China's literacy rate has received a thoughtful review by Wilt Idema in *T'oung Pao* LXVI.4–5 (1980), pp. 314–24, that should be read along with her book. Alexander Woodside has written a series of probing and provocative studies on literacy, including "Real and Imagined Communities in the Chinese Struggle for Literacy," pp. 22–45, in Ruth Hayhoe, ed., *Education and Modernization, the Chinese Experience* (Oxford: Pergamon Press, 1992). The conference volume that he and Benjamin Elman edited, *Education and Society in Late Imperial China, 1600–1900* (Berkeley: University of California Press, 1994), also contains much of interest for students of literacy in many dimensions, and Liang Qizi's 梁其姿 *Shishan yu jiaohua — Ming Qing de cishan zuzhi* 施善與教化—明清的

慈善組織 (Shijiazhuang: Hebei jiaoyu chubanshe, 2001) contains the most useful discussion of popular cults that promoted and honored literacy. For an intelligent treatment of readership and popular literature, Ann McLaren, *Chinese Popular Culture and Ming Chantefables* (Leiden: E. J. Brill, 2001) is an excellent guide.

All of these aspects of book history, from the bibliographical to the latest study of collecting and readership, are treated in the handsomely produced *The East Asian Library Journal* (previously known as *The Gest Library Journal*). Containing a wide variety of essays on Chinese, Japanese, Korean, and Vietnamese manuscripts and printed materials, this journal provides a fine outlet for the burgeoning number of studies on East Asian book culture. It merits the attention of anyone interested in keeping up-to-date with some of the best research done in this field today, as scholars increasingly see that the history of the Chinese book opens up a variety of productive approaches to understanding key dimensions and issues of Chinese history.

Finally, comprehensive bibliographies of primary and secondary sources concerned with the history of the Chinese book can also be found in Tsien Tsuen-hsiun's bibliographies in his *Paper and Printing* volume in the Needham *Science and Civilisation in China* series; his supplement to these in "Zhongguo yinshuashi jianmu 中國印刷史簡目," *Guoli Zhongyang tushuguan guankan* 國立中央圖書館館刊, n.s., 23. 1 (June 1990), pp. 179–99; the descriptive list in Wang Yuguan 王餘光, ed., *Cangshu siji* 藏書四記 (Wuhan: Hubei cishu chubanshe, 1998), pp. 353–80; and, the text and footnotes of Cynthia J. Brokaw's review of Inoue Susumu's book, *Chūgoku shuppan bunka shi*, in the *International Journal of Asian Studies* 2.1 (January 2005), pp. 135–65.

Glossary–Index

Five Classics. *See wujing*
Five Dynasties, 49, 214n17, 217n63, 228n89, 241n53
Four Books. *See sishu*
"Four Collecting Friends," 169
Four Treasuries Project, 73, 119, 137, 168, 169, 170, 190
French Royal Library, 124, 217n67
Fu Zengxiang 傅增湘, 182
fugui 富貴, 178
Fujian Province, 26, 32, 33, 48, 56, 57, 58, 60, 66, 67, 91, 100, 101, 102, 113, 114, 132, 207n90, 210n134, 215n33, 230n104, 231n113, 234n160. *See also* Fuzhou, Jianyang
Fuzhou 福州 (Fujian Province), 75, 97–8, 113, 118, 159, 235n2

Galileo, 252n83
Gao Panlong 高攀龍, 191
gazetteers, 56
ge 格, 68
ge er buxing 閣而不行, 68
Ge 葛 family of Yangzhou, 52
gewu 格物, 165
Geng Yu 耿裕, 59
Gernet, Jacques, 165, 252n83
Giles, Herbert, 229n91
gong 公, 118, 165, 252
Gong Cheng 龔橙, 76
gongpijia 攻皮家, 258
gongsheng 貢生, 104
Great Learning, 165
Grolier, Jean, 124
Gu 顧 (Suzhou family), 165
Gu Qiyuan 顧起元, 87
Gu Weiyue 顧維嶽, 250n57
Gu Yanwu 顧炎武, 57, 60, 66, 89, 91, 153, 159, 250n53
Gu Yuanqing 顧元慶, 84, 110
Guan Tong 管同, 256n21
Guanxian 官賢 quarter, Fuzhou, 113

Guanxiu 貫休, 62
Guangdong 廣東, 32, 97, 146
Gui Youguang 歸有光, 105, 111, 155, 224n26
Gui Zhuang 歸莊, 141
Guillaume, comte de Libri Carucci, 142
Guo Qinzhi 郭欽止, 150
Guoxue 國學, 108
Guozi jian 國子監, 127–8
Gutenberg, 21

Haechang temple (Canton), 23, 205n67
Han 韓 family of Shandong Province, 85–6
Han Learning, 168, 188, 191
Hangzhou, 92, 95, 220n101, 220n101; bookstores, 6, 95–8, 99, 100, 101–2, 113, 160; collectors, 52, 113, 135, 141, 167, 168, 169, 217n62, 256n27; commercial base for journeymen, 95; Ming publishing center, 6, 33, 35, 36, 54, 67; post-Sung decline, 52, 56–7, 230n106; Song publishing center, 5, 32, 48, 56, 57, 98, 108, 219n92; Southern Sung book shortages, 55, 56, 61,129; Yuan publishing center, 56–7
Hanji 漢記, 65
Hanlin 翰林 Academy, 91, 94, 141, 155, 167, 216n55, 241n50, 242n74, 243n81, 257n42
Hanshu 漢書, 55
Han Yu 韓愈, 56, 64, 98, 108
hao 號, 36, 187
Hayes, Dr James, 77
He Dacheng 何大成, 153, 157, 245n131
He Liangjun 何良俊, 53, 104
He Ning 何凝, 90
He Zhuo 何焯, 250n57

scripts, 206n85, 207n89, 219n92, 228n83; artisanal, 26–9, 73; Ou style, 29; standard style, 29

Seikadō bunko 靜嘉堂文庫, 46, 68, 167, 247n4, 264

Shaanxi Province, 32, 102

shan 杉, 38

Shang Jun, 152, 216n59

Shanghai, 12, 24, 52

Shang shu 尚書, 93

Shanhai jing 山海經, 64

Shanxi Province, 32, 33, 59, 151

Shao Bao 邵寶, 153

Shaoqing 昭慶 temple (Hangzhou), 101

Shaoxing (Zhejiang Province), 53, 54, 83, 138, 152, 180, 224n17, 234n147

She 歙 County Museum, Huizhou prefecture, 207n93

Shen Fang 沈芳, 54

Shen Kuo 沈括, 12, 13

Shen Yuwen 沈舉文, 75

Shen Zhou 沈周, 60, 87, 88

shengyuan 生員, 104–7, 109

shi 史 (history), 45

shi 詩 (poems), 181

shi 士 (scholars), 108, 188

Shi Miyuan 史彌遠, 108

Shiba Yoshinobu 斯波義信, 57

Shiguan 史館. *See* Historiography Institute

Shiguo jinian 十國紀年, 140

Shiji 史記, 53, 60, 64, 226n69

Shijing 詩經, 93

shilu 實錄, 127

Shilüe 史略, 93

Shilüe shiwen 史略釋文, 93

Shisan jing zhushu 十三經注疏, 99

shoe repairman, 186–7

shouchao 手抄/鈔. *See* manuscript, scripts, transcription

shufang 書坊, 67. *See also* publishing, commercial

shuji 書籍, 65

shupu 書舖, 228

shuyong 書傭, 37

shuyuan 書院, 85, 150, 151, 256n28

Shuyuan jinghua 書苑菁華, 75, 213n139

Sibu congkan 四部叢刊, 66

Sichuan, 91, 112 early printing center, 5, 9, 10, 11, 48, 56, 62, 85, 133, 217n63; Mongol invasion's blow to printing industry in, 57, 218n75; survival of imprints during Southern Song, 55, 150. *See also* Chengdu

Siku quanshu 四庫全書. *See* Four Treasuries

Sima Guang 司馬光, 51, 58, 59, 60, 89, 129

sishu 四書, 15, 56, 57, 58, 66, 93, 94

Sishu jizhu 四書集注, 56, 93

Sixtus VI, Pope, 142

Song Binwen 宋賓文, 176

Song Minqiu 宋敏求, 54, 150, 155, 156, 249n46

Song Shou 宋綬, 247n8

Song shi 宋史, 60, 64

Songjiang 松江, 60, 99, 110, 139, 215n38, 247n7

Songti zi 宋體字, 26

Sonkeikaku bunko 尊經閣文庫, 46

Stein collection. *See* Dunhuang

"stories," 63, 67–8, 110

Su Bian 蘇弁, 214n25

Su Shi 蘇軾, 58, 63, 187, 247n7, 259n72

Su Song 蘇頌, 54, 129, 153, 155

Su Yangzhi 蘇養直, 153

Sui dynasty, 213n16

Sui shu 隋書, 94

Sun 孫 family (in Sichuan), 85

Sun Daoming 孫道明, 108, 215n38

Sun Qingceng 孫慶曾, 94, 181

Sun Yunqie 孫允伽, 76

suren 俗人, 180